Freedom of speech, 1500–1850

Manchester University Press

Politics, culture and society in early modern Britain

General Editors
PROFESSOR ALASTAIR BELLANY
DR ALEXANDRA GAJDA
PROFESSOR PETER LAKE
PROFESSOR ANTHONY MILTON
PROFESSOR JASON PEACEY

This important series publishes monographs that take a fresh and challenging look at the interactions between politics, culture and society in Britain between 1500 and the mid-eighteenth century. It counteracts the fragmentation of current historiography through encouraging a variety of approaches which attempt to redefine the political, social and cultural worlds, and to explore their interconnection in a flexible and creative fashion. All the volumes in the series question and transcend traditional interdisciplinary boundaries, such as those between political history and literary studies, social history and divinity, urban history and anthropology. They thus contribute to a broader understanding of crucial developments in early modern Britain.

Recently published in the series

Chaplains in early modern England: Patronage, literature and religion
HUGH ADLINGTON, TOM LOCKWOOD AND GILLIAN WRIGHT (eds)

The Cooke sisters: Education, piety and patronage in early modern England GEMMA ALLEN

Black Bartholomew's Day DAVID J. APPLEBY

Insular Christianity ROBERT ARMSTRONG AND TADHG Ó HANNRACHAIN (eds)

Reading and politics in early modern England GEOFF BAKER

'No historie so meete' JAN BROADWAY

Writing the history of parliament in Tudor and early Stuart England
PAUL CAVILL AND ALEXANDRA GAJDA (eds)

Republican learning JUSTIN CHAMPION

News and rumour in Jacobean England: Information, court politics and diplomacy, 1618–25
DAVID COAST

This England PATRICK COLLINSON

Sir Robert Filmer (1588–1653) and the patriotic monarch CESARE CUTTICA

Doubtful and dangerous: The question of succession in late Elizabethan England
SUSAN DORAN AND PAULINA KEWES (eds)

Brave community JOHN GURNEY

'Black Tom' ANDREW HOPPER

Reformation without end: Religion, politics and the past in post-revolutionary England
ROBERT G. INGRAM

Connecting centre and locality: Political communication in early modern England
CHRIS R. KYLE AND JASON PEACEY (eds)

Revolution remembered: Seditious memories after the British Civil Wars EDWARD JAMES LEGON

Royalists and Royalism during the Interregnum JASON MCELLIGOTT AND DAVID L. SMITH

Laudian and Royalist polemic in Stuart England ANTHONY MILTON

The crisis of British Protestantism: Church power in the Puritan Revolution, 1638–44
HUNTER POWELL

Lollards in the English Reformation: History, radicalism, and John Foxe SUSAN ROYAL

The gentlewoman's remembrance: Patriarchy, piety, and singlehood in early Stuart England
ISAAC STEPHENS

Exploring Russia in the Elizabethan Commonwealth: The Muscovy Company and Giles Fletcher, the elder (1546–1611) FELICITY JANE STOUT

Loyalty, memory and public opinion in England, 1658–1727 EDWARD VALLANCE

Church polity and politics in the British Atlantic world, c. 1635–66
ELLIOT VERNON AND HUNTER POWELL (eds)

Full details of the series are available at www.manchesteruniversitypress.co.uk.

Freedom of speech, 1500–1850

EDITED BY ROBERT G. INGRAM, JASON PEACEY
AND ALEX W. BARBER

Manchester University Press

Copyright © Manchester University Press 2020

While copyright in the volume as a whole is vested in Manchester University Press, copyright in individual chapters belongs to their respective authors, and no chapter may be reproduced wholly or in part without the express permission in writing of both author and publisher.

Published by Manchester University Press
Oxford Road, Manchester M13 9PL

www.manchesteruniversitypress.co.uk

British Library Cataloguing-in-Publication Data
A catalogue record for this book is available from the British Library

ISBN 978 1 5261 4710 3 hardback
ISBN 978 1 5261 6706 4 paperback

First published 2020
Paperback published 2022

The publisher has no responsibility for the persistence or accuracy of URLs for any external or third-party internet websites referred to in this book, and does not guarantee that any content on such websites is, or will remain, accurate or appropriate.

Typeset in 10/12 Scala by
Servis Filmsetting Ltd, Stockport, Cheshire

Contents

NOTES ON CONTRIBUTORS—vii
ACKNOWLEDGEMENTS—x
ABBREVIATIONS—xi

1 Freedom of speech in England and the anglophone world, 1500–1850   1
  Jason Peacey, Robert G. Ingram and *Alex W. Barber*

2 Thomas Elyot on counsel, *kairos* and freeing speech in Tudor England   28
  Joanne Paul

3 Pearls before swine: limiting godly speech in early seventeenth-century England   47
  Karl Gunther

4 'Free speech' in Elizabethan and early Stuart England   63
  Peter Lake

5 The origins of the concept of freedom of the press   98
  David Como

6 Swift and free speech   119
  David Womersley

7 Defending the truth: arguments for free speech and their limits in early eighteenth-century Britain and France   135
  Ann Thomson

8 'The warr ... against heaven by blasphemors and infidels': prosecuting heresy in Enlightenment England   151
  Robert G. Ingram and *Alex W. Barber*

Contents

9   David Hume and 'Of the Liberty of the Press' (1741) in its original
    contexts   171
    Max Skjönsberg

10 The argument for the freedom of speech and press during the
    ratification of the US Constitution, 1787–88   192
    Patrick Peel

11 Before – and beyond – *On Liberty*: Samuel Bailey and the
    nineteenth-century theory of free speech   211
    Greg Conti

12 Unfree, unequal, unempirical: press freedom, British India and
    Mill's theory of the public   236
    Christopher Barker

INDEX—257

Notes on contributors

ALEX W. BARBER is Assistant Professor of Early Modern British History at Durham University. He has published articles in *Parliamentary History* and *History*. His *Communication of Sin: The Lapse of Licensing and the Circulation of Religious and Political Dissent in England, 1690–1720* is forthcoming from Boydell.

CHRIS BARKER is Assistant Professor of Political Science at the American University in Cairo and a former postdoctoral fellow with the George Washington Forum. His first book is *Educating Liberty: Democracy and Aristocracy in J.S. Mill's Political Thought* (2018). He has also published articles in *Contemporary Political Theory*, *Review of Politics*, *History of European Ideas* and *American Political Thought*.

DAVID COMO is Professor of History at Stanford University. He is the author of *Radical Parliamentarians and the English Civil War* (2018) and *Blown by the Spirit: Puritanism and the Emergence of an Antinomian Underground in Pre-Civil-War England* (2004). His articles have appeared in *Journal of British Studies*, *Past & Present*, *English Historical Review*, *Huntington Library Quarterly*, *Journal of Ecclesiastical History* and *Historical Journal*.

GREG CONTI is Assistant Professor of Politics at Princeton University. His first book is *Parliament the Mirror of the Nation: Representation, Deliberation and Democracy in Victorian Britain* (2019). His articles have appeared in *History of Political Thought*, *Journal of British Studies*, *Modern Intellectual History*, *History of European Ideas* and *Political Theory*.

KARL GUNTHER is Associate Professor of History at the University of Miami. He is author of *Reformation Unbound: Protestant Visions of Reform in England, 1525–1590* (2014), which was a finalist for the Royal Historical Society's Whitefield Prize and runner-up for the American Society of Church History's Brewer Prize. His articles have appeared in *Past &*

Present, *Journal of Ecclesiastical History*, *History Compass* and *Archiv für Reformationsgeschichte*.

ROBERT G. INGRAM is Professor of History at Ohio University and director of the George Washington Forum on American Ideas, Politics and Institutions. He is the author of *Reformation without End: Religion, Politics and the Past in Post-revolutionary England* (2018) and *Religion, Reform and Modernity: Thomas Secker and the Church of England* (2007). He has co-edited three books, including *God in the Enlightenment* (2016), *Between Sovereignty and Anarchy: The Politics of Violence in the American Revolutionary Era* (2015) and *Religious Identities in Britain, 1660–1832* (2005).

PETER LAKE is University Distinguished Professor of History at Vanderbilt University and a Fellow of the British Academy. A Ford Lecturer in British History at Oxford, he is the author of eight books, including *How Shakespeare Put Politics on the Stage* (2017); *Bad Queen Bess? Libels, Secret Histories and the Politics of Publicity in the Reign of Queen Elizabeth I* (2015); *The Antichrist's Lewd Hat* (2002); *The Boxmaker's Revenge* (2001); and *Moderate Puritans and the Elizabethan Church* (1982).

JOANNE PAUL is Lecturer in Early Modern History at the University of Sussex. She is the author of *Thomas More* (2016) and *Counsel and Command in Early Modern English Thought* (forthcoming). She has co-edited (with Helen Graham-Matheson) *Queenship and Counsel in the Early Modern World* (2017) and *Governing Diversities: Democracy, Diversity and Human Nature* (2012). Her articles have appeared in *Hobbes Studies*, *Renaissance Studies* and *Renaissance Quarterly*.

JASON PEACEY is Professor of History at UCL. He is the author of *Print and Public Politics in the English Revolution* (2013) and *Politicians and Pamphleteers: Propaganda in the English Civil Wars and Interregnum* (2004). He has also co-edited (with Chris Kyle) *Parliament at Work* (2002) and edited *The Regicides and the Execution of Charles I* (2001). He has published many articles and book chapters, some of which have appeared in the *Journal of British Studies*, *Historical Journal*, *English Historical Review*, *Historical Research*, *Media History*, *Parliamentary History* and *The Seventeenth Century*.

PATRICK PEEL is Lecturer in Political Science at the University of Michigan and a former postdoctoral fellow with the George Washington Forum. He teaches courses on political theory, American political development and law and has published articles in *Justice System Journal* and *Political Research Quarterly*. He is currently writing a book on the populist use of American state courts for building and reviving republican democracy.

MAX SKJÖNSBERG is a Postdoctoral Research Associate at the University of Liverpool, working on a collaborative project on libraries and reading communities in the eighteenth-century Atlantic world. He was formerly an Associate

Lecturer at the University of St Andrews and the University of York, and David Hume Fellow at the Institute for Advanced Studies in the Humanities at the University of Edinburgh. He has published in the *Historical Journal, Journal of British Studies, Modern Intellectual History, History of Political Thought, European Journal of Political Theory* and *History of European Ideas*, and his first book – *The Persistence of Party: Ideas of Harmonious Discord in Eighteenth-century Britain* – is forthcoming with Cambridge University Press in 2021.

ANN THOMSON is Professor of European Intellectual History at the European University Institute. Her books include *L'âme des Lumières: Le débat sur l'être humain entre religion et science Angleterre-France (1690–1760)* (2013), *Bodies of Thought: Science, Religion and the Soul in the Early Enlightenment* (2008) and *Barbary and Enlightenment: European Attitudes towards the Maghreb in the 18th Century* (1987). She has also published more than five dozen book chapters and three dozen articles.

DAVID WOMERSLEY is Thomas Warton Professor of English Literature at the University of Oxford and a Fellow of the British Academy. His books include *Divinity and State* (2010); *Gibbon and the 'Watchmen of the Holy City': The Historian and His Reputation, 1776–1814* (2002) and *The Transformation of the Decline and Fall of the Roman Empire* (1988). He is the general editor of Oxford University Press's *Writings and Correspondence of Edward Gibbon* and was general editor of the Cambridge Edition of the Works of Jonathan Swift. He has produced thirteen critical editions of eighteenth-century works and edited another five collections of essays.

Acknowledgements

This volume is possible thanks to the George Washington Forum on American Ideas, Politics and Institutions at Ohio University. We need especially to thank Nicole Gordon for her steadfast support of the GWF. We need also to thank James Bowman, Tim Lehmann, Heather Thomas, Winsome Chunnu-Brayda, Debora Shuger, Chloé Bakalar, Glauco Schettini, Drew Starling and Anton Matytsin for their valuable contributions.

Athens, London, Durham
July 2019

Abbreviations

Add.	Additional
AHR	American Historical Review
BL	British Library, London
Bodleian	Bodleian Library, Oxford
CCED	Clergy of the Church of England Database [www.theclergydatabase.org.uk]
CCO	Christ Church, Oxford, Library
CWJSM	J. Robson (ed.), Collected Works of John Stuart Mill, 33 vols (Toronto, 1963–91)
DHRC	J. Kaminski and G. Saladino (eds), The Documentary History of the Ratification of the Constitution, 26 vols (Madison, 1995–)
ECS	Eighteenth-Century Studies
EDH	D. Hume, Essays: Moral, Political and Literary, ed. E. Miller (Indianapolis, 1994)
EHR	English Historical Review
ELR	English Literary Renaissance
HJ	Historical Journal
HMC	Historical Manuscript Commission
HLQ	Huntington Library Quarterly
HPT	History of Political Thought
HR	Historical Research
IOR	India Office Records, British Library
JBS	Journal of British Studies
JEH	Journal of Ecclesiastical History
JES	Journal of English Studies
JHI	Journal of the History of Ideas
JMEMS	Journal of Medieval and Early Modern Studies
LPL	Lambeth Palace Library, London
LRO	Leicestershire Record Office

Abbreviations

ODNB	C. Matthew and B. Harrison (eds), *Oxford Dictionary of National Biography*, 60 vols (Oxford, 2004)
PBA	*Proceedings of the British Academy*
PH	*Parliamentary History*
P&P	*Past and Present*
PMLA	*Publications of the Modern Language Association*
PW	H. Davis and E. Herenpreis (eds), *The Prose Writings of Jonathan Swift*, 14 vols (Oxford, 1939–74)
RES	*Review of English Studies*
SCH	*Studies in Church History*
SCJ	*Sixteenth-Century Journal*
SRM	Societies for the Reformation of Manners
TCD	Trinity College, Dublin
TNA	The National Archives, Kew
TRHS	*Transactions of the Royal Historical Society*

The place of publication is London, unless otherwise noted. Where an archival source is cited in the notes, it is implied, unless otherwise noted, to be a manuscript.

Chapter 1

Freedom of speech in England and the anglophone world, 1500–1850

Jason Peacey, Robert G. Ingram and Alex W. Barber

Daniel Defoe was of two minds about freedom of speech. On the one hand, he reckoned that many had misused their liberty to express their views in print. It would, he lamented, 'be endless to examine the Liberty taken by the Men of Wit in the World, the loose they give themselves in Print, at Religion, at Government, at Scandal; the prodigious looseness of the Pen, in broaching new Opinions in Religion, as well as Politics, are real Scandals to the Nation, and well deserve a Regulation'.[1] The ideological cell-division catalysed by the Reformation had, by Defoe's day, made pluralism a fact of English life. And ideological battles first played out in print.[2] Yet Defoe also reckoned that government licensing of publications was itself inimical to liberty: 'I cannot see how the supervising, and passing all the Works of the Learned part of the World by one or a few men, and giving them an absolute Negative on the Press, can possibly be reconcil'd to the liberty of the English Nation'.[3] Print licensing was 'a Branch of Arbitrary Power in the Government'.[4] Moreover, Defoe insisted, that the English could express their views freely and openly had meant that the 'English Nation had always carried a figure equal to their Neighbours, as to all sorts of Learning, and in some very much superior'.[5] Freedom of speech and the allied freedom of the press, then, both encouraged learning amongst the English *and* potentially destabilised English society and politics. And though he disapproved of press regulation, Defoe's *Essay on the Regulation of the Press* (1704) none the less prioritised peace over liberty, and offered possible legal solutions that might ensure effective restraints on the promulgation of ideas which threatened the civil peace.[6]

Daniel Defoe, like most English men and women from the Reformation onwards, recognised that addressing freedom of speech meant dealing simultaneously with issues of liberty, pluralism, politics and restraint. This book about the early history of freedom of speech also highlights the connections between liberty, pluralism, politics and restraint. It covers the period

I

from the early sixteenth century to the mid-nineteenth century and treats that stretch of time as a coherent period, one which was not unvariegated but one in which there nonetheless existed a set of coherent practical and theoretical problems which animated the discussion and practice of free speech.

Freedom of speech is a topic that has long been an unapologetically Western liberal ideal. Those living in the English-speaking world are especially prone to be adherents of 'free speech fundamentalism'.[7] A number of reasons account for the Western liberal valorisation of freedom of speech. Firstly, the right to speak freely flows naturally from the anthropology of liberalism itself. The *individual*, as Larry Siedentop has argued, is 'the organizing social role in the West'; and *civil society* 'emerged, with its characteristic distinction between public and private spheres and its emphasis on the role of conscience and choice' from the primacy of the individual in the West.[8] *Liberalism*, in turn, is the Western ideology which most wholly prioritises the *individual*, conceiving of the individual as an autonomous self which reaches its fullest realisation through its ability to make unfettered choices.[9] It hardly surprises that Western liberals explicitly link the ability to speak freely with the full realisation of the individual self. Timothy Garton Ash recently defended free speech by saying that 'we need freedom of expression to realise our full individual humanity', and '[i]f we are prevented from exercising it freely, we cannot fully be ourselves'.[10] Other more obvious reasons have also recommended free speech as a Western virtue. Most notably, modern repressive regimes have been anti-liberal ones which have always stifled freedom of speech, even as they have often paid lip service to protecting free speech and the free press.[11] Nowhere was this more evident than in twentieth-century Communist regimes, so that, with Communism's fall in the late 1980s and early 1990s in the Soviet bloc, Western liberals could look with satisfaction at the apparent victory of their own cultural and political values.[12] Indeed, many interpreted Communism's collapse as a sign of the latent desire amongst all people for the democratic values championed by free Western societies.

Freedom of expression also lay at the heart of post-Second World War political projects. The *Universal Declaration of Human Rights* (*UDHR*) (1948) – inspired by Franklin Delano Roosevelt's proclamation of the 'four freedoms' – declared there to be a number of fundamental human rights, including freedom from slavery, freedom of movement within borders and freedom of conscience. Yet Article 19 – 'everyone shall have the right to hold opinions without interference ... everyone shall have the right to freedom of expression' – undergirded the basic concepts of dignity, liberty, equality and brotherhood.[13] The *UDHR* reckoned that freedom of speech would buttress future democratic states, all of which struggled to recover from their catastrophic recent – and unfree – pasts. For the *UDHR*'s architects assumed that the document would be adopted by Western countries precisely because they inhabited a civilisation with long-held traditions of personal liberties and freedom.[14] That the countries which refused to adopt the *UDHR* – the Soviet

Union, Czechoslovakia, Poland, Yugoslavia, Ukraine, Belorussia, Saudi Arabia and South Africa – were totalitarian, theocratic or apartheid states only deepened the Western, liberal conviction that freedom of expression posed an existential threat to illiberal regimes.

However, the view that freedom of speech was both the prerequisite for and the bulwark of a stable liberal state has recently come under severe pressure on two broad fronts, one concerning religious expression – especially regarding Islam – and the other concerning hate speech. The response to Salman Rushdie's *Satanic Verses* (1988), which questioned the status of the Prophet Muhammad, exposed a crack in the liberal edifice of free speech fundamentalism.[15] In response to Ayatollah Khomeini's *fatwa* condemning Rushdie and his publishers to death for having committed blasphemy against Islam, many reacted angrily to attempts to banish Rushdie's book from the public sphere but reserved most ire for, in their view, tepid defenders of free speech.

The *Satanic Verses* affair traded on and destabilised the legacy of a commonplace version of the Enlightenment. Modernity – read most reductively as secular liberalism – is understood by many as a unitary version of public life in which all matters can be discussed freely *and* in which religion is banished from the public sphere.[16] The Rushdie affair called into question the supposedly inherent connection between free speech, secularism and political stability. Many liberal commentators reckoned that mobs demanding that Rushdie's book should be withdrawn directly challenged a home-grown English version of liberal progress. England, so it was claimed, was 'the home of freedom' and it was a full-frontal assault upon that memory to witness 'the burning of books and an openly homicidal witch-hunt'.[17] And yet, those on both the left and right who defended Rushdie and the absolute freedom of speech had to confront uncomfortable truths. Geoffrey Robertson's praise of the Home Office's decision to discontinue any further blasphemy prosecutions, for instance, reminded many that blasphemy remained illegal in Britain late into the twentieth century.[18]

This was just the start of the problem. The Rushdie affair, the *Jyllands-Posten* publications of 2005, the *Charlie Hebdo* murders in 2015 and the 2018 verdict of the European Court of Human Rights – which deemed certain criticisms of Muhammad to be blasphemous – have led many to ask whether the liberal model of public debate (secular) might be inadequate in today's hyperpluralistic world.[19] This inadequacy comes through most clearly in the European Court of Human Rights' ruling that it is blasphemous to accuse the Prophet of being a paedophile. On the one hand, the court affirmed that 'freedom of expression constitutes one of the essential foundations of a democratic society and one of the basic conditions for its progress'. On the other hand, it contended that the exercise of freedom of expression 'carries with it duties and responsibilities', which include 'the duty to avoid as far as possible an expression that is, in regard to objects of veneration, gratuitously offensive to others and profane'. The reason these duties and responsibilities exist is to preserve the public peace: 'Where such expressions go beyond the limits of a critical denial of other people's religious beliefs and are likely to incite religious intolerance ... a State may legitimately consider them to be incompatible with respect for the freedom of thought, conscience and religion and take proportionate restrictive measures'.[20]

The European Court of Human Rights was not the first in the postwar era to insist that some things cannot be said publicly. Just as the Soviet Union had believed that the West used the *UDHR* deliberately to sanctify certain rights to make a partisan political point, so too did some Islamic countries and Muslim scholars object to what they believed was a system in which religious belief and human rights were made deliberately incompatible. The dispute between Islamic countries at the UN General Assembly about whether the *UDHR* should be adopted has never gone away. Instead, it has encouraged further debate and thinking about how the relationship between religion and public debate might best be constructed, culminating in the signing of the *Cairo Declaration on Human Rights* (1990) by the Organisation of Islamic Co-operation. Whilst the *Cairo Declaration* has largely been dismissed in the liberal West as being incompatible with human rights, its specific sections on freedom of opinion offer insights into the religious and ideological multivalence of *freedom of speech* in non-Western societies, beyond resorting to binaries of 'repression' and 'freedom'.[21] 'Information', the *Cairo Declaration* accepts, is 'a vital necessity to society. It may not be exploited or misused in such a way as may violate sanctities and the dignity of prophets, undermine moral and ethical values or disintegrate, corrupt or harm society, or weaken in faith'. This, in turn, means that 'everyone shall have the right to advocate what is wrong and evil according to the norms of Islamic Shari'ah'.[22] Faced with such claims, critics of Islam reiterated that freedom of speech is a primary value: it cannot be divided and it undergirds democracy.[23]

More recently, the primacy of the right of free speech among liberal values has come under attack by those who believe that legal protections need to be enacted to protect people from *hate speech*. Many have made the case that free speech protections should not extend to putative hate speech, but Jeremy Waldron's arguments are especially influential. On Waldron's reading there is 'a sort of public good of inclusiveness that our society sponsors and that it is committed to'. The problem with hateful speech, in Waldron's view, is that it 'undermines the public good, or it makes the task of sustaining it much more difficult than it would otherwise be'. Not protecting people who are the targets of hate speech fails to protect their *dignity* and 'social standing', 'the fundamentals of basic reputation that entitle them to be treated as equals in the ordinary operations of society'.[24] Moreover, not to punish hate speech threatens the peace and stability of any liberal society. Put another way, Waldron turns on its head the arguments of free speech fundamentalists: where free speech absolutists hold that liberal societies cannot subsist without the untrammelled right to free expression, Waldron reckons that untrammelled free expression actually threatens the peace and stability of liberal societies. And Waldron, at least in part, justifies delimiting freedom of speech on Enlightenment grounds.[25]

Both those who valorise freedom of speech and those who now want to curb what they see as its excesses have thought about the subject not just in terms of the present but also historically. Thus far, it has been mostly political theorists, literary critics and legal scholars who have tried to excavate the histories of free speech, while historians have largely stood away from these investigations. In doing so, they have failed to grasp what might be called a new politics of discourse, and mostly concentrated either on understanding the effectiveness of censorship or on tracing freedom of speech as a distinct – almost elemental – category of political thinking.

Freedom of Speech, 1500–1850 brings together historians, political theorists and literary scholars of early modern England in one volume, to bring their different perspectives to bear on the very modern debate about free expression, particularly given that freedom of speech – or, more obviously, freedom of the press – first emerged in early modern England and its North American colonies. As such, this book revisits, and offers fresh perspectives on, this history, by exploring how contemporaries grappled with the issue from the sixteenth to the mid-nineteenth centuries. Such a *longue durée* approach is unusual for a volume of scholarly essays, but is particularly useful on this occasion for at least three reasons.[26] Firstly, it reflects the necessity of integrating religion into the history of free speech. Early debates about free speech were fundamentally debates about the freedom of *religious* speech. Secondly, from this period emerged texts – not least by John Milton and John Stuart Mill – which subsequently achieved canonical status in a putatively coherent tradition justifying unqualified free expression. Those texts and the moments from which they emerged, though, need to be properly contextualised in relation to contemporary ideas and practices, not least to recognise the complexity of the claims that were – and were not – being made. Finally, thinking about free speech between the sixteenth and nineteenth centuries points up the problems with the triumphalist – 'Whiggish' – accounts of free speech that undergird free speech fundamentalism.

Two variants of the triumphalist story – the one Macaulayan, the other Habermasian – stand out. The Macaulayan version traces back to Thomas Babington Macaulay's *History of England* (1848), in which the lapse of the Licensing Act was the axial moment in the history of free speech. Macaulay recognised that in 1695 the Licensing Act lapsed by accident, but argued that politicians and the public quickly embraced the free press, which became a permanent component of the English constitution. On Macaulay's reading, post-1695 politicians reckoned that the unhindered spread of information helped to create political and religious stability. Free speech soon became part of a series of accepted *rights*, including religious pluralism, toleration

5

and freedom of conscience. The wider public, eager to participate further in political life, also embraced the theories being advanced by government, and soon objected to all forms of censorship. By the middle of the eighteenth century, almost all English people believed that freedom of the press was an indivisible element of the English constitution based on rights theory. As Macaulay explained it, 'English literature was emancipated, and emancipated for ever, from the control of the government'.[27]

Macaulay's story has close affinities with Jürgen Habermas's more recent account, for Habermas too identified the late seventeenth century as a pivotal moment in the story of freedom of speech. Habermas anatomised the modern social space – separate from church and state – in which individuals could engage with one other and provided an account of its emergence. Before the late seventeenth century, there was a 'display oriented' public sphere; afterwards, there emerged a 'discourse oriented' bourgeois public sphere. In Habermas's story of the transformation of the old into the new public sphere the lapse of licensing, the entrenchment of parliamentary elections and the creation of the Bank of England provided the conditions in which people could discuss ideas publicly, freely and reasonably. That, in turn, created and empowered public opinion. Like Macaulay, Habermas argued that the Licensing Act's lapse heralded the 'elimination of the institution of censorship'.[28]

The initial Habermasian approach to the waxing importance of public opinion during the early eighteenth century obscured the tangled connection between religion and free speech, and Habermas's early take on religion has been characterised as 'antireligious'.[29] Historians have followed his lead in positing a causal connection between the emergence of a powerful public and a shift in how religion was defined and debated.[30] On this reading the public, not priests, became the authoritative judge of religion, and this, in turn, catalysed secularisation. Freedom of expression yielded freedom from religion. More recently, Habermas has changed his mind on the importance of religion to the early modern period.[31] For Habermas has recognised that religious believers do not – and, crucially, did not – accept the totalising claims to authority made by the modern secular state, or the supposedly attendant necessity for the public sphere to be a *secularised* public sphere. He related this directly to modern free-speech debates: 'it is not permissible to challenge opinion- and will-formation by censoring speech or cutting it off from possible sources of meaning ... [T]he respect that secularised citizens owe their religious fellow-citizens also has an epistemic dimension.'[32] Most historians who remain committed to Habermasian public-sphere theory, however, have been reluctant to pursue the implications of Habermas's change of view. To do so requires reckoning with religion's role in the history of freedom of speech, and thinking about the primary venue in which public debates, religious or otherwise, got played out: print. So, while modern debates about the challenges surrounding freedom of speech have inspired this book, it most substantively involves an engagement with prevailing Whiggish – whether Macaulayan or Habermasian – narratives about the history of press freedom in the early modern period.

The historiography on freedom of expression in the early modern period has involved two discrete modes of analysis. Firstly, scholars have examined press regulation and censorship, and analysed the latitude that authors, journalists and publishers possessed.[33] Secondly, they have analysed whether the 'print revolution' led to the emergence of a 'public sphere' of free and rational debate.[34] Far less attention has been paid to whether or not contemporaries developed ideas about – and justifications for – free expression. Historians have focused, in short, more on the *reality* of press restraint than on the *theory* of press freedom. We need especially to think carefully about both the *intention* and *power* of early modern governments.

At their heart, scholarly debates about print culture in early modern England have centred on detecting a 'struggle' over freedom of the press, and have yielded up overly polarised accounts that mask a remarkable degree of consensus.[35] The scholarship that has proved most contentious – by emphasising the 'tyranny' of early modern press regimes – was a product not just of the times in which it was written but also of scholars who were not historians. F.S. Siebert's *Freedom of the Press in England, 1476–1776* (1952), which appeared at the height of the Cold War and which drew explicit comparisons between the tyranny of early modern regimes and Eastern Bloc repression, was especially influential. Siebert was dean of Michigan State University's college of communication, and his 'presentist' book reflected an interest in the origins of the US Constitution and in modern jurisprudence. It emphasised not just repression and struggle but also change and development.[36] Equally 'presentist' was a Marxist historian like Christopher Hill, who compared the press policies of early modern England unfavourably with those of repressive modern regimes and who emphasised how the English revolution – temporarily – eased regulation.[37] Although such scholarship nowadays attracts attention for its worst elements, more recent literary scholars have likewise insisted that government 'repression' was 'systematic'.[38] Annabel Patterson's influential account of authorial practices under the shadow of the censor was predicated upon ideas about the 'repressive culture' of the early modern period and on the existence of 'pervasive' censorship.[39]

If these accounts are Whig and Marxist histories of free speech and the free press, it is also the case that these histories did the valuable work of trying to understand change over time. If their accounts were reductive it was because of their presuppositions about the more or less linear progress of history, especially regarding the freedoms valued in modern liberal societies. Whilst this book does not share their presuppositions, it does aim to chart change over time regarding both *freedom of speech* and *freedom of the press*. What emerges is a story of messy, non-linear, reversible developments across the early modern period, particularly those involving motives and strategies that were not necessarily 'liberal'. Whilst there is certainly no consensus – and perhaps no really convincing evidence – that freedom of expression emerged in the 'long' early modern period in ways that fit with modern ideas, the chapters in this book illustrate that government practices changed dramatically over time, and that freedoms of both speech and the press emerged as contested but valued – and perhaps even normative – concepts by the eighteenth century's end.

Revisionist scholars first made clear the failings of both Whig and Marxist approaches to press freedom. They produced more rigorously contextualised accounts of the aims and effects of early modern policies, and of the nature – or indeed absence – of demands for greater press freedom.[40] For instance, they rethought institutions like High Commission and Star Chamber, which had previously been regarded as organs of state repression, and reconsidered well-known but unusual episodes, like the punishment of John Stubbes and the trials of William Prynne. They also reappraised contemporary comments that apparently signalled an intention to behave repressively, from James I's complaint about 'the itching in the tongues and pens of most men' to Shakespeare's reference to art being made 'tongue tied by authority'.[41]

The most systematic – and nuanced – revisionist case, particularly relating to the Elizabethan and Jacobean periods, was developed by Cyndia Susan Clegg, who argued that previous scholarship involved 'decontextualised facts, overgeneralisation and half-truths'.[42] Clegg's account clarifies four key elements of the revisionist case. Firstly, censorship was unsystematic and unpredictable, lax and inefficient, and usually involved specific issues like national security, as well as a 'pragmatic situational response to an extraordinary variety of particular events'. It could also be performative and function as political propaganda.[43] As such, censorship was a 'playing card in a complex political game', rather than a 'policy' or a 'strategic agenda'.[44] Because censorship was 'local' and 'multivocalic', we must explore the specific 'rationale' for individual incidents of censorship, and acknowledge the importance of 'varied and often contradictory and competing interests'.[45] Censorship, then, involved multiple actors with different agendas at different times. This meant that specific books received different treatments at different moments,[46] and that 'patronage, personalities, historical events and political conditions' determined a book's 'reception'.[47]

Secondly, revisionists reinterpreted the Stationers' Company's role in the book trade and distinguished between censorship and commercial regulation.[48] From the Tudor period onwards, one of London's trade guilds or livery companies implemented press policy. That body was not simply an instrument of state power, but also aimed to protect its members and its monopoly interests. Revisionists argued, therefore, that as much as anything pre-publication licensing – which was used for only a small proportion of books – was a method for protecting the financial interests of stationers – as a form of copyright – rather than for ensuring that a book's content was thoroughly scrutinised. The official licence was a mark more of *privilege* than of *orthodoxy*.[49]

Thirdly, revisionist accounts questioned the intentions of the authorities, insisting, for instance, that the action taken against specific books tended to reflect concern about tone rather than substantive content; about their *manner* rather than their *matter*. So, the vigorous response to the Marprelate tracts and to those by Stubbes and Prynne is said to have reflected a reaction to the fiery style of such tracts, rather than determination to punish dissent.[50] Debora Shuger argued that historians need to recover the 'system of beliefs and values that made the regulation of language ... seem a good idea' and stressed that censorship related to persons rather than ideas. Early modern regimes, she insisted, sought to enforce 'civility rules'; and even occasional draconian attempts to constrain the press reflected 'deeply consensual norms' relating to charity, defamation, 'name-calling' and 'hate speech'. The problem, on this account, was 'licentiousness'.[51]

Finally, revisionist scholars denied that the period witnessed a 'struggle' for press freedom, and insisted that contemporaries lacked a principled conception of the value of free expression. Thus, while it might be possible to identify complaints about censorship before 1640, these involved people who claimed freedom to express their *own* ideas and opinions, rather than to a *general* freedom of expression. Moreover, they often involved the demand to be able to engage in fairly restrained kinds of religious *disputation*, rather than in unfettered political *debate*.[52] As such, revisionists insisted that those who defended themselves in the face of censorship tended to insist that their views ought to be heard because they were 'true', not because freedom was inherently desirable.[53]

Revisionism's impact has been considerable and mostly salutary. It is no longer credible to argue that censorship was monolithic or systematic, and we now know that censorship could be ineffective, not least because censored books became much more popular.[54] Nevertheless, there remains considerable scope to critique revisionist claims, and post-revisionists have certainly done so. They have argued that revisionists dispatched a straw man, since even Whiggish and Marxist scholars recognised that censorship was neither entirely efficient nor effective, and that there had always been underground presses which printed and distributed illicit texts. Beyond this, revisionists were wrong to suggest that censorship was *merely* a matter of tone rather than substance: whether or not their policies were effective, Henry VIII sought a 'purge' of 'pernicious doctrine'; Elizabeth I tried to silence radical forms of unsound doctrine; and James I targeted 'apostacies', 'heresies' and 'great errors'.[55]

Moreover, as Anthony Milton argued, the 'obsession with proving or denying' censorship is a 'red herring'. While uncertainty about what might be censored may have created suspicion and dampened discussion and debate in print,[56] Milton's approach involved conceding that there was more going on than simply a 'struggle' between the government and an 'opposition'. Licensing and censorship involved fragmented authority and competing interests, but the result was that some opinions were silenced and that print became a less available option for some people. So long as works were moulded and shaped by authority, even if they were not suppressed, then official licences were simultaneously marks of respectability and demarcations of acceptable terrain for debate. Indeed, even if this terrain may have been capacious, and even if the boundaries of acceptable discourse may have been contested and subject to change, restraints still existed and were far from neutral. It remained perilous to print texts that were beyond the pale. Most now accept that 'censorship' was 'less a matter of silencing authors or ideas than an instrument for defining, policing and negotiating what counted as orthodoxy'.[57]

Put simply, censorship was an everyday fact of life, and something that could involve pre-publication licensing, post-publication punishment and the use of royal proclamations and prerogative power. While contemporaries did not consider regulation to be inherently problematic its effects were real. While there was scope to express dissenting views, regulation was a powerful reality, and authors felt compelled to navigate controls in a variety of ways, including employing manuscripts, overseas presses and underground networks.[58]

Moreover, whilst post-revisionists insist that the decades before the English Civil Wars were less consensual than revisionists claimed, and that press regulation was a more or less significant phenomenon, they also stress the need to recognise change over time. Firstly, post-revisionists encourage us to think afresh about the rise of printed news. News was a promiscuous and popular commodity, and the governments of James I and Charles I paid particularly close attention to 'current affairs' printing from the early 1620s onwards.[59] Whilst regulation of the news reflected a conventional concern with the discussion of foreign policy, comments about the 'licentious' nature of print culture also reflected nervousness about tone, manner and style. There reached a point in the early seventeenth century when print discussion of 'matters of state' became intrinsically problematic. Moreover, the government sought to control print's likely *audience*, fearing that news texts would reach the 'foolish vulgar'.[60] It may be in this respect, and only in this respect, that Tudor and early Stuart governments were concerned about *printing*, rather than about the availability of texts *per se*. Their aim, in other words, may not have been to silence all forms of discourse and criticism, or even to proscribe certain kinds of material, but rather to ensure that certain things – irrespective of their tone and substance – were not *readily* available in print and for an indiscriminate audience.[61]

Secondly, post-revisionists alerted us to the ways in which Charles I and Archbishop Laud were responsible for a new and distinctive approach to print culture, not least regarding religious debate. This involved using High Commission and Star Chamber in innovative ways. Thus, whilst Prynne may indeed have been prosecuted for sedition over *Historiomastix*, interpretations of sedition, and of how it could be proved, were being tightened.[62] Demonstrating that new parameters for printing emerged under Laud and Charles has involved highlighting clear patterns regarding works that did and did not face official sanction. Before the late 1620s, the licensing of texts by episcopal chaplains was not *necessarily* censorious and could involve 'benign' interventions to prevent Puritan works getting into print. Over time authors and publishers could still 'shop around' to find lenient licensers, but this itself indicated that authors increasingly felt constrained by the licensing system.[63] Thus, while it is wrong to suggest that Laudian press policy was supremely *effective*, evidence abounds of a more concerted official attempt to suppress unacceptable views; of favour being shown towards a new kind of conformity; of the deliberate and one-sided dampening of debate; and even of greater tolerance for Catholic texts.[64] As such, whilst it is undoubtedly correct to point out that one of the most severe cases of 'ideological censorship' of the early Stuart period actually involved *Parliament* taking action against an Arminian (Richard Montagu) rather than the *Crown* moving against Puritans, the broader context involved heightened religious tension and the development of what became the Laudian press policy in *response* to Montagu's treatment.[65] Afterwards, texts that had once been acceptable became subject to restraint.[66] Puritans increasingly *sensed* that the Laudian licensing system was stacked against them, and reacted accordingly, and this made it more likely that religious debates would spill out into print; ensured that more concerted efforts were made to 'stir up' popular support with aggressive polemics; and led some authors to turn to European presses to get their works into print. As such, it is possible to accept that the late 1630s 'show trials' – of men like Burton, Bastwick, Prynne and Lilburne – were anomalous, while also recognising that they made things worse.[67]

During Charles I's reign, licensing came under attack, so that censorship – and free speech – became matters of debate, whether on principled or pragmatic grounds.[68] Ben Jonson claimed that 'the punishment of wit doth make [its] authority increase', while Thomas Scott argued that censorship encouraged defiance, 'for ... if one pen, or tongue be commanded to silence, they will occasion and set ten at liberty to write and speak'. Writing, Scott claimed, was like grass, in that 'the more it is depressed, the thicker it will spread and grow'.[69] Francis Bacon agreed, noting that while 'libels and licentious discourses against the state' were 'signs of trouble', suppression was not necessarily a remedy, 'for the despising of them many times checks them best, and the going about to stop them doth but make a wonder long-lived'.[70]

Scholars have challenged the notion that contemporaries lacked ideas about free speech and have demonstrated that free speech was indeed conceptualised and validated, in certain settings for certain people who behaved in certain ways. David Colclough highlighted the importance that some contemporaries attached to *parrhesia* – frank or justified speech – as a mode of political counsel, tracing the ancient lineage of such ideas; highlighting claims about the wisdom of the 'plain' or common person; and recovering the value that was attached to the active, informed and truth-telling citizen, not least at moments of crisis. Occasionally, such notions involved ideas about the compulsion to speak out, and about the value of prophet-like counsellors, as with the poet-pamphleteer George Wither, who styled himself England's 'remembrancer', or Thomas Scott, *Vox Populi*'s author.[71]

It is upon such foundations that this volume makes notable contributions. Joanne Paul (Chapter 2) develops different dimensions of contemporary ideas about *parrhesia*, not least the sense that free or frank speech was regarded less as a right than as a *duty*. The work of Thomas Elyot clearly highlights a fundamental difference between early modern and modern conceptualisations of free speech and demonstrates that *freedom* was not necessarily regarded as *restraint*'s opposite, not least in the sense that it was considered possible to be liberated by speaking out, irrespective of the consequences. These themes of restraint and the duty of free speech are also picked up by Karl Gunther (Chapter 3), and in ways that complicate matters. Gunther shows that restraint – including, crucially, self-restraint – was practised and valued even by those who accepted that free speech might be a duty. As Gunther shows, restraint was not something that was imposed upon authors by the authorities, but rather something that could be self-imposed, as part of a process of reflecting on audiences and contexts and of seeking to avoid harm, offence or indeed violence. Peter Lake (Chapter 4), meanwhile, develops ideas about the importance that was placed upon *counsel*, by highlighting the non-theoretical and not necessarily oppositional ways in which moments of crisis from the late sixteenth century to the Spanish Match in the 1620s generated *outbreaks* of free speech. These involved commentators from both within and beyond the political establishment, some of whom sought 'popularity', while others deployed a rhetoric of emergency to justify the promiscuous use of printed and scribal texts, including libels. All of these early modern authors, Lake argues, made appeals to various kinds of 'public', and it was such tactics – and at least tacit claims to free speech – that provided the context and pretext for the kinds of heightened restraint that marked the early Stuart period.[72]

Central to Colclough's account of free speech was Parliament. Parliament has long been recognised as being central to the history of free speech, even if only in terms of the privilege (and perhaps *right*) for MPs to speak freely at Westminster. Whig historians, for instance, detected tension with the Crown over how – and on what issues – such freedoms could be used. They also noted that such claims provoked resistance from monarchs like

James I, in terms of the need to avoid 'licentiousness', and to decide who would be responsible for maintaining decorum. In such tussles, of course, it becomes clear that contemporary fears about licentiousness – the *manner* of discourse – proved hard to separate from questions about the substance, or *matter* of, debate.[73] Colclough also claimed that the Commons broadened its remit and came to associate its own freedoms with the 'liberties of the subject'. He argued, furthermore, that parliamentary free speech shaped how people engaged in political debate beyond Westminster, not least through the circulation of news and scribal documents.[74] David Como (Chapter 5) demonstrates in other ways how parliamentary culture shaped public debate. This involved claims that presses should be free 'in time of parliament', largely because *Parliament* could take action against anyone who behaved indecorously: free speech implied neither absence of control nor licentiousness. For the pre-war period, then, the chapters in this volume significantly enhance our appreciation of how contemporaries conceptualised free speech; how they did so in a variety of ways that were not necessarily 'modern'; and how *change* occurred within political culture regarding free expression.

Recognising the need to acknowledge and explain change is a particular strength of post-revisionist scholarship. None the less, problematic notions about a 'collapse' of censorship, like the 'explosion' of cheap print which seems to have been its effect, remain commonplaces of scholarship on the 1640s and 1650s. In fact, there is plentiful evidence that attempts to reimpose press control emerged almost immediately after the outbreak of civil war, with demands that printed texts should contain the names of authors and publishers (so that post-publication punishments could be imposed), with the passage of new legislation, and with the appointment of new licensers.[75] To be sure, the period witnessed unprecedented possibilities for printing novel and unorthodox opinions.[76] Yet many at the time decried the new situation as anarchic, bemoaned the instability of the print medium and demanded new forms of restraint.[77] Seditious texts could still be censored and their authors and printers punished, and if the pre-civil-war period can no longer be described as one of 'pervasive' censorship, then neither were the revolutionary decades devoid of press control. This was very obviously true in terms of the news press, where government control eventually – if briefly – became total.[78]

The upheavals and experiences of the mid-seventeenth century had a lasting effect. Press culture and press regulation were transformed during the mid-century. Firstly, the period after 1641 involved a qualitative shift towards more ephemeral kinds of print, aimed at an increasingly broad audience, and, although the 'explosion' of titles, if not printing, was not universally admired, it was hard to reverse. Secondly, the experience of the Civil Wars made it clear that licensing was a political tool. The licensers appointed after 1643 contributed to the existing sense that licensing was a discredited method for regulating the press, and it became much harder to use an official licence as a marker of authenticity or orthodoxy. Thirdly, the parliamentarian and commonwealth regimes experimented with methods of press regulation that deployed state officials – not the Stationers' Company – to enforce laws.[79] Fourthly, the practice of civil war and interregnum governments involved *monitoring* the press: they mostly gathered information on journalists, printers and publishers to censure – as much as punish – them. This represented a fairly novel approach to press regulation, which involved the *policing* and perhaps *harassing* of the press, as much as it did *controlling* it.

Novel arguments regarding press freedom accompanied the new press policies, although any engagement with the ideas that emerged from the 1640s must involve great care, lest scholars find proto-liberalism in texts like Milton's *Areopagitica*.[80] Neither Milton nor his contemporaries offered a 'rights'-based approach to press freedom, and few were prepared to grant such freedom to Catholics. Indeed, opponents of Caroline press policy called for fairly strict press controls in the 1650s, while Milton not only disparaged the capacities of the 'vulgar sort' but also wrote of the need to 'clip' Presbyterians 'as close as Marginal Prynne's ears', and then served as a press licenser during the republic. Like other contemporaries, Milton was more animated by *clerical* licensing, which privileged perspectives other than his own, than by oversight of the press *per se*.[81]

Nevertheless, taking such cautions on board should not mean overlooking the emergence of intriguing ideas in the 1640s. David Como has argued that the discourse around press controls during the 1640s involved 'ideological fragmentation and escalation', wherein defences of religious toleration touched on press freedom and were seen as part of a wider political programme. Thus, while a radical like William Walwyn accepted the need to suppress books that were 'scandalous or dangerous to the state', he nevertheless offered 'the closest thing to a defence of press freedom that civil war England had yet seen'. Central here was an unprecedented degree of support for *debate* as something that was *necessary*.[82] By January 1649, Levellers were prepared to argue that 'liberty' of the press was 'essential unto freedom' and that licensing always bred tyranny.[83] Another way of explaining what was happening here, as Como's chapter in this volume suggests, is that claims about presses being free 'in the time of parliament', which began to emerge in the 1620s, came to be expressed much more generally after 1640, to the point where they could be invoked at *any* time, to hold *all* forms of authority to account, and in ways that became intimately linked to constitutional reform. By the late 1640s free speech was justified even without Parliament acting as the arbiter of decorum, and as something that was essential to the prevention of political and constitutional corruption.

However, what the Levellers did not make explicit was that they were (mostly) opposed to pre-publication censorship rather than to all forms of control. When their vocal supporter Gilbert Mabbott decried the system of licensing, he not only expressed opposition to *monopolies*, but also argued that 'it is lawful to print any book ... without licensing, so [long] as the authors and printers do subscribe their names thereunto, that so they may be liable to answer to the contents thereof'.[84] Like the Levellers, Mabbott was on the radical fringes of contemporary debates, but such commentators expressed a clear preference for post-publication punishment rather than pre-publication censorship, and considered this to be compatible with 'liberties' and 'freedom', even if they hinted at something more radical.

The mid-seventeenth century, in other words, witnessed messy experimentation but also new ways of thinking and acting, and the development of ideas that had begun to emerge before 1640 and that involved striking notions about press freedom. Important changes also took place after 1660, above and beyond the brief experiment with looser control that accompanied moves towards religious 'indulgence' in the early 1670s. Charles II's government declined to turn back the clock by reviving the prerogative courts, opting instead to achieve press control through legislation.[85] In addition, particularly close attention was paid to printed news, by means of a government monopoly, and Sir Roger L'Estrange, press overseer, was determined to control what was available to the 'unruly populace'. Indeed, for L'Estrange, the preoccupation with audience was perhaps as important as press restraint more generally, and he is notorious for complaining that cheap print – particularly news – 'makes the *multitude* too familiar with the actions and counsels of their superiors'.[86] Mark Knights, meanwhile, has argued that the later Stuart period witnessed profound nervousness about print culture, and that in a context of highly partisan politics there emerged a crisis of truth-telling.[87] Equally clear is that the shift towards a legislative approach to press regulation, involving acts that needed to be renewed periodically, created moments when control 'lapsed'. This occurred in 1679, during the Exclusion Crisis, leading to a 'flood' of print. Although judges declared that Charles II could prohibit newspapers and pamphlets using prerogative powers, renewed control proved difficult before 1685, to the point where Oxford University took matters into its own hands.[88] The late 1670s and early 1680s, therefore, were a period of mass Whig propaganda, of mass petitioning and of the 'outrageous liberty of the press', before some kind of order was restored with the 'Tory reaction'.[89] The years after the Glorious Revolution witnessed measures that were *intended* to make press regulation possible, more obviously than it did their effective implementation.[90]

As such, the story of the seventeenth century is not simply one in which it became harder to sustain effective press control, or in which control was patchy and erratic. Governments gradually demonstrated greater concern about audience, and about the news medium, as opposed to merely what ideas were available; regimes continued to be divided over the merits of relying upon the Stationers' Company; and faith in the value of pre-publication censorship began to wane. Charles Blount – the most obvious heir to John Milton as an advocate of 'liberty of the press' – explicitly demanded an end to licensing, but *not* to the censuring of offensive texts.[91]

These developments provide the backdrop to the Licensing Act's 1695 lapse, a lapse which has generated bold historiographical claims. Paul Monod argued that censorship was 'buried' in 1695; that 'ideological control was no longer effective at the level of the educated elite'; and that 'political consciousness extended itself rapidly among the popular classes'. What resulted was 'compromise' rather than 'control': afterwards 'a less censored press' and 'greater tolerance of the press' became 'a necessary condition of party politics'.[92] John Feather likewise argued that England witnessed 'a degree of freedom unique in a major country in eighteenth century Europe', even if such freedom was 'hedged about' with various restrictions.[93] Such conclusions are at least partly endorsed by contributions to this volume. David Womersley (Chapter 6) notes the increasingly clear connection that contemporaries made between free-thinking and freedom of expression and that claims about press freedom became more universal and less qualified.

The significance of 1695 has, however, been debated. Womersley also points out that writers like Jonathan Swift had profound reservations about the merits of free-thinking, let alone free expression. Elsewhere, scholars have noted that the decision not to renew press legislation reflected opposition to the Stationers' Company monopoly, rather than a conscious decision to liberate the press, and that numerous attempts were made to find other means to ensure some kind of regulation. This suggests that contemporaries were divided over the means – not the desirability – of press control.[94]

A more crucial issue involves contemporary thinking on how to deal with undesirable texts, especially ones regarding religion. Swift, as Womersley shows, was concerned about heterodox opinions, but did not favour the use of state power to deal with them, and relied instead upon the need for self-restraint. Others, however, continued to believe in press restraint, not least because souls needed to be saved by protecting truth from falsity.[95] In Chapter 8, Robert Ingram and Alex Barber reflect on the importance of, and the fate of, blasphemy legislation, successfully introduced in 1698, but then unsuccessfully re-enacted in 1721. They demonstrate the importance that continued to be attached to restraint as a necessary means of protecting 'truth', but also challenge the idea that the failure of the 1721 bill reflected principled support for free speech, even if some contemporaries certainly feared the prospect of 'persecution'. The key, they argue, is that ideas about restraint were predicated upon the need to protect truth *and* civil peace, and in the end the failure to pass the blasphemy bill in 1721 reflected changing views about the conditions in which restraint should be effected, and a recognition that this might not serve the interests of the state and the achievement of civil peace.

What certainly happened was that greater importance was attached to post-publication regulation, by prosecuting people for seditious libel. Publishers (Edmund Curll), journalists (John Tutchin) and pamphleteers (Daniel Defoe), and ultimately priests (Henry Sacheverell) were all targets of legal prosecution. Seditious libel was defined very broadly: it could involve questioning the succession, commenting on foreign and military affairs, and challenging the church's position within the constitution, or launching personal attacks on the monarch and courtiers. Nevertheless, zealous searches for illicit texts gradually fell out of fashion, and successful prosecutions were relatively rare, outside of fairly specific periods, such as 1704–8. As such, whilst there were *moments* when the press came under particularly intense pressure – as in 1714–16 – the system has more generally been described as 'haphazard', and Alan Downie argued that Robert Harley, more interested in propaganda than in suppression, actually contributed to 'the rise of a free press'. Indeed, to the extent that attempts were made to tighten control and close loopholes in the decades that followed, successive ministries encountered difficulties in securing convictions, and 'surrendered to impotence'.[96]

Of course, as Max Skjönsberg (Chapter 9) demonstrates, there were moments when threats to freedom of expression became much more real. He points to the late 1730s, when Walpole's ministry introduced pre-performance censorship of stage plays and clamped down on the reporting of parliamentary debates. At the same time, he also notes that such measures prompted vigorous debate (including the reprinting of Milton's *Areopagitica*), and indeed Hume's famous essay on the liberty of the press (1741). More obviously, governments subjected authors and stationers to *harassment*, and it seems likely that the threat of prosecution generated nervousness about printing scandalous things and encouraged self-restraint. Nevertheless, the use of informers and press spies constituted a system of surveillance, intimidation and *policing* more obviously than a policy of control.[97]

In short, the government tried to ensure that authors and publishers were *held to account* for the publication of unacceptable works. In passing judgement on Tutchin in 1704, for instance, Chief Justice Holt stated that 'if men should not be called to account for possessing the people with an ill opinion of the Government, no Government can subsist'.[98] Defoe, writing in 1714, advocated taking action against the hawkers of cheap print because such material made governments 'familiar' and 'contemptible' to the people'.[99] Yet again the concern was with material that reached a mass audience.

Crucially, however, a system based on the absence of pre-publication licensing, but with the capacity for post-publication censorship, was described throughout the eighteenth century as *constituting* a free press, and as a 'bulwark of our liberty'. Defoe denied that 'liberty' would be 'abridged' even if outspoken authors and their printers were 'punished', and the *Craftsman* explained in 1726 that press freedom involved 'an unreserved, discretionary power for every man to publish his thoughts on any subject, and in any manner, which is not expressly forbidden by the laws of the land, without being obliged to apply for a license or privilege for so doing'. 'Freedom of speech', in short, was thought to be compatible with the punishment of offensive literature, because people could 'publish and be damned'. As such it is not implausible to argue that 'the end of licensing was liberty of the press'.[100] Indeed, as Skjönsberg demonstrates, the laxity of press regulation in Britain by the mid-eighteenth century was often deemed vital to the maintenance of a balanced constitution. It is even plausible to suggest that Chief Justice Mansfield expressed a more or less *consensual* position in 1783 by ruling that 'the liberty of the press consists in printing without any previous license, subject to the consequences of law', before adding that the 'licentiousness of the press is Pandora's box, the source of every evil'.[101]

Thus, while press control was not discussed in the 1689 Bill of Rights, it is wrong to say that there was no theoretical framework for press freedom after 1695.[102] It is true that few people made principled or philosophical claims for unlimited press freedom, although, as Ann Thomson shows (Chapter 7), it is possible to find spirited challenges to censorship and defences of press freedom from men like John Toland. Such claims could be made on Miltonic grounds – in order to encourage the search for truth – although for Toland another issue was the need to be able to expose abuses of power. As Thomson shows, moreover, defences of press freedom tended to relate to philosophical enquiry, rather than other political and religious issues; tended to involve claims about freedom for an intellectual elite; and tended to involve works for which there would likely be a limited audience. Free-thinkers distinguished between textual freedom and freedom of speech and were willing to countenance the punishment of sedition and treason. Their claims were thus not about unfettered freedom.

Of course, the situation remained somewhat *unstable* for most of the eighteenth century, and disputes persisted about the degree of acceptable press freedom. For some scholars the Wilkite campaign to overturn restrictions on newspaper reporting represented the 'final step in the campaign for a free press'.[103] John Wilkes certainly described press freedom as the 'birthright of a Briton, and … the firmest bulwark of the liberties of this country'.[104] Others too made impassioned pleas for free expression, justifying libels and journalism that held public figures to account, and by this stage it was possible to argue that the press constituted a 'fourth estate', wherein journalists had 'an undoubted *right* publicly to complain of the conduct of ministers when they do wrong'.[105] By the 1770s there was widespread support for a version of press freedom that could distinguish *freedom* from *licentiousness*, and this too was reflected in legal pronouncements.[106] Blackstone declared that liberty of the press was 'essential to the nature of a free state', adding that 'this consists in laying no previous restraints upon publications and not in freedom from censure for criminal matter when published'. For Blackstone, every free man had a *right* to 'lay what sentiments he pleases before the public', but, if anyone published things deemed 'improper, mischievous or illegal', they needed to accept the consequences. This did not involve, he insisted, any 'restraint' being 'laid upon freedom of thought or inquiry'.[107]

Such views perhaps involved *qualified* support for press freedom, and care is needed about precisely what kind of 'rights' were thought to be involved and what this term meant. Concerns certainly persisted about 'lively and controversial journalism', about mass audiences and about 'popularity', whereby a politician might make himself 'an eternal slave to the wills, opinions and judgments of those whom he seeks for his followers'.[108] Hume, as Skjönsberg recognises, edited his essay on press freedom in 1770, in order to offer a much less ringing endorsement of press freedom, and did so in direct response to the perceived threat that Wilkes posed to political stability.

For other scholars, however, the Blackstonian position was not the end of the story. Patrick Peel (Chapter 10) challenges the notion that Blackstone's vision prevailed in revolutionary North America. In ways that echo David Como's chapter he emphasises the importance of petitions, which opens up his exploration of a distinctively 'free state' approach to citizenship. This emphasised the power of the 'people' and placed greater emphasis on the importance of press freedom as the 'channel through which the oppressed may utter their injuries', and indeed as a *right*. Intriguingly, Peel notes that these ideas gave way to a more circumscribed vision only after the 1840s.[109] As such, there is scope – as some historians of the English press have argued – to focus upon Fox's Libel Act (1792) as the moment that constituted the 'final check' on government power, because it empowered juries to do more than merely judge 'facts'. This arguably made it possible for 'public opinion' to intervene between a government and its critics. The 1792 act was not immediately effective, given the prosecution of Thomas Paine and the more repressive measures of the 1790s, but such retrenchment did little to halt the decline in the use of seditious libel in the early nineteenth century.[110] Indeed, in 1792 Lord Erskine referred to Paine by stating that 'every man, not intending to mislead, but seeking to enlighten others and what his own reason and conscience ... have dictated to him as truth, may address himself to the universal reason of the whole nation, either upon the subjects of government in general, or upon that of our own particular country'.[111] As such, some have argued that a version of freedom of the press finally became *normative*, even if disputes remained over 'the exact location of that fine line separating liberty from license'.[112]

Nevertheless, as the two final chapters in this volume suggest, there is considerable value in looking *beyond* the 1790s. For key themes from the previous two centuries resonated into the nineteenth century. Greg Conti (Chapter 11) draws much-needed attention to Samuel Bailey, an early nineteenth-century author whose *Essays on the Formation and Publication of Opinions* (1829) predates John Stuart Mill's more famous treatment of the subject. Bailey's

Essays were more radical than Mill's treatment, in terms of their treatment of social intolerance and the tyranny of public opinion and their emphasis on the value of a marketplace of ideas for the achievement of truth and peace. Bailey represents a distinctly new phase in thinking about press freedom, although he was not reflecting on the negative effects of democracy, or on the tyranny of the *majority*. More importantly, while Bailey clearly regarded free speech as a right, he also signalled continuity with the past by insisting that it was also a *duty*, even if he regarded this as a duty to express things that were thought to be true, rather than to *find* the truth.

Finally, Chris Barker (Chapter 12) draws attention to how even John Stuart Mill delimited free expression. It has long been recognised that Mill insisted on protecting the private lives of public individuals and worried that speech acts that might provoke violence. What Barker crucially draws attention to, however, is Mill's attitude towards press freedom in imperial India, where there were *ongoing* issues over whether it was better to engage in pre-publication censorship or post-publication control and where Mill advocated imposing restraints. What seems clear is that his attitude was utilitarian, not absolutist; his approach was contextual, and he regarded freedoms as *conditional*. For Mill, in other words, press freedom was *inappropriate* in an Indian context, given what he viewed as the existing nature of the Indian public.

This is an unsettling but important conclusion to a survey of scholarship on how press control and press freedom were thought about, discussed and practised before the mid-nineteenth century in the English-speaking world. Nevertheless, this survey and this volume are clearly significant. The chapters comprising this book indicate that there was no linear path towards press freedom and that great care is needed when discussing what freedom of the press and freedom of speech meant over time. Both in theory and in practice such things were – as they remain – unstable, and we must recognise both complexity and contingency.[113] This means recognising that contemporaries may have worried more about *manner* than *matter*; about the tone of printed texts ('licentiousness') more than their substantive content; and about texts that reached mass audiences more than those that were more exclusive. Decision-making about particular texts was influenced by considerations of genre, theme, style and audience. And different texts got treated differently. This perhaps made it possible to think afresh about religious discourse, printed news and political commentary. It also means thinking about both the aims and the effectiveness of press control, not just in terms of whether licensing represented *control* rather than *influence* but also in terms of whether it makes sense to read *intention* from *effect*, and it is also vital to recognise that the challenge of ensuring effective control had an impact on governmental ambitions. Indeed, it also makes sense to recognise that press 'control' took many forms, from pre-publication censorship to post-publication restraint, as well as surveillance, intimidation and harassment, and the policing of opinion.

Likewise, it is also necessary to reflect carefully on how contemporaries made claims – or demands – about press freedom. No matter how much more vocal exponents of free speech became, there remained many who were nervous about, or opposed to, the waning of restraint, not least because of concerns about the need to protect truth, ensure salvation and maintain peace. It is also important to be cautious about regarding such demands as involving unconditional or unfettered freedom, and about the basis on which free speech was validated. Freedom of expression could be regarded as a duty rather than a right, and contemporaries also recognised situations in which self-restraint was necessary. In that sense, restraint was not necessarily something that needed to be *imposed*. It also seems clear that, whilst some linked freedom of expression to freedom of thought, and to the search for truth, others were motivated by the need to ensure effective accountability and oversight, to prevent corruption and the abuse of power, and to maintain the constitution and the people's liberties. Beyond this, there were also many different reasons for opposing certain forms of press control, most of which did not involve a principled demand for freedom, and many of those who demanded free speech accepted the need for some kind of control or restraint, in terms of licentiousness, sedition and treason, and perhaps heresy. As such, it is unnecessary to equate freedom with the absence of control, or to suggest that limitations on free speech necessarily involved the infringement of liberties, not least when civil peace was at stake.

Such cautions are vital to the history of free speech, and they might even be salutary in relation to modern debates. Ultimately, however, it is also necessary to acknowledge that amid all of the continuities of thought and practice from the sixteenth to the nineteenth century, things looked very different by Victoria's reign compared with the reign of Henry VIII. What gives this period coherence was not that things remained the same over time, but rather how differently free speech was discussed in the early modern compared to the modern world. This might even prove instructive, not least by recognising how both religious and constitutional issues were central to debates about free speech, and became intertwined with each other in complex ways. Such coherence also involves our ability to recognise that, while any appreciation of free speech needs to recognise how public discourse worked in contextual moments, and that most demands for free speech involved contextualised forms of lobbying, it is also possible to observe the slow gestation and crystallisation of key ideas: *distrust* in pre-publication censorship; the relationship between free speech, anti-corruption and political accountability; and the notion of restraint being compatible with freedoms and liberties. Ultimately, the period witnessed messy and somewhat fraught change – non-linear, contested and perhaps dialectical – in terms of the degree to which it was thought necessary and possible to suppress unwelcome ideas, and in terms of the fact that there emerged a widely endorsed language of press freedom involving notions of rights and liberties. It is possible to recognise such changes while also acknowledging that press freedom was rarely if ever the same as freedom of expression, amid the persistence of ideas that the press needed to be monitored and policed, and that licentiousness ought to be punished somehow.

NOTES

1. D. Defoe, 'An Essay on the Regulation of the Press (1704)', in W. Owens (ed.), *The Political and Economic Writings of Daniel Defoe. Volume 8: Social Reform* (2000), 145.
2. R. Ingram, *Reformation without End: Religion, Politics and the Past in Post-Revolutionary England* (Manchester, 2018).
3. Defoe, 'Essay on the Regulation of the Press', 147.
4. Ibid., 146.
5. Ibid., 150.
6. Ibid., 149.
7. T. Bejan, *Mere Civility: Disagreement and the Limits of Toleration* (Cambridge, MA, 2018).
8. L. Siedentop, *Inventing the Individual* (Cambridge, MA, 2014), 2.
9. See, for instance, P. Deneen, *Why Liberalism Failed* (New Haven, 2018), 31–4.
10. T. Garton Ash, *Free Speech* (New Haven, 2016), 207. See also R. Dworkin, *Matter of Principle* (Cambridge, MA, 1985), 335–87; *Justice for Hedgehogs* (Cambridge, MA, 2011), 364–79, esp. 372–4.
11. S. Fitzpatrick, *Everyday Stalinism: Ordinary Life in Extraordinary Times: Soviet Russia in the 1930s* (Oxford, 1999), 164–89.
12. F. Fukuyama, *The End of History and the Last of Man* (New York, 1992).
13. H. Hannum, 'The Status of the Universal Declaration of Human Rights in National and International Law', *Georgia Journal of International and Comparative Law* 25 (1995–96), 25.
14. J. Winter and A. Prost, *René Cassin and Human Rights: From the Great War to the Universal Declaration* (Cambridge, 2013).
15. A. Mondal, *Islam and Controversy: The Politics of Free Speech after Rushdie* (Basingstoke, 2014), 97–146.
16. W. Bulman, 'Introduction: Enlightenment for the Culture Wars', in W. Bulman and R. Ingram (eds), *God in the Enlightenment* (Oxford, 2016), 1–41.
17. Quoted in P. Weller, *A Mirror for Our Times: 'The Rushdie Affair' and the Future of Multiculturalism* (2009), 21.
18. L. Maer, *The Abolition of Blasphemy Offences* (2008).
19. See *Ethnicities* 9 (2009), 291–447.
20. *Case of E.S. v. Austria* (25 October 2018).
21. H. Bielefeldt, N. Ghanea and M. Wiener, *Freedom of Religion or Belief: An International Law Commentary* (Oxford, 2016).
22. 'Cairo Declaration of Human Rights', in T. Stahnke and P. Martin (eds), *Religion and Human Rights* (New York, 1998), 185–9.

23 R. Dworkin, 'The Right to Ridicule', *New York Review of Books* (23 March 2006).
24 J. Waldron, *The Harm in Hate Speech* (Cambridge, MA, 2012), 4, 5. See Ivan Hare and James Weinstein, *Extreme Speech and Democracy* (Oxford, 2009), 123–285.
25 Waldron, *Harm*, 204–33. See also J. Waldron, *God, Locke and Equality: Christian Foundations of Locke's Political Thought* (Cambridge, 2002). Cf. Bejan, *Mere Civility*.
26 Cf. E. Powers (ed.), *Freedom of Speech: The History of an Idea* (Lewisburg, 2011), which focuses on the eighteenth century.
27 T. Macaulay, *The Works of Lord Macaulay* (1871), IV, 126.
28 J. Habermas, *The Structural Transformation of the Public Sphere*, trans. T. Burger (Cambridge, MA, 1989), 58.
29 C. Calhoun, 'Introduction', in C. Calhoun (ed.), *Habermas and the Public Sphere* (Cambridge, MA, 1992), 35–6.
30 M. Knights, 'How Rational Was the Later Stuart Public Sphere?', in P. Lake and S. Pincus (eds), *The Politics of the Public Sphere in Early Modern England* (Manchester, 2007), 252–67.
31 J. Habermas, *Between Naturalism and Religion* (Cambridge, 2008), 99–147.
32 Ibid., 5.
33 J. Clare, 'Censorship', in A. Kinney (ed.), *Oxford Handbook of Shakespeare* (Oxford, 2011), 276–94; M. Dzelzainis, 'Managing the Later Stuart Press, 1662–1696', in L. Hutson (ed.), *Oxford Handbook of English Law and Literature, 1500–1700* (Oxford, 2017), 507–28, 529–47.
34 J. Peacey, 'The Revolution in Print', in M. Braddick (ed.), *Oxford Handbook of the English Revolution* (Oxford, 2015), 276–93; P. Lake and S. Pincus, 'Rethinking the Public Sphere', in P. Lake and S. Pincus (eds), *The Politics of the Public Sphere in Early Modern England* (Manchester, 2007), 1–30.
35 The treatment of slanderous and seditious *speech* has more or less been the preserve of social historians: D. Cressy, *Dangerous Talk: Scandalous, Seditious and Treasonable Speech in Pre-Modern England* (Oxford, 2010); A. Bellany, 'Libel', in J. Raymond, *Oxford History of Popular Print Culture: Volume One: Cheap Print in Britain and Ireland to 1660* (Oxford, 2011), 141–63.
36 F. Siebert, *Freedom of the Press in England, 1476–1776* (1952). See also W. Clyde, *The Struggle for the Freedom of the Press from Caxton to Cromwell* (1934).
37 C. Hill, 'Censorship and English Literature', in *Collected Essays of Christopher Hill* (Brighton, 1984), I, 32–71.
38 J. Clare, *Art Made Tongue-tied by Authority: Elizabethan and Jacobean Dramatic Censorship* (Manchester, 1999).
39 A. Patterson, *Censorship and Interpretation: The Conditions of Reading and Writing in Early-Modern England* (Madison, WI, 1984), 17.
40 P. Lake, 'Post-Reformation Politics, or on Not Looking for the Long-term Causes of the English Civil War', in M. Braddick (ed.), *Oxford Handbook of the English Revolution* (Oxford, 2015), 21–42.
41 S. Lambert, 'State Control of the Press in Theory and Practice: The Role of the Stationers' Company before 1640', in R. Myers and M. Harris (eds), *Censorship and the Control of Print in England and France, 1600–1900* (Winchester, 1992), 1–32; B. Worden, 'Literature and Political Censorship in Early Modern England',

in A. Duke and C. Tamse (eds), *Too Mighty to Be Free: Censorship and the Press in Britain and the Netherlands* (Zutphen, 1987), 45, 48. See also D. Loades, 'The Press under the Early Tudors: A Study in Censorship and Sedition', *Transactions of the Cambridge Bibliographical Association* 4 (1964), 50; D. Loades, 'The Theory and Practice of Censorship in Sixteenth-century England', *TRHS* 24 (1974), 141–57; L. Rostenberg, *The Minority Press and the English Crown: A Study in Repression, 1558–1625* (Niewkoop, 1971), 81.

42 C. Clegg, *Press Censorship in Elizabethan England* (Cambridge, 1997), 219.
43 D. Shuger, *Censorship and Cultural Sensibility: The Regulation of Language in Tudor-Stuart England* (Philadelphia, 2006), 243.
44 Clegg, *Elizabethan England*, 5, 75, 79–102, 138–69; C. Clegg, *Press Censorship in Jacobean England* (Cambridge, 2001), 23, 68–89.
45 Clegg, *Jacobean England*, 20, 66–7.
46 Clegg, *Elizabethan England*, 103–22; Clegg, *Jacobean England*, 123, 194; C. Clegg, *Press Censorship in Caroline England* (Cambridge, 2008), 16, 25, 30, 39, 115; R. McCabe, '"Right Puisante and Terrible Priests": The Role of the Anglican Clergy in Elizabethan Censorship', in A. Hadfield (ed.), *Literature and Censorship in Renaissance England* (Basingstoke, 2001), 75–94; Shuger, *Censorship*, 236.
47 Clegg, *Elizabethan England*, 122.
48 Loades, 'The Press', 49.
49 Clegg, *Elizabethan England*, 6, 10–11, 13, 19, 20–1; Clegg, *Caroline England*, 9, 29, 31–2, 35–6; G. Johnson, 'The Stationers versus the Drapers: Control of the Press in the Late Sixteenth Century', *Library* 10 (1988), 1–17; F. Nash, 'English Licenses to Print and Grants of Copyright in the 1640s', *Library* 4 (1982), 174–84; M. Bell, 'Entrance in the Stationers' Register', *Library* 16 (1994), 50–4; W. Greg, 'Entrance, License and Publication', *Library* 25 (1994), 1–14.
50 Clegg, *Elizabethan England*, 170–217; R. McCabe, 'Elizabethan Satire and the Bishops' Ban of 1599', *Yearbook of English Studies* 11 (1981), 188–93.
51 D. Shuger, 'Civility and Censorship in Early Modern England', in R. Post (ed.), *Censorship and Silencing: Practices of Cultural Regulation* (Los Angeles, 1998), 91; Shuger, *Censorship*, 4–5, 6, 69, 77, 103, 165, 219, 231–2, 272.
52 Worden, 'Literature', 47; Lambert, 'State Control', 7.
53 Shuger, *Censorship*, 236.
54 T. Cogswell, 'Thomas Middleton and the Court, 1624: *A Game at Chess* in Context', *HLQ* 47 (1984), 273–88; N. Mears, 'Counsel, Public Debate and Queenship: John Stubbs's *The Discoverie of a Gaping Gulf*, 1579', *HJ* 44 (2001), 629–50; M. Kishlansky, 'A Whipper Whipped: The Sedition of William Prynne', *HJ* 56 (2013), 603–27.
55 D. Woodfield, *Surreptitious Printing in England, 1550–1640* (New York, 1973); Clegg, *Caroline England*, 11, 14, 24.
56 Patterson, *Censorship*, 75; P. Finkelpearl, '"The Comedians' Liberty": Censorship of the Jacobean Stage Reconsidered', *ELR* 16 (1986), 125.
57 Shuger, *Censorship*, 244.
58 T. Freeman, 'Publish and Perish: The Scribal Culture of the Marian Martyrs', in J. Crick and A. Walsham (eds), *The Uses of Script and Print: 1300–1700* (Cambridge, 2004), 235–54; S. Foster, *Notes from the Caroline Underground* (Hamden, CT, 1978).

59 R. Cust, 'News and Politics in Early Seventeenth-century England', P&P 112 (1986), 60–90, J. Boys, *London's News Press and the Thirty Years War* (Woodbridge, 2011).
60 Clegg, *Jacobean England*, 161–96; Clegg, *Caroline England*, 191–4.
61 Shuger, *Censorship*, 238–9; D. Ginsberg, 'Ploughboys versus Prelates: Tyndale and More and the Politics of Biblical Translation', *SCJ* 19 (1988), 45–61.
62 Clegg, *Caroline England*, 89, 108–12, 115, 120–1, 124, 166–78. Cf. Kishlansky, 'A Whipper Whipped'.
63 A. Hunt, 'Licensing and Religious Censorship in Early Modern England', in A. Hadfield (ed.), *Literature and Censorship in Renaissance England* (Basingstoke, 2001), 135.
64 F. Williams, 'The Laudian imprimatur', *Library* 15 (1960), 96–104; W. Schleiner, '"A plot to have his nose and eares cut off": Schoppe as Seen by the Archbishop of Canterbury', *Renaissance and Reformation* 19 (1995), 69–86; N. Bawcutt, 'A Crisis of Laudian Censorship: Nicholas and John Okes and the Publication of Sales's *An Introduction to a Devout Life* in 1637', *Library* 1 (2000), 406–22; Clegg, *Caroline England*, 45, 60–7.
65 Shuger, *Censorship*, 263.
66 P. Lake, *The Boxmaker's Revenge: 'Orthodoxy', 'Heterodoxy', and the Politics of the Parish in Early Stuart London* (Stanford, 2002).
67 Clegg, *Caroline England*, 41, 45, 95, 65–7, 78, 164, 181.
68 Ibid., 219–20.
69 Patterson, *Censorship*, 52, 77.
70 Ibid., 4.
71 D. Colclough, *Freedom of Speech in Early Stuart England* (Cambridge, 2005), 209–11; M. O'Callaghan, *The 'Shepheards Nation': Jacobean Spenserians and Early Stuart Political Culture, 1612–1625* (Oxford, 2000), 147–96.
72 See also, Bellany, 'Libel'; T. Cogswell, 'Underground Verse and the Transformation of Early Stuart Political Culture', *HLQ* 60 (1998), 303–26.
73 J. Neale, 'The Commons Privilege of Free Speech in Parliament', in E. Fryde and E. Miller (eds), *Historical Studies of the English Parliament* (Cambridge, 1970), II, 147–76; H. Hulme, 'The Winning of Freedom of Speech by the House of Commons', *AHR* 61 (1956), 825–53.
74 Colclough, *Freedom*, 184, 194–250.
75 J. Peacey, *Politicians and Pamphleteers: Propaganda during the English Civil Wars and Interregnum* (Farnham, 2004), 132–62.
76 Hill, 'Censorship', 50.
77 C. Blagden, 'The Stationers' Company in the Civil War Period', *Library* 13 (1958), 1–17; T. Clancy, 'The Beacon Controversy, 1652–7', *Recusant History* 9 (1967), 63–74; H. Plomer, 'Some Dealings of the Long Parliament with the Press', *Library* 10 (1909), 90–7.
78 T. Nexo, 'Between Lies and Real Books: The Breakdown of Censorship and the Modes of Printed Discourse during the English Civil War', in M. Laerke (ed.), *The Use of Censorship in the Enlightenment* (Leiden, 2009), 77–94; L. Miller, 'The Shattered *Violl*: Print and Textuality in the 1640s', *Essays and Studies* (1993), 25–38.
79 Peacey, *Politicians*, 132–62; Clegg, *Caroline England*, 231.

80 Worden, 'Literature', 47.
81 B. Hoxby, '*Areopagitica* and Liberty', in N. McDowell and N. Smith (eds), *Oxford Handbook of Milton* (Oxford, 2009), 218–37; D. Como, 'Print, Censorship and Ideological Escalation in the English Civil War', *JBS* 51 (2012), 843.
82 Como, 'Ideological Escalation', 821, 837; Clegg, *Caroline England*, 232; *Two Treatises* (1645).
83 *To the Right Honourable the Supreme Authority of this Nation* (1649).
84 *Perfect Diurnall* 304 (21–8 May 1649), 2531.
85 J. Walker, 'The Censorship of the Press during the Reign of Charles II', *History* 35 (1950), 219–38; M. Treadwell, 'Stationers and the Printing Acts at the End of the Seventeenth Century', in J. Barnard and D. McKenzie (eds), *The Cambridge History of the Book: Volume 4: 1557–1695* (Cambridge, 2002), 755–76.
86 Hill, 'Censorship', 51.
87 M. Knights, *Representation and Misrepresentation in Later Stuart Britain: Partisanship and Political Culture* (Oxford, 2004).
88 Hill, 'Censorship', 53; T. Crist, 'Government Control of the Press after the Expiration of the Printing Act in 1679', *Publishing History* 5 (1979), 49–77; L. Schowerer, 'Liberty of the Press and Public Opinion, 1660–1695', in J. Jones (ed.), *Liberty Secured? Britain Before and After 1688* (Stanford, 1992), 199–230.
89 T. Harris, *London Crowds in the Reign of Charles II* (Cambridge, 1987), 62–129; M. Knights, *Politics and Opinion in Crisis, 1678–81* (Cambridge, 1994).
90 L. Schwoerer, 'Press and Parliament in the Revolution of 1689', *HJ* 20 (1977), 545–67; P. Monod, 'The Jacobite Press and English Censorship, 1689–95', in E. Cruickshanks and E. Corp (eds), *The Stuart Court in Exile and the Jacobites* (1995), 127–34.
91 C. Blount, *A Just Vindication of Learning* (1679); C. Blount, *Reasons Humbly Offered for the Liberty of Unlicens'd Printing* (1699).
92 Monod, 'Jacobite Press', 141–2.
93 J. Feather, 'The English Book Trade and the Law, 1695–1799', *Publishing History* 12 (1982), 52.
94 L. Hanson, *Government and the Press, 1695–1763* (Oxford, 1967), 8–9. For other means to control the press, see R. Astbury, 'The Renewal of Licensing Act in 1693 and Its Lapse in 1695', *Library* 33 (1978), 296–322; J. Feather, 'The Book Trade in Politics: The Making of the Copyright Act of 1710', *Publishing History* 8 (1980), 19–44; J. Downie, *Robert Harley and the Press: Propaganda and Public Opinion in the Age of Swift and Defoe* (Cambridge, 1979), 149–61; J. Downie, 'The Growth of Government Tolerance of the Press to 1790', in R. Myers and M. Harris (eds), *Development of the English Book Trade, 1700–1899* (Oxford, 1981).
95 A. Barber, '"Why don't those lazy priests answer the book?": Matthew Tindal, Censorship, Freedom of the Press and Religious Debate in Early Eighteenth-century England', *History* 98 (2013), 680–707; A. Barber, 'Censorship, Salvation and the Preaching of Francis Higgins: A Reconsideration of High Church Politics and Theology in the Early 18th century', *PH* 33 (2014), 114–39.
96 Hanson, *Government*, 36–73; M. Ezell, *The Later Seventeenth Century* (Oxford, 2017), 445–54.
97 J. Hyland, 'Liberty and Libel: Government and the Press during the Succession Crisis in Britain, 1712–1716', *EHR* 101 (1986), 863–88; Hanson, *Government*,

39–44; H. Snyder, 'The Reports of a Press Spy for Robert Harley: New Bibliographical Data for the Reign of Queen Anne', *Library* 22 (1967), 326–45; M. Treadwell, 'A Further Report from Harley's Press Spy', *Library* 2 (1980), 216–18; Patterson, *Censorship*, 118.
98 Quoted in P. Hamburger, 'The Development of the Law of Seditious Libel and the Control of the Press', *Stanford Law Review* 661 (1985), 735.
99 Quoted in Hyland, 'Liberty and Libel', 863.
100 Ibid.; G. Kemp, 'The "End of Censorship" and the Politics of Toleration, from Locke to Sacheverell', *PH* 31 (2012), 53, 64.
101 Quoted in J. Oldham, *English Common Law in the Age of Mansfield* (Chapel Hill, 2004), 229.
102 Hanson, *Government*, 2; Schwoerer, 'Liberty of the Press'.
103 Hanson, *Government*, 30–2; Downie, 'Growth', 60.
104 R. Rea, '"Liberty of the Press" as an Issue in English Politics, 1792–1793', *Historian* 24 (1961), 26.
105 E. Hellmuth 'The Palladium of All Other English Liberties: Reflections on the Liberty of the Press in England during the 1760s and 1770s', in E. Hellmuth (ed.), *The Transformation of Political Culture: England and Germany in the Late Eighteenth Century* (Oxford, 1990), 490–4.
106 Ibid., 478.
107 Quoted in ibid., 479–80.
108 Ibid., 481, 485.
109 See also M. Warner, *The Letters of the Republic: Publication and the Public Sphere in Eighteenth-century America* (Cambridge, MA, 1990).
110 T. Ross, *Writing in Public: Literature and the Liberty of the Press in Eighteenth-century Britain* (Baltimore, 2018).
111 Siebert, *Freedom*, 392.
112 Rea, 'The Liberty of the Press', 26.
113 Patterson, *Censorship*, 3.

Chapter 2

Thomas Elyot on counsel, *kairos* and freeing speech in Tudor England

Joanne Paul

What makes speech free? It is usually taken that speech is 'free' if it is not met with punishment from governing authorities.[1] 'Freedom of speech' involves a right to speak without fear of governmental reprisal. A focus on the debates surrounding 'liberty of speech' in the Tudor period, however, leads us to another way of considering the 'freedom' of speech: that it is not the absence of punishment which makes speech free, but rather the choice to speak freely regardless of such reprisal.[2] In this way, the discussion shifts from the limits and boundaries of free speech to the way in which speaking truth is itself freeing, regardless of the consequences.

In Tudor England, these debates centred on the delivery of political counsel. There was both a 'paradox of counsel' and a 'problem of counsel' in Tudor England. The paradox existed in the expectation that rulers must take counsel to legitimise their rule, even though such counsel – if obligatory – could limit their power. The problem came from the perspective of the counsellors themselves: they ought to speak truth to power but doing so in non-ideal circumstances could lead to that counsel being ignored, or, worse, to their imprisonment or death. The key word often used to describe such dangerous counsel was *parrhesia*, variously understood as 'plain speaking' or 'liberty of speech'.

No Tudor writer had more to say about counsel and frank speech than Thomas Elyot, whose thought on the topic was shaped by the increasingly restricted space for counsel-giving in England in the 1530s.[3] Elyot, especially in his writings of 1533, tackled both the paradox and the problem of counsel head on. Drawing particularly on the work of Isocrates and Plutarch, Elyot sets out that the demands of 'right timing' (*kairos*) necessitate frank speech in order to limit the otherwise unrestrained passions of a monarch, regardless if these will be met with punishment or not. Such speech, Elyot maintains, is not just free in itself but is itself liberating: for the speaker – no matter the consequences; for the listener – even when forced to listen or obey; and for the commonwealth. As such, Elyot answers both the paradox and the problem of counsel: the king's power is not diminished by obeying virtuous counsel, but enhanced, and the counsellor is not endangered by giving his counsel, but freed. In the absence of an unrestricted space for communicating ideas, for Elyot truthful frank speech still must be delivered, which serves to free the speaker, even if it results in physical enslavement. It is a different view of free speech from most modern interpretations and has the potential to offer another way of thinking about free speech – and its issues – today.

From the classical to the modern period *parrhesia* can be seen to have four essential elements:

- *(primarily)* a truthful speech act
- *(which contains)* a critique of either speaker or audience (usually the latter)
- *(given in the context of)* a power differential (speaker must be less powerful than the audience)
- *(resulting in)* a sense of risk or danger in speaking this truth.[4]

Despite these central elements, *parrhesia* has been interpreted various ways throughout its very long history. In particular, work has been done in the last decade to show the ways in which the Foucauldian interpretation of *parrhesia* is in many ways at odds with – or is at the least another side of – an older notion of *parrhesia*, which highlighted its offensive licentiousness.[5] Plato both recommends and condemns *parrhesia*, suggesting that it ought to be restricted to the law-maker, as its use by other classes can produce civil discord.[6] The great rhetorician Quintilian (highly influential in the Renaissance) places *parrhesia* (or *'licentia'*) amongst his figures of speech, noting that it 'may frequently be made a cloak for flattery'.[7] As Matthew Landauer points out, ancient *parrhesia* had both a positive and a negative connotation. Pejoratively, it could be 'thoughtless, careless, impudent speech'.[8] On the other hand, it could also be the sort of free speech that served 'as a possible antidote to secure the epistemic properties crucial to a successful debate', thus securing democracy.[9] This can also relate to a confusion and conflation of *parrhesia* and an older term, *isegoria*, which tended to have more positive connotations, relating to the opportunity for all to speak freely.[10] It was *parrhesia* that proved the more enduring term, absorbing rather than ending the debates about what 'free speech' ought to mean.

The connection between notions of 'free speech', *parrhesia* and counsel-giving in early modern England has long been established. David Colclough's work on *Freedom of Speech in Early Stuart England* has been especially influential in showing that 'At the heart of early Stuart debates on free speech was the question of how best to advise a prince – the question of counsel'.[11] *Parrhesia* was the key rhetorical figure in these discussions, which becomes interwoven with the paradox and problem of counsel:

The counsellor's freedom of speech was a prerequisite for the proper fulfilment of his duty, and both republican and imperial versions of the classical past insisted that frankness was a central virtue of the advisor. The compulsion to speak out thus came from a desire or necessity to be virtuous, as well as from the firmly held belief that ultimately the safety of the realm was more important than either one's own safety or the comfort of the ruler.[12]

Parrhesia was associated with a Ciceronian duty to protect the commonwealth over and above other interests, especially one's own self-interest.

The most influential Tudor handbook on rhetoric, Thomas Wilson's *The Arte of Rhetorique*, first published in 1553, defines *parrhesia* as 'when we speake boldly, & without feare, euen to the proudest of them, whatsoeuer we please, or haue list to speake'.[13] Henry Peacham's *The Garden of Eloquence* (1577) echoes this idea, also bringing in the notion of the permissibility of such speech: '*Parrhesia*, when speaking before them whome we ought to reuerence and feare, & hauing somthing to say, which either toucheth the[m]selues, or their friends, do desire them to pardon our boldness, shewing that it were great pittie, yf for lack of admonitio[n], vices should be maintained, & vertues oppressed.'[14] In using this figure, Peacham goes on, 'the time, the place, and chiefly the persons, ought wel to be considered of'.[15] Likewise George Puttenham, Elyot's own nephew, writes in his *Defense of English Poesie* (1589) that '*Parhsia*' can be said to be in use 'when [the persuader's] intent is to sting his aduersary, or els to declare his mind in broad and liberal speeches, which might breede offence or scandall, he will seeme to bespeak pardon before hand, whereby his licentiousnes may be the better borne withall'.[16] *Parrhesia* is thus not free speech itself for these writers, but carries within it the request for freedom of speech. In the absence of institutionalised universal rights, frank speech to those in power requires the indulgence of the listener in each instance. For this reason, *parrhesia* brings together two otherwise apparently contradictory notions: dangerous speech and free speech.

Attention to the way in which Thomas Elyot fits into this story, and perhaps even complicates it, has developed in the last ten years, particularly in the work of Arthur Walzer. Whereas Colclough focused on the rhetorical emphasis on *decorum* – 'the time at which, the place in which, and the persons to whom one was speaking'[17] – Walzer and others have focused on another Greek concept: *kairos* – the 'right' or 'opportune' moment.[18] Walzer makes the argument that Elyot's *Of the Knowledge Which Maketh a Wise Man* and *Pasquil the Playne*, both produced in 1533, treat the issues of right-timing, counsel and *parrhesia* in ways that highlight the Janus-faced nature of this last concept, drawn from the classical debates regarding its use in both democratic and non-democratic contexts.[19] As Walzer notes, in non-democratic institutions (he gives the examples of 'Imperial Rome and Early Modern England') the '"ideal counselor" replaces the "ideal orator" as the normative idea of the rhetor' who uses *parrhesia*.[20]

It is especially in the works of classical philosophers on which Elyot draws

– Isocrates and Plutarch – that *parrhesia* becomes connected to ideas about advising the ruler, as well as *kairos*.[21] Isocrates' *Ad Nicoclem* advises the king to grant freedom of speech to 'those who have good judgement' to advise him,[22] and he puts himself consciously in the position of *parrhesiast* in his address to Philip and in the *Antidosis*.[23] In Plutarch *parrhesia* reaches new levels of importance, reflecting the tension between the need for the free speech of men of prudence, and the ways in which it could be a cover for the flatterer.[24] Plutarch sets out a series of tests to uncover such a one: the most crucial distinctions between the flatterer and a true friend is in the nature of their advice, and, especially, that the latter gives frank advice (*parrhesia*) at the right time (*kairos*). In particular, 'frankness, like any other medicine, if it be not applied at the proper time [*kairos*], does but cause useless suffering and disturbance, and it accomplishes, one may say, painfully what flattery accomplishes pleasantly. For people are injured, not only by untimely [*akairos*] praise, but by untimely blame as well.'[25] By missing the proper moment, such speakers can 'deliver' the listener readily into the hands of flatterers. In trying to avoid the accusation of flattery, in other words, friends must be careful they do not go too far the other way in giving unseasonable criticism, and Plutarch proceeds to give detailed advice about the proper nature of frank speech. Plutarch summarises: 'In what circumstances, then, should a friend be severe, and when should he be emphatic in using frank speech? It is when occasions demand [*kairos*] of him that he check the headlong course of pleasure or of anger or of arrogance, or that he abate avarice or curb inconsiderate heedlessness.'[26] A true friend will watch for such occasions, and not let them 'slip'. For this reason, Plutarch concludes that 'it is necessary to treat frankness [*parrhesia*] as a fine art, inasmuch as it is the greatest and most potent medicine in a friendship, always needing, however, all care to hit the right occasion [*kairos*], and a tempering with moderation'.[27] It is important, Plutarch makes clear, to grasp the occasion for frank speech, in order to mitigate the influence of the passions in the counselled. This is the purpose or function of *parrhesia* for Plutarch, one of the most influential classical writers on the subject in Tudor England.

The classical tradition, however, as the Renaissance humanists found, raised more questions than it provided answers. How could this opportune moment be identified? How could a frank speaker deliver advice to one not inclined to hear it, especially if an ideal opportunity does not present itself? In particular, they were interested in the way in which counsel might provide for the freedom of the people, by countering the tyrannical tendencies of a single ruler.[28] As Erasmus puts it in his *Education of a Christian Prince*, it would be best if the people could elect their ruler, but 'Where there is no power to select the prince, the man who is to educate the prince must be selected with comparable care'.[29] Erasmus in this text is ambivalent about the efficacy of the counsellor, as opposed to the tutor, of a prince, ascribing to the former the role of establishing virtue in the prince and, thus, in the people as a whole.[30] From the prince flows all the good and ill of the commonwealth, and it is the man who instructs him in the virtues who determines the nature of what the prince disseminates to his people: 'a country owes everything to a good prince; but it owes the prince himself to the one whose right counsel [*recta ratio*] has made him what he is'.[31] Erasmus also observed the ways in which speech to a powerful figure could be freeing. As he writes in his description of his *Panegyricus*, 'I realized that this literary form [the panegyric] cannot be handled without flattering. However, I have adopted a novel approach – being very free in my flattering and very flattering in my freedom'.[32] That being said, Erasmus sides with Plutarch in maintaining that the worst sort of flattery is one that involves a 'touch' of *parrhesia*.[33]

It is in coming up against Lutheranism that Erasmus is clearest on the relationship between free speech and correct timing. He writes to Lorenzo Campeggio in 1520 that he gave advice to Martin Luther:

> that he should spare the dignity of rulers, for if they are inopportunely insulted or admonished they do not improve, but rather become embittered and sometimes stir up dangerous storms. As a result, the critic loses his authority and sometimes his life, and the advice its effect. While it is never lawful to oppose the truth, still it is sometimes expedient to conceal it at the right time.[34]

In these few lines, Erasmus expresses succinctly the humanist 'problem of counsel' and its connection to right timing. If the right moment is identified correctly, the problem of counsel will be avoided. Silence is often necessary, depending on the demands of the moment.

Erasmus's friend and contemporary Thomas More appears to have the same model in mind in Book I of his *Utopia*, in which he sets out a debate between a Platonic defence of the contemplative life and a Ciceronian argument for the active life, expressed in terms of whether an experienced scholar – in this case Raphael Hythloday – should become a counsellor to a prince.[35] The character of Morus argues for duty and *decorum*: Hythloday's advice would do the commonwealth good, and thus he ought to give it; in so doing, he ought to alter his advice according to the circumstances, not attempting to impose unbending principles regardless of circumstance. Hythloday resolutely holds that his counsel would be of no benefit outside of the ideal context of Utopia, a place in which there is nothing private, and thus no self-interest or pride. Importantly, Hythloday holds that to enter into service to a prince would in fact be servitude, in contrast with the freedom that he enjoys outside of the court. His advice would meet with only ridicule or punishment. If he adopted the compromising 'indirect' approach suggested by Morus, it would no longer be virtuous advice, becoming as corrupted as that around it. Book I of *Utopia* is a debate regarding the problem of counsel, without a clear resolution.[36]

In general, More does advocate for the active life of politics, but is cautious when it comes to frank speech. Speech is better than silence, when it tends to the reformation of the company, but this is dependent on the nature of the occasion. In his *Four Last Things*, written in about 1522, he sets out that there is 'as scripture saith, time to speke & time to kepe thy tong', a reference to the appearance of *kairos* in Ecclesiastes 3:7.[37] When encountering 'nought and vngodly' speech, keeping silent is only the second-best path of action, and is entirely self-serving. Instead, it is better to 'breake into some better matter' and thus benefit all those assembled as well.[38] If, however, speech will not change them and will only 'irritate them to anger', then silence is the best option.[39]

Such speech ought to take place, however, in private. In Utopia it is a capital offence to speak of public matters outside the public assembles, and, like Erasmus, More is especially clear about the limitations to free speech after the Reformation. As he writes in his *Confutation of Tyndale's Answer* in 1532–33, it 'were a lewd thing to suffer any prince, estate, or governor, to be brought in slander among the common people'. It is the responsibility of the prince's 'confessors and counsellors' to keep him in line.[40] More himself fiercely enforced bans on seditious and heretical texts, even though he had – reportedly – also advocated for freedom of speech in Parliament.[41]

More's position is soundly critiqued by his contemporary Thomas Starkey in his *Dialogue between Pole and Lupset*. For Starkey, seeking an opportunity for speech means not, as Hythloday would have it, waiting for the ideal opportunity but seizing any that comes along. This might mean, in contrast to More's comments above, that it becomes necessary to present one's advice outside of the institutionalised forums for doing so.

The *Dialogue* begins in much the same way as *Utopia*: two interlocutors – Thomas Lupset and Reginald Pole – engage in a discussion of the merits and disadvantages of counsel-giving. Lupset attempts to convince Pole that he ought to offer his counsel to a prince for the good of the commonwealth. Pole agrees in principle that every able man ought to offer his counsel in this way, but the issue remains of 'time and place'.[42] In a tyranny, he objects as Hythloday had, either good counsel will be laughed at and rejected or the counsellor himself will become corrupted (the 'problem of counsel' again). Lupset immediately recognises this objection, criticising those who 'too narrowly and so curiously they ponder the time and the place, that in all their lives they nother fine time nor place', vainly looking for 'Plato's common weal'.[43] Instead, the focus should be on 'taking the time when it is, and taking occasion when it offereth itself ... Let not occasion slip; suffer not your time vainly to pass, which without recovery fleeth away; for, as they say, occasion and time will never be restored again.'[44] Pole (and thus Hythloday) has missed the point of an emphasis on *kairos*. According to Starkey's Lupset, it is not about delaying until the perfect moment but about seizing an available opportunity with the aim of doing one's 'office and duty', which is to speak truth to power.[45]

Starkey suggests that hereditary monarchy is a problem; it does nothing to ensure that a monarch will be led by reason, rather than the affections. As such, the prince must, in turn, be ruled by his counsellors. In the vision set out by Pole, this means making the monarch subject to a series of councils, which in fact hold sovereign power in the state. Pole, in the end, however, maintains that he lacks the opportunity to communicate this advice to the Parliament or king, and will wait until such an opportunity presents itself. Such 'tarrying of time', Lupset objects, will in fact lead to the 'destruction of all'.[46] It is on this note that the dialogue ends, and it was never published. Awaiting the opportunity to safely deliver one's advice limits the scope for speaking. Erasmus and More advocate silence in such occasions; Starkey worries that awaiting the ideal moment to speak has destabilising effects on the commonwealth.

Elyot's contemporaries grappled with the issues of free speech, freedom and right timing, but with little concrete resolution. The problem and paradox of counsel still persist in these writings. Added to them is confusion about what exactly constitutes the right moment and what sort of speech should be used in it. It is in Elyot's works, especially those published in 1533, that resolutions to these issues are put forward. Elyot defines clearly the opportune moment for frank speech, demonstrates under what conditions frank speech should break the bounds of propriety and *decorum*, and solves both the problem and paradox of counsel by highlighting the freeing nature of *parrhesia*, even (or perhaps especially) in the context of tyranny.

Thomas Elyot was part of the humanist circle around Thomas More. He entered the service of Henry VIII shortly after More had, in 1523, as senior clerk of the king's council.[47] He, however, lost his position in the wake of Cardinal Wolsey's fall in 1529, and so was forced to work his way back into the king's favour. The result was *The Boke Named the Governour*, published in 1531, and designed to show off Elyot's relevant skills and suitability for a political posting. It is, perhaps for that reason, a fairly conservative text. Elyot places greater emphasis on the maintenance of existing social hierarchies than do More or Starkey. Although he borrows from Isocrates and Plutarch in exclaiming 'O what damage have ensued to princes and their realms where liberty of speech hath been restrained!', giving the example of Alexander, who fell into hatred and eventual death because of his silencing of freedom of speech, he does not address the issue of what an individual should do in tyrannous circumstances.[48] In short, in the *Governour* he does not explicitly confront the problem nor the paradox of counsel. In fact, he expresses a Hythloday-esque scepticism in regard to liberty of speech, given the corrupt context in which it must operate. Since 'this liberty of speech is now usurped by flatterers', it is difficult to distinguish it from flattery.[49] The receiver of advice must therefore determine whether the adviser is a friend or not. The problems encountered by those wishing to give truthful advice are not considered.

Two years after writing the *Governour*, Elyot's context had changed dramatically, and with it his approach to these questions.[50] Elyot served as ambassador to Spain for four months from 1531 to 1532, sent to try to bring Charles V around on the issue of the annulment of the marriage of his aunt, Catherine of Aragon, to Henry VIII. Elyot did not support Henry's 'Great Matter'; as Greg Walker establishes, Elyot seems to have had a private meeting with Henry in June 1532 in which he expressed his views on the annulment of Henry's first marriage.[51] Elyot was replaced by Thomas Cranmer and when he returned to England was out of money and favour. For this reason the 1533 texts convey a greater sense of urgency in considering the role of the counsellor, and contain a deeper reflection especially on the themes of *kairos* and *parrhesia*.

In particular we are concerned with *Pasquil the Playne* and *Of the Knowledeg*[52] *which Maketh a Wise Man*, both published in 1533.[53] Walzer suggests that they present a critique of unrestrained, indecorous and ill-timed frank speaking, noting the conflict between 'two different versions of the rhetoric of counsel ... one based on principles of philosophy and one based on strategic rhetoric', in many ways mirroring the opposition that had been presented in Book I of More's *Utopia*.[54] In what follows, I maintain that Elyot does not simply rearticulate this problem, but presents a resolution, by ruminating on the role of *parrhesia* in securing liberty.

In *Pasquil*, plain speaking is represented by the title character, a personification of the Pasquino statue in Rome, upon which residents could post complaints and satires.[55] Through this practice, Elyot notes, he has become 'rude and homely'.[56] Pasquil debates with two embodiments of flattery, noted to be 'cosens' as there is 'small diuersite betwene [their] condicions':[57] Gnatho, who 'alway affirmed, what so euer was spoke[n] of his maister', and Harpocrates, who favours silence.[58] Elyot ends his address to the reader with the plea that 'if it seme to you, that Pasquill sayeth true' then 'in declaringe howe moche ye do fauoure truthe, defende hym ageyngst venemous tunges and ouerthwart wittis', for these 'doeth much more myschieffe, than Pasquillus babillinge', a plea that Pasquil repeats in the final line.[59] Elyot thus accepts from the outset the Janus-faced nature of *parrhesia*, yet concludes that the opponents of truth-speaking are far more dangerous than those who – in an effort to speak truth – offend or prattle, as Pasquil does.

Pasquil's discussion with each counsellor centres on the interpretation of a quotation from Aeschylus's *Libation Bearers*.[60] The quotation as Gnatho gives it is 'holding thy tonge wher it behoueth the. And spekyng in tyme that whiche is conuenient.'[61] In Aeschylus's original, the character of Orestes addresses the chorus, instructing them to 'be silent when there is need and speak only what the occasion demands'.[62] The dialogue becomes a debate about how best to interpret this line, and – in essence – how best to determine what *kairos* really means in regards to giving counsel.[63] Gnatho gives his reading first. He interprets the statement as meaning that 'it behoueth a man to holde his tunge, whan he aforeseeth by any experience, that the thinge, whiche he wolde purpose or speke of to his superior, shall neyther be pleasantly herde nor thankefully taken'.⁶⁴ He suggests that, when it comes to words, 'oportunitie & tyme alwaye do depende on the affection and appetite of hym that hereth them'.⁶⁵ Of course, anyone well read in their Plutarch, as Elyot was, would know that this was an interpretation of *kairos* completely at odds with the one that a good counsellor was meant to adopt. The good counsellor ought to use *kairos* to restrain affections, not to play to them.

In response, Elyot has Pasquil reiterate much of Plutarch's doctrine of *kairos*:

> Oportunite consisteth in place or tyme, where and whan the sayd affections or passion of wrath be mitigate and out of extremitie. And wordes be called conueniente, whiche haue respecte to the nature and state of the person, vnto whom they be spoken, and also to the detriment, whiche mought ensue by the vice or lacke that thou hast espied, & it ought not to be as thou hast supposed. For oportunite & tyme for a counsayllour to speke, do not depend of the affection and appetite of hym that is counsayled: mary than counsaylle were but a vayne worde, and euery man wolde do as hym lyste.⁶⁶

The affections should not be entered into a consideration of opportunity except in terms of their being 'out of extremitie'. Gnatho is thus correct that Pasquil ought to consider 'what, and to whome, and where thou spekist', but he considers the wrong factors in relation to these, and with the wrong ends in mind.⁶⁷ Gnatho seeks promotion, Pasquil truth. That is part of what makes Gnatho such a dangerous flatter: he seems to be speaking sense, but in fact is self-serving – precisely the problem that Elyot had identified in the *Governour*.

Gnatho is also correct that Pasquil 'rayles', but this has to do with the pressing needs of Pasquil's context. As Pasquil states at the end of the dialogue, he would 'speake neuer a worde, but sit as styll as a stone' if those 'that be called, wolde alwaye playe the partis of good Counsaylours'.⁶⁸ But the world is turned upside-down, so that 'stones do grutche' and 'counsailours be spechelesse'; the statue Pasquil speaks while advisers say nothing.⁶⁹ This idea that the world 'is rou[n]d, and therfore it is euer tournynge' so that 'nowe the wronge side vpwarde, an other tyme the ryghte' runs throughout the text, especially in Pasquil's greetings to Gnatho and Harpocrates.⁷⁰ Pasquil opens by declaring 'It is a wonder to see the world: Now a daies, the more straunge the better lyked, therfore vnnethe [scarcely] a manne maye knowe an honest man from a false harlotte', upon which enters Gnatho.⁷¹ When Harpocrates enters, he declares that he will give his master counsel after they both have eaten, prompting Pasquil to declare 'Lo is it not as I sayde, a wonder to se this worlde?' as in 'olde tyme' men used to attend to such important matters in the morning, before dining, recalling Pasquil's juxtaposition of the right timing of eating and counselling.⁷² Now 'after noone is tourned to fore noone, vertue into vice, vice into vertue, deuotio[n] into hypocrisie, and in some places men saye/ fayth is torned to herisye'.[73] In other words, the timing of affairs has turned virtues into vices. In such a world, Pasquil's bluntness, usually inappropriate, is the only option.[74] As he says, he might otherwise give his counsel in private, but, since he is not invited into the chambers of the mighty to correct their vices, he must publish it publicly, so that shame might be a motivating factor for a vice-ridden leader.

Gnatho's suggestion, then, that Pasquil's counsel is not listened to because it is too harsh misses the point: Pasquil's counsel is harsh because he was not listened to. Pasquil's bluntness is a last resort, caused by the evil counsellors – the Gnathos and Harpocrates – of the world. In some ways this is a position much like Hythloday's – a truth-speaker excluded because of already-existing bad counsel – but Pasquil is no Hythloday in his counsel, and is desperate, not reluctant, to give his advice. He is not awaiting a utopian scenario, but rather has been shut out. This was Elyot's own position in 1533, supplanted by Gnathos and Harpocrates and forced to articulate his counsel publicly. The opportunity he had described is not possible, so instead it becomes a question of when the urgency of the situation demands the cessation of silence.

This is the question taken up in Pasquil's exchange with Harpocrates. Challenging Harpocrates's dedication to silence, Pasquil asks him 'If I perceyued one at thy backe with a swerde drawne, redy to strike the, woldest thou that I shulde holde my peace, or else tell the?'[75] Harpocrates responds that 'Naye, sylence were than oute of season' – 'season' being another translation for *kairos*.[76] Pasquil responds that Harpocrates 'wyll season silence' and jokes that 'Marye I wene my lorde shulde haue a better cooke of you thanne a counsayllour'.[77] He asks Harpocrates 'howe thou doest season thy sylence[?]'[78] Harpocrates responds that he does so 'with sugar, for I vse lyttell salte', and Pasquil retorts that this 'maketh your counsayl more swete than sauery'.[79] Harpocrates' choice of 'season' makes his advice pleasant but not wholesome.

Harpocrates has also misunderstood the situation which would necessitate plain speaking. He wishes to insist that he needs to speak out only when the danger to his master is imminent, as the sword drawn at his back. Their debate thus hinges on the meaning of the word 'imminent', which Pasquil notes is 'a worde taken out of latine, and not co[m]menly vsed'.[80] Harpocrates defines 'imminent' as 'whan it appereth to be in the instante to be done or to happen: and afer some mens exposition, as hit thretned to come'.[81] Pasquil insists, however, that Harpocrates has misunderstood this word, for 'the instant whan it appereth/ that your frend shall be slayne/ and the instante whan he is in sleinge' are in fact not the same, but 'diuerse'.[82] To speak in Harpocrates' 'imminent' moment is to be too late, for then 'it is in the instance of doinge or happening'.[83] Speech is 'in good season' when the danger is imminent in Pasquil's understanding of the term.[84] Pasquil and Harpocrates agree that before this moment speech is dangerous to the speaker, and, after it, dangerous to the hearer.⁸⁵ This exact moment must be hit, then, to benefit both counsellor and counselled. The problem of counsel comes down to understanding *kairos*. *Pasquil*, however, does not solve the problem of counsel, though it clarifies it, and like *Utopia*, and Starkey's *Dialogue*, it ends without a clear resolution.

These issues come together, and are addressed in full, in Elyot's *Of the Knowledge Which Maketh a Wise Man*, a dialogue between two parties, Plato and Aristippus, the former of whom is the Socratic teacher, the latter the learner. Aristippus, as he appears in Laertius, is a hedonist, which makes Plato's later lessons about the rule of reason stand out all the more clearly.⁸⁶ Crucially as well, Aristippus is described as having been much favoured by Dionysius because 'He was capable of adapting himself to place, time and person, and of playing his part appropriately under whatever circumstances'.⁸⁷ Like Gnatho, this flattering opportunist makes an ideal foil for the *parrhesiastes*.⁸⁸

Plato appears in the text in slave's garb, having been sold and almost killed (twice) for offering his frank counsel to the tyrant Dionysius, as recorded to Diogenes Laertius's life of Plato:

> But when Plato held forth on tyranny and maintained that the interest of the ruler alone was not the best end, unless he were also pre-eminent in virtue, he offended Dionysius, who in his anger exclaimed, 'You talk like an old dotard.' 'And you like a tyrant,' rejoined Plato. At this the tyrant grew furious and at first was bent on putting him to death; then, when he had been dissuaded from this by Dion and Aristomenes, he did not indeed go so far but handed him over to Pollis the Lacedaemonian, who had just then arrived on an embassy, with orders to sell him into slavery.⁸⁹

Notably, in Elyot's version, Plato responds that Dionysius's words 'sauored of Tyranny', which the character of Plato later claims demonstrates his temperance and reserve in counselling the king, as it was not a straightforward accusation of tyranny against the king himself.⁹⁰ This rejoinder is, according to Elyot, 'that whiche is best worthy to be called wysedome'.⁹¹ The immediate lessons, then, of this text appear to be similar to those of *Pasquil*: blunt frank speech is sometimes necessary in order to correct the vices of kings, even under threat of death. But what is to be done about those consequences?

Aristippus, like Gnatho to Pasquil, accuses Plato of speaking 'vnaduisedly', for, knowing the 'nature and disposicion' of the listener, he should not have spoken in the way that he did. Plato explains to Aristippus that, as his purpose in coming to Sicily was not to advise the king, he resisted the call to attend Dionysius until he was convinced. Dionysius wished to see Plato, the two agree, because of the 'reporte' he had heard of Plato's 'wisedome and knowledge'.⁹² As this is what prompted Dionysius's call, Plato reasons to Aristippus, Plato was required to fulfil this expectation and both act and speak accordingly. Aristippus is forced to agree: Plato ought to 'tell [Dionysius] truthe/ & accordinge to [Plato's] profession'.[93] As Plato's profession is 'That no man is happy, except he be wise and also good', the two embark on a discussion of what wisdom is, or rather what kind of knowledge constitutes wisdom.[94]

After a long discussion, they conclude that this knowledge is self-knowledge, which gives knowledge – in turn – of others: 'the knowlege of hym selfe: wherby also he knoweth other', which is to know things 'intelligible' rather than 'sensible', and thus resides in the soul.[95] Plato draws the image of the soul as ruler over the passions, with understanding 'for a chiefe counsayllour'.[96] If the imagination does not consult 'king cou[n]saylle of vnderstandyng' it can be moved and persuaded to think that vices be 'good pleasant & profitable'.[97] Without such counsel, the soul becomes 'ministre vnto the sences/ which before were her slaues' and 'holly at their co[m]mandment'.[98] The internal persuasion of the soul is echoed by the same externally, for 'vicious co[m]munication, yl counsayle, and flatery' lead to 'the venemous humour of ylle opinion, wherof commeth vice'.[99] For Elyot's Plato, the rule of understanding's counsel guards against the enslavement of the soul, leading to vice. This model of internal counsel mitigating enslavement parallels the model that Plato will also use in which relationship with the king, in which he takes the role of 'king cou[n]saylle of vnderstandyng' over Dionysius's soul.

When the invitation came at last to Plato to speak on the nature of kingship, Plato 'reioyced, wenyng to haue founde the oportunitie to speake that I so longe loked for.'[100] Having this opportune moment, Plato was required to live up to the expectation of wisdom Dionysius had of him, and declare the contents of the knowledge which makes him wise: that the ideal king is one 'in whom the soule had intiere & ful auctorite ouer the sensis & alway kept the affectis in due rule & obedie[n]ce, folowyng only the counsayle of Vndersta[n]ding'.[101] Plato ends his counsel to Dionysius on the image of the tyrant, who loses understanding as a counsellor, and is thus ruled by the appetites and falls easily into the 'snares' of such flatterers, ignoring the words of those who would seek to correct him.[102] As Plato explains, one who does not follow the counsel of understanding is enslaved, king or no.

Plato's 'knowledge' resolves the paradox of counsel – the king is freed, not restrained, by listening to wise advice – but it does not solve the problem. Aristippus protests that Plato endangered himself in speaking to Dionysius this way, 'without hope of benefite'.[103] Plato maintains, however, that Dionysius 'had no power to indamage my soule, by whose operation I was called a wyse man', whereas, if he had chosen not to speak out of fear of bodily harm, he would have 'proued my selfe to haue ben a foole and no wyse ma[n]'.[104] Plato 'declared that my mynde was not subiecte to corporall passions, and consequently not to sensuall affections' in speaking the truth to Dionysius.[105] Thus, 'by takyng libertie from me, and makyng me a slaue, he more declared mi wordis to be true'.[106] Plato is untouched by his physical enslavement because his soul remains free through his choice to speak truth to power. Dionysius, on the other hand, is shown starkly in his enslavement. Plato concludes that he was indeed never lost, as he 'was neuer transformed or out of that astate, where in a wise man ought alway to be', whereas Dionysius 'hath bothe lost him selfe' by refusing Plato's knowledge, and has lost Plato 'which by [his] counsaile shuldist haue ben to hym so royall a tresure'.[107] Freedom can be found by the rule of reason, which Plato demonstrates through his act of *parrhesia*. Thus, Elyot answers both the paradox and the problem of counsel: wise counsel should indeed rule the king, and the counsellor ought to have no fear of consequences in the performance of his duty. All are made free through freeing speech.

If one accepts, as Elyot does, that the rule of reason over the passions is what preserves liberty, then it is easy to see how frank speech to those in power can be liberating. If the auditor heeds the advice then he is freed even as he is ruled, as are those he governs because he ceases to be a tyrant. If he does not, then the counsellor is still free – no matter what might be done to him physically – as he has not been governed by his passions in avoiding such a confrontation.

Modern notions of freedom of speech are centred on the observance of individual universal rights by a governing power. If this is lost, then no freedom of speech can be said to exist. In Elyot's work, the act of speaking truth to power is itself freeing, no matter the consequences, and is in fact necessary. In this view, then, freedom of speech moves from a right to a duty, and the mechanism of freedom from the extent of governmental control to the speech act of the individual. This freeing speech can (and ought to for Elyot) exist in contexts in which modern notions of freedom of speech does not.

This notion of freeing speech existed in Tudor England alongside the ancestor of the government-granted rights-based understanding of freedom of speech, traditionally expressed in Parliament. It is the latter which won out, largely, as Colclough has demonstrated, through the greater power of Parliament, and as I have attempted to show elsewhere, due to the lessening position of the political counsellor.[108] It has long been held one of the roles of the history of political thought to unearth forgotten or discarded ways of conceptualising those ideas taken to be 'givens', such as the notion of free speech, a practice which is often held to be necessarily emancipatory. By tracing *parrhesia* and its encounter with *kairos* in the work on the counsellor in the early Tudor period, we come across a way of thinking about free speech that presents an alternative perspective. Conceiving of free speech as a duty, requiring deep reflection, education and self-sacrifice, taking place in the context of a situation of unfreedom, shifts the rhetoric around the term, as well as the burden of responsibility or agency. It is not something that can be 'taken away' by governmental powers or other citizens, but rather something that can be neglected or abused by those citizens who refuse to take it up or do so in ways that are self-serving and thus necessarily detrimental to the commonwealth in which they live (as well as themselves). The goal of this notion of free speech is defined as the good of the commonwealth, rather than the preservation of an individualistic notion of rights. It seeks to correct corrupted (self-interested) governmental authorities for the freedom of all.

None of this is to suggest that the modern rights-based notion needs to be replaced wholesale by this duty-based concept of free speech. I leave it up to others who have thought more deeply about how freedom of speech functions (or fails to function) in modern polities to theorise the ways in which these two perspectives on the concept might work together. Nevertheless, it is a tradition that needs to be held in remembrance: first, because it helps us to understand the intervention made by Elyot in the context of Tudor 'tyranny'; and second, because recalling this alternative view might itself free us from some very modern problems surrounding the idea of freedom of speech.

NOTES

1 Freedom of speech is often understood in terms of Berlin's negative conception of liberty: N. Warburton, *Free Speech: A Very Short Introduction* (Oxford, 2009), 7–8.
2 This is to say not that they were not also concerned with the boundaries between liberty and licence, or indeed about government limitations on free speech but that there was another element to the debate, which has been lost to modern discussions of freedom of speech.
3 See R. Sullivan and A. Walzer (eds), *Thomas Elyot: Critical Editions of Four Works on Counsel* (Leiden, 2018), 'Introduction', chapter 2; J. Paul, *Counsel and Command in Early Modern English Thought* (Cambridge, 2020), chapter 2.
4 From J. Paul, 'Serving the Public by Advising the Ruler', in P. Overeem and F. Sager (eds), *The European Public Servant: A Shared Administrative Identity?* (Colchester, 2015), 45; see M. Foucault, *Fearless Speech* (Los Angeles, 2001).
5 See C. Atack, 'Plato, Foucault and the Conceptualization of *Parrhesia*', HPT 40 (2019), 23–48.
6 See Plato, *Laws*, trans. R. Bury (Cambridge, MA, 1967–68), 1.649b, 2.671b, 3.694b, 7.806c, 8.829d, 10.908c–d.
7 Quintilian, *Quintilian: With an English Translation*, trans. H. Butler (Cambridge, MA, 1922), 9.2.27.
8 M. Landauer, '*Parrhesia* and the Demos Tyrannos: Frank Speech, Flattery and Accountability in Democratic Athens', HPT 33 (2012), 187.
9 Landauer, '*Parrhesia*', 185–208, adds the feigned and unfeigned variants as well, in line with the *Ad Herennium*.
10 T. Bejan, 'The Two Clashing Meanings of "Free Speech"', *The Atlantic* (2 December 2017).
11 D. Colclough, *Freedom of Speech in Early Stuart England* (Cambridge, 2005), 3.
12 Ibid., 6.
13 T. Wilson, *The Arte of Rhetorique*, quoted in ibid., 47.
14 H. Peacham, *The Garden of Eloquence*, quoted in ibid., 53.

15 Ibid., 53.
16 H. Puttenham, *The Arte of English Poesie* (1589), 189–90.
17 Colclough, *Freedom of Speech*, 5.
18 A. Walzer, 'The Rhetoric of Counsel and Thomas Elyot's Of the Knowledge Which Maketh a Wise Man', *Philosophy and Rhetoric* 45 (2012), 24–45; A. Walzer, 'Rhetoric of Counsel in Thomas Elyot's Pasquil the Playne', *Rhetorica: A Journal of the History of Rhetoric* 30 (2012), 1–21; see also J. Paul, 'The Use of Kairos in Renaissance Political Philosophy', *Renaissance Quarterly* 67 (2014), 43–78.
19 Which he demonstrates in A. Walzer, 'Parrēsia, Foucault, and the Classical Rhetorical Tradition', *Renaissance Society Quarterly* 43 (2013), 1–21; see also Landauer, 'Parrhesia', 185–208.
20 Walzer, 'Parrhesia', 3.
21 Elements of what follows have been drawn from Paul, *Counsel and Command*.
22 Isocrates, 'Ad Nicoclem', in *Isocrates with an English Translation in Three Volumes*, trans. G. Norlin (Cambridge, MA, 1980), 2.28.
23 Isocrates, 'To Philip', in *Isocrates with an English Translation in Three Volumes*, trans. G. Norlin (Cambridge, MA, 1980), 5.72; Isocrates, 'Antidosis', in *Isocrates with an English Translation in Three Volumes*, trans. G. Norlin (Cambridge, MA, 1980), 15.179. See also his letter to Antipater, as treated by Landauer, 'Parrhesia', 190. Kairos is essential to the orator or counsellor, defining the very bounds of deliberation; see Paul, *Counsel and Command*.
24 These themes were anticipated to a certain extent by Isocrates, see Landauer, 'Parrhesia', 190.
25 Plutarch, 'Quomodo adulator ab amico internoscatur', in *Moralia with an English Translation*, trans. F. Babbitt (Cambridge, MA, 1927), 25.
26 Ibid., 29.
27 Ibid., 36.
28 This was also a theme in the medieval discourse of counsel. Medieval *speculum principis* books often emphasised counsel as the remedy to the necessarily limited abilities of a prince, as well as his tendency towards tyranny; see Paul, *Counsel and Command*. John of Salisbury's *Policraticus*, one of the first works in this genre, also makes the suggestion, developed by Thomas Elyot, that wise counsel frees the listener from vice, which enslaves, and so 'man is to be free and it is always permitted to a free man to speak to persons about restraining their vices'; John of Salisbury, *Policraticus: Of the Frivolities of Courtiers and the Footprints of Philosophers*, ed. C. Nederman (Cambridge, 1990), 180. He suggests, on this basis, that freedom of speech ought always to be in operation.
29 Erasmus, *The Education of a Christian Prince*, trans. L. Jardine (Cambridge, 1997), 6.
30 This stems from the positions posited in Letters 94 and 95 of Seneca; see Paul, *Counsel and Command*.
31 Erasmus, *The Education of a Christian Prince*, 6.
32 Erasmus, *Erasmus and His Age: Selected Letters of Desiderius Erasmus*, ed. H. Hillerbrand (New York, 1970), 47, see also 85; Latin: Erasmus, *Opvs Epistolarvm Des. Erasmi Roterdami*, ed. P. Allen (Oxford, 1992), I, 405.
33 See Colclough, *Freedom of Speech*, 44.

34 Erasmus, *Erasmus and His Age*, 160.
35 Q. Skinner, *Visions of Politics: Volume 2* (Cambridge, 2002), 213–63.
36 J. Hexter, 'Thomas More and the Problem of Counsel', in R. Sylvester and G. Marc'hadour (eds), *Quincentennial Essays on St. Thomas More* (Boone, 1978), 55–66.
37 T. More, *English Poems, Life of Pico, the Last Things*, ed. A. Edwards, K. Gardiner Rogers and C. Miller (New Haven, 1997), 136.
38 Ibid., 136.
39 Ibid., 137.
40 T. More, *The Confutation of Tyndale's Answer*, ed. L. Schuster, R. Marius and J. Lusardi (New Haven, 1973), 561.
41 See Colclough, *Freedom of Speech*, 131–2.
42 T. Starkey, *A Dialogue Between Pole and Lupset*, ed. T.F. Mayer (1989), 36.
43 Ibid., 38.
44 Ibid., 38–9.
45 Ibid., 39.
46 Ibid., 191.
47 See Sullivan and Walzer (eds), *Thomas Elyot*, 'Chapter 2'.
48 T. Elyot, *The Book Named The Governor*, ed. S. Lehmberg (New York, 1962), 108.
49 Ibid., 151.
50 For the dramatic effect this period had on Elyot see K.J. Wilson, 'Introduction', in *The Letters of Sir Thomas Elyot*, Studies in Philology 73 (Chapel Hill, 1976), xii–xiii. It is also evidenced in Elyot's 1532 letters to Cromwell in this text (7–16), in which he speaks of his disappointment at not being a member of Henry's counsel, and the poverty that has followed on the heels of his embassy.
51 G. Walker, *Writing under Tyranny: English Literature and the Henrician Reformation* (Oxford, 2007), 123–5.
52 This is an error in the original; I will refer to the text as *Of the Knowledge*, however, in what follows.
53 Also relevant is his translation of Isocrates' letter to Nicocles, published as the *Doctrinall of Princes* in the same year, in which he repeats Isocrates' advice that the prince ought to 'Geue to wise men libertee to speake to thee freely', T. Elyot, *The Doctrinall of Princes* (1533), 11r; Isocrates, 'Ad Nicoclem', 2.28.
54 Walzer, 'Thomas Elyot's *Of the Knowledge Which Maketh a Wise Man*', 24; see also Walzer, 'Thomas Elyot's *Pasquil the Playne*'. A similar position is expressed in Sullivan and Walzer (eds), *Thomas Elyot*.
55 For Elyot's awareness of the Pasquino statue and verses in December 1532 see Walker, *Writing under Tyranny*, 182–3. As Walker points out, if this is indeed when Elyot became inspired to write *Pasquil*, then he wrote the first edition of text quickly and in intense circumstances, which may explain why it is more vehement than other texts, and why he seems to endorse Pasquil's bluntness.
56 Elyot, *Pasquil the Playne* (1533), fol. 2r. There are two 1533 editions of *Pasquil*, both produced by Thomas Berthelet, the king's printer. One acknowledges Elyot's authorship in the address to the reader, the other does not (and they differ in pagination). I have used the former, which was actually the second of the two to be produced, with Elyot's revisions.

57 Ibid., fols 11v–12r. In this edition it reads 'cosen germanes remoued', in the other 1533 edition it reads 'right cosens' (fol. 12r).
58 Ibid., fol. 2r. Walker, *Writing under Tyranny*, 184–5, gives several possible contemporary identifications for Gnatho, and one for Harpocrates: Thomas Cramner.
59 Elyot, *Pasquil*, fols 2v, 30v.
60 See Paul, 'Use of *Kairos*', 52.
61 Elyot, *Pasquil*, fol. 5r.
62 Aeschylus, *Aeschylus, with an English Translation*, ed. H. W. Smyth (Cambridge, MA, 1926), II, 580. Note that the form here is *kairios*, a variant of *kairos*.
63 As Walzer, 'Rhetoric of Counsel', 8, puts it: 'The theme of *Pasquil the Playne* is the timing of appropriate counsel.'
64 Elyot, *Pasquil*, fols 5v–6r.
65 Ibid., fol. 6r.
66 Ibid., fols 8v–9r.
67 Ibid., fol. 4r. Elyot translates *decorum* in his *Dictionary* of 1538 as 'a semelynesse, or that which becommeth the person, hauynge respecte to his nature, degree, study, offyce, or professyon, be it in doinge or speakynge, a grace. sometyme it sygnifyeth honestie'; T. Elyot, *The Dictionary* (1538), sig. XXXv. Notably this definition has no temporal dimension. Elyot did not blur *kairos* and *decorum*, but rather saw them as mutually supportive for efficacious speech.
68 Ibid., fols 29r–v.
69 Ibid., fol. 29v.
70 Ibid., fols 15r–v; See E. Howard, 'Sir Thomas Elyot on the Turning of the Earth', *Philological Quarterly* 21 (1942), 441–3; J. Redmond, 'A Critical Edition of Sir Thomas Elyot's "Pasquil the Playne"' (Purdue University PhD, 1971), 165–6.
71 Elyot, *Pasquil*, fol. 3r. 'Harlott' here means 'a false or evil man, not a loose woman', Redmond, 'A Critical Edition', 154.
72 As Redmond, 'Critical Edition', 163, points out, this was also in line with expectations of the time; the 1528 Eltham reform paper requires counsellors to 'apply themselves diligently, meeting at ten o'clock in the morning at the latest, and again at two in the afternoon'.
73 Thomas Elyot, *Pasquil*, fol. 13r. This 'turning virtue into vice' speaks to the tradition of *paradiastole*. Notably, Elyot may have been the first English writer to attempt to define *paradiastole* in his *Dictionary* of 1538 (sig. Qivr): '*Paradiastole*, a dilatinge of a mater by an interpretation'. Elyot's comment on heresy here is one of two thinly veiled critiques of the Reformation in *Pasquil*. Earlier, Pasquil seems to suggest that had 'Popes, emperours/ kinges/ and cardinalles' listened to his advice, it might have been prevented (fols 9v–10r).
74 This is consistent with Isocrates' use of *parrhesia* as well, as Colclough, *Freedom of Speech*, 25, puts it 'The kind of frankness undertaken by both Isocrates and Demonthenes is represented by them as necessary only because the people are under the sway of flatterers'. In fact, as Colclough goes on to say, in these contexts it is only free speech (or only remarkable free speech) if it does in fact break the bounds of decorum.

75 Elyot, *Pasquil*, fol. 13v.
76 Elyot, *Pasquil*, fol. 13v. For the translation of *kairos* as 'season', see J. S. Baumlin, 'Ciceronian Decorum and the Temporalities of Renaissance Rhetoric', in P. Sipiora and J. S. Baumlin (eds), *Rhetoric and Kairos: Essays in History, Theory and Praxis* (New York, 2002), 141–4. 'To season' in English has its root in the temporal meaning of 'season', originally referring to allowing fruits, etc. to 'season' – i.e. 'to render (fruit) palatable by the influence of the seasons' – before picking them. Thus 'right time' is etymologically linked to this sense of seasoning, and Elyot's pun has even greater meaning.
77 Elyot, *Pasquil*, fols 13v–14r.
78 Ibid., fol. 15v.
79 Ibid., fols 15v–16r.
80 Ibid., fols 19r–v.
81 Ibid., fol. 19v.
82 Ibid.
83 Ibid.
84 Ibid., fo. 20r.
85 Ibid.
86 Walzer, 'Thomas Elyot's *Of the Knowledge*', 27–8.
87 D. Laertius, *Lives of Eminent Philosophers*, trans. E. Hicks (Cambridge, MA, 1972), 66. Notably, this is not a case in which the original in Greek is *kairos*, neither is the Greek *prepon* (Latin *decorum*) used here. See Sullivan and Walzer (eds), *Thomas Elyot*, 30–1, 213.
88 See also Walker, *Writing under Tyranny*, 198.
89 D. Laertius, *Lives of Eminent Philosophers*, 18–19. As Walzer, 'The Rhetoric of Counsel and Thomas Elyot's *Of the Knowledge Which Maketh a Wise Man*', 25, points out, this was a popular story in Renaissance England, appearing, for instance, in More's *Utopia* in the debate between Morus and Hythloday. See also Sullivan and Walzer (eds), *Thomas Elyot*, 210.
90 Elyot, *Of the Knowledeg*, fols 101r–2v.
91 Ibid., fol. A6v.
92 Ibid., fol. 6r.
93 Ibid., fols 14v–15r.
94 Ibid., fol. 15r.
95 Ibid., fol. 27r.
96 Ibid., fol. 51r.
97 Ibid., fol. 52r.
98 Ibid., fol. 52r.
99 Ibid., fol. 71r.
100 Ibid., fol. 95r. Plato and Aristippus also discuss the issue of right-timing in regard to Plato's rejoinder, which Aristippus suggests should have awaited 'more oportunitie' once Dionysius's 'fume had been passed' (fol. 102v). Plato rejects this suggestion, however, suggesting that such a delay would have in fact lost the opportunity, for Dionysius would have quickly forgotten the exchange, and his words would have had no effect. A philosopher like Plato looks to Providence, not Fortune in the deciding of time; he spoke as he must in the opportunity that had been provided to him. Plato thus does not reject *kairos*, as

Sullivan and Walzer (eds), *Thomas Elyot*, 222–6, seem to suggest, but places it in the giving of Providence, not Fortune.
101 Elyot, *Of the Knowledeg*, fol. 95v.
102 Ibid., fol. 97v.
103 Ibid., fol. 105r.
104 Ibid., fol. 105v.
105 Ibid., fol. 106r.
106 Ibid., fol. 106v.
107 Ibid., fol. 107r.
108 Colclough, *Freedom of Speech*; Paul, *Counsel and Command*.

Chapter 3

Pearls before swine: limiting godly speech in early seventeenth-century England

Karl Gunther

Some time in the late 1620s an English minister named William Hinde penned a lengthy and laudatory biography of the recently deceased Cheshire Puritan John Bruen. Leaving no virtue unremarked, Hinde drew attention to the godly patriarch's 'holy conversation' with all manner of people.[1] Bruen offered 'wholesome instructions, loving admonitions, godly exhortations, and good directions' to 'the tender Babes, Plants, and Lambes of Christ Jesus'.[2] To 'such as were yet in their sins, blind, ignorant, popish, or prophane', Bruen spoke words of rebuke: 'How, often as he hath by occasion seene them in the midst of their Heathenish sports, and Idolatrous feasts, either kissing the Calves, or dancing about them, hath he looked angerly upon them, and spoken roughly unto them, yet mourning for the hardnesse of their hearts.'[3] Yet Hinde also noted occasions when Bruen refused to admonish certain sinners or make a bold defence of the gospel before them. 'If he by occasion did meet with such persons as were mockers, contemners of God, and despisers of good things', Hinde wrote, 'hee would not cast Pearles before Swine, nor holy things before Dogs, but turne away his face from them, and not so much as salute them, nor speak one word unto them.'[4]

Given what we know about Puritans' principled propensity to meddle in their neighbours' sins, as well as the pressure they felt to maintain a holy witness in the midst of the ungodly, we might expect Hinde to criticise Bruen's silence in the face of mockers and 'contemners of God' as a moral failing. Yet this was not at all how Hinde depicted it, instead interpreting Bruen's behaviour as righteous obedience to Christ's command to the disciples in Matthew 7:6 to 'Give not that which is holy unto the dogs, neither cast ye your pearls before swine, lest they trample them under their feet, and turn again and rend you'.[5] This was a familiar adage in early Stuart England – one that Hinde's fellow Cheshire Puritan John Leycester memorably crossreferenced in 1623 with the Roman dramatist Plautus's even more evocative advice to 'Cast not thy meat into a Pispot' – and one that was put to many

47

different uses throughout the sixteenth and seventeenth centuries.[6] Matthew 7:6 was frequently invoked to argue that 'dogs' and 'swine' must be prevented from receiving the sacrament of communion, while Roman Catholic theologians read the text as offering a clear prohibition on the publication of vernacular Bibles and, in one extreme Henrician case, as a prohibition on even preaching to the laity.[7] Preachers made the text serve an admonitory function in their jeremiads, warning their audiences that God would cease to cast his pearls among them if they continued to wallow in their swinish ways. In a topical pamphlet of 1624, the text was even used to argue against intermarriage with papists, 'forasmuch as we may not give holy things unto Dogs, nor cast our pearles before Swine, and therefore much lesse give our selves to such as are called Dogs and Swine'.[8]

But, as Hinde's use of Matthew 7:6 reveals, Christ's prohibition on casting pearls before swine could also be read as placing fundamental limitations on Christian speech. The idea that early modern Protestants might want to place limits on godly speech strikes us as counterintuitive, to say the least. Protestants placed the written and spoken word at the centre of their vision of the Christian commonwealth, with the Word to be proclaimed from the pulpit, written on the walls of churches and common rooms, and on the lips of the godly at all times. As David Colclough and Diane Parkin-Speer have shown, moreover, English Protestants believed that they had 'a duty and a right' to exercise something they called 'liberty' or 'freedom' of speech.[9] When using this phrase, of course, Protestants were not proclaiming a universal human right to free expression. Instead, they viewed freedom of speech as a biblically mandated duty to speak the *truth* fearlessly and boldly, rebuking sin and proclaiming the gospel even if it meant facing persecution and martyrdom for so doing. When Puritans faced attempts to circumscribe their free speech, they refused to acknowledge the legitimacy of these limits: when pressed in 1573 to subscribe that he would not speak against the legally established Church of England or the Book of Common Prayer, for example, the Puritan minister Robert Johnson refused because he 'would not consent to that abridging of that libertie whiche I ought to have and freedome to speake against whatsoever fault shalbe publiklie mainteyned'.[10] As Jane Kamensky has shown, while Puritans were certainly willing and eager to proscribe speech they deemed unchristian, they sought ever greater freedom for their own godly speech.[11]

In this chapter, however, I will argue that early Stuart Protestants placed limits on their *own* freedom of speech. For the Protestants I will discuss below – almost all of them ministers and most of them Puritans – truthfulness was not the only criteria for assessing the propriety of Christian speech. As we will see, they devoted considerable attention to the proper contexts and audiences for godly speech, as well as the dangerous potential for godly speech to cause 'harm', give 'offence' or incite violence – terms and considerations that remain, with shifting meanings, at the heart of our own modern debates about freedom of speech. Examining their arguments will enable us to understand why a Puritan like John Bruen might have refused to cast his pearls before swine and give us a fuller understanding of the development of freedom of speech in early seventeenth-century England.

The Bible commanded Christians to engage in several forms of godly speech. 1 Peter 3:15 demanded profession of faith, instructing Christ's followers to 'be ready always to give an answer to every man that asketh you a reason of the hope that is in you with meekness and fear' while 2 Timothy 4:2 insisted that Christians 'reprove, rebuke, exhort with all long suffering and doctrine'. Early Stuart Puritans took these duties very seriously and issued fearsome warnings to those who would shirk them. The Northamptonshire minister Robert Bolton denounced those who 'never open their mouth' and maintained a 'sinfull silence' in the face of blasphemy and sin as 'vile cowards' and 'a kind of traitors to the state of Christianitie'.[12] Those who could listen to blasphemy and 'swallow up al in sencelesse silence', wrote the author of a lengthy 1625 dialogue on reproof, could not truly be 'in the state of saving grace', since even the smallest spark of love for God would 'set our tongues on worke' to defend God's honour.[13] Silence in the face of sin revealed not only a lack of love for God but hatred for one's neighbour, since the Christian who refused to do the charitable work of brotherly correction was guilty of soul murder.[14] Indeed, neglecting reproof made one complicit in the specific sins of others, since 'in God's Consistory, the not corrector as well as the law-breaker is both guilty of the sinne and subject to the same reward'.[15]

Protestant moralists insisted that the duty of 'admonishing and reproving ... appertaines to all degrees, and states of men, superiours, inferiours, [and] equals', but they were not able to offer equally universal instructions about how or when to speak words of brotherly correction and admonition.[16] In part, this had to do with the way that they characterised the biblical commands requiring Christians to speak words of reproof. Deploying a medieval scholastic distinction, early seventeenth-century Protestant commentators regularly and crucially distinguished between 'negative' and 'affirmative' commandments in scripture.[17] A negative commandment was framed as a prohibition and 'binds a man to obedience alwaies, and to all and every time'.[18] Affirmative commandments, by contrast, were injunctions to perform a certain godly duty. Whilst Christians were always required to obey them, 'affirmative precepts doe not bind you to doe at al times that which is commanded ... they necessarily binde us to observe them, when occasions, time and place require them to be done; when charity requireth the performance of them'.[19] According to this distinction, then, Christians must spend every waking moment refraining from actions like murder, adultery, blasphemy and idolatry, but they need not constantly keep the Sabbath, honour their mothers and fathers, fast, give alms or speak words of admonition and reproof to sinners. Whilst they must be *ready* at all times to perform these affirmative duties – and, in this sense, they were said to 'binde alwaies'[20] – Christians were commanded to actually do them only in the appropriate circumstances. Affirmative duties were good not 'simply' in themselves but 'in regard of all circumstances at that instant concurring', and a good action ceased to be good 'when it is not seasonably done'.[21] Even reading the Bible could be sinful, Thomas Gataker explained in a 1619 pamphlet, if a servant was reading it 'when he should be serving in his Masters supper'.[22]

This conception of admonitory speech as an 'affirmative duty' – always binding, yet only to be done in the right circumstances – explains why early Stuart discussions of reproof did not simply demand bold speech. The Northamptonshire Puritan minister Richard Trueman's 1629 treatise on the *Doctrine of Reproof* provides a representative example. Trueman vehemently argued that failing to reprove sinners was deeply uncharitable and also made the non-reprover complicit in the sinner's sins. Christians, he argued, must spare no sin and no person from courageous and loving words of reproof.[23] Yet Trueman also argued that 'every man is not bound to reprove, being but a private man, but when conveniencie doth offer it selfe'.[24] As it turned out, there were many situations in which reproving a sinner would be inconvenient and inappropriate. Trueman argued, for example, that words of reproof should be spoken at a time 'when the delinquent is most capable of reproofe'.[25] This ruled out reproving 'when a man is in distresse and perplexity', since 'a troubled spirit is unwilling to heare rebuke'.[26] It also meant that 'wee must not reprove in time of excesse and riot', most specifically when the sinner was drunk.[27] Citing 1 Samuel 25 and Abigail's decision to 'not tell *Nabal of his drunkennesse till he was awake from his wine*', Trueman noted that 'she knewe that a distemper was no season for a man to be bettered by reproofe'.[28] In this situation the sinner was likely to lash out violently, as Alexander the Great had done when he 'killed *Clitus* his intimate and familiar, because he [Clitus] reproved him of drunkennesse, in the midst of his cups'.[29] When speaking words of reproof, then, the Christian 'had need take heed, that he runne not upon his owne mischiefe and ruine ... for our owne safety, and for the benefit of the reproved, let us be carefull to make choice of such a time, when his heart is most pliable to correction and discipline, and this will adde grace and comelinesse to our reproofe'.[30] None of this necessarily absolved the Christian from the duty of reproving once these people had come to their senses or sobered up, but it was undoubtedly welcome advice to the godly who would find themselves among drunken strangers or neighbours, licensing silence in situations where rebuking sinful behaviour would have been a most unpleasant and potentially dangerous activity.

Trueman argued that reproof had to be done not only at the proper time but in a way that took into account the sinner's disposition, personal history and social standing. This knowledge would typically enable Christians to effectively tailor their words of reproof to match the sinner, but it could sometimes require them simply to remain silent and choose not to admonish. If one knew that a brother had sinned, for example, but discerned 'manifest signes of speedy amendment', Trueman argued that 'now here there is no place left for reproofe, but love *must cover a multitude of sinnes*: and indeed he that cannot wisely according to time and place digest and winke at small faults, when there are true and strong probabilities of amendment, from the party offending, is unfit to be a reprover'.[31] Since it was essential to know some things about the person you were about to reprove, Trueman argued that it was not necessarily a good idea to reprove strangers. The Christian 'that will take upon him to reprove hee knowes not whom, in an abrupt and unseemely manner, performes hee knowes not what, and his action is strained, as if a *Justice of peace* should looke for as much authority in another country, as he can challenge at home'.[32] With the sinning stranger, silence was probably the best course of action: the 'best reproofe in this kinde, is our dislike, and resolution on the contrary, with *Joshua, I and my house will serve the Lord*; or with the *Prophet David, I will not sit or remaine with the wicked*; that at least, if we cannot better them, wee may keepe our selves from infection'.[33]

Sinning strangers were not the only people whom early Stuart Protestants were advised to refrain from admonishing. Some people mocked and scorned Christian truth so openly that they were obviously impervious to words of admonition or reproof. In a 1604 addendum to William Perkins's commentary on Galatians 1–5, the Cambridge Puritan Ralph Cudworth argued that 'A man is not to reproove, if he be certaine his reproofe will doe no good: for when the ende ceaseth, all things tending to the end do likewise cease; therfore if there be no hope of amendment (which is the ende of reproofe) reproofe is to be omitted; specially if it be so farre from bettering the partie, that it make him much worse'.[34] When faced with open scorners and persecutors, 'it were great folly to spend labour in vaine, in telling them of their faults, when our schooling will not better them, but incense them more and more: It were better to be silent, or to separate from them, then to stirre up hornets, or to thrust our hands into a wasps neast',[35] The Puritan divine John Dod was even more explicit about this in his 1606 commentary on the Book of Proverbs. Proverbs 9:7–8 instructed readers that 'He that reproveth a scorner getteth to himself shame: and he that rebuketh a wicked man getteth himself a blot. Reprove not a scorner, lest he hate thee: rebuke a wise man, and he will love thee.' Dod explained that this prohibition on rebuking scorners taught Christians 'to bee very circumspect what persons we deale with, that there bee some hope of successe'.[36] Dod repeated a common theme when he stressed that Christians must not be too hasty when identifying the incorrigible and 'obstinate sinner', but he and others insisted that such knowledge was not only possible but actionable. When the incorrigible 'upon sufficient triall have declared themselves by a continued obstinacie to bee so', then the godly should not offer them '[t]he benefite of Christian counsell', because 'it is a certaine losse of labour to deale with them, and to as good purpose to lay a plaister to a dead mans wound, as to endeavour to heale them'.[37] Samuel Gardiner likewise urged caution when identifying the 'contumacious companion', but instructed his readers 'that wee should not loose our labours' by admonishing those who had proven 'uncapable of reproofe'.[38] As Roger Ley preached at Paul's Cross in 1621, true Christians would 'reprove sinne', but 'when there are apparent testimonies, no good can come, it is in vaine to stirre. One may better spare the labour, then put the Scripture to a swearing man in a drunken fit, or counsaile a man bent to scorne and derision.'[39]

Some critics disagreed, arguing that Christians should not worry about success or failure when admonishing others. In a 1617 pamphlet on Luke 15:41–4, F.S. argued that Christ's example 'doth teach all his Ministers, yea, and all Christians, to open their bowels of mercie, even towards the obstinate, not rashly to forsake them, and depart from them, and to give them over; but rather to labour to winne them unto Christ, and to omit no time, to spare no labour to effect it, and to bring it to passe'.[40] It might 'be objected that it is in vaine and but labour lost, *to cast pearles before Swine, and to give that which is holy unto Dogges*', but F.S. replied that 'we ought not so to thinke by and by of such as are obstinate and ingratefull, of such as are froward and stubborne, for God can suddenly change them'.[41] Even if such persons would never change, the possibility of success should not enter into the Christian's calculus when speaking 'admonitions and exhortations'. Christians should simply 'doe our diligence, and commit the successe unto God'.[42] From this perspective, casting pearls before swine was inevitable, the cost of doing business if a Christian were to obey God's command to admonish and reprove.[43]

But to Puritan ministers like William Sclater the cost of indiscriminate speech was simply too high. When discussing the duty of admonition in his oft-republished 1619 commentary on 1 Thessalonians, Sclater criticised the practice of Diogenes and the Cynics, who 'were wont promiscuously to admonish all they met with. What if they fell on deafe men? They answered, Words were gratuitous, and cost them nothing. Besides, though they missed their end in many, yet admonishing all, they might doe good to some.'[44] There were 'many' in England who, with 'like zeale, shall I say? or passion', were also 'prodigally casting away *sacred and precious admonitions upon Dogs and Swine*', contrary to the instructions of Christ who commanded his followers to cautiously 'make choice of such, as wee must admonish by the Word of God. Though words bee gratuitous, yet Gods Word is sacred and precious: *We may not cast holy things to Dogs, nor Pearles before Swine.*'[45]

As Sclater's words suggested, the problem was not simply that casting pearls before swine was useless. It could actually do harm. On one level, it would harm the Word of God itself by subjecting it to blasphemy and defilement. In his 1626 collection of sermons delivered in Northamptonshire, Robert Bolton argued that Christ prohibited casting pearls before swine because of his 'holy jealousie over the glory and Majestie of his owne blessed Word'.[46] Words of reproof were words of Scripture, which were the purest and holiest words imaginable, issuing forth directly from God's 'owne infinite understanding'.[47] The swine were those 'who doe scornefully and contemptuously trample under foote all holy instructions, reproofes, admonitions, tendred unto them out of the Word of Truth', and Christians must not offer these holy words to the swinish in order to prevent them from treating 'so glorious a message from the mighty God of heaven with contempt and scorne'.[48] In 1627 John Carter wrote that Christians must take great care when 'we take in hand to teach, admonish, or reprove', since in doing so 'we speake the words, or *oracles of GOD*', and these precious pearls of 'good counsel and instruction, out of Gods most holy Word' must not be 'abased and abused by malicious and filthy wretches'.[49]

Speaking words of reproof to a 'dog' would also likely result in physical harm. Christ's command to not give holy things to dogs who would 'turn again and rend you' was widely read as a counsel of self-preservation. 'Dogges flie upon such as endevour to put them from their carrion they have seazed upon', Samuel Gardiner wrote in 1606, 'so such hell-houndes will violently rise up against such, as shall goe about to withdraw them from their filthinesse'.[50] Christ had such love and concern for his followers, Bolton argued, that 'he would not have his child to vouchsafe so much as a reproofe to any blasphemous wretch, or desperate Swaggerer, that would furiously flie in his face for offering him a Pearle'.[51] John Carter told his readers that in Matthew 7:6 Christ 'willeth us in all our instructions, admonitions, and reproofes, to have an eye to our owne safetie, that we bring not an old house upon our heads'.[52] Indeed, as several commentators pointed out, since Christ specifically prohibited Christians from admonishing the dogs, they should expect no providential protection if they proceeded to do so: 'if thou goe beyond thy boundes against the rule of Christ', the London minister Edward Elton preached, 'where is thy warrant of safetie against the malice of the wicked and violent persons?'[53] Writing several decades later in 1660, the Somersetshire minister Henry Jeanes offered several vivid examples of how a Christian's inappropriate exercise of free speech could imprudently provoke both blasphemy and violence. '[E]very private man', Jeanes argued,

> is not bound to runne into an ale-house, or taverne, there to reprehend a company of desperate drunkards, who would looke upon his reprehension as an act of pragmaticalnesse, and insolency, and for it be ready to quoite [i.e., throw] him downe the Staires, or run him through with their swords: and as imprudent an act would it be, *in Spaine*, to run into their Churches, and there to cry against the Idolatry of the Masse; and in the Streets of *Constantinople* to declame against the impostures of *Mahomet*; for hereby we should scandalize them indiscreetly, and foolishly occasion them, as to blaspheme our religion, so to cut us in pieces.[54]

Jeanes concluded that 'Promulgation of a truth, and Christian reproofe, are duties commanded by God, and yet are to be sometimes abstained from, for scandals taken by, not onely the weake, but all[so?] malitious'.[55]

Others stressed that Christians must consider not only their own safety when speaking words of reproof but the safety of other Christians as well. In a sermon printed in 1605, Egeon Askew identified godly silences in the biblical text that he argued served as a model for Christians to emulate at the present day. St Paul 'in his Epistle to the *Romains* did not so much as touch *Nero* their bloud-thirsting Emperour (but willed every soule be subject to his power) lest that Lion (as wisely not in that, but truly in another Epistle he tearmed him) being awaked by reproofe, should roare after his prey, and seeke whom he might devoure'.[56] The Church fathers had followed Paul's example and chosen 'not to rebuke a tyrant in his furie, lest that should more incense his rage against the Church'.[57] When spoken to a dog, words of brotherly admonition and charitable reproof became fighting words, and should not be spoken.

Finally, seventeenth-century English Protestants regularly noted that admonishing a dog or swine would not only be fruitless but would actually 'be so farre from bettering the partie, that it make him much worse'.[58] The Herefordshire Puritan minister John Tombes spelled out this argument in great detail in his 1641 treatise *Christs Commination against Scandalizers.*[59] Tombes defined offensive acts as 'all such acts whereby mens minds are harmed', specifically acts that would induce others to commit sin.[60] There was a spectrum of scandalous and offensive behaviour, but among the worst was occasioning the 'Apostasy of some, hardening of others, occasioning others to blaspheame the name of God, to inveigh against the truth, Gospell, Religion, &c'.[61] Scripture was full of fearsome warnings against offending and scandalising others, which was most easily done by Christians behaving sinfully themselves, but could also be done by Christians performing godly duties in inappropriate ways. For example, Tombes argued that 'reproving of our neighbour is a duty enjoyned by God, yet to be omitted at some times, when the person to be reproved would bee likely rather hardened, then amended by reproofe'.[62] Affirmative duties like reproof 'are commanded principally to this end, that they may doe good to men for the curing of their evills, the furthering of vertue in them. Wherefore when prudence shewes that such actions would bee either fruitles in respect of their end, or contrariwise harmfull, they are to bee forborne: in this case there is a *Libertas non faciendi, a liberty not to doe them*, or rather hee ought not to doe them.'[63] When speaking words of reproof, then, 'our liberty is to bee restrained to avoyde scandall', to avoid offending or harming others by driving them deeper into sin, rather than drawing them forth from it.[64]

Tombes's argument strikingly drew together a series of terms that, with very different meanings and content, continue to shape debates about free speech and its proper limits. Christians, Tombes claimed, should not engage in 'offensive' speech that would cause 'harm' to others. For Tombes, this meant speech that would cause certain sorts of people to sin, blaspheme and destroy their own souls. The godly's 'liberty' to speak the hard truths of

Christian admonition had to be restricted in this case, with what they were free to say being subordinated to what they ought to say (or rather not say). With apologies to Kierkegaard, we might say that Tombes was outlining situations that required a teleological suspension of a Christian's freedom of speech.

When discussing these limits on godly speech, most Protestant commentators made a special point of noting that they were placing limits only on private speech. John Dod, for example, stressed that Solomon's instructions to 'rebuke not a scorner' did not apply to ministers like himself or magistrates. While 'private reproofes are to be spared' when encountering scorners, 'yet must they publikely bee pursued by the ministrie, and censured by the Church, and punished by the magistrate'.[65] Scorners were unworthy of reproof, but they were ripe for smiting.[66] For Arthur Hildersam, the line between private and public ran right through the person of the minister. Taking Christ as his model, Hildersam noted in a lecture of 1610 that when Jesus was 'in the presence of wicked men, he kept silence from good words', but this was only when Herod, the high priests, and Pilate were questioning him as a 'private person'.[67] In his 'publike ministry', by contrast, Jesus 'spake good things, and taught the will of God nevertheless freely and boldly, though the Pharisees, and other wicked men were present, when he taught'.[68] The minister who followed Christ's example would need to speak differently in different situations, therefore, remaining silent before scorners as a private man, but boldly teaching and reproving the dogs and swine in his public capacity, regardless of 'the presence of any wicked man whatsoever he be'.[69] Furthermore, while we have seen many commentators argue that private Christians should consider their own personal safety when offering reproof, John Carter Jr argued that this consideration did not apply to the public ministry. In a sermon preached at Norwich in 1650, Carter argued that ministers would face 'great opposition' as they rebuked people's sins, but 'the Minister of Christ must not feare the faces of men; but with liberty and freedome of speech utter the message of the Lord ... Ministers that cast the Pearles of reproofes before Doggs and Swine, must expect that such brutish creatures will fly in their faces, and if it be in their power, will rent and teare them.'[70] Ministerial freedom of speech, in other words, permitted – indeed, required – clergy to speak publicly in ways that would potentially provoke violence.

But some Protestants thought that Christ's prohibition on casting pearls before swine *did* apply to ministers' public speech. This was the view taken by no less than William Perkins, the great Elizabethan Puritan theologian whose writings influenced generations of English Puritans. In *The Arte of Prophecying*, Perkins's manual on preaching, he made the commonplace claim that the godly preacher must apply doctrine to his audience in ways that were 'diverslly fitted according as place, time, and person doe require'.[71]

Perkins identified seven sorts of people whom the minister must consider when preaching, the first of which were the '*Unbeleevers who are both ignorant and unteachable*'.[72] Ministers should spare no effort to prepare such people to learn godly doctrine, disputing with them and reproving their sins so that 'they may become teachable'.[73] If the minister had some success and developed 'hope that they are become teachable and prepared', he was then to open Christian doctrine to them gradually, but 'if they shall remaine unteachable without hope of winning them, they are to be left' – advice he followed by quoting Matthew 7:6 and Proverbs 9:8.[74]

The godly clergymen who read Perkins's manual undoubtedly considered many of their parishioners to be 'unbeleevers who are both ignorant and unteachable'. When Arthur Hildersam (Perkins's fellow student at Cambridge in the 1570s) argued that ministers were duty-bound to preach to the dogs and swine, for example, he admitted that it was very discouraging for a minister to preach to 'such as he seeth no hope to do good upon' and to see 'notorious drunkards, or whoremongers, or blasphemers, or prophane fooles, that scorne all goodnesse, come to heare us'.[75] But with attendance at Sunday services mandated by law, ministers in the Church of England seemed to have no choice but to preach to such people. They could 'leave' the unteachable, of course, by leaving their congregation. In his 1585 commentary on the minor prophets, translated into English and published at Cambridge in 1594, the French Reformed theologian Lambert Daneau had written that it was 'lawfull for the true Ministers of GOD in the ende to leave those flockes, in the which after sufficient and long time, and daylie patience, and a great while waiting they see no fruite of the word of God ... when as the hearers become not the better, but the worse by the preaching of the worde, they are to bee left, as swine, unto whome God his pearles are not to bee cast any longer, as Christ himselfe doth counsell Matth. 7. ver. 6.'.[76] But clergy with livings and careers in the national church were highly unlikely to follow this advice.

Perkins never explained how the unteachable were to be 'left' in *The Arte of Prophecying*, but he returned to the subject in his commentary on Matthew 5–7 (Christ's 'sermon on the mount'), published posthumously in 1608. According to Perkins, it was the dogs and the swine who must leave the congregation, not the minister. Matthew 7:6 taught ministers to '*have regard how, & to whom ye dispense the word and sacraments*'.[77] The dogs and swine were '*malitious obstinate enemies*, manifestly convicted of their enmitie to Gods word & doctrine, of whose amendment there is no hope'.[78] Private people should not attempt to identify these people, for 'it is not in the power and libertie of any private man to give judgement of another that he is a *dogge* or a *swine*; but it is a publike dutie belonging to the ministers and governours of the Church to give judgement in this case'.[79] Ministers were bound to 'first preach & publish the word of God to al men without exception', but if there were obstinate enemies who maliciously railed against godly preaching and showed no signs of amendment, 'then are they to be cast out by the Church, and to be accounted as dogges, and to be barred from the word of life till they repent'.[80] The dogs and swine must be excommunicated and barred 'from the use of the Churches Ministerie in the word, praier, and sacraments' in order to prevent at least two 'daungerous events which would ensue by communicating holy things unto dogges and swine'.[81] First, because the dogs and swine would respond to sermons with contempt and mockery, preaching to them would defile the holy Word of God and 'the holy things of God must not be prophaned and abused, therefore they must not be communicated unto wilfull enemies of the grace of God'.[82] Second, the dogs and swine not only would profane the Word of God, but 'annoy & hurt by reviling and persecution those that be the messengers of the word unto them'.[83]

Perkins offered here an institutional solution that would enable the clergy to exercise their ministry without fear of the 'daungerous events' that preaching to dogs and swine would provoke. In practice, however, whilst the Church of England had a system of excommunication, it was hardly as comprehensive or as intensely enforced as what Perkins envisioned here. For ministers who shared Perkins's concern, therefore, the problem was how to avoid casting pearls before swine in an environment where (as the London Puritan minister John Randall put it) 'it is not in our power, still to make choise of such Auditors as shall be fit for our instructions'.[84] In a sermon published posthumously in 1622, Randall claimed that Christ himself was always 'very wise and wary in disposing of the mysteries of God' in his preaching ministry, 'making speciall choise of tractable and towardly minds, to whom he doth deliver this Doctrine'.[85] Randall pointed to many examples from the gospels of Christ refusing to teach people who were not 'fit' to receive his message, like the Canaanite woman in Mark 15 to whom Christ said '*it was not meet to take the childrens bread and to give it unto dogges*'.[86] Randall found it particularly significant that Christ did not preach the Sermon on the Mount (Matthew 5–7) to the multitudes or to the high priests, but only to the apostles in private. This was a 'matter of Imitiation for us that are of the Ministery, teaching us, after the example of our Saviour, not to impart the mysteries of salvation to all men indifferently, but rather in wisedome to make choise of our Auditors, as neere as wee can, to whom wee deliever them'.[87] But since it was 'a thing impossible' for ministers to 'make speciall choise of our Auditors for every thing we speake', ministers must assess their audiences and adjust their messages. To the 'prophane and wilfull ... if thou speakest any thing, thou must speake of the judgements of God', but to 'more towardly & tractable spirits', the minister was to impart a 'kindly lesson'.[88] Ministers 'must be wise in making choise of such instructions as shall be fit for our Auditors', Randall insisted, and 'chary ... in delivering the mysteries of God' so that 'we doe not give such holy things unto dogs, nor cast his precious pearles before swine'.[89]

In this chapter I have adopted an unconventional approach to early Stuart thought about freedom of speech. Rather than focusing on defences of freedom of speech against royal or ecclesiastical censorship, I have considered the theoretical limits that Protestants placed on their *own* freedom of speech. I have focused, moreover, on the rules that Protestants applied to the exercise of what we might call 'everyday' freedom of speech: frank speech between family members, neighbours, parishioners and strangers about matters of right and wrong, sin and salvation. Early modern debates about freedom of speech in Parliament and regarding political counsel were, of course, enormously important for the conceptual and legal history of free speech. But the everyday exercise of freedom of speech was a far more significant aspect of people's lives in early Stuart England, and contemporary discussions about it deserve close attention as well.[90]

Early Stuart Protestants viewed admonition and reproof as essential Christian duties and as a matter of freedom of speech. The godly minister was to reprove sin 'with all liberty and freedome of speech and spirit ... wheresoever he finds it'.[91] Thomas Gataker praised Richard Stock, pastor of All-Hallowes Bread Street, London, for 'his freedome of speech ... in reproving of sinne, and that even to the faces of the gr[av?]est, both in publike and private, when occasion required it'.[92] Friends were to exercise '[p]lainnesse and freedome of speech ... admonishing each other of the sinnes and faults they commit, if they be any thing palpable, and offensive, and well entertaining such admonitions'.[93] As we have seen, however, early Stuart Protestants also placed crucial limits on this duty to speak freely. As Joanne Paul shows in Chapter 2 above, the question of when to speak boldly and when to be silent was discussed throughout the classical and humanist rhetorical tradition. Yet while the university-trained authors examined in this chapter would have been familiar with those debates, their discussions of free speech were fundamentally shaped by theological concepts and biblical injunctions. When John Bruen refused to speak to the 'contemners of God', he was doing little more than following the advice contained in the margin of the Geneva Bible next to Matthew 7:6: 'Declare not the Gospell to the wicked contemners of God whom thou seest left to them selves and forsaken'.[94]

Few readers will be surprised to learn that early seventeenth-century Protestants sought to limit theological speech that they deemed inappropriate. It is surprising, however, to see Puritans (of all people) sometimes putting godly rebuke and admonition in this category, placing boundaries on the free expression of what they considered undoubted truths. Freedom of speech was not an absolute good for early Stuart Protestants, who argued that it should always be exercised in the service of other, higher goods.[95] Specifically, speech should promote God's glory and the good of those who heard it. There were some circumstances in which even truth-full, godly speech would not serve these ends, instead provoking blasphemous counter-speech and violence, and ultimately harming others, including those whom the speech was supposed to help. Lay people – and perhaps even ministers – had to assess the situation and calculate the likely consequences of their speech. In many (perhaps most) situations, free speech was a necessary duty, even if the response would not be particularly pleasant for the speaker. But if the godly were 'certaine' that Christian admonitions 'will doe no good', as Edward Elton put it in 1615, or 'when there are apparent testimonies, no good can come' as the London minister Roger Ley put it in 1621, then the godly had (as we have heard John Tombes put it in 1641) 'a liberty not to doe them, or rather hee ought not to doe them'.[96] This combination of the word 'liberty' with the assertion of an *obligation* to speak (or not speak) runs counter to the most common modern understanding of 'freedom', with its emphasis on autonomous individual choice. But it takes us to the dynamic heart of how early modern Protestants understood the proper exercise of 'freedom', in which the Christian (and his or her speech) was simultaneously supposed to be both 'a perfectly free lord of all, subject to none' and 'a perfectly dutiful servant of all, subject to all'.[97]

NOTES

1. W. Hinde, *A Faithfull Remonstrance of The Holy Life and Happy Death of John Bruen* (1641), 183.
2. Ibid., 184.
3. Ibid., 183.
4. Ibid., 183–4.
5. Unless otherwise noted, all biblical quotations are KJV.
6. J. Leycester, *Enchiridion, Seu Fasciculus Adagiorum Selectissimorum* (1623), b3r.
7. S. Hozjusz, *Of the Expresse Worde of God* (Louvain, 1567), 103r–v; on the Henrician example, see S. Brigden, 'Youth and the English Reformation', *P&P* 95 (1982), 55 n, 103.
8. *Certaine Advertisements for the Good of the Church and Common-wealth* (Amsterdam, 1624?), 36.
9. D. Colclough, *Freedom of Speech in Early Stuart England* (Cambridge, 2005), 4; also see D. Parkin-Speer, 'Freedom of Speech in Sixteenth Century English Rhetorics', *SCJ* 12 (1981), 65–72.
10. *A parte of a register* (1593), 94, 96; see Parkin-Speer, 'Freedom of Speech', 71.
11. J. Kamensky, *Governing the Tongue: The Politics of Speech in Early New England* (Oxford, 1997), chapter 1.
12. R. Bolton, *Some Generall Directions for a Comfortable Walking with God* (1626), 119. On Bolton's views, also see P. Lake and I. Stephens, *Scandal and Religious Identity in Early Stuart England* (Woodbridge, 2015), 128–32.
13. A.L., *Spirituall Almes: A Treatise wherein is set forth the Necessity, the Enforcements, and Directions of the duty of Exhortation* (1625), 70, 22, 62.
14. Fra. G. Affinati d'Acuto Romano, *The Dumbe Divine Speaker, Or: Dumbe speaker of Divinity. A Learned and excellent Treatise, in praise of Silence*, trans. A. Munday

(1605), 262–6; T. Cooper, *The Converts First Love Discerned, Iustified, Left, and Recouered* (1610), 6–7; Bolton, *Some Generall Directions*, 119; A.L., *Spirituall Almes*, 85–7, 96, 99.
15. R. Trueman, *A Christian Memorandum, or Advertisement wherein is handled the Doctrine of Reproofe* (Oxford, 1629), 119–20.
16. H. Holland, *The Historie of Adam* (1606), 55r.
17. For explications of this distinction, see G. Widley, *The Doctrine of the Sabbath* (1604), 90; G. Downame, *The Christians Sanctuarie* (1604), 11; T. Bell, *The Regiment of the Church* (1606), 216–17; J. Corderoy, *A Warning for Worldlings* (1608), 319–20; W. Perkins, *A Godly and Learned Exposition of Christs Sermon in the Mount* (1608), 187; W. Loe, *The Merchant Reall* (Hamburg, 1620), 97; J. Mayer, *The English Catechisme Explained* (1622), 192; J. Downame, *A Treatise Against Lying* (1636), 57.
18. Perkins, *A Godly and Learned Exposition*, 187.
19. Corderoy, *A warning for worldlings*, 320.
20. Perkins, *A Godly and Learned Exposition*, 188.
21. T. Gataker, *Of the Nature and Use of Lots* (1619), 188.
22. Ibid., 188.
23. On these points, see Trueman, *Christian Memorandum*, 84–8, 118–25.
24. Ibid., 9.
25. Ibid., 33.
26. Ibid., 33.
27. Ibid., 34.
28. Ibid., 34.
29. Ibid., 35.
30. Ibid., 36. This ran somewhat contrary to his later advice to '[l]et us not sticke to touch the hole of the *Aspe*; and to lay our handes upon the den of the *Cockatrice*' (86).
31. Ibid., 18.
32. Ibid., 10.
33. Ibid., 10–11.
34. W. Perkins (and R. Cudworth), *A Commentarie or Exposition, upon the five first Chapters of the Epistle to the Galatians* (Cambridge, 1604), 478–9.
35. Cudworth, *A Commentarie*, 479.
36. J. Dod, *A Plaine and Familiar Exposition of the Ninth and Tenth Chapters of the Proverbs of Salomon* (1606), 19.
37. Ibid., 18–19.
38. S. Gardiner, *A Booke of Angling, or Fishing* (1606), 19–20.
39. R. Ley, *The Bruising of the Serpents Head. A Sermon Preached at Pauls Crosse September 9. 1621* (1622), 45.
40. F.S., *Jerusalems Fall, Englands warning* (1617), 7.
41. Ibid., 7–8.
42. Ibid., 8. Richard Trueman likewise argued that 'God requires not at our handes the cure of the partie wee deale with, that must be wrought by his owne hand and mercy; only wee are commanded to have a care over one another': *Christian Memorandum*, 101.
43. Also see A.P., *The compasse of a Christian* (1582), 7.

44 W. Sclater, *An Exposition with Notes upon the first Epistle to the Thessalonians* (1619), 480.
45 Ibid. Some might wonder whether Christians really must 'silently suffer Gods Name to be blasphemed', but Sclater assured them that 'There is a reall reproofe to be given to such, by *separating from their societie*' (480).
46 Bolton, *Some Generall Directions*, 114.
47 Ibid., 115.
48 Ibid., 115–16.
49 J. Carter, *A Plaine and Compendious Exposition of Christs Sermon in the Mount* (1627), 103–4.
50 Gardiner, *Booke of Angling*, 20.
51 Bolton, *Some Generall Directions*, 114.
52 Carter, *Plaine and Compendious Exposition*, 104.
53 E. Elton, *An Exposition of the Epistle of St Paule to the Colossians, delivered in sundry Sermons* (1615), 1320.
54 H. Jeanes, *A Second Part of The Mixture of Scholasticall Divinity, with Practical* (Oxford, 1660), 97.
55 Ibid., 107 (n.b., incorrect pagination).
56 E. Askew, *Brotherly Reconcilement* (1605), 7. Half a century later, Edward Reyner would argue that Paul's decision 'to forbear speaking against the great *Diana* at *Ephesus*, at least directly, and by name' was a model for Christians to remain silent 'when wee see no hope of doing good by reproof': *Rules for the Government of the Tongue* (1656), 197–8.
57 Askew, *Brotherly Reconcilement*, 7.
58 Cudworth, *A commentarie*, 478; also see Askew, *Brotherly Reconcilement*, 7; Trueman, *Christian Memorandum*, 23–4; A. Hildersam, *CVIII Lectures Upon the Fourth of John* (1632), 293.
59 1641; Wing T1802.
60 Tombes, *Christs Commination*, *5v.
61 Ibid., 79.
62 Ibid., 164–5.
63 Ibid., 167–8.
64 Ibid., 168.
65 J. Dod and R. Cleaver, *A Plaine and Familiar Exposition: Of the Eighteenth, Nineteenth, and Twentieth Chapters of the Proverbs of Salomon* (1610), 18. On this distinction, also see Holland, *The Historie of Adam*, 53r; Trueman, *A Christian Memorandum*, 9.
66 Dod and Cleaver, *Plaine and Familiar Exposition*, 91–3.
67 Hildersam, *CVIII Lectures*, 293–4.
68 Ibid., 294.
69 Ibid.
70 J. Carter (Jr), *The Tomb-Stone* (1653), 143–4. Carter stressed that God would deliver them.
71 W. Perkins, *The Arte of Prophecying*, trans. T. Tuke (1607), 99. The text was originally published as *Prophetica* (Cambridge, 1592).
72 Ibid., 102.
73 Ibid., 103.

74 Ibid., 104–5.
75 Hildersam, *CVIII Lectures*, 294–5.
76 Lambert Daneau, *A Fruitfull Commentarie upon the twelve Small Prophets*, trans. J. Stockwood (Cambridge, 1594), 1059.
77 Perkins, *Godly and Learned Exposition*, 441.
78 Ibid., 439.
79 Ibid., 440.
80 Ibid., 441–2.
81 Ibid., 444. Perkins allowed that if someone had been excommunicated 'for some particular crime, and there be hope of his repentance, because he doth not shew himselfe a dogge or a swine, by wilfull obstinacie in his sinne and contempt of the Church', he should only be excluded from the Sacraments and from prayer, but 'admitted to the hearing of the word, because that is a means to humble him for his sinne, and to bring him to repentance' (444).
82 Ibid., 445.
83 Ibid., 445.
84 J. Randall, *The Necessitie of Righteousnes* (1622), 16.
85 Ibid., 14, 13. Similarly, Perkins had argued that Christ initially preached his gospel to all of the Jews, but when he 'saw some of them [the Jews] maliciously obstinate, then he propounded *his doctrine unto them in parables unto them*, that they might be hardened in sinne: and after expounded the same privately to his Disciples'. The apostles followed this pattern after Christ's ascension, preaching first to the Jews, 'even when they were persecuted by them: but at length when as they saw that of obstinate malice they oppugned the truth', the apostles '*turned to the Gentiles, Act. 13.46*'. Perkins, *Godly and Learned Exposition*, 442.
86 Randall, *Necessitie of Righteousnes*, 14.
87 Ibid., 15.
88 Ibid., 16–17.
89 Ibid., 16.
90 On the limitations of adopting a legal approach to studying freedom of speech, see T. Garton Ash's comments in *Free Speech: Ten Principles for a Connected World* (New Haven, 2016), 82. For a discussion of very different proposals for limiting potentially incendiary religious conversation in seventeenth-century England, see T. Bejan, *Mere Civility: Disagreement and the Limits of Toleration* (Cambridge, MA, 2017).
91 J. Downame, *A Guide to Godlynesse* (1622), 125.
92 Gataker, *Abrahams Decease* (1627), 11.
93 W. Whately, *A Pithie, Short, and Methodicall opening of the Ten Commandements* (1622), 101.
94 *The Bible* (Geneva, 1561), AA4v.
95 According to Stanley Fish, free speech is *always* a subordinate good; see the title essay in S. Fish, *There's No Such Thing as Free Speech* (Oxford, 1994).
96 Elton, *An Exposition*, 1320; Ley, *The Bruising of the Serpents Head*, 45.
97 M. Luther, 'The Freedom of a Christian', in T. Lull (ed.), *Martin Luther's Basic Theological Writings* (Minneapolis, 1989), 596.

Chapter 4

'Free speech' in Elizabethan and early Stuart England

Peter Lake

I need to start with if not an apology then at least a request for the reader's indulgence, because I am going to start with the argument of two books that I recently published, neither of which directly addresses the topic of freedom of speech anything like head-on, but both of which are concerned with the limits of the sayable, and the ways in which things that were formally unsayable got said, and were subsequently discussed in post-Reformation England. Throughout there will be more than an element of (self-)synthesis going on in this chapter, as I try to arrange things that I and a range of other scholars have said about the nature of public politics, and the existence and limits of something that I have called elsewhere 'the post reformation public sphere'[1] around the topic of 'free speech'. I will, to some extent, be repeating myself, but hopefully mainly to make connections between different elements in my own work, and more importantly between those elements and a body of emerging research by a number of other scholars, all of which can be made to reflect on the topic of free speech, even when that has not (always) been a central concern or organising concept in that research itself.

To do that I am going to begin with the topic of counsel.[2] It was a truth universally acknowledged, by advocates of even the most authoritarian or absolutist theories of monarchy, that rulers needed counsel. They needed it because they had to be able to be told the truth about the situation of their realm and the condition of their subjects, and because, in its absence, they could all too easily become the prisoners of their own intimates and favourites; persons whose interest in the retention of royal favour could make it all too necessary and indeed easy for them to tell the prince what he or she wanted, rather than needed, to hear. There needed to be, in short, persons able to tell something like truth to power. This was a role best discharged, indeed, it could only legitimately be discharged, by 'public men', that is to say persons – and, in this period, they were always men – charged with various sorts of office under the Crown; office that enabled them to tell the prince what he or she needed to know. In ecclesiastical affairs that role was played by the clergy in general and the bishops in particular. Their publicness stemmed from their office-holding, and from the fact that they were dealing with public matters, i.e. matters that concerned the public good. But there was a paradox at the heart of this notion of publicness, for, because the matters about which the ruler most needed advice concerned the so-called *arcana imperii*, the counsel-giving functions of the public man could be discharged only in private; that is to say behind the closed doors of the Council chamber. Thus the public duty of public men in giving counsel had nothing to do with the public, defined as a wider body of subjects (or citizens) before whom such counsel-giving should take place, or to whom any of it ought to be directed.

The one exception to this rule was, of course, provided by Parliament, where men rendered public by their status as peers of the realm, or by their election to the House of Commons, were not merely allowed but supposed to counsel the prince. Here was the classic locus, perhaps the only locus outside the Council chamber or the court, in which the subject could exercise *parrhesia*, the frank or free speech which all good counsellors owed to their princes. Again, this was public business; quintessentially concerned with the public, that is with the common good, and, in certain aspects, justified by the claim that what was being presented here for royal consideration represented the grievances of the subject. What the prince was learning about in these exchanges was the truth about the real condition of his or her realm, a truth which might otherwise be hidden by the very necessary remoteness or apartness that defined the nature of royal power in post-Reformation England.

A good deal of stress has been placed of late on the social depth of early modern English government; that is to say on the extent to which office-holding, often directly dependent on appointment by the Crown or its agents, penetrated down the social scale and into the localities.[3] At its most coherent and aggressive this analysis has led some historians more or less to categorise post-Reformation England as a monarchical republic, and to discern, lurking beneath the persona as subjects of many of those involved in the doing of the Crown's, the commonwealth's, or indeed, as many came to describe it, their 'country's', business, a semi-covert, which is also to say a semi-overt, identity as 'citizens'. But here it is worth remembering that for the most part, while the active co-operation of such people was absolutely necessary for the workings of the state, the business thus conducted and the institutional channels in and through which it was transacted were administrative and legal, rather than political. There has been a tendency, of late, to pooh-pooh such distinctions as anachronistic, and consequently to see virtually everything to do with the exercise of power and jurisdiction during this period as inherently political. And it is true that a good deal of business that we would organise under the sign of politics was conducted through legal and administrative means and modes. Calling such mechanisms and modes of power simply political does indeed get at something important about the way the post-Reformation polity worked, but in so far as the notion of politics retains any sense of self-conscious judgement, of overt communication and critique, of formal deliberation and consent, then too promiscuous use of the word *political* serves to obscure something rather important about the polity of early modern England. In short, and put in crude terms, in certain renditions of the period and of the polity, the republican bit of the monarchical republic is in danger of sometimes obscuring the monarchical part.[4] And concentrating on just who got to have a formal say, in other words who got to counsel the prince, and under what circumstances and where, is as good a way as any both to redress that balance and to begin a discussion of free speech during this period. For even substantial members of the gentry only got to say anything like what they thought about the affairs of the day in Parliament. And, as a myriad revisionist historians of that institution have told us, Parliament sat only intermittently and when the monarch chose to call it.

It was a truth (almost) universally acknowledged – although not perhaps by James I, and certain royal apologists, who insisted that the Parliament-men remember that, while their standing as such was ephemeral, their status as subjects was permanent – that you could say things and address topics in Parliament that, said or addressed anywhere else, would get you locked up. Of course, sometimes people misjudged even that degree of licence and got locked up anyway, for there were always considerable limitations on what could be discussed or said even there. Moreover, while there was something quintessentially public about these exchanges in Parliament, they, too, were at least supposed to happen in secret. Outsiders were barred from observing the proceedings of the House and members were at least supposed not to report on the doings of the Parliament.[5]

The precise limits of parliamentary speech, and the extent to which the proceedings of the House really were secret, were always open to intermittent contest and experiment, and sometimes became the subject of rather fractious debate between the Crown and the Parliament-men. However, it remains the case that, throughout the Elizabethan and early Stuart periods, central aspects of royal policy – religion, royal marriage, the conduct of foreign policy, for example – were at least in theory completely off limits and those who insisted on talking about them, when the monarch did not want them discussed, were consistently subject to discipline and restraint. The resulting spats were the stuff of which the narrative histories of Sir John Neale and other 'Whiggish' historians of Parliament were made.[6]

Even in ecclesiastical affairs the necessity for the monarch, in discharge of the Royal Supremacy, to consult the clergy or the bishops, while acknowledged on all sides, was not, in practice, all that clear cut. While all agreed that, as a lay person, the monarch ought to take clerical advice in ecclesiastical affairs, whether he or she was obliged to take that advice remained an open question. Over the prophesyings, Grindal thought that Elizabeth was so obliged, but she did not. Just as Grindal maintained that she had not taken counsel before making her decision, the queen insisted that she had, and we know who won that one.[7] Whitgift conceded that it was 'the part of a wise and godly prince to have' 'weighty matters of doctrine (being in controversy) decreed and determined by such as, for their authority, wisdom and learning, are most fit to entreat of such matters', but insisted that this did not detract from the power of the civil magistrate to make 'orders in the church or ecclesiastical laws, for even those orders and laws which were made in such [church] councils were made by the authority of the emperor', after, that is, the emperor himself had called, presided over and even voted in the councils involved.[8] John Bridges made much the same point by comparing the relation enjoyed by the prince with his secular and his ecclesiastical counsellors. In 'civil affairs', he maintained, 'it was not counted a subjection' 'for a prince to follow the advice of wise and faithful councilors', since 'for all their duty in giving him faithful advice and his duty to follow their advice', when it came to making law, while they might maintain that 'thus it should be', it was the prince 'that determineth thus it shall be. So that their determination is indeed properly no determination of the matter but deliberation and advisement.' In both civil and ecclesiastical affairs, he concluded, the prince was obliged to do 'nothing rashly, but, if the matters be doubtful, with good counsel and advice of them that be learned in these matters'. But just because 'he should do nothing without their advice', that did not mean that 'he can do nothing without their authority'. 'Just as no wise prince will suffer' his councillors to arrogate such power to themselves, so 'no truly faithful counsellors will so take upon them'. 'Though he follow in all points the advice of his councilors, yet have not they the chief authority.' This was a point Bridges insisted upon against the clericalist pretensions of both the presbyterians and the papists.[9]

Thus the dynamics of what we might call free speech were worked out in a series of tensions, and sometimes conflicts, between the duty of certain public men to defend the public interest – crudely that of the commonwealth and of true religion, and the constraints placed on who got to talk about such things and where and to whom they got to talk about them. The result was a very restricted circle of persons comprising in secular affairs Privy Counsellors, in practice certain courtiers and favourites, and, in ecclesiastical matter the bishops and certain godly learned clergy, and, on some topics but not on others, Parliament-men.

Under the right circumstances, most often those created by actual or perceived crisis and threat, these very restricted ranks of the counsel-giving classes could be expanded. The books I mentioned at the beginning of this chapter dealt with the nature of such circumstances during the reign of Elizabeth I. One of them, *Bad Queen Bess?*, described how and when, under the threat of popish rebellion, or of incipient popish rule, to be effected through the accession of Mary Stuart, the regime, or rather elements within it – that is to say groups around and under the queen, but not necessarily the queen herself – widened the basis of the political nation. They did so, in part, to put pressure back on the queen to act, having failed to convince her to do so in debates and manoeuvres conducted behind the closed doors of the court and Council chamber, and in part to energise and activate various sorts of publics – crudely the Protestant state's most engaged supporters, aka the godly – so that, if the worst were to happen and the papists rose or Elizabeth died with Mary Stuart still above ground – they would do the right thing, establish the Protestant succession and thus preserve both the cause of the gospel and the current structures of power and patronage from the depredations that would inevitably follow the accession of a Catholic ruler. What was at stake here was a public politics of appeal to various strands of Puritan/Protestant, and therefore zealously loyalist, opinion. The limits of the counsel-giving classes were being expanded, and the structures of the monarchical republic, seen as a hierarchy of office-holders, was being turned at least, *in potentia*, into a cadre of active citizens who could be depended upon, if and when the (Marian and papist) balloon ever did go up, and the realm was stripped of any locus of monarchical legitimacy, to autonomously do the right thing, and defend the Protestant succession and state.

The regime's moves, in this mode, to mobilise popular and parliamentary Protestant opinion against Mary and the Duke of Norfolk, provoked a Catholic reaction. This involved trying, through the pamphlet press, to tell the truth about what was really happening; that is to say about the real conspiracy against monarchical legitimacy, England, the commonwealth and true religion. That conspiracy was based on a clique of ambitious and atheistical evil councilors determined to render the queen dependent upon them and their supporters, remove Mary Stuart and then divert the throne in their own interests. It was the pressing nature of that conspiracy that both necessitated and legitimated appeals to the public, appeals designed to tell the truth about who the real villains of the piece were, so that, when the crisis hit, people would know what to do, which was to rally, not to the leaders of the monarchical republic, here redescribed as a noxious atheistical clique of self-serving evil-counsellors, but also the one true heir, Mary Stuart.

These Catholic ripostes were contained in a number of texts which I have described elsewhere as libellous secret histories, elaborate accounts of what was really going on and who the real conspirators were, and where the real threat to political stability and monarchical legitimacy lay. There were three major statements of this position, the first in the early 1570s being *The Treatise of Treasons*, the second in 1584 being *Leicester's Commonwealth* and the third in the early 1590s the group of tracts that went collectively under the nickname of *Cecil's Commonwealth*. Each of them constituted, in the terms set by David Colclough's magisterial book on *Freedom of Speech in Early Stuart England*, complex acts of *parrhesia*;[10] that is to say, the very nature of the crisis and the conspiracy laid out in the body of the text provided the legitimating occasion for the act of (very) free speech which in fact laid that crisis, and the sinister machinations that lay behind it, before the reading public.

This was to invert the values and claims of the 'monarchical republic', which is best conceived as a particular version of the workings of the monarchical state, conceived as a form of mixed, counsel-led monarchy; a vision legitimated, and, it was claimed, animated by, civic republican discourses of political virtue, service to the commonweal, good counsel. This was, in Norman Jones's resonant phrase, 'government by virtue', and to Burghley and his admirers its epitome was Jones's hero, Lord Burghley himself, who, it was said, never left home without a copy of Cicero's *De officiis* in his pocket.[11] On the official account, this idyll of Protestant zeal and humanist virtue was under threat from ambitious, atheistical plotters and fanatical Catholics, a *mésalliance* of zealots and malcontents. Driven by a mixture of popish zeal and antichristian spite, on the one hand, and by the ruthless pursuit of power, and, to this point, disappointed self-interest, on the other, this was a conspiracy comprised of foreign Catholics, the agents of, variously, the Catholic League, the Duke of Guise, Spain and the Pope, together with a range of English Catholics, both exile and native, and various malcontents and outs, bent on upending the status quo in order to repair their own ruined careers, and put themselves in power, Mary on the throne and the mass back in every church in England. This view of the situation was based upon and sustained by the series of Catholic plots that punctuated the reign. Ranging from the revolt of the Northern earls, through the Ridolfi, Throckmorton, Parry, Babington and Squire plots, these were both very real and heavily ginned up, involving not merely willing agents and allies of the Guise and zealous Catholics, willing to risk everything in order to rescue their country from heresy and Mary from prison, to conspirators as ludicrous as Dr Parry and unlikely as Dr Lopez.

What was at stake in these exchanges was not a theoretical, freestanding debate about the rights and wrongs, the proper limits on and privileges of, 'free speech' but rather the use of the allegedly pressing threats represented by these rival conspiracy theories, as legitimations for orgies of truth-telling designed to persuade a series of overlapping publics of what was really going on and of the real dangers with which the realm was confronted.

Nor should we necessarily assume that we are dealing here with weapons of the weak, expedients which those on the outs with the state were forced to use in order to protest the tenor of official policy and their own parlously marginalised or persecuted status. On the contrary, if anything, this move was first made by people near the centre of the regime and their hangers-on and supporters in order to force action against Mary and the Duke of Norfolk. The Catholic resort to libellous plot talk and secret history started out as a response to this move by the powers that were. In *Bad Queen Bess?* I argued that the result was a dialogic, even dialectical, struggle between the regime and its Catholic critics and enemies, in which each side accused the other of libelling, that is to say, of telling lies to popular audiences about the secret doings of princes. In the Catholic telling, supporters of the regime told lies about the King of Spain, the Catholic league, the seminary priests and the papacy, while the regime replied that it was the Catholics who were defaming the Elizabethan state. By the end, each side was accusing the other of essentially the same things, deploying parallel, indeed functionally identical, versions of monarchical dysfunction and tyranny, different claims about the identity of the rogue state whose outrageously aggressive and unscrupulous behaviour was plunging the whole of Western Europe into chaos. For the Catholics, of course, that rogue state was Elizabethan England, and for the Elizabethan authorities and their supporters it was the Spain of Phillip II, backed up by the pope and the Duke of Guise.[12]

Not, of course, that the Catholics and their enemies within the regime were the only people engaging in this sort of public politics, using all of the available media to make a case about the need to protect the cause of true religion and the commonweal from the threat of false religion, evil counsel and corruption. English Puritans, too, felt compelled to do something of the same thing. To do so the Puritans used three genres, each wreathed in certain assumptions about, or pretensions to, something we might want to call 'free speech'. The first is the sermon, which of course had built into its DNA an obligation to tell truth to power, by applying the insights and admonitions of Scripture to the sins and enormities of the day. There was a longstanding tradition of so-called commonwealth preaching in this mode that stretched back at least as far as Edward's reign.[13] There was, of course, always a ritual element involved here, as the standard sins received the standard rebukes, all in a public effort to purge the system of faults which all too often were endemic to it, through the purely formal means of routinised clerical denunciation, rather than through any very practical process of reform or reformation. But it would be too cynical to leave the analysis there. After all, within all of the positive, even idealised, stereotypes of the godly prince, magistrate, bishop or minister, which were the common stock of the preacher called to address, praise or maintain the authority structures of the post-Reformation church and state, there lurked (admittedly often implicit) anti-types, visions of what ungodly versions of said offices and functions would or might look like. As Kevin Sharpe pointed out years ago, very often compliment implied criticism and vice versa, and it was the job of the skilful preacher to exploit those ambiguities in order to tell saving truth not only to the members of his own congregation but also, when the opportunity presented itself or the circumstances demanded it, to the powers that were.[14]

For there was also the continuing fantasy about the spiritual power of the word preached, to which was attributed a capacity to cut through all the error and self-interest of a fallen world, to penetrate the walls of flattery, indirection and deceit that all too often surrounded the prince and powers in the realm.

If the hearts of kings really were in the hands of the lord, his most common instrument in softening those hearts with his grace and bending them to his will was the word preached. Thus, the Puritans consistently sought to mobilise the power of preaching behind their various quests for further reformation, appealing not only to their own auditories, and the more general public described by the promiscuous reach of print but also, when the opportunity arose, to the monarch himself or herself. The most spectacular instances of this propensity tended to cluster around moments of contention or crisis, like the opening moves of the Elizabethan Puritan movement, which saw Edward Dering get into such hot water for a sermon preached before the queen and the authorities seek to crack down on who got to preach at Paul's Cross; or the campaign for further reformation at the start of James's reign, which saw John Burgess imprisoned, interrogated and finally silenced and deprived for a sermon upbraiding the king for the course of ecclesiastical policy after the Hampton Court conference; or, later on, the Spanish match, when court and City preachers like Andrew Willet and John Everard were imprisoned for preaching against the match; or later still the fuss over the rise of Arminianism.[15]

As in the cases of Dering and Burgess, these confrontations between the prerogative of the godly preacher to tell truth to power and royal authority all too often ended in tears. But that some people either got it wrong, or thought it worth the risk to take their moment in the limelight to push things further than prudence would otherwise have seemed to dictate, shows not merely the latent potential within the ideal of the godly preaching minister but the positive impulse, the obligation, if you will, for the preacher to discharge his conscience and do his duty by telling his auditory, no matter how exalted, the unvarnished truth.

Throughout the 1570s and 1580s, the Puritan movement marshalled the assumptions, latent in the godly sermon, in an aggressive campaign against the faults and corruptions of the contemporary ecclesiastical status quo, and in an equally explicit canvassing of the Presbyterian platform as the God-designed answer to many of the realm's most pressing practical and spiritual problems. In so doing they not only harnessed the impulse towards 'free speech' implicit in the role of the godly preaching minister but also those to be found in the formal religious disputation. There, on the basis of a set of texts and modes of argument the authority of which was agreed by all the participants, a series of propositions were debated back and forth with every argument answered by another, and every cited authority responded to. The assumption was that through the punctilious observation of the appropriate modes of discourse and argument, truth would emerge and error be confuted. An extra edge was added to these assumptions by the rise of post-Reformation confessional conflict, since what was now at stake were the truth claims of two rivals for the mantle of the true church. Since the basic text at stake here was the Bible, certainly for Protestants, the assumption was that final resolution on the basis of a proper understanding of the word of God was not only available but to be expected if all parties to such proceedings accorded their behaviour to the relevant norms. Catholics of course, shared these assumptions, hence Campion and Parsons demanded that they be allowed to dispute the crucial points at issue between the Protestant Church of England and the Church of Rome before the queen. Here, if anywhere, in this period we have a model of 'free speech', that is to say of untrammelled rational debate. Indeed, on that basis, Deborah Shuger has claimed that it was in the university disputation, more than anywhere, that the post-Reformation got closest to achieving something like a genuinely Habermasian public sphere for the exercise of public reason.[16]

Because of that, the Presbyterians continually demanded to be allowed to dispute the issue of church government before the queen, certain, as they were, that, unleashed through the forms of syllogistic debate and properly scholarly interpretation and application, scriptural truth would out, and the gospel defeat its human opponents and triumph in the final establishment of the form of church government laid down by Christ and the apostles. Unsurprisingly these requests were unsuccessful, although the fact that, in 1584, they did achieve the concession of a formal disputation about the controverted ceremonies in front of an audience of Privy Counsellors including Leicester and Burghley, just as the regime had, in the end, conceded that formal disputation to the Jesuit Edmund Campion, albeit under extraordinarily disadvantageous circumstances in the Tower, showed just how much traction repeated appeals for a free disputation could exert. In certain situations, and for certain purposes, the demand for free speech could be powerful enough to constrain the actions of authorities who, as in the case of the incarcerated Campion, seemed to have all the cards in their own hands.[17]

Denied access to such officially sanctioned public forums, the Presbyterians did the next best thing, which was insistently to claim the promiscuously public forum of print as their own. More intermittently, they tried to recruit the space afforded by Parliament, for their attempts to strong-arm the regime into further reformation. In print they conducted what were in effect formal disputations, or rather they forced representatives of the regime to engage them in such disputations. For, once they had thrown down the gauntlet of a formal challenge, that is to say, an elaborated statement of the case for the discipline, which first Field and Wilcox and then Thomas Cartwright did in the early 1570s, the authorities clearly felt that they could not afford to allow such statements to pass unanswered. A similar dynamic drove the process of anti-papal polemic as a series of divines, like William Whitaker and William Fulke, in large tomes mostly in Latin and dedicated to leading members of the regime, repeatedly took on leading Catholic polemicists like Stapleton, Sander or Bellarmine, in the process, of course, publicising the very arguments they were trying to refute. In this way, the dynamics of religious disputation in an age of confessional conflict summed up many of the paradoxes surrounding the notion of free speech, and its constraint, in post-Reformation England.[18]

Not that the ideologues and polemicists of the Puritan movement limited themselves to the genres of the godly sermon or formal polemic, to legitimate their own public pitch for further reformation. They also had recourse to libellous, *ad hominem* attacks centred on various sorts of conspiracy theory, very similar to those launched by the Catholics. This was, in many ways, to piggy-back off the official narrative about the popish threat. It was just that, through their analysis of the popish corruption still afflicting the worship and government of the national church, which culminated in their analysis of episcopacy as a frankly antichristian institution, the Puritans located popery very close to the centre of the ecclesiastical status quo in England. On that basis, they came to view the bishops as parties to an increasingly self-serving, authoritarian and corrupt conspiracy to keep things the way they were. All of which, they claimed, gave help and succour to the large number of actual or potential papists still lurking, often enough in plain sight, in the midst of English society. They were referring here to the so-called 'church papists', sinister figures whose presence in various establishments was currently being connived at by a variety of corrupt or complacent authorities in church and state, but whose malice and popery would be revealed and expelled by the operations of the discipline, if it could once be established. In these ways, the conformist conspiracy to mislead the queen about the discipline and the Puritans became associated with the wider popish threat, against which the Puritans represented themselves as the realm's and the queen's last and best defence. Thus, on the Puritan view, the real conspirators were the bishops and their clerical hangers-on, everybody, in fact, who had a stake in the ecclesiastical status quo, and, in obstructing the progress of further reformation, was preferring their narrow private interests before those of the church and commonwealth. To get around this blockage, it was necessary to appeal over the heads of these conspirators, who, it was feared, currently had a lock on the royal ear, by appealing, not merely to the parliamentary classes but, even, on the most radical statement of the case, to the 'people'.[19]

Initially, the Puritans had had recourse to what John Field called 'suit and dispute',[20] through their conduct of religious polemic in the pulpit and the press, their demands that they be allowed a public disputation before the queen and their efforts to achieve reformation through Parliament. When those efforts failed, broken on the intransigence of the queen and an increasingly assertive cadre of conformist clergy, fronted by Whitgift, the Puritans, or at least some of them, responded by transposing many of the propaganda modes perfected by that *éminence grise* of the Puritan movement, John Field – the surveys of the ministry, the collection of damning detail about the corruptions, exorbitances and repressions of the bishops and their hangers-on, the increasingly insistent statement of the Presbyterian case against the status quo and for the discipline – into the realm of cheap print.

I am referring here, of course, to the infamous Marprelate tracts, in which a no-holds-barred exposition of the case for Presbyterian reformation was combined with the popular libel in a full-throated, populist, often hilariously demotic denunciation of the bishops and their creatures as the real villains of the piece, the great obstacle that was standing between England and the God-satisfying security from irreligion and popery that only the Presbyterian platform could supply. [21]

Where previous Presbyterian polemic had always been comprised of formal scholarly disputation, in which argument was matched with argument, authority with authority, with a *soupçon* of libellous, *ad hominem* vitriol mixed in on the side – the conformists had of course responded in kind – now the *parti pris* allegations of Martin pushed things over the edge, with the result that mainstream Presbyterian ideologues, who throughout the protracted exchanges about the discipline had clung to their status as godly learned divines, were outraged. Martin left them with no foothold within reformed respectability and allowed the Puritan movement to be denounced as the populist threat to all order in church and state that conformist apologists like Whitgift had always claimed that it was.[22]

Accordingly, not only was the Martinist press hunted down and suppressed, the entire Puritan movement was rolled up and definitively denounced. Many of its leading figures appeared first in High Commission and then in Star Chamber; some on the radical fringes died in jail, or even on the scaffold. Cartwright went into exile in the Channel Islands and the rest of the movement disappeared underground. All of which was accompanied by the ultimate in libellous secret history; that is to say, by Richard Bancroft's two accounts of the enormities of the Presbyterian movement, *Dangerous Positions* and *A Survey of the Pretended Holy Discipline*, both of which contained heavily documented, but utterly *parti pris*, accounts of the classis movement construed as a subversive conspiracy against all order in church and state. These last provided contemporaries with a detailed kiss-and-tell narrative of the populist enormities of the Puritan movement, and Collinson with the basic template for his own research and narrative. Thus began an absolutist reaction, centred on divine-right theories of monarchy and episcopacy, which was to reach its apogee under James I, but which started in the 1590s with the reaction against Presbyterianism.[23]

Thus, on all sides of the argument – Catholic, Puritan and conformist – exercises in 'free speech' were always legitimated by the rhetoric of conspiracy and emergency. Each group presented its recourse to such methods as exceptions that proved the rule that, under normal circumstances, such behaviour was entirely illicit. In each case the perpetrators portrayed themselves as reacting to an emergency, as often as not one prompted by the conspiratorial efforts of the other side, whether Puritans or papists, Spain or the papacy, evil counsellors, popish conspirators or corrupt prelates. In those circumstances, with the monarch deluded by some conspiracy of evil counsel, with the commonwealth, the church or both threatened by some malign faction or other, the usual constraints upon broaching affairs of state before the people simply had to be laid aside. In effect, the parties to these exchanges announced their own privately decided states of emergency or exception, the exigencies of which did not merely license but demand orgies of 'free speech', through which the real truth was to be told to the monarch certainly, but also to promiscuously popular audiences, the nature and extent of which were determined solely by the reach of the media being used to send the message.

The end of Elizabeth's reign and start of James's featured a spasm of such emergencies, occasioned by a number of conspiracies, both real and imagined, and a series of pleas and counter-pleas for various sorts of political and religious settlement, all designed to come out of the process of regime change, as, to appropriate a commonly used contemporary metaphor, one sun set and another rose. The appeals were organised, variously, around the war with Spain and the rights and wrongs of peace; the personality and fate of the Earl of Essex; the Archpriest controversy, itself a dispute not merely about the right relation between different sorts of Catholic and the Protestant state but also about the succession, toleration and the nature of the Puritan and papist threats. The accession of James prompted various, both Catholic and Puritan, agitations about, in the Puritan instance, the cause of further reformation in church and state, and, in the Catholic one, toleration (for Catholics, if not for Puritans). These various mini-crises, and the very different (often mutually exclusive) perceptions of, and agendas for, the current conjuncture, all merged together to produce an ongoing sense of flux, indeed of crisis, as many of the fixed points of the previous regime seemed to disappear, and many of the issues seemingly closed down by an Elizabethan settlement that had in fact settled very little, were reopened and relitigated. It was a period characterised by both fake and real conspiracies, ranging from the Essex conspiracy to the Bye and Main plots to the gunpowder treason, and by a series of public agitations and pamphlet wars, featuring not merely printed texts but a range of circulating manuscript tracts and petitions, manuscript libels and position papers.[24]

In the course of these ructions, new or emergent genres – modes of communication that were to dominate the conduct of public politics, and modulate and enable the practice of 'free speech' in the early Stuart period – came into in play. I refer here primarily to the verse libel and the manuscript separate.[25] These were all in prominent evidence in the political practice of, and contemporary comment upon, the Essex circle. As Paul Hammer and Alex Gadja have shown, Essex himself was a pertinacious, and, in some ways, skilful, if perhaps rather intemperate, user of the manuscript separate as a way to promote his person and cause.[26] The circulation in manuscript (and then, almost certainly despite his best intentions, in print) of his *Apology*, which took debates on the rights and wrongs of peace and war out of the closed circles of the court and the Council, into a still nascent and ill-defined yet palpable 'public sphere', is just the most notorious of his efforts in this direction. As he languished in the Tower, and, much to the regime's distress, the London pulpits echoed with prayers for his good health, and, if I am right about certain of Shakespeare's plays – amongst them the Henry IV plays, *Henry V, The Merry Wives of Windsor, Julius Caesar* and *Hamlet* – the exigencies of his later career did not pass without the commentary, delivered more or less in real time, of the public theatres.[27] The events surrounding the earl's fall were the subject of a plethora of anonymous manuscript libels, distributed around the City and court. His trial and execution were followed by the circulation of a variety of rather different manuscript separate accounts of his trial, and, as Andrew McCrae and Alastair Bellany have shown, the start of the new reign saw a series of verse libels apportioning blame for his grizzly end around and amongst the survivors.[28] As the seminal work of Arnold Hunt has shown, the regime responded to all this with a co-ordinated propaganda campaign delivered both in the pulpit and in print.[29]

In a great deal of recent work it has become conventional to deal with verse libels and manuscript separates as largely early Stuart phenomena, and it is certainly true that they grew enormously in number and circulation during the later period, but on this evidence they were of a distinctly Elizabethan provenance; products, in fact, of the long succession and accession crises that did so much to shape the politics of the post-Reformation in late sixteenth-century England. One might say the same about the propensity to view politics as a sort of palimpsest, a mess of conspiracy and counter conspiracy, that had to be decoded by the clued-up spectator or commentator. By the late sixteenth century this capacity, in Noah Millstone's resonant phrase, 'to see like a statesman' was becoming a much-sought-after commodity.[30] And it was doing so not merely through the operation of illicit Catholic tracts and commentaries like *The Treatise of Treasons, Leicester's* or *Cecil's Commonwealth*, the production of which dated back to the early 1570s, but through the popular theatre, which, in a succession of history plays, purported to show just what the politics of the royal court and Council were really about, what the great and the good were really doing, even as they claimed, with the likes of Lord Burghley, to be serving only the highest of moral ends and pursuing only the interests of the Crown, the church and the commonwealth. Indeed, as Andras Kisery has argued, through the publication of plays like *Hamlet* and Jonson's *Sejanus*, some plays were being converted into printed texts from which the sorts of insights, the apophthegms, the moral and political saws and *sententiae*, necessary to understand and comment upon the process of politics could be extracted and commonplaced away.[31] Here was a certain skill set, a mode of viewing events, interrogating texts and interpreting politics well on its way to becoming a form of social distinction, or cultural capital; that is to say, a necessary part of the cultural apparatus of the properly cultivated member of the political or cultural elite.

Since this sort of free speech, or recourse to the politics of the public sphere, was legitimated by the rhetoric of the emergency or state of exception, once the emergency of the moment was over, and the relevant threat or conspiracy had been unmasked and seen off, the need for such extraordinary measures was supposed to disappear. These were emergency expedients, designed to meet extreme circumstances, not features of a political and cultural scene in which free speech or the recourse to some sort of public sphere was going to be, or even ought to be, either normal or normative. On the contrary, once the circumstances which had prompted such behaviour had ceased to pertain, things ought to go back to a form of monarchical normality in which the public authority personated in the monarch, counselled by a narrow range of counsellors, persons rendered genuinely public by their appointment by the Crown to the proper counsel-giving offices under the Crown, did the business of the church and commonwealth, safe from the prying eyes and ears of the populace. It was the function of such persons to issue orders and instructions, perhaps attended with brief rationales for what they were doing, exhortations to obedience and virtuous compliance and assertions of the legitimacy of the authority by which said instructions were being issued, but not to engage in argument or elaborate explanation or defence of the course chosen.

Once the accession crisis that had ended Elizabeth's and opened James's reign was over, that is to say by 1606 or so, one might think that optimum conditions for such a return to normality now pertained. The Protestant succession had been secured. The monarch was an adult male Protestant, with a male heir. The war with Spain was over, and the religious issues opened or reopened by the accession had been decided. There was to be no toleration even for loyalist Catholics, and no Puritan further-reformation of the church. By the same token, at the level of ideology, the accession of James I had seen what appeared to be the definitive triumph of divine-right absolutism over monarchical republicanism. We have a similar vision of the government of the church, presided over by the divine right powers of the prince and the bishops, the latter of whom were now established, at least to James's and their own satisfaction, as holders of genuinely apostolic office.

But James's accession, and the apparent resolution of many of the most pressing issues that had framed the politics and culture of the previous reign, did not usher in a return to some idyllic monarchical normal. They did not for a variety of reasons, some, as it were, contingent, that is to say determined by particular political issues or events, others more structural or generic. To start with the latter, while never normative, nor ever accepted as simply normal, recourse to the politics of the public sphere, what we might term the dark arts of what its critics called 'popularity' had been deployed so often by such a diverse range of political actors that, by the end of the sixteenth century, such behaviour had become part of the practised *modus operandi* of the actual or wannabe statesman or 'politician'. There were even those, like Sir Francis Bacon, willing to give advice on the limits and uses of popularity; in other words accounts of how to do it properly, and how to avoid its pitfalls.[32] Again, if I am right about certain Shakespeare plays of the 1590s, that discussion had already gone public, even popular, through the staging of such issues and debates in the commercial theatre.[33] Similarly, the genres through which such appeals might be conducted, and either satiric or substantive comment made on the course of events – crudely the verse libel and the manuscript separate – had established themselves as both practices and commodities, with settled assumptions about how they could and should be best produced, circulated and consumed, without attracting the destructive opprobrium of the state. Of course, every now and again, someone – like the unfortunate Lewis Pickering[34] – went too far, or got caught out, but, in general terms, there were rules for these particular games, which now started to take on an intermittent, but also, in some sense, settled, role in the political lives of increasing numbers of people. The same might be said for the conventions, the implicit trade-offs and compromises, the unwritten rules, if you like, that enabled the theatre to keep commenting on the course of politics. Again, as the early career of Ben Jonson shows, that envelope could always be pushed a little too far, and particular texts and authors could get into real trouble, but, for the most part, the ground rules were set, and people know both how to produce and how to read or view plays directly connected to the issues or events of the day.

All of which produced some paradoxical outcomes, not the least of which was the propensity of King James himself, even as he proclaimed his own absolute God-given powers as king and opined about the impenetrability of the *arcana imperii*, to engage with his critics, not merely in copious volumes of polemical divinity but also by replying to them in kind in doggerel verse. Indeed, as the researches of Matt Growhoski are revealing, in the case of John Barclay's *Satyricon*, James was even willing to use complex verse satires, indeed even libels, as instruments of state.[35] What was involved here was more than James I's personal foibles or literary and theological proclivities, but rather an expression of the paradoxes of absolute monarchy operating in a version of the post-Reformation public sphere, a space or context in many ways defined by the intermittent exercise of certain sorts of free speech by individuals or groups responding to what they took to be the moral imperatives and opportunities offered by the rhetorical ideal of *parrhesia* and the current political circumstances. And in fact, in his intermittent interventions into the resulting debates and exchanges, James himself might be thought to have been committing that paradoxical thing, an act of royal *parrhesia*. That is to say, each descent from the majesty that ought to hedge a king into the prolixity of argument and self-justification was intended as a one-off, an expedient, whereby a situation discombobulated by popular or tribunician spirts would be returned to a monarchical normal defined by James's view of the right relation between the royal prerogative and the liberties of the subject, the Parliament's right to give counsel and his own right to rule. James's public statements were then intended to act not as provocations to further conversation but rather as something like definitive, because royal, statements of the way things were and thus as end points to, rather than as continuations of, the current cacophony. Although it has also to be admitted that James also liked to govern by setting and resetting limits to what was acceptable discourse, and often overestimated the capacity of his own persuasive powers to do that. As Ken Fincham and I observed in 1985, James often seems not to have realised that he 'won' arguments, and imposed relative silence on certain opinions, not because he was 'right' but because he was king. That meant that the suppressed opinions and concerns did not go away, but simply festered, although, as an inveterate political tactician rather than strategist, that might well have seemed enough to James.[36]

As for the substantive, political reasons why things did not go back to some pre-lapsarian normal, these centred on different versions of the same mixture of the dynastic and the confessional that had dominated the politics of the previous reign and were to remain the central political issues of the post-Reformation for decades to come. These concerned issues of peace and war and of royal marriage, but also featured, in the English case, the after-effects of the half-completed, always already contested, attempts at reformation and counter-reformation of the last century.

One of the things that was happening here was the transfer of modes of communication and analysis that had previously been the preserve of popish critics of the Elizabethan state into what we might call the mainstream of English protest discourse. This was enabled by the end of the war with Spain, and the emergence of real Catholic and crypto-Catholic interests at court. Central here was the rehabilitation of the Howards, and the rise in particular of Henry Howard, Earl of Northampton, an erstwhile supporter of Mary Stuart who for all his closeness at the end of the reign with Essex had always been on the outs with the Elizabethan regime.[37] Now, under James, he emerged as a central figure, second only to Cecil in the inner councils of the king. This enabled tropes about popish conspiracy, which under Elizabeth and during the war, had nearly always acted centripetally, to be become centrifugal forces.[38] No longer uniting a Protestant regime and its supporters together against an external popish threat, under the changed circumstances of James's reign, these same tropes and assumptions now allowed the growing perception of a popish presence within the court to prompt Protestant criticism of the regime itself. This was a propensity that could only strengthen when the prominence of the Spanish ambassador at court was compounded by the imminence of a Spanish match.[39]

The continuing fiscal crises that beset the Jacobean state, produced in part at least by the extravagance of the king and the corruption of many of his officers and courtiers, provided fertile ground for the application of the rhetoric of corrupt, evil counsel, of malign self-seeking men battening off the Crown in the pursuit of their private, rather than the public, interest. Again, this propensity was compounded by the presence of rather a lot of Scots at court, and the existence of real-enough sex scandals surrounding the king's favourite Robert Carr and Frances Howard, the Essex divorce and the Overbury murder.[40] All of which lent itself to a style of *politique* analysis centred on court conspiracy and evil counsel, of precisely the sort to which the Catholics had subjected the Elizabethan regime. Here was *Leicester's Commonwealth*, with its sex scandals and poisoning, come home to roost.

As Alastair Bellany has shown, the result was in part a mixture of sex and money, of (often misogynist) tropes for luxury and both popish and financial corruption, entirely recognisable to any one at all conversant with current American politics, and, in part, a mélange of fantasies about witchcraft and magic, and the voraciously emasculating effects of female desire, more peculiar to the early modern period. The presence of this lurid cocktail all over the revenge tragedies of Webster or Ford was almost certainly not accidental.

All of which came together in a critique of James's style of rule and a 'monarchically republican' vision of how the English polity ought to work, based on assertively masculine and Protestant notions of political virtue and active citizenship. How this all worked can best be gleaned from the works of Thomas Scott, a Norfolk minister and latterly religio-political exile in the Low Countries, and the author of, amongst other equally incendiary works, the notorious *Vox Populi*. Scott envisioned Parliament as the central means whereby the political virtue, and indeed the just grievances and true condition, of the king's subjects could be brought into remediating contact with the workings of the court and the Council. Without the regular, supervisory attentions of Parliament, the natural propensity towards corruption, inherent in the very structures of the court, would, Scott maintained, run out of control. For, left to its own devices, the court was a place where the pursuit of private ends, in private, through the politics of access, flattery and deceit, would always produce various forms of corruption. The monarch's structural position, surrounded by the machinations of his courtiers, who would always be tempted to prefer their own interests before those of the commonwealth, rendered it all but impossible, even for the most virtuous of rulers, to effect the necessary reforms and impose the necessary controls. What was required to enable the Crown to put its own affairs in order was contact with the necessarily public authority and truth-telling testimony of Parliament, which, alone of the institutional mechanisms of monarchical rule, could be relied upon to inform the king of the real condition and concerns of his subjects, and thus bring the propensity towards corruption endemic in the court under control. Or so Scott claimed. To take up Conrad Russell's famous *bon mot*, for Scott Parliament was not only most definitely an institution not an event, it also was an institution whose regular operation was absolutely essential to the moral, political and religious health of the kingdom.

This represented a systematic application of 'evil counsellor' theory to early Stuart politics. The analysis here was not merely moral and *ad hominem* but systemic, at issue not merely the personal corruptions and depravities of individual counsellors but rather the structural propensities of royal courts and personal monarchy, not only to enable, but serially to reproduce, a certain sort of corruption, to the containment of which the regular meeting of the Parliament was absolutely essential. Scott's vision was topped off by the quintessentially popish and foreign figure of Gondomar, the Spanish ambassador, who, in his rendition of the current conjuncture, played the central role of evil counsellor-in-chief. In a malign alliance with English Catholics certainly, but also with a range of corrupt, careerist courtiers, all of them desperate to avoid the reforming gaze of Parliament, and therefore ready to exalt the prerogative and push the Spanish match, Gondomar represented the point where Scott's rabid anti-popery and his diagnosis of court-based corruption met. The result, according to Scott, was the Spanish Match, which he portrayed as a central part of what he described as the long-standing Spanish conspiracy to achieve world domination.[41]

Here, then, was the emergency which legitimated Scott going public with his analysis of what ailed the nation, which, of course, he did in that most promiscuously uncontrollable medium of print, first in *Vox Populi* and then in a series of other tracts printed, for the most part, abroad. Not that print was the only medium in play here. *Vox Populi* also circulated as a manuscript separate, and a range of court, City and provincial preachers, like Andrew Willett, John Everard and, in Ipswich, Samuel Ward, got into hot water for denouncing the match in the pulpit, and, in Ward's case, in a remarkable printed image featuring the Armada and the gunpowder plot. Here was the ultimate instance of the exercise of free speech or *parrhesia* by true patriots, calling, in effect, on the king to call Parliament, so that he could listen to the 'representatives of the people' assembled there telling him the unvarnished truth about the current situation of his kingdom, and thus enabling him to come to the rescue of a church and commonwealth currently threatened by both popery and corruption.

On the one hand, this looks like a classically oppositionist agenda and ideology, a clear instance of 'free speech' 'telling truth to power'. But we should beware of a Whiggish concentration on 'Puritan' opposition to the match, for, as Tom Cogswell first pointed out years ago, the match provoked, not univocal opposition, but debate, with various groups and individuals making a case for, as well as against, it, and in particular for the virtues of peace over the uncertainties and hardships of war.[42] And as Conrad Russell observed even longer ago, this was a moment to which it is all but impossible to apply traditional dichotomies between 'court and country', 'government and opposition', since the court itself was split between the king, who wanted to pursue his traditionally pacific policies, and his son and favourite, who did not.

Scott himself became embroiled in a pamphlet exchange with the veteran Catholic polemicist Verstegan, who produced a series of tracts aping the format, titles and arguments of Scott's oeuvre, arguing in favour not of 'the Protestant' but rather of a version of the 'Catholic cause'. In England itself, in order to convince the papacy to issue the requisite dispensation for the match, James had to sustain the impression that English Catholics were not subject to any form of persecution. This meant the release of large numbers of Catholic priests and widespread semi-public expressions of Catholic belief and practice, particularly in London around the foreign embassies, but not only there. In response to this heightened Catholic activity, and in particular to stem the tide of high-profile conversions to Catholicism, including that of Buckingham's mother, a series of semi-public disputations were held between representatives of the church of Rome and various stands of English Protestant opinion. These occurred at court and in the City, and many of them produced or provoked rival accounts of what had happened, spread in manuscript and in print.[43] Following the return from Madrid this febrile atmosphere was compounded by public expressions of joy at Charles's return without a Spanish bride, and heightened debate about the prospect of war with Spain. In short, the Palatine crisis and the match provided precisely the sort of emergency, the sustained state of exception, which allowed or enabled the exercise of free speech by all sorts of contending groups and individuals.

It was the combination of virulent Puritan, but not only Puritan, opposition to the match, with the increased levels of Catholic visibility and activism epitomised by various high-profile conversions, particularly amongst the ladies of the court, that provided the context if not for the 'rise of Arminianism' *tout court*, then certainly for Richard Montague's two infamous books, *A New Gag for an Old Goose* and *Appello Caesarem*. These did double, both anti-popish and anti-Puritan, duty, since on Montague's account the Church of England was rendered vulnerable to Catholic critique by the Calvinism which all too many of its own members attributed to it. It was only by repudiating the effects of this decades-long Puritan conspiracy to Calvinise the Church of England in ways that its foundation documents simply did not allow, that the Catholic threat could be repelled. There could scarcely be a clearer instance of the way in which the crisis provoked by the match called the conventional boundaries of acceptable speech into radical question, allowing certain styles of both Catholic and Arminian speech out into the open, while calling into question the propriety, the assumed claim to represent publicly authorised orthodoxy, of certain styles of Calvinist or (allegedly) Puritan discourse. As ever, claims to free speech advanced by, or for, some (previously marginalised) groups meant the threat of proscription or silence for others.

The tergiversations of this continuing political crisis ensured that even Thomas Scott's status as the poster child for 'Puritan opposition' was not secure. From the outset, Scott had been careful to frame his position as both a construal and a defence of what he took to be the status quo ante, looking back to a golden age of Elizabethan Protestant zeal and anti-Catholic and anti-Spanish activism to legitimate his current stance, and construing his view of the way the polity worked as the traditional one. He had also been careful to type the tendencies against which he was speaking out as both novel and other, that is to say as popish, court-centred and, in the case of Gondomar, simply Spanish. He larded his tracts with quotations from the works of James himself in order the better to be able to claim to be agreeing with the king, whom he claimed to be defending from the corrupting influence of evil counsel and court corruption.

So much was perhaps to be expected. It was, of course, the whole point of the evil counsellor manoeuvre that it should allow those deploying it to cast themselves as the best friends of the prince, even as they excoriated central elements of his or her policies and central figures in his or her regime. But interestingly Scott himself, and even more the agenda of which he was perhaps the most outspoken advocate, enjoyed an intensely ambiguous relationship with the regime, or at least with central elements within it. A virulent critic of court corruption, when Buckingham – who was, in many ways, the epitome of everything that the likes of Scott took to be wrong with the Jacobean court – came back from Madrid, Scott hailed him as the saviour of the nation. He did so because the duke was returning as the nemesis of the hated Spanish Match,[44] and was about to embark on what Tom Cogswell has termed the 'blessed revolution', a *renversement d'alliances* that saw James's son and favourite embrace the cause of war and seek the alliance of patriot voices in the House of Commons.[45]

However, having embraced this mode of discourse in 1624, Charles and the duke were eaten up by it in 1625–26, as elements at court, in the Commons and in the wider political nation turned on Buckingham as the architect of a (failed) war effort that had in fact been sabotaged by James himself during the last months before his death. Crucially for the argument being pursued here, a major role was played in this turn of events by a piece of classic black propaganda, an exercise in libellous secret history designed to unmask the nefarious doings of a malign evil counsellor straight out of the *Treatise of Treasons / Leicester's Commonwealth* school of political commentary. This was a tract called *The Forerunner of Revenge*, written by a Catholic spy, one Dr Eglisham, and printed in Flanders, as an exercise in Catholic disinformation. Remarkably given its Catholic origins, this text, which alleged that James I had been poisoned by Buckingham (and perhaps by Charles), rapidly entered the mainstream of English political discourse, and, as Alastair Bellany and Tom Cogswell have shown, played more than a walk-on role in the impeachment of the duke in 1626.[46]

As Bellany, Cogswell and Noah Millstone have also shown, the dramatic events that ensued – the impeachment of the duke, the Forced Loan, the

Petition of Right, the murder of Dr Lamb, the assassination of Buckingham, the execution of his assassin Felton, the spectacular failure of the 1629 Parliament – were all commented upon and publicised by a range of verse libels and manuscript separates of an unprecedented profusion and sophistication.[47] Very significantly, this chorus of illicit commentary was again anything but uniformly oppositional in tone or content; we are still not dealing here simply with the weapons of the weak; modes of action and genres of expression resorted to only by those critical of the regime and thus denied access to other more licit or respectable forms of communication. On the contrary, while the chorus of verse comment that greeted the assassination of Buckingham and the trial and execution of his assassin, John Felton, certainly featured paeans of praise to Felton as a sort of martyr, a true patriot, who had sacrificed himself in order to save his country and the commonweal, it also contained denunciations of Felton as a subversive enemy to all order in church and state and tributes to Buckingham as his innocent victim.[48]

The significance of the rise of the parliamentary separate, charted with such exactitude by Noah Millstone, resided, amongst other things, in its capacity to transfer the effects of the freedom of speech available to Parliament-men within the chamber, where they could broach subjects and say things that anywhere else would get them into serious trouble, to the wider political nation, or to at least those parts of it that were either directly or indirectly exposed to these accounts of the Parliament's proceedings. The separates, and to a lesser extent the libels and satirical verses, acted as an echo chamber to the speeches being made, and the causes being canvassed, in and though Parliament. In this way, the effects of parliamentary *parrhesia* were spread around the kingdom.

Not only that, but, as Noah Millstone has shown in the case of Sir John Eliot and his allies, we have the emergence of political actors self-consciously playing the game of publicity, ensuring that their parliamentary speeches circulated in manuscript, even circulating versions that were not actually given, and thus plotting a politics of free speech and publicity that was self-consciously intended to operate outside as well as inside the chamber.[49] Indeed, Millstone convincingly suggests that such impulses and calculations lay behind the famous scene at the conclusion of the 1629 Parliament when the Speaker was held in his chair in order for a final parliamentary remonstrance to be loosed on the world. As Conrad Russell observed long ago, such extreme behaviour represented a striking (implicit) acknowledgement that all of the conventions that rendered Parliament viable as a channel of communication, a source of counsel, a site of criticism and compliment to the Crown, and thus as a source both of redress of grievances for the subject and of supply for the Crown, had broken down.[50] On Millstone's argument, Eliot and his confrères knew as much. Theirs was not (merely) a passionate admission of failure, a (pointless) gesture of defiance, a swansong of desperate protest directed at the Crown, it was rather a message designedly sent from

Parliament, via manuscript circulation, to the nation at large; one designed, on Millstone's account, to stir up the merchant community to levels of resistance that would drive the Crown once more to the negotiating table.

In taking that tack, Eliot and his allies were merely adopting to their own peculiarly aggressive purposes a tactic adopted throughout the decade by the House of Commons, which throughout the 1620s tried to issue various collective statements of intent or vindication of itself, which of course were to be spread around the kingdom through manuscript circulation. Such attempts were made in 1621, 1625, 1626 and 1628, but perhaps the best example here is the *Commons Remonstrance* of 1628, which according to Millstone was 'among the most widely circulated scribal texts of the entire era'.[51] It was also the document that John Felton famously carried sewn into his hat when he stabbed the Duke of Buckingham to death at Portsmouth in August 1628.[52] Increasingly, as Richard Cust has highlighted, these collective statements elicited formal replies from Charles I, replies which often took the form not merely of royal speeches but more significantly of printed declarations explaining just why he had been forced to dissolve this or that parliament.[53]

It was here that we find some of the best evidence of the anti-popular, absolutist reaction that these developments came to elicit from the king and the court. For in these texts we find an explanation of current events in terms of a popular and Puritan conspiracy against monarchical power in both church and state. Confronted by the failure of parliament after parliament to respond to his just demands for supply in time of war, a war into which Charles felt he had been urged by the Parliament of 1624, Charles had recourse to his own version of an evil-counsel narrative. Both the people and the House of Commons, Charles claimed, had fallen victim to a conspiracy of popular spirits, *tribuni plebis* as both he and his father had called them, who, desperate to enhance their own reputation and power, had ingratiated themselves with the people, inculcating a sense of grievance and claiming to take the part of the people's liberties against the prerogatives of the Crown. Gradually these men had risen to prominence in the House of Commons, the rank and file membership of which they had likewise duped into taking their lead. By gaining control of crucial committees they had started to entrench upon the powers of the Crown. These men were the prime practitioners of popularity, presenting themselves to the people as so called 'patriots', defenders of the commonweal, against the supposed depredations of the court.[54] For Charles, Sir John Eliot was the epitome of this populist conspiracy, and, as John Reeve has shown, having consigned Eliot to the Tower for his actions in 1629, Charles was for a long while determined to have him arraigned for treason, despite the fact that the judges were unanimous that no such charge was legally viable.[55]

While Charles concentrated on the threat posed to monarchical government by such secular politicians, others, court preachers and prelates, dwelt on the similarly popular threat posed by the Puritans. Here perhaps the stand-out example is a court sermon preached by Matthew Wren before the king in February 1628. There Wren lambasted a threat to all order in church and stated represented by people who 'reckon them that stand least upon points with God in worshiping of him, the godliest men and the best Christians', and 'them that stand most upon points with the king, against obeying of him, the best subjects, or (as it now goes current in their own coin) "good patriots"'. Such people were so sure of their own spiritual superiority that they 'count it a shrewd wrong to be but told what's right' and, if any man displayed, to God, 'a better devotion', or, to the king, 'a better allegiance', than themselves, they were immediately besmeared with the charges of 'dangerous superstition', in the first instance, and of 'ambitious flattery', in the second.[56] Denouncing the lack of reverence displayed by such people in the worship of God, Wren also noted what he presented as their concomitant lack of obedience in the service of the king, maintaining that it was impossible properly to discharge one's duty of right worship towards God, if one did not do the same towards the king, and vice versa.[57]

This was to associate the threat of a populist Puritanism with that posed by the 'good patriots', the *tribuni plebis*, denounced by Charles as the real cause of his dysfunctional relationship with Parliament. And, of course, it was as the best way to meet that threat, as it had revealed itself in the vociferous opposition to the Spanish Match, that an Arminianising Laudianism had first risen in the counsels of the Crown, at the end of James's reign, and then established itself at the centre of royal favour, if not, until the early 1630s, of ecclesiastical policy and power, under Charles. Wren's sermon was preached in the period between December 1627 and March 1628 when a fierce debate was raging at court and in Council about whether Charles should continue with the sort of new counsels that had produced the Forced Loan or return to more conventional parliamentary ways of funding the war effort. It can, therefore, be construed as a sort of Laudian offer sheet, an aggressively anti-Puritan, distinctively Laudian, set of new counsels in ecclesiastical affairs, perfectly suited to parallel and support those under way in secular affairs. As Richard Cust has described, as it turned out Charles ended up taking the parliamentary route,[58] and it was not until that had ended in complete disaster in the assassination of Buckingham and the debacle of the 1629 Parliament, that Charles was free to adopt something like the complete Laudian package, which, of course he proceeded to do over the course of the 1630s.

The king's patronage of Laudianism was part of what Kevin Sharpe has described as a full-on attempt to re-educate the English in the habits of obedience, reverence and awe in the face of both royal and divine authority. That lesson was to be taught not so much through the word, that is to say through exhortation and argument, either in the pulpit or on the printed page, as through performance, and visual representation. Crucial here was the participation in, and observation of, various acts of outward worship, highly scripted ritual or ceremonial performances, through which the outward individual was to be schooled in reverence, decorum and obedience and thus the appropriate inward virtues of obedience, fear and awe inculcated. The master discourse here was provided by the Laudian ideal of the beauty of holiness, and, in particular, by the Laudian obsession with schooling ordinary Christians in the right ritual and ceremonial responses to the divine presence in church. This was paralleled by the Caroline obsession with enforcing the correct levels of decorum and respect before royal authority, whether that authority was instantiated in the royal person or in its representation or in other of the forms or workings of royal authority. In the court masque the revelation of, and exposure to, the authority of the Crown, and indeed the person of the monarch, were seen to have a curative effect on all that ailed the kingdom. Again, many of the portraits of Van Dyck, or the court plays performed for Henrietta Maria, portrayed the virtue and decorum of the royal person, and the unity and affection of the royal marriage, as object lessons in the meld between obedience and love, reason and passion, that ought to characterise the king's relation with his subjects and his realm.[59]

This was a comprehensive royal reaction to what we might term an excess of 'free speech'; a response which, unlike that of his father, James, did not involve a voluble continuation of the conversation, a back-and-forth sustained even as the king himself spoke volubly about the mystery of the *arcana imperii* and the subject's duty to watch and admire the monarch's mastery of the arts of kingcraft. On the contrary, here Charles was meeting the excessive speech of his subjects with (relative) silence. That excess had reached its peak in the later 1620s in a cacophony of comment, conversation and critique conducted through print, manuscript and oral communication, in a variety of venues, stretching from the Parliament house to the alehouse, and the manor house. Here was Charles trying stop that conversation, by shutting down many of the central modes and sites of communication which had enabled it to start in the first place. And here Parliament's status as the prime site within the polity for the exercise of free speech, and the tight connection between the production and consumption of manuscript separates and the proceedings of Parliament (noted by Millstone) were both key, as were Laudian efforts if not to silence, then certainly to redefine, constrain and control the preaching of God's word. If one were to adopt the argot of the most portentous sort of cultural historian, one might talk of a fundamental shift between the ear and the eye as the dominant sense, the preferred recipient of the political and religious communication coming out of the Caroline regime in church and state. Hence the Laudian turn away from the word preached to the sacraments as the chief means of grace and to collective prayer and divine worship as the major mode of edification in the church. On this view, it was no accident that it was in the 1630s that Ben Jonson finally lost his long-running argument with Inigo Jones about the relative significance of the scenic and performative effects of the masque, conceived and realised by the dramaturge (Jones), as opposed to the words scripted by the poet (Jonson).

According to Sharpe, that disinclination to explain himself set in at the start of the Personal Rule and did not break down until the crisis of the early 1640s forced Charles to act more as faction leader than monarch, but, in fact, that turns out not to be true. As early as 1637, in the co-ordinated campaigns launched against both the Puritan triumvirs, Burton, Bastwick and Prynne, and Bishop John Williams, the regime – if not Charles himself, then some of his most trusted mouthpieces, like Laud and Heylyn, as well as some rather more obscure hangers-on, like Christopher Dow – returned to systematic political case-making. The official campaign against them simply inverted their case against the regime, which involved a conspiracy of evil counsel, driven on the bishops, who were bent on introducing a form of popery into the English church, while encouraging the king into ever greater encroachment on the liberty of the subjects; encroachments which took on their most blatant form in the treatment meted out to the Puritan triumvirs and other Puritan critics of the regime. Heylyn and Dow countered by unmasking what they claimed was the real conspiracy, that being hatched by popular Puritans and tribunician spirits, to drive a wedge between the prince and his people. For, according to Heylyn, the Puritan triumvirs were merely continuing the earlier subversive activities of the *tribuni plebis* who had subverted the parliaments of the later 1620s so effectively. They were doing so through accusations of evil counsel lodged against the bishops but in fact designed to criticise the king himself. As a systematic attempt to alienate the king from his subjects and the subjects from their prince, this was tantamount to treason, an offence, these tracts alleged, with which the triumvirs were extremely lucky not already to have been charged.

The claim was that the Puritans held a radical version of monarchical republicanism, a vision of the polity that in effect reduced the authority of the prince to that of a doge of Venice. Royal authority, they claimed, was subject to the authority of positive law, in effect abolishing the basis for any effective version of the royal prerogative and leaving the operations of royal power subject to the criticism of the subject. On this view, the obedience of free subjects was conditional on the king's observing the terms of the legal covenant that bound him to his subjects, and his subjects to him. Burton, in particular, argued that Charles had reaffirmed that covenant in secular affairs, through the Petition of Right, and, in religious affairs, by his profession that he would not change the religion of the Elizabethan church. According to Burton, since making those commitments in the late 1620s Charles had systematically broken both of them; the first through the regime's treatment of Burton, Bastwick and Prynne, which represented a persecutory, indeed a positively tyrannical, abuse of power, and the second through his sponsorship of Laudian and Arminian policies in the church. On this basis, Burton and his mates pronounced their own state of emergency, a state of affairs that more than justified their present exercise in *parrhesia*, their going promiscuously public with their allegations about the bishop-centred threat to the rights, liberties and religion of all English people. According to Heylyn, Burton regarded himself and Prynne as self-appointed tribunes of the people.[60] Prompted by conscience and the word of God to speak truth to power, Burton used much the same pitch to call on the people to support him; citing as he did so what Heylyn termed that principle of '*parrhesia* which you so commend against all kings and princes'[61] as though 'you would have every man ... as bold a bravo as yourself, to bid defiance to the king, at least to stand it out against all authority'.[62] For Burton was out 'to make the common people think that they have more than private interest in the things of God, and in the government of states; nothing more plausible nor welcome to some sort of men, such whom you either make or call "free subjects"'.[63]

Over against what he presented as Burton's more or less classic restatement of monarchical republicanism and Calvinist resistance theory, Heylyn conjured an equally classic restatement of Jacobean divine-right absolutism; affirming that 'kings do hold their crowns by no other tenure than *dei gratia* ... what power soever they have, they have from God, by whom kings reign and princes decree justice', and asking 'how and by whom do you conceive they should be limited?' No doubt Burton would reply by the law, to which claim Heylyn responded, with James I, that the origin of such laws as might be taken to limit the king was the king himself,[64] and thus the liberties of the people were themselves the product of royal law-making. Besides, Heylyn added, monarchy was founded upon natural, not upon positive, law, which was why 'princes in themselves are above the laws, as princes are considered *in abstracto,* and extent of power. How far that extent may reach, you may see in the first of Samuel and chapter 8.' This was the passage in which Samuel explains to the children of Israel just what subjection to a king could entail; a text cited for precisely this purpose by James I in his *True Law of Free Monarchies*. Of course, in practice, or, as Heylyn put it, '*in concreto*, a just prince will not break those laws which he hath promised to observe', but he could, and, if he did, his subjects would be left with no redress. Thus, Heylyn asked Burton to suppose that the king were restrained by human positive law, 'after the manner that you would have', and that he then went on to neglect 'those laws whereby you apprehend his power is limited, how would you help yourself by this limited power? I hope you would not call a consistory and convent him there, or arm the people to assert their pretended liberties, though, as before I said, the puritan tenet is that you may do both.'[65] For Heylyn, it was 'a kind of disobedience and disloyalty to question what a king can do, being God's deputy here on earth'.[66] As for the ordinary subject, he or she should remember that 'the safest man is he that thinks no evil, and entertains not rashly those unjust reports which are devised and spread abroad by malicious wits of purpose to defame their betters, that they themselves may gain applause and be cried up, and honoured, yea, *tantum non*, adored, by poor ignorant men, who do not understand aright what their projects aim at'.[67]

But Heylyn was not merely refighting Jacobean battles, he sought to return his readers' minds to the *Sturm und Drang* of the late Elizabethan confrontation with the Presbyterian movement, reminding Burton that Greenwood, Penry and Udall, amongst others, 'zealous puritans all', had been 'condemned to death, and the more part executed'.[68] Burton, then, should beware lest he suffer the same fate as that Elizabethan firebrand, John Udall, who had, of course, died in jail, under sentence of death.[69]

On this account, the likes of Burton, Bastwick and Prynne were lucky that they had not already suffered such a fate, but Heylyn was quick to remind them that the leniency of their current treatment would not be repeated. This was a decidedly one-off job. As Heylyn explained it, the authorities had decided, just this once, that 'an answer should be made unto all your quarrels, that so the people, whom you have seduced, might see the error of their courses' and 'your proselytes may perceive what false guides they follow, and all the world may see how much you have abused the king and his ministers with your scandalous clamours'. But these exchanges were most definitely not the beginning of a conversation, an opening of the public sphere through a series of Puritan challenges and official responses, during which the regime would reply to each and every of the 'scandalous and seditious pamphlets that are now grown so rife that every day produces new monsters'. That way madness lay; it would not only 'encourage you on your courses' but also 'suddenly dissolve the whole frame of government'. On the contrary, the current flurry of official responses represented a once-and-for-all drawing of a line, a definitive statement of the official position, after which there would be silence, and, if the objects of the government's ire did not cease and desist, real repression, of the sort that had brought the Elizabethan Puritan movement to such a shuddering halt. For, as Heylyn warned, 'princes have other ways to right themselves, and those which are in authority under them, than by the pen, and such as will fall heavier, if you pull them on you'.[70]

What was at stake here, firstly in the royal declarations of the late 1620s, and now in Heylyn's, Dow's and Laud's denunciations of Burton, Bastwick and Prynne of 1637, was the application of a species of evil counsellor theory, this time not to the court of the prince but rather to the relation pertaining, in the first instance, between the House of Commons and a small group of *tribuni plebis*, and, in the second, between the Puritan *boutefeu* and their popular following. In each case, a mass of at least potentially loyal persons was being misled and seduced into calamitously subversive attitudes and actions by a small group of malign private and popular spirits. This conspiracy was unmasked in a burst of royally sponsored *parrhesia*, an extraordinary expedient, adopted in response to an immediate crisis, in this case not by the (either Catholic or Protestant) critics of the monarchical state but rather by its defenders, who had been forced to act by a conspiracy of popular spirits, self-appointed spokesmen for and evil counsellors to the people, out to subvert all authority in both church and state. As in all such outbreaks of plain speaking, this one was intended not to start but rather definitively to end a conversation, as things were returned to a decidedly authoritarian, both Laudian and absolutist, version of monarchical normality. This was to be achieved, on the one hand, by a mixture of privileged public speech, exemplary punishment and the threat of future repression on a scale unseen since the crack-down on the Elizabethan Puritan movement, and, on the other, by the silently incremental effects of repeated exposure to, and participation in, the formalities of Laudian worship and the forms of Caroline government.

If Charles, writing in the late 1620s, and his spokespersons writing in the later 1630s, are to be believed, we are dealing here with a longstanding contest between, on the one hand, a popular and Puritan opposition, dedicated to a monarchically republican, covenant-based view of the polity and of kingship, an anti-episcopalian, at best implicitly Presbyterian, view of church government, and a subversively Calvinist style of piety, and, on the other, a royal establishment, organised around a divine-right view of both royal and episcopal government, and a decidedly Arminian style of piety. This, of course, is a decidedly 'Whiggish' vision of the period, which might be taken rather to confirm my (admittedly only half-serious) suggestion that Charles I was indeed the first Whig historian of early Stuart politics; the only difference between Charles's view and the Whig version being that he viewed as entirely malign developments what the likes of Wallace Notestein took to be central to the emergence of parliamentary power, which, of course, they viewed entirely favourably and Charles, naturally enough, did not.

But, in taking that view of the period seriously – and since it clearly was the view held by Charles I and his inner circle, as historians, we really do have to do that – we do not also have simply to accept or endorse it.[71] Certainly, on the subject of free speech, what has emerged here is anything but a typically Whiggish view of the matter. Rather, we have a series of claims and practices, to which intermittent recourse was made by a variety of groups and individuals. Each such recourse was prompted and legitimated by some sort of actual or perceived emergency; a crisis so severe that only resort to extraordinary, and ordinarily illicit, modes of communication could possibly meet it. This was not, either in its origins or its inherent nature, a weapon of the weak; an argument or manoeuvre restricted to opponents of royal power. On the contrary, as we have seen, it was first used, at the beginning of our period, by elements in the Elizabethan regime in order to legitimate their campaign against Mary Stuart, and, at its end, by spokesmen for the Caroline regime to justify their multimedia campaign against Burton, Bastwick and Prynne and behind them Bishop Williams.

If this manoeuvre reached its most virulent and developed stage early on in the period in the hands of Catholic opponents of the regime, it did so only in response to the efforts of the Elizabethan state to do in Mary and Norfolk, while typing English Catholics as so many rebels and traitors waiting to happen. Moreover, its use did not end there. As we have seen, spokesmen for the regime continued to push their own anti-popish conspiracy theory, telling their own libellous secret histories about English Catholics, the seminaries and the machinations of the Pope, the League and the King of Spain, while Puritan critics of the ecclesiastical status quo told an anti-episcopal version of essentially the same conspiracy theory to effect their (reforming) purposes; purposes which they represented as but the continuation, indeed the completion, of the regime's own essentially repressive anti-Catholic, disciplinary agenda.

These outbreaks of 'free speech' were largely occasioned by two structural features of the Elizabethan post-Reformation. Most importantly, by the succession and accession crises *in potentia*, that shaped the politics of the reign, and secondly by the 'but halfly reformed' nature of the Elizabethan church settlement, and the Puritan movement for further reformation that it produced. Taken together these ensured that by the second-half of the reign many of the features usually assigned to the early Stuart period – the manuscript libels, and satirical verses, the libellous secret histories, circulation of manuscript position papers and separates, the obsessions with court corruption and evil counsel – were all in place. Indeed, they could all be found honed to high levels of sophistication and self-consciousness both in the practice of the Essex circle itself and in the wider responses to and perceptions of that circle's activities. Thus, it was within the Essex circle that the hostile *politique* analysis of the court, of the sort perfected by the regime's Catholics critics, was first systematically applied by Protestants to the workings of the Elizabethan regime, as, under the influence of the likes of Antonio Perez and Anthony Bacon, the Essexians came to view the Cecils as a malign conspiracy to mislead the queen, make peace with Spain and sell the succession, in their own interest, to the Spaniard.[72]

Thus, one of the big stories in the period was the process whereby such hermeneutic habits and suspicions migrated from largely Catholic circles into the Protestant mainstream, where they allowed heightened levels of suspicion and critique to be directed at the Jacobean court. With the end of the war with Spain and the accession of an adult male Protestant endowed with an heir, and pretty soon a spare as well, many of the central organising themes at the centre of the so-called succession and accession crises that had done so much to define the politics of Elizabeth's reign, and beset the opening years of James's, had played themselves out. All of which allowed what had been the largely unifying force of anti-popery to be directed inward at the emergent Catholic and crypto-Catholic, and then finally Spanish presences within the Jacobean court and establishment. The impact of this shift was compounded by James's financial woes, which were in part a product, and in part a cause, of the contemporary fuss about royal extravagance and court corruption. Associated with a variety of foreign, or at least un-English, influences – Scots courtiers and favourites, Catholics, Gondomar – the consequent negative perceptions were exacerbated by a series of sex scandals that beset the court throughout the 1610s.

All of which provided the occasion for an orgy of both *parrhesiastic* (and at times) voyeuristic commentary and criticism conducted sometimes in Parliament, but more often and more intensively through verse libels and circulating manuscripts. The climacteric point arrived with the fuss over the Spanish Match, which provoked not only an orgy of *parrhesia*-fuelled opposition from a range of preachers and pamphleteers but also genuine debate. Not only did the match have its defenders, but its impact, and the reaction to the adverse reaction against it, opened up space for the public statement of opinions, and performance of identities, both Catholic and Arminian, that had previously been kept well under wraps. Having tried, in 1624, to harness the political and emotional energies of the patriot and Protestant cause, Charles and Buckingham fell victim to a backlash against their failed efforts to fight the right sort of war; a backlash that fed off those very same energies. Out of the resulting cacophony developed what one might term a royalist conspiracy theory, centred on the popular spirits allegedly leading both the Commons and the people astray, and announced in a series of royal acts of *parrhesia*, in which, against his best instincts, Charles deigned to explain his actions to his subjects; an act of condescension both prompted and legitimated by the depth of the crisis into which said critics had plunged the realm. Thereafter followed the experiment in political and moral re-education, based on the eye and not the ear, on performance and visual representation, rather than argument or even exhortation, that was the Personal Rule, as Kevin Sharpe has described it.[73] Which idyll ended in another outbreak of officially sponsored *parrhesia* designed once and for all to shut down the counter-narrative, the alternative evil-counsellor-centred conspiracy theory, being propagated by Burton, Bastwick and Prynne.

Whilst one should not ignore, or even play down, the contingency of the political events that drove this narrative, one can also surely see a dialectical progression at work here, as acts of free speech, each designed to describe, unmask and denounce various conspiracy-based emergencies, practised by one group or another – by the state and its (either Catholic or Puritan) critics, by various Parliament-men and the defenders of the court, or the Crown, or indeed by the monarch himself, by the opponents or defenders of the Spanish Match – elicited other such acts from their opponents. The result was a series of claims to and outbreaks of 'free speech' of increasing frequency, if not intensity. But what this was not was the rise of free speech in anything like the modern sense, since the aim of each of these exercises in *parrhesia* was to achieve a situation in which certain groups got to speak and certain things got to get said while others most definitely did not. The role of Catholicism in these discussions is always a dead give-away. As Hall and Alford could testify, in the Elizabethan House of Commons any attempt to say things designed to save Mary Stuart from the block got short shrift from both the House itself and the powers that were, and, in 1621, the same Parliament that was so protective of its own right to free speech expelled one of its own members for protesting against the unequal treatment serially meted out by parliaments to papists and Puritans and sought to discipline Edward Floyd, who was not even a member of the House, for saying slighting things about the Elector Palatine and his wife.[74] Whether, then, this period has much of anything to say to historians of free speech seems to me to be very much an open question, one to which the other contributors to this volume are far more qualified to speak than I.

NOTES

1 P. Lake and S. Pincus (eds), *The Politics of the Public Sphere in Early Modern England* (Manchester, 2007), esp. introduction and chapter 1.
2 J. Guy, 'The Rhetoric of Counsel in Early Modern England', in D. Hoak (ed.), *Tudor Political Culture* (Cambridge, 1995), 47–71; J. Rose, 'Kingship and Counsel in Early Modern England', *HJ* 54 (2011), 47–71; J. Rose (ed.), *The Politics of Counsel in England and Scotland, 1286–1707* (Oxford, 2016). See also forthcoming work from Joanne Paul, and her 'The Best Counsellors Are the Dead: Counsel and Shakespeare's Hamlet', *Renaissance Studies* 30 (2015), 646–65.
3 See S. Hindle, *The State and Social Change in Early Modern England, 1550–1640* (Basingstoke, 2000); S. Hindle, 'Hierarchy and Community in the English Parish: The Swallowfield Articles', *HJ* 42 (1999), 835–51.
4 P. Collinson, 'The Monarchial Republic of Elizabeth I', *Bulletin of the John Rylands Library* 68 (1987), 394–424; P. Collinson, 'The Elizabethan Exclusion Crisis and the Elizabethan Polity', *PBA* 84 (1994), 51–92; J. McDiarmid (ed.), *The Monarchical Republic of Early Modern England: Essays in Response to Patrick Collinson* (Aldershot, 2007); M. Goldie, 'The Unacknowledged Republic', in Tim Harris (ed.), *The Politics of the Excluded* (Basingstoke, 2001), 153–94. See K. Thomas, 'The Levellers and the Franchise', in G.E. Aylmer (ed.), *The Interregnum: The Quest for Settlement, 1646–60* (1972), 57–78.
5 O. Arnold, *The Third Citizen: Shakespeare's Theatre and the House of Commons* (2007); for the realities of the situation see C. Kyle, *Theater of State: Parliament and Political Culture in Early Modern England* (Stanford, 2012); and C. Kyle and J. Peacey (eds), *Parliament at Work: Parliamentary Committees, Political Power and Public Access in Early Modern England* (Woodbridge, 2002). Also see P. Lake and M. Questier, 'Thomas Digges, Robert Parsons and Sir Francis Hastings and the Politics of Regime Change in Elizabethan England', *HJ* 61 (2018), 1–27.
6 Of course, for revisionists like Geoffrey Elton, the resulting debates were so much fuss and bother, mere distractions from the real business of Parliament, which for Elton was legislation, rather than part of any wider processes of political communication, substantive or symbolic. While such claims are debatable, in a volume dedicated to the issue of 'free speech' such historiographical debates need

not detain us to the extent that they would were this a volume concerned with the functions and fortunes of Parliament as an institution.

7 P. Collinson, 'The Downfall of Archbishop Grindal', in *Godly People: Essays on English Protestantism and Puritanism* (1982), 371–97; P. Collinson, *Archbishop Grindal, 1519–1583: The Struggle for a Reformed Church* (1979); P. Lake, 'A Tale of Two Episcopal Surveys: The Strange Fates of Edmund Grindal and Cuthbert Mayne Revisited', *TRHS* 18 (2008), 129–63; P. Lake, '"The Monarchical Republic of Queen Elizabeth I" (and the Fall of Archbishop Grindal) Revisited', in J. McDiarmid (ed.), *The Monarchical Republic of Early Modern England: Essays in Response to Patrick Collinson* (Aldershot, 2007), 129–47.

8 J. Ayre (ed.), *The Works of John Whitgift* (Cambridge, 1851–3), III, 306–7.

9 J. Bridges, *A Defence of the Government Established in the Church of England for Ecclesiastical Matters* (1587), 1368–70; J. Bridges, *The Supremacy of Christian Princes Over all Persons Throughout their Dominions in all Causes Ecclesiastical as Temporal* (1573), 212.

10 For *parrhesia* as a 'figure of excusing for speaking boldly' and 'the act of speaking boldly itself' see D. Colclough, *Freedom of Speech in Early Stuart England* (Cambridge, 2005), 57.

11 N. Jones, *Governing by Virtue* (Oxford, 2015).

12 P. Lake, *Bad Queen Bess? Libels, Secret Histories and the Politics of Publicity in the Reign of Queen Elizabeth I* (Oxford, 2016).

13 Colclough, *Freedom of Speech*, 77–119; C. Davies, *A Religion of the Word* (Manchester, 2002).

14 K. Sharpe, *Criticism and Compliment: The Politics of Literature in the Reign of Charles I* (Cambridge, 1987); Colclough, *Freedom of Speech*, 77–93.

15 For Dering see P. Collinson, 'A Mirror of Elizabethan Puritanism: The Life and Letters of "Godly master Dering"', in Collinson, *Godly People: Essays on English Protestantism and Puritanism* (1982), 289–324, and P. Lake, *Moderate Puritans and the Elizabethan Church* (Cambridge, 1982), 16–24; for Burgess, see P. Lake, 'Moving the Goal Posts? Modified Subscription and the Construction of Conformity in the Early Stuart Church', in P. Lake and M. Questier (eds). *Conformity and Orthodoxy in the English Church, c. 1560–1660* (Woodbridge, 2000), 179–205.

16 D. Shuger, 'St Mary the Virgin and the Birth of the Public Sphere', *HLQ* 72 (2009), 313–46.

17 P. Collinson, *The Elizabethan Puritan Movement* (1967); P. Lake and M. Questier, 'Puritans, Papists and the "Public Sphere" in Early Modern England: The Edmund Campion Affair in Context', *Journal of Modern History* 72 (2000), 587–627.

18 Lake, *Moderate Puritans*, 93–115; R. Bauckham, 'The Career and Theology of Dr William Fulke, 1537–89' (Cambridge University PhD, 1973).

19 P. Lake, *Anglicans and Puritans? Presbyterianism and English Conformist Thought from Whitgift to Hooker* (1988), chapter 2; Lake, *Moderate Puritans*, 25–35.

20 P. Collinson, 'John Field and Elizabethan Puritanism', in Collinson, *Godly People: Essays on English Protestantism and Puritanism* (1982), 335–70.

21 Lake, *Anglicans and Puritans?*, 81–5; P. Collinson, 'Ecclesiastical Vitriol: Religious Satire in the 1590s and the Invention of Puritanism', in J. Guy (ed.), *The Reign*

of *Elizabeth I* (Cambridge, 1995), 150–70. And now see the definitive account in J. Black, *The Martin Marprelate Tracts* (Cambridge, 2008), introduction.
22 P. Lake and M. Questier, *The Antichrist's Lewd Hat: Protestants, Papists and Players in Post-Reformation England* (New Haven, 2002), 509–63.
23 Collinson, *Elizabethan Puritan Movement*, part 8; P. Collinson, *Richard Bancroft and Elizabethan Anti-Puritanism* (Cambridge, 2013), 28–128.
24 P. Lake and M. Questier, *All Hail to the Archpriest* (Oxford, forthcoming), esp. introduction.
25 A. Bellany, '"Raylinge rymes and vaunting verse": Libelous Politics in Early Modern England, 1603–1628', in K. Sharpe and P. Lake (eds), *Culture and Politics in Early Stuart England* (1994), 285–310, 367–71; T. Cogswell, 'Underground Verse and the Transformation of Early Stuart Political Culture', in S. Amussen and M. Kishlansky (eds), *Political Culture and Cultural Politics in Early Modern England* (Manchester, 1995), 277–300; A. McRae, *Literature, Satire and the Early Stuart State* (Cambridge, 2004); Colclough, *Freedom of Speech*, 196–250; Richard Cust, 'News and Politics in Early Seventeenth-century England', *P&P* 112 (1986), 60–90; N. Millstone, *Manuscript Circulation and the Invention of Politics in Early Stuart England* (Cambridge, 2016).
26 P. Hammer, 'The Smiling Crocodile: The Earl of Essex and Late-Elizabethan "Popularity"', in P. Lake and S. Pincus (eds), *The Politics of the Public Sphere in Early Modern England* (Manchester, 2007), 95–115; A. Gajda, *The Earl of Essex and Late Elizabethan Political Culture* (Oxford, 2012); A. Gajda, 'Debating Peace and War in Late Elizabethan England', *HJ* 52 (2009), 851–78; A. Gajda, 'The Earl of Essex and "Politic History"', in A. Connolly and l. Hopkins (eds), *Essex: The Cultural Impact of an Elizabethan Courtier* (Manchester, 2013), 237–59.
27 Lake, *Bad Queen Bess?*
28 *Early Stuart Libels* [www.earlystuartlibels.net], accessed 26 October 2019.
29 A. Hunt, 'Tuning the Pulpits: The Religious Context of the Essex Revolt', in L. Ferrell and P. McCullough (eds), *The English Sermon Revised* (Manchester, 2001), 86–114.
30 N. Millstone, 'Seeing like a Statesman in Early Stuart England', *P&P* 222 (2014), 77–127.
31 A. Kisery, *Hamlet's Moment* (Oxford, 2016).
32 Colclough, *Freedom of Speech*, 73–6.
33 Lake, *Bad Queen Bess?*
34 A. Bellany, 'A Poem on the Archbishop's Hearse: Puritanism, Libel and Sedition after the Hampton Court Conference', *JBS* 34 (1995), 137–64.
35 M. Growhoski, 'The Secret History of a "Secret War": John Barclay, His *Satyricon* and the Politicization of Literary Scholarship in Early Modern Europe, 1582–1621' (Princeton University PhD, 2015).
36 K. Fincham and P. Lake, 'The Ecclesiastical Policy of James I', *JBS* 15 (1985), 169–207.
37 *ODNB*.
38 T. Scott (?), *Philomythie or Phylomythologie* (1616).
39 C. Wiener, 'The Beleaguered Isle: A Study of Elizabethan and Early Stuart Anti-Catholicism', *P&P* 51 (1971), 27–62.

40 A. Bellany, *The Politics of Court Scandal in Early Modern England* (Cambridge, 2002).
41 P. Lake, 'Constitutional Consensus and Puritan Opposition in the 1620s: Thomas Scott and the Spanish Match', *HJ* 25 (1982), 805–25; M. Peltonen, *Classical Humanism and Republicanism in English Political Thought, 1570–1640* (Cambridge, 1995), 229–70; Colclough, *Freedom of Speech*, 102–19.
42 T. Cogswell, 'England and the Spanish Match', in R. Cust and A. Hughes (eds), *Conflict in Early Stuart England* (Harlow, 1989), 107–33.
43 M. Questier, *Stuart Dynastic Policy and Religious Politics, 1621–1625* (Cambridge, 2009), 26–128.
44 Lake, 'Thomas Scott'.
45 T. Cogswell, *The Blessed Revolution* (Cambridge, 1989).
46 A. Bellany and T. Cogswell, *Murder of King James I* (New Haven, 2015).
47 Ibid.; A. Bellany, 'The Murder of John Lambe: Crowd Violence, Court Scandal, and Popular Politics in Early Seventeenth Century England', *P&P* 200 (2000), 37–76; T. Cogswell, 'John Felton, Popular Political Culture and the Assassination of the Duke of Buckingham', *HJ* 49 (2006), 357–85.
48 A. Bellany, '"The Brightnes of the Noble Leiutenants Action": An Intellectual Ponders Buckingham's Assassination', *EHR* 118 (2003), 1243–63.
49 Millstone, *Manuscript Circulation*, 202–7.
50 C. Russell, *Parliaments and English Politics, 1621–9* (Oxford, 1979).
51 Millstone, *Manuscript Circulation*, 231, 224, 117–19.
52 Cogswell, 'John Felton'.
53 R. Cust, 'Charles I and a Draft Declaration for the 1628 Parliament', *HR* 63 (1990), 143–61; R. Cust, 'Charles I and Popularity' in T. Cogswell, R. Cust and P. Lake (eds), *Politics, Religion and Popularity in Early Stuart Britain* (Cambridge, 2002), 235–58.
54 Cust, 'Charles I and Popularity'; Lake, 'From Revisionist to Royalist History: Or Was Charles I the First Whig Historian?', *HLQ* 78 (2015), 657–81.
55 J. Reeve, *Charles I and the Road to Personal Rule* (Cambridge, 1989), 118–71, esp. 120–1.
56 M. Wren, *Sermon Preached before the King's Majesty* (Cambridge, 1628), 35.
57 Ibid., 41–2.
58 R. Cust, *The Forced Loan and English Politics, 1626–8* (Oxford, 1987), 72–90; R. Cust, *Charles I* (Harlow, 2005), 62–82, 104–32.
59 K. Sharpe, 'The King's Writ: Royal Authors and Royal Authority in Early Modern England', in K. Sharpe and P. Lake (eds), *Culture and Politics in Early Stuart England* (Stanford, 1993), 133–4. Also see M. Smuts, *Court Culture and the Origins of a Royalist Tradition in Early Stuart England* (Philadelphia, 1987), 217–92; M. Smuts, 'Force, Love and Authority in Caroline Political Culture', in I. Atherton and J. Sanders (eds), *The 1630s* (Manchester, 2006), 28–49.
60 P. Heylyn, *Brief and Moderate Answer to … Henry Burton* (1637), 80.
61 Ibid., 52.
62 Ibid., 58.
63 Ibid., 188–9. Heylyn was here referring to a passage in which, after citing two examples of outrageously frank denunciatory speech – the first by the prophet Nehemias to confront King Ahab, and the second, by a blind bishop of Chalcedon,

to face down Julian the Apostate – Burton had asserted that 'this *parrhesia*, this liberty and freedom of speech, in such cases is not without fear of God, but a branch and fruit that springeth of it'. H. Burton, *For God and the King* (1636), 26–7.
64 Ibid., 32.
65 Ibid., 33–4.
66 Ibid., 179.
67 Ibid., 190.
68 Ibid., 187–8.
69 Ibid., 193.
70 Ibid., 191–3.
71 Lake, 'From Revisionist to Royalist History?'.
72 Gajda, *Earl of Essex*.
73 K. Sharpe, *The Personal Rule of Charles I* (New Haven, 1992).
74 Lake, *Bad Queen Bess?*; Colclough, *Freedom of Speech*, 173.

Chapter 5

The origins of the concept of freedom of the press

David Como

This chapter investigates the origins of concepts of press freedom in the anglophone world. It might seem surprising that there is anything left to contribute on a topic of such obvious significance and scope. That there remains much to be said may be ascribed, in large part, to the inescapable association of the subject with the Whig-Liberal historical approach. What could be more unapologetically Whiggish than a search for the origins of a bedrock principle of modern liberal democracy? And, beginning in the 1970s, this sort of Whiggery came under withering attack among early modernists, who began to spurn grand, progressive narratives as anachronistic, presentist, and hopelessly triumphalist. Investigations into the long-term origins of press freedom, with a handful of exceptions, more or less ceased, relegated to the historiographical graveyard, along with the other supposedly barbaric vestiges of Whig teleology.[1]

Nevertheless, the stubborn fact remains that, between 1600 and the middle of the eighteenth century, novel concepts and practices of press freedom were not only articulated in the anglophone world but gained very wide purchase, reshaping political life in profound ways. This is not a development that can or should be ignored by historians. The challenge is to reconstruct histories of long-term, overarching change, without distorting or misunderstanding the categories, modes of thought and practices of the people of the past by imposing our own, anachronistic presuppositions. The present chapter attempts such an investigation: I hope to reveal the process by which, through a set of assumptions that were indeed rather alien to modern sensibilities, within the crucible of early Stuart political crisis, something recognisably similar to our own conceptions of press freedom began to come into being.

Early seventeenth-century England, like other Western European polities of the day, had developed complex mechanisms to regulate the printing press. A system of pre-publication censorship evolved under the Tudors, embodied in a series of Crown injunctions and decrees, implemented and supplemented through careful oversight of London's Stationers' Company, the printers' and booksellers' guild mainly responsible for enforcement.[2] Under these rules, all printed books were supposed to be pre-approved by qualified licensers, chiefly episcopal chaplains, before publication. Frequently, although not uniformly, books so authorised were then entered in the Stationers' Company registers. At the end of the sixteenth century, there is little sign that anyone questioned the underlying premises of this censorship regime: no one thought (or at least openly said) that the presses should be open to everyone, or that there was anything inappropriate about the state and church suppressing dangerous or heretical books. The burden of this chapter is to help explain how that consensus collapsed, and how, within a few decades, the logic of press control and censorship was turned inside-out, with momentous effects.[3]

To understand this monumental collapse, the problem will be considered within two overlapping theoretical and practical contexts. Firstly, in keeping with the governing theme of this volume, I will begin with the concept of freedom of speech. This was often where early Whig historians started. In particular, they drew attention to the emergence, in the Tudor period, of very specific claims to freedom of speech in Parliament. There was a double allure to this: Whigs saw here two epic developments, intertwined – the rise of Parliament, alongside a burgeoning notion that MPs should be free from harassment or imprisonment for words uttered in Parliament. This doctrine of parliamentary free speech was well established by the early seventeenth century, and to Whiggish scholars, the language of freedom suggested the primal eruption of more general principles of liberty of expression.[4]

But there were major problems with this line of argument. Far from being a grand, general principle, parliamentary free speech was a privilege, requested of, and in turn granted by, the king. If in the late sixteenth century, pushed by assertive Puritan MPs, it acquired the sheen of an entrenched custom, bordering on a right, it was still a right that extended only to Parliament, and only for activities undertaken in session.[5] Moreover, crucially, the privilege of parliamentary free speech was expressly to be exercised in conditions of secrecy. Nothing uttered in Parliament was supposed to be repeated or published outside the two houses. Parliament, the notion went, assembled as the king's great council, providing frank advice and information, channelled to the monarch through the two Speakers, and members' speeches and internal deliberations were supposed to remain private and privileged, shielded from prying eyes of both monarch and broader public – as one MP put it, 'like the Sibylline oracles anciently kept in Rome, which were *arcana sacra* and not to be divulged'.[6] It is hard to see how this circumscribed principle – operative only when Parliament was sitting, and by its very intent secretive, closed and privileged – might have seeped out to become something like a broader, universalised principle of liberty of speech, still less of the press.

An additional major complication for this Whiggish approach was that, when early Stuart subjects used the phrase 'freedom of speech', they did not intend what twenty-first-century people mean. Instead, they were generally inspired by classical rhetoric, in particular the figure of *parrhesia*, which had been developed in ancient Greece and transmitted via Roman rhetoricians and the New Testament. Here 'freedom of speech' meant not freedom from external coercion or censorship, in the way moderns tend to imagine it, but something more like 'boldness of speech', willingness to speak frankly, even in the face of danger. The definitive study of this motif is David Colclough's elegant *Freedom of Speech in Early Stuart England*, which demonstrates how insurgent humanism ensured that the *parrhesia* figure was widely used by the early seventeenth century, and that, to an extent, it shaped newly assertive claims of parliamentary free speech, which were imagined as providing essential, frank counsel to the monarch. But, with typical aversion to the dead hand of Whiggery, Colclough also pointedly suggested that his classically informed 'freedom of speech' was far removed from abstract modern rights-claims, and that his account of *parrhesia* 'resists attempts to uncover a teleology of free speech in a recognizable form'.[7]

If 'freedom of speech' provides one important context for my investigation, the second is found in an even more ubiquitous characteristic of early Stuart political culture – the practice of petitioning. Petitioning, of course, was common throughout much of the early modern world. In England, recourse to petitioning the Crown was ancient and well established, and took multiple forms.[8] Equally well entrenched, by the seventeenth century was the practice of petitioning Parliament – or the king-in-Parliament – during those periods when the two houses were sitting.[9] Again, this relates to Parliament's chief function as a kind of point-of-contact between the Crown and the country, a brief conjuncture during which the people could lay at their governors' feet grievances and supplications, to be redressed through wholesome legislation or adjudication. Petitions to Parliament had been submitted for generations, but there are signs that in the early seventeenth century, for various reasons, the practice of petitioning the two houses underwent a renaissance, assuming newly intense and sophisticated forms.[10] An important feature of this newly sophisticated culture of petitioning Parliament was the fact that, by the 1620s, a growing number of petitions to Parliament were actually being printed. Sometimes these petitions were produced as cheap broadsides designed to place copies into every member's hands; at other times, petitions were evidently printed in editions crafted for broader public consumption, that is, as pieces of propaganda, aimed at ginning up public support for particular programmes or causes.[11]

Having laid out these contexts, I will in the remainder of this chapter explore a pair of intertwined problems. Firstly, I will seek to show how the parliamentary custom-cum-right of free speech did in effect leak into the wider world, and to demonstrate how, when combined with increasingly assertive assumptions about petitioning, it began to inform novel cases for imposing limits on government controls on the press.[12] Secondly, in revealing how this happened, I will suggest that the classical figure of 'freedom of speech' underwent subtle mutation, and came to undergird more general visions that imagined concrete limits on the state's capacity to control or stifle public discourse.

PRINT IN THE TIME OF PARLIAMENT: RELIGIOUS CONFLICT, PETITIONING AND THE PRESS IN THE 1620s

The crucial initial phase in this story, and one largely overlooked by previous scholars, came in the 1620s. This was a decade of roiling political instability, marked by failed parliaments, failed wars, and politico-religious confrontations, all capped by King Charles I's decision to govern without Parliament after the tumultuous 1629 session. The issues at stake in the contentious parliaments of the 1620s will be familiar to students of the period: they included, in the first instance, whether England was to enter the Thirty Years War; how to finance and fight this war, once it started; how to cope with the supposedly unparliamentary, illegal taxation and coercion that the government subsequently used to raise money; what to do about the influence of Charles's favourite and war-master, the Duke of Buckingham; and finally, looming over all, was fear that the Stuart kings were drifting closer to Roman Catholicism through a programme of sacramentalising the English church. Amidst the distempered parliaments of the 1620s, we see incipient hints that something unusual happened in the domain of print.

The key launching pad for our investigation is a brief passage (the importance of which was first highlighted by Jason Peacey) drawn from Peter Heylyn, sometime chaplain to Charles I. In his post-Restoration hagiographic defence of Archbishop William Laud, Heylyn recalled the religio-political battles of 1626, and, in particular, the attacks in Parliament and press on the alleged Arminianism of Richard Montagu. Montagu was a controversial cleric who published two books in the 1620s, assailing the dominant Calvinism of the early Stuart church. His works elicited a firestorm, conjuring fears of potential slide back towards Rome.[13] On 18 April 1626, the House of Commons branded Montagu a disturber of the church, who sought 'to reconcile' English subjects 'to Popery'. On Heylyn's account, Parliament's attack emboldened Montagu's enemies. Having 'perceived' that he had 'been smitten' by the move, and desperate 'not to lose the opportunity of a Parliament-time (when the Press is open to all comers)', Montagu's critics piled on, publishing numerous books against him. Heylyn's striking phrase suggested that, among some, there was a recognised sense that, while Parliament sat, the rules of licensing and enforcement were somehow loosened or suspended, throwing the 'Press ... open to all comers'. Whether Heylyn was merely ascribing this view to Montagu's Calvinist critics, or whether Heylyn himself acknowledged it, is unclear. But the mere suggestion that such an assumption existed in any quarter is significant.[14]

It is interesting to speculate as to where such a conception might have originated. One fragment of evidence hints that the idea described by Heylyn may have had its genesis, at least in inchoate form, in the mid-Elizabethan period. In 1572, during controversies over *An Admonition to the Parliament*, the ministers Thomas Wilcox and John Field, imprisoned for contriving this notorious Puritan tract, told a conformist interlocutor that 'We wrote a boke in the parliament tyme (which should be a free tyme of speakinge or wrytinge), justly craveinge a redresse and reformation of many abuses, and for that we are imprisoned and so uncourtiouslie intreated'. This comment, uttered in private conversation, but then packaged by the imprisoned preachers for manuscript circulation (with a view towards eventual print publication), suggests that more aggressive Protestant critics of the Elizabethan settlement hit upon this eccentric notion – that somehow 'the parliament tyme ... should be a free tyme of speakinge or wrytinge' – as part of their escalating print campaign against the ceremonial and disciplinary order of the church.[15] It is unclear if this was an off-the-cuff argument, invented by two clerics who had published themselves into legal jeopardy, or whether it represented a more widely shared 'talking point' in godly circles. Nevertheless, Field and Wilcox articulated, in rough terms, the principle that Heylyn saw taking shape by the 1620s, perhaps suggesting that similar sentiments may have been nurtured in intervening decades within coteries of hardline Protestants.[16]

Surviving evidence suggests that only after the collapse of the 1626 Parliament were ideas about printing in Parliament-time sharpened and codified. In the following months, the authorities suppressed a series of Calvinist books – even as Arminian and sacramentalist sermons and tracts were reportedly vented with impunity – intensifying fears that Charles's evil counsellors were bent on promoting crypto-popish forms of divinity.[17] That England now found itself involved in a two-front war against Europe's Catholic titans, Spain and France, did surprisingly little to allay these anxieties. The need to fund the war compelled Charles to summon another Parliament in 1628. During this Parliament, amidst seething discontent and hopes of a political turnabout, we see clearer articulations of the notion that the licensing regime was somehow transformed during the convention of the two houses. As soon as Parliament met, determined Calvinists who had been silenced in the previous two years plunged back into print, frequently without seeking licence.[18]

Among these Calvinist activists were the lawyer William Prynne and his publisher Michael Sparke. Prynne's career as a political and religious firebrand was launched in 1626, when he released a book challenging Montagu. From here, his conflicts with the Caroline authorities escalated, and, after Parliament gathered in March 1628, Prynne issued *A Briefe Survay and Censure of Mr Cozens His Couzening Devotions*, a tirade attacking the supposedly Arminian and crypto-popish sacramentalist John Cosin. Prynne and his bookseller Sparke had attempted to publish this book earlier, but had been foiled by the episcopal chaplain Dr Thomas Worrall.[19] Prynne and Sparke now entered print without licence. Prynne's book bore a dedication to Parliament, complaining of the treatment he and other allegedly orthodox Protestants had received from the ecclesiastical authorities, and urging MPs to follow through on their intended course, during the 1626 session, to crack down on Montagu and other Arminian ideologues. Prynne's address to Parliament illustrates the logic animating him to defy the licensing regime:

> is it not then high time for your *Honours* to engage, bestirre, and shew your zeale in the cause, the quarrel and patronage of our Church and Faith, when *Popery* and *Arminianisme* are growne now so potent, so head-strong, so impudent, sawcy, and audacious, as to over-top ... the very truth and *Doctrines of our Church*; to *stop their pleas*, and barre their passage to the Presse in a peremptory and presumptuous manner, even whiles the Parliament doores of Justice stand wide open to heare their pressures, and avenge their wrongs; bidding particular and personall defiance to these two spreading and combinings [sic] errors which threaten ruine and surprisall to them?

Here Prynne complained that even while Parliament was sitting, while its 'doores of Justice stand wide open', wicked ecclesiastical licensers were obstructing 'passage to the Presse' of righteous books defending Protestant truth. Because of this obstructionism, 'to you alone (right *Christian Senators*, and *valiant worthies* of the Lord) they now address their tongue-tide grievances, and silenced complaints: to you they flye for present succour and redresse against their adverse and prevailing powers; and now implore your aide, your justice, doome, and finall sentence ... against those open and professed enemies'.[20] My claim here is not that William Prynne was defending anything like freedom of the press; this is a man who clearly wanted Parliament to crush authors like Montagu and Cosin. But Prynne's words do suggest a more restricted, but no less interesting assertion: that Parliament, the greatest court in the land, as well as the king's greatest council, while its 'doores of Justice stand wide open', was rightly to receive the complaints and grievances of subjects, including printed supplications of the type that Prynne here offered up.

It was left to Prynne's publisher, Michael Sparke, to articulate the principle in more general terms. Sparke, an inveterate Puritan bookseller, underwent repeated arrests and investigations in the 1620s and 1630s for venting anti-Arminian and puritanical books, including several by Prynne. In the course of Sparke's later legal entanglement in Star Chamber for printing Prynne's *Histrio-mastix*, the authorities interrogated a witness who claimed that, during the Parliament of 1628–29, Sparke declared 'that in Parliament tyme hee woulde undertake to print any thinge'. The Attorney General seized on this, telling the court that 'Sparkes ... is a man that giveth out, That in

Parliament tyme hee will print any thinge'. The alleged boast clearly caught the court's attention, and in sentencing Sparke, at least two judges invoked the complaint that 'In Parliament tyme hee cares not what hee prints'.[21] Sparke thus reportedly opined that Parliament's convention somehow changed the dynamics of the press, providing licence to publish 'any thinge'. Indeed, Peter Heylyn's recollections were likely based at least partly on the *Histrio-mastix* case, in which Heylyn was deeply involved.[22] Whether Sparke believed that this alteration during 'Parliament-time' was a matter of proper constitutional practice or whether he was simply stating his own brazen willingness to defy the licensing regime is not really important.[23] The fact that people were openly articulating the concept that conditions of press licensing shifted during time of Parliament is crucially significant.

The words of Prynne and Sparke, taken together, suggest that, among some, there was a gathering sense that parliamentary sessions comprised a kind of numinous moment, during which the boundaries of political life were momentarily realigned. Members of Parliament experienced this, of course, in the privilege of freedom of speech that governed their deliberations. But the implication here is that the reordering of the boundaries of public discourse extended beyond the precincts of Westminster.

Further light is cast on the matter in the most inflammatory book printed for the same Parliament, Alexander Leighton's *An Appeal To the Parliament; or Sions Plea against the Prelacie* (1629), a work nakedly framed as a direct address to Parliament. In his epistle to the two houses, Leighton explicitly invoked the figure of *parrhesia*: 'as for freedome of speech ... wee hope your Honours will impute it to the present danger: for who will not cry ... when his mother is like to be murthered before his eyes'. Leighton then launched a diatribe against the entire episcopal order. Naturally, the book was not licensed, and its incendiary content meant that it had to be printed in the Dutch republic. To Leighton's misfortune, this ensured that copies arrived in England after Charles had dissolved the Parliament, amidst extraordinary scenes of acrimony, in March 1629. The radicalism of Leighton's *Sions Plea* sparked immediate fury, and the government soon arrested him.[24]

Under interrogation, Leighton provided insight into the logic of the position emerging here. He explained that he undertook the work at the behest of 'some well-affected people to frame a draught of their desires to the Parliament then being, which all the Kings leige people might doe'. His book was thus a kind of petition, designed to inform Parliament of the grievances and will of the people, during the critical moment of contact between Crown and country. Leighton's interrogators predictably pressured him 'to give up the names of those' who had urged him to the work. He refused, explaining that 'as it was done in time of Parliament, when every subject might without impeachment unfold a *publique grievance* so if that high Court were in being, and should call them to it, they should either avouch the act; or I would deliver ... their names'.[25] When Parliament sat, just as MPs needed to be able to offer up frank counsel to represent the ailments of the commonwealth, so also subjects had to be free to 'unfold' the nation's grievances 'without impeachment'. When questioned on the charge that he had produced one thousand copies of *Sions Plea*, Leighton in fact tried to translate the book's suppositious function as a petition to Parliament into an explicit defence. He maintained that 'hee intended the said Booke onely for the parliament, and therefore printed not soe manie Coppies as are layd Downe in the information', instead printing only 'betweene Five and six hundred', a number fewer than those adequate 'to serve the severall members of both the howses' with individual copies. His book, Leighton thus implied, should be treated not as the work of virulent anti-episcopal propaganda it manifestly was but rather as a kind of humble supplication, intended only for the eyes of the Lords and Commons at Westminster, 'Parliament/ being a body Politike as this Defendant Conceived/ to which the meanest members of the Commonwealth might intimate there Cares and feares Concerninge the Dangers and Deliverances of the said Common wealth/ being the Mother of us all'.[26]

If Leighton's words hint at the coalescence of a sophisticated defence of loosened printing restrictions 'in time of Parliament', they also reveal a crucial obverse side of the argument: the printed presentation of grievances to Parliament offered no threat of sedition or disruption because, while Parliament sat, it could 'call' the interested parties to account, thereby judging or disciplining those who wrote, supported or published such books. Parliament was not merely England's legislature and the king's supreme council but the realm's highest court, possessing power to punish malefactors. Hence Leighton's justification of his action did not imply an absence of all constraint or control.

Nevertheless, his justification hinted that the 'time of parliament' afforded a unique moment, in which rules of political discourse were transformed, not just in the rarefied spaces of the two houses, but beyond, manifesting the logic behind the claims, reported by Heylyn, and allegedly voiced by Sparke, that the press should be open in time of Parliament. The authorities did not agree, and Leighton was sentenced to be fined, whipped, pilloried, branded to have ears cut off, and to be imprisoned indefinitely. In notes prepared for Leighton's sentencing, Attorney General Robert Heath took stock of the disturbing purport of Leighton's arguments, remarking that the doctor had maintained 'That he intended to present it to the parliament ... as if it were lawfull and tollerable to sclaunder the King or the government in parliament'. As Heath explained, Parliament was 'but [the king's] counsell; not his Governors'. The Attorney General thus sounded an alarm about the entire practice of printing petitions to Parliament, suggesting that it provided a vehicle for slander and sedition: 'this also is a[n] irreguler and an insufferable way grown too frequent of late. To put all informations, petitions, breviatts: intended for the parliament in Print'. This practice, he complained, 'is but a newe way', and Heath thus proposed to the councillors in Star Chamber that

Leighton's case afforded the opportunity to smother the entire practice in its infancy: 'I humbly move it, and offer it to your judgments, as a fitt thinge to be suppressed for the future'.[27]

Heath's recommendation laid bare the submerged fallacies of Leighton's self-defence. On its face, *Sions Plea* – like other printed 'petitions' to Parliament – was ostensibly directed only to the two houses. But in putting such petitions and supplications to print, authors and petitioners were obviously making their arguments available to audiences far beyond Westminster. Deploying the figure of *parrhesia*, and embedding it in a *de facto* right to petition Parliament through print, these authors were, through a kind of transitive move, suggesting that during Parliament-time, much as MPs had a right and duty to speak freely in the two chambers, subjects should be free to print and broadcast grievances abroad, for the information of MPs, and ultimately for the greater good of the commonwealth. Try as Leighton might to plead that his book was intended for MPs' eyes alone, Heath's complaints about printed petitions correctly grasped that this self-justification was disingenuous, and that the act of printing projected arguments to a much broader readership. The slippery, transitive move made by the likes of Sparke and Leighton indeed inverted a key component of Parliament's privilege of free speech – that the words of the Lords and Commons were expressly to remain secret. By contrast, the printed supplications of 'petitioners' such as Leighton were trumpeted to the public at large, for the better information (or, as Heath would have judged, perversion) of the commonwealth as a whole.

THE ENGLISH CIVIL WAR: FROM PARLIAMENT-TIME TO 'THE FREEDOM OF THE PEOPLE'

The arguments proffered by Prynne, Sparke and Leighton were tactical in nature and tightly related to the unusual conjuncture of the 1620s. It is possible that if the political tensions of that decade had subsequently been defused, or if Charles had succeeded in rendering permanent his experiment of Personal Rule without Parliament, this bubble of interestingly innovative argument might simply have popped and been forgotten. However, Charles did not succeed, and in 1640, after provoking a crisis and rebellion in his northern kingdom of Scotland, he was forced to recall Parliament. With the convention of the Short and Long Parliaments, the potency and prevalence of the ideas described here became manifest.

In 1640 it became clear that *some* people *did* believe the press should be open to all comers in Parliament-time. Hints arrived within weeks of the opening of the Long Parliament in November 1640. I have elsewhere described a secret press, which operated in London in 1640–41, publishing diatribes against episcopacy, separatist polemic and Scottish Covenanter propaganda. This press, responsible for many of the most challenging unlicensed books of that year of political crisis, was managed partly by Richard Overton, the future Leveller theorist.[28] For present purposes, two books produced by this secret press are of particular importance. *A Dialogue. Wherin is Plainly Layd open the Tyrannicall Dealing of the Lord Bishops against Gods Children* had first been published in 1589 as part of an earlier, storied battle between Puritans and the bishops, the so-called Martin Marprelate controversy. Resurrected by the secret press in the final days of 1640, the tract's title page noted that it was 'Reprinted in the time of *Parliament*'. Soon after, the press issued a second tract 'Printed in the time of *Parliament*'.[29] While no explication was offered, the phrasing suggests that the secret press's operators believed that during Parliament-time rules governing publication were somehow altered, thus justifying their unauthorised enterprise. How many publishers and authors shared this conviction is uncertain, but, as soon as Parliament met, a flood of unlicensed books cascaded from city presses. This was partly a result of the retreat of the licensing authorities, but it perhaps also emanated from belief among some stationers that Parliament intended to protect them from punishment.

This principle was explicitly articulated in July 1641, with the publication of Henry Burton's notorious *The Protestation Protested*, a work which elicited indignation in the Commons, on the grounds that it presumed to reinterpret Parliament's recent Protestation. Burton argued that acceptance of the Protestation implied total rejection of the Church of England, maintaining that the church's true constitution was 'the Church-way of independency'. In the ensuing controversy, the printer, Gregory Dexter, was arrested. He was interrogated by Sir Edward Dering's committee for printing, a body created by the Long Parliament to investigate abuses of licensing under Laud. When asked by what authority he printed the book, Dexter responded that 'he had no authority for setting his letters to this treatise, but the generall liberty ... used whilst this parliament is sitting'.[30] Here was explicit testimony that some stationers believed the sitting of the Long Parliament entailed a 'generall liberty', eliminating requirements for formal licensing.

It should be emphasised that Dexter was no ordinary printer. Like Overton and those behind the secret press of 1640, Dexter was a radical Puritan, involved in clandestine printing since his apprenticeship in the 1630s, when he had surreptitiously produced some of Prynne's books. Dexter would print many of the civil war's most notorious works, including tracts by Roger Williams, John Milton and others.[31] So we should beware suggesting that his sentiment was universal. However, among a subset of godly extremists, the basic idea had taken hold by mid-1641. It is, moreover, not accidental that this conceit was embraced especially by radical Puritans – congregationalists, separatists, anabaptists and other sectaries, all of whom would soon be labelled as 'independents'. The reasons for this are complex, and constraints of space do not permit a fuller account, but, once England's civil war erupted in 1642, arguments about printing in 'Parliament-time' were undoubtedly propagated chiefly by extreme independents, often alongside calls for wider religious toleration.[32]

Crucially, these extremists were emboldened not merely because they thought that such a 'generall liberty' existed but also because they believed Parliament had endorsed this liberty. Indeed, it was commonly suggested by more radical Puritans that, early in the Long Parliament, MPs had explicitly affirmed the 'generall liberty' of the press in Parliament-time, meaning that the newly anarchic print trade was not merely a result of benign neglect but a deliberate policy of the two houses. In effect, these propagandists claimed, the Long Parliament had explicitly extended its own 'freedom of speech' to the wider world (or at least to those with access to printing presses).

This belief was openly uttered only after the outbreak of the civil war and the reinstitution of a new system of press oversight in Parliament's Licensing Ordinance of June 1643. The Licensing Ordinance famously re-erected a regime of censorship, replacing the old episcopal licensers with godly, orthodox divines. Although ostensibly directed against royalists, the system was quickly mobilised to constrain radical Puritan publication, by early 1644 eliciting intense anxiety among some of Parliament's most ardent supporters. Dexter, for instance, had his premises raided and his presses seized, forcing him from the business.[33] In July 1644 the first sustained critique of the Licensing Ordinance appeared in William Walwyn's *The Compassionate Samaritane*, a book justly renowned for its arguments in favour of wide religious toleration. Walwyn's opening epistle to Parliament recalled that 'In the beginning of Your Session, when our Divines ... wrote freely against the Bishops, and the Bishops made complaint to You for redresse; some of You made answer that there was no remedy, forasmuch as the Presse was to be open and free for all in time of Parliament', and Walwyn presented his tract as 'lay[ing] claime to that priviledge'.[34] Having searched diligently the records and speeches of Parliament between 1640 and 1642, I have yet to find an account confirming that any MPs issued such a statement – pronouncing 'the Presse ... open and free' in Parliament-time – either formally or in passing. Possibly, Walwyn referred to transactions in Dering's committee for printing, the deliberations of which are mostly lost. Perhaps the incident or incidents did not take place at all. But if that was the case, the mythical exchange Walwyn reported soon assumed a life of its own, retailed as proven fact in subsequent works.

Walwyn further complained that although Parliament's ordinance 'was purposed ... to restraine ... the Kings writings and his Agents, yet it hath by reason of the qualifications of the Licensers ... stopt the mouthes of good men'. This was part of the crafty design by which clergymen aimed at 'making themselves masters of the people'. Through the 'Licensers (who are Divines and intend their interest) ... nothing may come to the Worlds view but what they please, unless men will runne the hazard of imprisonment'; meanwhile 'scandalous books' were 'still disperst' with impunity. For Walwyn, this was a travesty. He argued that the press must be free, and those confident of their opinions 'should desire that all mens mouthes should bee open, that so errour may discover its foulnesse, and truth become more glorious by a victorious conquest'.[35] This was the broadest statement of press freedom that had ever appeared in English. Walwyn insisted that there was a wide domain of public discourse that Parliament should not touch.

Importantly, however, Walwyn was not proposing absolute liberty of the press. Parliament clearly had the right to suppress books 'scandalous or dangerous to the State'.[36] He did not specify how this regime of oversight was to operate, but, as in Leighton's case fourteen years earlier, Walwyn presumably believed that Parliament's sitting meant offenders could be punished *ex post facto* by the two houses. Nevertheless, despite this important caveat, Walwyn's tract represented a significant escalation upon previous arguments: while embracing the claim that during Parliament-time the press should be free (and suggesting that MPs had endorsed this as conscious policy), Walwyn was also massaging the boundaries of the case, and hinting that it was not merely the magical aura of a parliamentary session which undergirded this privilege but a more general principle whereby authors and speakers should be afforded liberty of expression, extended until their words proved positively dangerous to the state.

Of course the most famous formulation of this more expansive position came four months later. *Areopagitica; A Speech of Mr. John Milton For the Liberty of Unlicenc'd Printing, To the Parliament of England* argued against all forms of pre-publication licensing. Milton suggested that, while retrospective punishment for printed libel or other gross offences was appropriate, prior restraint on publication through censorship damaged the commonweal. *Areopagitica* has been subjected to intensive analysis by generations of students and thinkers. What has been overlooked, however, is that Milton acknowledged and incorporated the argument germinating since the 1620s. Like Walwyn, Milton identified a creeping Presbyterian conspiracy, embodied in the Licensing Ordinance:

> Who cannot but discern the finenes of this politic drift ... that while Bishops were to be baited down, then all Presses might be open; it was the peoples birthright and priviledge in time of Parlament, it was the breaking forth of light. But now the Bishops ... voided out of the Church ... liberty of Printing must be enthrall'd again ... the privilege of the people nullify'd ... the freedom of learning must groan again, and to her old fetters; all this the Parlament yet sitting.[37]

This was only one of many arguments canvassed by Milton, and it was hardly the chief strand of his case, but it showed that he had absorbed the now common assertion that the press should be open in time of Parliament. He apparently concurred that this was 'the peoples birthright', and decried the danger to 'liberty of Printing' in Parliament-time, but he also transcended this argument, and maintained that at all times, both during and outside of parliamentary sessions, prior restraint through licensing contravened the public good.

The core claim about 'Parliament-time' was recycled with increasing insistence as the battle between so-called 'independents' and 'Presbyterians' began to convulse Parliament's coalition. Thus, the godly martyr and separatist propagandist John Lilburne in 1645 bewailed that Presbyterians 'have not dealt fairly ... in stopping the *Presse* against us, while things are in debate, yea robbing us of our Liberty ... in time of freedome, when the *Parliament* is sitting, who are sufficiently able to punish that man ... that shall abuse his penne'. The press should be open in Parliament-time, partly because Parliament was fully capable of correcting offenders, but also because parliamentary sessions represented an extraordinary moment of 'debate', in which subjects had liberty to publish whatever conduced to the public welfare. Yet, like Walwyn and Milton, Lilburne, in claiming that the press should be free in Parliament-time, also began to assert more general principles. He urged that 'the Presse might be as open for us as for you, and as it was at the beginning of this *Parliament*, which I conceive the *Parliament* did of purpose, that so the freeborne *English* Subjects might enjoy their Liberty and Priviledge, which the Bishops had learned of the *Spanish Inquisition* to rob them of'. As in *Areopagitica*, press censorship was presented as a vestige of benighted popery, the legacy of the Spanish inquisition, passed down to the bishops, whose spirit had now infected putatively godly Presbyterians; while Lilburne did not elaborate, it is difficult to see how such practices might be defensible outside of parliamentary sessions.[38] In *Englands Birth-Right Justified*, nine months later, Lilburne and his collaborators used a new metaphor for the press as a marketplace of ideas, complaining of the Stationers' efforts 'violently (even now in Parliament time, which should be like a cryed *Faire*, and each one free to make the best use of their *Ware*, both for the publick, and their own private good) to suppress every thing which hath any true Declaration of the just Rights and Liberties of the free-borne people'.[39] Here, the now familiar view of a free press in Parliament-time was laced with other threads of argument: firstly, Parliament-time was presented as a kind of commercial competition, a freewheeling bazaar of ideas and proposals, which was being stifled not just by the Licensing Act but also by a cabal of monopolists, the Stationers' Company, which had suborned the machinery of the commonwealth for private interests; and, secondly, Lilburne suggested that an open press was not merely the due of English subjects but was actually a crucial instrument for clarifying and securing all other rights and liberties of the people.

In all this, we see a tendency to expand upon and generalise from more limited propositions. The basic claims that the press should be free in Parliament-time, and that the two houses had somehow endorsed this principle, had mutated into a series of more comprehensive arguments. Chief among these was the idea that the two houses were now backsliding from their original defence of press freedom by conniving with priests and monopolists to reimpose servitude. This became a mantra, particularly in the circles surrounding Lilburne, by 1646: one pamphlet asserted that 'It is a *priviledge* in *Parliament* time, due to the *freeborn Subjects* of *England*, that the *Printing Presses* should bee free', a privilege 'being now *Monopolized* from them by the *persecuting Presbyters*'.[40] Another tract, produced by Richard Overton's latest secret press, asked 'Is it *seditious*, for a *Free-man* unjustly imprisoned, to publish the same to all the World? It was not so judged in the beginning of this Parliament; but then was *the beginning of Freedome*, and it seemes, *Wee are at the end thereof*: and at the *beginning of a new bondage*.'[41] Another defence of Lilburne, *Vox Plebis, Or, The Peoples Out-cry Against Oppression*, bore a title page declaring itself 'printed 1646. in the sitting of Parliament; during which time the Presse ought to be free and open, as the Parliament declared to the Bishops at the beginning thereof'. Again, however, there were also elaborations and clarifications of this basic suite of arguments. In June 1646 the author of *A Pearle in a Dounghill* lamented 'That the Presse should be stopt in time of Parliament, as barring all free informations, and admitting only what *appointed* Lycencers shall allow'.[42] Here, in brief, was a universalisation of the underlying logic that had been articulated by Alexander Leighton, now abstracted out of the specific context of petitioning the two houses: 'free informations' needed to flow to Parliament and public during this paramount moment of national deliberation.

Thus, radical independent propagandists insistently repeated that the press should be open in Parliament-time, along with the (possibly spurious) claim that MPs had declared this to be so. But they also decisively expanded the boundaries of this case. Firstly, it was now asserted that the privilege of free printing, initially imagined as relating specifically to presentation of grievances or petitions to Parliament itself, had both a broader ambit and a broader purpose. 'Free informations', like Lilburne's 'Declaration[s] of the just Rights and Liberties of the free-borne people', were to be circulated not solely for the use of representatives at Westminster but rather for the enlightenment of the public as a whole. To be sure, the underlying justification for this privilege was partly religious, since it was increasingly assumed that the best way to foster 'the breaking forth, encrease and growth of knowledge' was through unconstrained, open discourse.[43] But in civil affairs, too, the general publication of necessary truths was deemed essential to the freedom and safety of the commonwealth. Thus, the notional audience for published information was shifting. This was closely tied to a deeper shift in theory and practice, wherein 'the people' came to be imagined not as passive subjects of governance but rather as central agents in political processes, perhaps even the ultimate sovereign power in the state, meaning that ordinary individuals (rather than MPs) were now conceived as the rightful consumers and arbiters of printed appeals.[44]

Secondly, while advocates continued to repeat the original formula that 'Parliament-time' created special conditions, several commentators pushed beyond this proposition, stating or implying that practices of licensing – if not other forms of press regulation – were always illegitimate and contrary to the public good. In part, this shift was a result of the extension of the Long Parliament, which, now in its fifth year, had ceased to be a temporary event, and had become something more like a permanent fixture of governance, thereby blurring the boundary between 'Parliament-time' and other times. But partly, too, authors had clearly begun to universalise the logic of their case, and to suggest that the same popish or oppressive principles which made censorship illegitimate during sessions of Parliament also rendered it dangerous to the commonwealth at other times.

This last shift was clearly facilitated by a third development, a rising sense that Parliament itself was incapable of justly policing the public sphere of print. Walwyn, Milton and Lilburne had hinted that licensing was unnecessary because Parliament, while in session, possessed authority to punish malefactors *ex post facto*. Indeed, this putative authority was arguably crucial to the notion, originally conjured by Leighton and others, that subjects required freedom to print petitions in Parliament-time. Accordingly, attempts were initially made in the 1640s to suggest that the escalating violence and abuses of the new licensing system were not Parliament's doing, but were rather the handiwork of malign private interests, such as Presbyterian clergymen or the stationers. As conflict mounted, and as militant parliamentarians found themselves harassed or imprisoned by Parliament for publishing unlicensed material, it became more difficult to sustain this narrative, and Parliament's own competency to police print began to look increasingly suspect, resulting in ever more expansive versions of the arguments here.

In some cases, theorists began to valorise a more global condition of discursive freedom as essential for the common good. An illustrative example is found in the tract *Strong Motives, Or Loving And Modest Advice, Unto the Petitioners for Presbiterian Government*, published in October 1645, which accused Presbyterian ministers of seeking to silence their opponents for personal gain: 'for if there be once graunted a freedome of speech, an opening of the Presses, and toleration of all Opinions, and immediately downe goeth the glory of the Clergy', along with their power and profits.[45] Here, not only do we see the suggestion that the press should be open as a matter of principle (alongside 'toleration of all Opinions') but we also observe a subtle recalibration of the phrase 'Freedome of speech'. This is not mere early modern *parrhesia*, connoting boldness of speech; rather, it is something closer to an understanding of freedom of speech as an absence of external restraint, and construed as a positive good. Against claims that this would lead to an orgy of sedition and heresy, advocates insisted it was in fact the ideal way to resolve public controversies: 'let any mans experience witnesse whether freedome of discourse be not the readiest way both to give and receive satisfaction in all things'.[46] While we should beware of equating this position with a fully modern vision of free speech as an unfettered, abstract individual right

– several thinkers cited here also contemplated peculiarly alien schemes for constraining outrageously libellous or false utterances – it cannot be denied that these arguments marked a quiet modification of the more familiar parrhesiastic 'freedom of speech'.[47] This recalibrated conception of 'free speech' remained atypical in the later seventeenth century – where it competed with more traditional renderings as biblical or classical *parrhesia* – but its eruption into political discourse during the Civil Wars marks an important watershed.[48]

Between 1646 and 1649, as the battle to determine the settlement of the nation intensified, the polemic against licensing and press controls grew more insistent. As is clear, the arguments discussed here were deployed above all in the circle of activists around John Lilburne; by late 1647, as this group assumed a clearer identity, mobilising petitions and campaigns to shape the final settlement, its leaders and backers came to be branded with the epithet 'Leveller'. Demands for press freedom were, unsurprisingly, now folded into 'Leveller' declarations. The apogee of this process came in January 1649, soon after Pride's Purge, and as the king's trial was beginning. The Leveller coalition in London organised a petition to the Commons, objecting to a recent army warrant for suppressing unlicensed books. The petition launched the most thoroughgoing statement on the press seen during England's conflicts of the 1640s and 1650s. Denouncing all 'specious pretences ... to over-aw the Press', the petitioners rejected the entire practice of licensing. The 'liberty' of 'the Press' was 'so essential unto Freedom, as that without it, its impossible to preserve any Nation from ... the worst of bondage'. The petition warned, 'if Government be just in its Constitution ... it will be good, if not absolutely necessary for them, to hear all voices and judgement, which they can never do, but by giving freedom to the Press'. The basic principle of press liberty in Parliament-time was expanded to all government in all times: presses needed to be free to provide a conduit for the recommendations and voices of the people. Moreover, the petition hinted that not only prior censorship but also retrospective punishment was inadvisable: 'in case any abuse' the governors' 'authority by scandalous Pamphlets, they will never want able Advocates to vindicate their innocency'. Argument, not coercion, was the proper corrective to dangerous or seditious publications. Thus, to 'refer all Books ... to the judgement ... Licensers, or to put the least restraint upon the Press, seems altogether inconsistent with the good of the Common-wealth, and expressly opposite and dangerous to the liberties of the people'. The Commons were thus urged to revoke all measures that constrained 'the Freedom of the People; as in other things, so in that necessary and essential part, of speaking, writing, printing, and publishing their minds freely'.[49]

This petition represented the most comprehensive version of the arguments traced in this chapter. It may therefore stand as the endpoint of the process described here, whereby a limited notion that licensing restrictions were somehow loosened in Parliament-time metamorphosed into a totalising claim that 'restraint upon the Press' was always illegitimate and dangerous to the common good. Future scholarship will need to trace the fate of these conceptions of press freedom in the later seventeenth century. To be sure, disputes persisted into the 1650s, with repeated demands for press freedom enunciated in Leveller-inspired petitions. These expansive, absolutist arguments jostled alongside more restrictive opinions, including the idea that constraints should be relaxed, but not totally, and robust claims that strong press controls and prior censorship were necessary.[50] With the Restoration, these battles continued, and the recurrence of arguments against press censorship can be traced after 1660, along with ferocious conflicts over the issue, blazing into the early eighteenth century.[51] This is not to suggest that the halting, contested retreat of censorship and press control can be explained solely by surveying printed treatises and tracts for changes in formal political theory; rather, shifts in formal theory were closely linked to more informal assumptions and practices dictating the conduct of political and religious life, along with commercial forces that simultaneously worked to undermine older assumptions about press management. The domain of formal theory must be examined in conjunction with the actual practice of politics, the changing dynamics of the book trade and the vicissitudes of political contingency. Only then will we emerge with a fuller picture of how and why licensing was abandoned in the anglophone world, to be followed in the early eighteenth century by the more general embrace of concepts of a free and open press, together with a more capacious vision of freedom of speech, liberated from external constraint.

I would argue that it is critical to do so. While we need to be cautious not to ascribe anachronistically modern conceits to early modern actors, and while we should avoid imagining this story as a triumphant, uncontested and unbroken march, it is in my view essential for historians to grapple with long-term processes of critical importance to the development of political societies in the English-speaking world and beyond, an enterprise that is ever more significant given the current global conjuncture.

NOTES

1. For a notable exception, see R. Martin, *The Free and Open Press: The Founding of American Democratic Press Liberty, 1640–1800* (New York, 2001), some of whose arguments prefigure those made in this chapter. The author would like to thank Noah Millstone for helpful discussions on this broader subject; earlier iterations of the essay benefited from presentation at Ohio University, Princeton, Stanford, and the Newberry Library.
2. For different views of this system and its evolution, see F. Siebert, *Freedom of the Press in England, 1476–1776* (Urbana, 1952), 21–87; C. Clegg, *Press Censorship in Elizabethan England* (Cambridge, 1997), 30–65.
3. In examining the origins of arguments against pre-publication censorship, this chapter departs from recent work, which deals chiefly with how the

censorship regime operated and how effective it was, often assessing attendant cultural and political effects. C. Hill, 'Censorship and English Literature', in Christopher Hill, *The Collected Essays of Christopher Hill* (Amherst, MA, 1985), I, 32–71; A. Patterson, *Censorship and Interpretation: The Conditions of Writing and Reading in Early Modern England* (Madison, 1984); B. Worden, 'Literature and Political Censorship in Early Modern England', in A. Duke and C. Tamse (eds), *Too Mighty to Be Free: Censorship and the Press in Britain and the Netherlands* (Zutphen, 1987); Clegg, *Elizabethan England*; C. Clegg, *Press Censorship in Jacobean England* (Cambridge, 2001); C. Clegg, *Press Censorship in Caroline England* (Cambridge, 2008); D. Shuger, *Censorship and Cultural Sensibility: The Regulation of Language in Tudor-Stuart England* (Philadelphia, 2006); J. McElligott, *Royalism, Print and Censorship in Revolutionary England* (Woodbridge, 2007). For debate over religious censorship, see S. Lambert, 'Richard Montagu, Arminianism and Censorship', *P&P* 124 (1989), 36–68; A. Milton, 'Licensing, Censorship, and Religious Orthodoxy in Early Stuart England', *HJ* 41 (1998), 625–51; S. Mutchow Towers, *Control of Religious Printing in Early Stuart England* (Woodbridge, 2003).

4 Siebert, *Freedom of the Press*, 100–4; H. Hulme, 'Our American Heritage: Freedoms Derived from the English Constitution', *American Bar Association Journal* 32 (1946), 898.

5 J. Neale, 'The Commons' Privilege of Free Speech in Parliament', in R. Seton-Watson (ed.), *Tudor Studies* (1924), 257–86; H. Hulme, 'The Winning of Freedom of Speech by the House of Commons', *AHR* 61 (1956), 825–53.

6 For this (and evidence the theory was routinely flouted), see J. Peacey, '"Rushworth Shall Not Take Any Notes Here": Journals, Debates and the Public, 1640–60', *PH* 33 (2014), 426.

7 D. Colclough, *Freedom of Speech in Early Stuart England* (Cambridge, 2005), 15, 120–95; for earlier discussion, see D. Parkin-Speer, 'Freedom of Speech in Sixteenth-century English Rhetorics', *SCJ* 12 (1981), 65–72.

8 For the ubiquity of petitioning by the early Tudor period, see R. Hoyle, 'Petitioning as Popular Politics in Early Sixteenth-century England', *HR* 75 (2002), 365–89.

9 For the medieval origins, see G. Dodd, *Justice and Grace: Private Petitioning and the English Parliament in the Late Middle Ages* (Oxford, 2007).

10 For the importance of petitioning (and print), see D. Zaret, *Origins of Democratic Culture: Printing, Petitions, and the Public Sphere in Early-Modern England* (Princeton, 2000). Zaret argues the 1640s were transformative, but significant changes in petitioning were afoot earlier. For upsurge in petitioning the Lords from 1621, see J. Hart, *Justice upon Petition: The House of Lords and the Reformation of Justice* (Cambridge, 1991).

11 C. Kyle, *Theater of State: Parliament and Political Culture in Early Stuart England* (Stanford, 2012), 158–74; C. Kyle, 'From Broadside to Pamphlet: Print and Parliament in the Late 1620s', *PH* 26 (2007), 17–29; C. Clegg, 'Print in the Time of Jacobean Parliaments', in P. Langman (ed.), *Negotiating the Jacobean Printed Book* (Farnham, 2011), 66–8.

12 The relationship (or lack thereof) between 'freedom of speech' and 'freedom of the press' remains a pressing question in American jurisprudence, owing to the inclusion of these two parallel rights in the First Amendment. See A. Bhagwat,

'Posner, Blackstone, and Prior Restraints on Speech', *BYU Law Review* 2015 (2015–16), 1151–82. While not directly addressing the issues controverted by US judges and legal scholars, the present chapter suggests that the concepts of 'freedom of speech' and 'freedom of the press', although distinct, were closely linked and were mutually constitutive from the beginning of sustained theoretical arguments over press controls in the seventeenth century.

13 See N. Tyacke, *Anti-Calvinists: The Rise of English Arminianism, c. 1590–1640* (Oxford, 1990).

14 P. Heylyn, *Cyprianus Anglicus* (1671), 148; J. Peacey, *Politicians and Pamphleteers: Propaganda during the English Civil Wars and Interregnum* (Aldershot, 2004), 330; *Journals of the House of Commons*, I, 845–7. Heylyn was likely correct that some of Montagu's critics published without licence during the 1626 session. Only two anti-Montagu books were entered in the Stationers' Register, William Prynne's *The Perpetuitie of a Regenerate Mans Estate* and *A Joynt Attestation, Avowing the Discipline of the Church of England* (both registered during Parliament's session). Unregistered predestinarian books by Bishop Carleton, Francis Rous, Anthony Wotton and Samuel Ward preceded Parliament's dissolution; others by John Yates and Henry Burton cannot be dated precisely. Prynne claimed, however, that most of the anti-Montagu books were 'licenced by Archbishop Abbots Chaplines', suggesting some may have been licensed, but not entered in the Register. W. Prynne, *Canterburies Doome* (1646), 159; C. Elrington (ed.), *The Whole Works of the Most Rev. James Ussher, D.D.*, 17 vols (Dublin, 1864), XV, 339; E. Arber (ed.), *A Transcript of the Register of the Company of Stationers of London, 1554–1640* (1875–94), V, 95–137.

15 A. Peel (ed.), *The Second Parte of a Register: Being a Calendar of Manuscripts under that title intended for publication by the Puritans about 1593* (Cambridge, 1915), 87-8; the passage was first noted in Siebert, *Freedom of the Press*, 90. I am grateful to Karl Gunther for bringing it to my attention.

16 See, for example, the arguments in H. Barrow, *A petition directed to her most excellent Maiestie* (1591), 40–1.

17 H. Burton, *A Narration of the Life of Mr. Henry Burton* (1643), 4; D. Featley, *Cygnea Cantio* (1629), 41–2; Prynne, *Canterburies Doome*, 159; R.C. Johnson, M.F. Keeler, M.J. Cole and W.B. Bidwell (eds), *Commons Debates 1628* (New Haven, 1977–83), III, 151.

18 See, for example, H. Burton, *Israels Fast* (1628); H. Burton, *A Tryall of Private Devotions* (1628), Ar; Henry Burton, *Babel No Bethel* (1629).

19 Johnson et al. (eds), *Commons Debates 1628*, III, 151.

20 W. Prynne, *A Briefe Survay and Censure of Mr Cozens His Couzening Devotions* (1628), 3r–v.

21 Houghton Library, Harvard University, MS. Eng. 1359, Feb. 7 (deposition of Joseph Hunt, stationer); Feb. 7 (Attorney General Noy's speech); Feb. 13 (Sir Thomas Richardson's sentence). These passages, drawn from the most extensive MS transcript of the *Histrio-mastix* trial, are echoed and confirmed in variant accounts of the proceedings. See the MS of Lord Cottington's sentence in Samuel Hartlib's papers: Sheffield University Library, Hartlib Papers, 68/10/8A in M. Greengrass, M. Leslie and M. Hannon, *The Hartlib Papers* (Sheffield, 2013); J. Rushworth, *Historical Collections. The Second Part* (1680), 224, 226.

22 A. Milton, *Laudian and Royalist Polemic in Seventeenth-century England: The Career and Writings of Peter Heylyn* (Manchester, 2007), 44–5.
23 If indeed Sparke did utter these words, it was one of a battery of arguments he developed against licensing. In May 1629, he pronounced the Star Chamber decrees of 1586 'of no validity or force to binde his Majesties Subjects', as they were not 'ratifyed by act of Parliament'. TNA, SP 16/142/22, fol. 28r.
24 A. Leighton, *An Appeal to the Parliament; or Sions Plea against the Prelacie* (1629), 'To The right Honourable and High Court of Parliament'. On Leighton, see S. Foster, *Notes from the Caroline Underground: Alexander Leighton, the Puritan Triumvirate, and the Laudian Reaction to Nonconformity* (Hamden, 1978).
25 A. Leighton, *An Epitome or Briefe Discoverie* (1646), 12–13.
26 BL, Sloane MS 41, fols 2r–v; this manuscript, recording Leighton's answer to the articles against him, was later folded into Leighton, *Epitome*, 26–8.
27 TNA, SP 16/168, fol. 25v; for earlier signs of elite discomfort with the printing of parliamentary petitions, see Kyle, 'From Broadside to Pamphlet', 17–18.
28 D. Como, *Radical Parliamentarians and the English Civil War* (Oxford, 2018), 50–88.
29 *A Dialogue. Wherin is Plainly Layd Open the Tyrannicall Dealing of the Lord Bishops Against Gods Children* (1640), t.p.; L.F., *A Speedy Remedie against Spirituall Incontinencie* (1640), t.p.
30 M. Jansson (ed.), *Proceedings of the Opening Session of the Long Parliament: House of Commons*, 7 vols (Rochester, NY, 2000–7), V, 688–9, corrected against BL, Stowe MS 354, fol. 111. See also Como, *Radical Parliamentarians*, 94–7.
31 W. Parker, 'Contributions toward a Milton Bibliography', *Library* 16 (1936), 425–38; B. Swan, *Gregory Dexter of London and New England, 1610–1700* (Rochester, NY, 1949); D. Como, 'Print, Censorship, and Ideological Escalation in the English Civil War', *JBS* 51 (2012), 831–2, 849–57; Como, *Radical Parliamentarians*, 36–9, 113–15, 123–6, 134–6, 196–201, 234–9, 435–6.
32 See further, Como, *Radical Parliamentarians*, 119–22, 180–211, 233–9, 260–7.
33 Como, 'Ideological Escalation', 829–36; Como, *Radical Parliamentarians*, 194–201, 234–9.
34 [W. Walwyn,] *The Compassionate Samaritane: Unbinding the Conscience* (1644), A4r; Martin, *Free and Open Press*, 16–25, first noted this line of argument beginning with Walwyn in the mid-1640s.
35 *Samaritane*, A4v, 38–9, 58–60.
36 Ibid., A4r, 38–9, 76.
37 J. Milton, *Areopagitica* (1644), 25–6.
38 J. Lilburne, *A Copie of a Letter, Written by John Lilburne Leut. Collonell* (1645), 2–3; cf. Milton, *Areopagitica*, 7–8, 24–5.
39 *Englands Birth-Right Justified* (1645), 10, usually ascribed to Lilburne and certainly produced by Richard Overton's secret press. D. Adams, 'The Secret Printing and Publishing Career of Richard Overton the Leveller, 1644–46', *Library* 11 (2010), 4, 13, 30, 45–7.
40 *The Tender Conscience Religiously Affected* (1646), 'To the Reader'.
41 *An Alarum to the House of Lords* (1646), 7; Adams, 'Secret Printing', 3–4, 23, 30, 66.
42 *A Pearle in a Dounghill* (1646), 3.

43 [R. Overton,] *Divine Observations* (1646), 11.
44 For a classic example of this theoretical move, see, e.g., *A Remonstrance of Many Thousand Citizens, and other Free-born People of England* (1646); see further Como, *Radical Parliamentarians*, esp. 420–7.
45 *Strong Motives, Or Loving and Modest Advice* (1645), 4; Como, *Radical Parliamentarians*, 339–46.
46 [W. Walwyn,] *A Helpe to the right understanding of a Discourse Concerning Independency* (1645), 8.
47 [W. Walwyn,] *A Demurre to the Bill for Preventing the Growth and Spreading of Heresie* (1646), A2r, A3r; J. Lilburne, *A Whip for the Present House of Lords* (1648), 4.
48 Preliminary investigation suggests that construal of 'freedom of speech' as an absence of restraint on discourse and positive political good (as opposed to *parrhesia*) became widespread only in the early eighteenth century. See R. Crosfeild, *The government unhing'd* (1703), 17; [J. Addison,] *The Thoughts of A Tory Author, Concerning the Press* (1712).
49 *To the Right Honourable, the Supreme Authority of this Nation, the Commons of England in Parliament assembled. The humble Petition of firm and constant Friends* (1649).
50 *To the Commons of England, Assembled in Parliament. The Humble Petition of the well-affected* (1649), 2; *To the Honourable, the Commons assembled in Parliament. The Humble Petition of divers well-affected People* (1650); *To the Supreme Authority, the Parliament of the Common-Wealth of England. The humble Petition of divers constant Adherers* (1652); *The Beacons Quenched: Or The Humble Information of divers Officers in the Army* (1652), 12; W. Ball, *A Briefe Treatise Concerning the Regulating of Printing* (1652).
51 See G. Kemp, 'L'Estrange and the Publishing Sphere', in J. McElligott (ed.), *Fear, Exclusion and Revolution: Roger Morrice and Britain in the 1680s* (Aldershot, 2006), 84; E. Sirluck, 'Milton and a Forgotten Licensing Controversy', *RES* 11 (1960), 260–74; E. Hickeringill, *A Speech Without-Doores* (1689), E4v–Fv; M. Knights, 'Parliament, Print and Corruption in Later Stuart Britain', *PH* 26 (2007), 49–61; A. Barber, '"Why Don't Those Lazy Priests Answer the Book?" Matthew Tindal, Censorship, Freedom of the Press and Religious Debate in Early Eighteenth-century England', *History* 98 (2013), 680–707.

Chapter 6

Swift and free speech

David Womersley

'Strenuum pro virili libertatis vindicem.' Swift so arranged it that the very last of his many acts of self-representation brought him before the reader of his epitaph assuming the identity of a strenuous defender of manly liberty.[1] An essential part of that strenuousness was an effort of discrimination. Swift was no defender of all the activities that had been, or were in his own day busily being, dignified with the adjective 'free'. In particular, he held no brief for either free speech or its close associate, free-thinking. So it is a repeated feature of his writings that he implicitly distinguishes his own satiric outspokenness from its degraded counterpart, the free speech of those who speak irresponsibly, or blasphemously – those, in other words, whose speech is free only in the low sense of being gratuitous.

Swift repeatedly availed himself of the freedom from pre-publication censorship that followed on from the lapse of the Licensing Act in 1695, and he regularly ran the risk of falling foul of the post-publication censorship (in the form of prosecutions for seditious libel) which still obtained.[2] In March 1714 *The Public Spirit of the Whigs*, Swift's biting mockery of Richard Steele's pamphlet *The Crisis*, had been the subject of a royal proclamation in which £300 had been offered for information about the author, and the printer of the pamphlet, John Barber, had been taken into custody and interrogated. In 1720 Edward Waters had been prosecuted for publishing Swift's *A Proposal for the Universal Use of Irish Manufacture*. In 1724 certain passages in one of the *Drapier's Letters* (*A Letter to the Whole People of Ireland*) had been condemned by the Irish Privy Council as 'Seditious and Scandalous'. Once again, £300 had been offered for information about the author, and the printer, John Harding, had been taken into custody and examined. So it was more than just a sally of humour when in September 1725 Swift brought Pope up to date about the progress he had made with *Gulliver's Travels*, and informed him that they were 'intended for the press when the world shall deserve them, or rather when a Printer shall be found brave enough to venture his Eares'.[3] And nor would Swift have been surprised in 1738 when Erasmus Lewis, having read the manuscript of Swift's *History of the Four Last Years of the Queen*, was so shocked by the portraits of leading politicians it contained that he warned the author that, if the manuscript were published as it stood, 'nothing could save the Author's Printer and Publisher's from some grievous punishment'.[4] Nevertheless, Swift harboured profound misgivings about what he saw as the rising tide of free-thinking, free speaking and free publishing.

THE EXPANSION OF THE CLAIM TO FREE SPEECH: EURIPIDES TO THE UNITED NATIONS

If one reviews salient instances from antiquity to the mid-twentieth century in which a right to free speech is either claimed or celebrated, one is struck by the tendency for those claims over time to be couched in terms ever more universal, ever less qualified by circumstance and ever less (at least overtly) consequentialist in form, to the point where the right to free speech has come to seem in our day almost autotelic, or an end in itself.

In ancient Greece, assertions of the right to free speech or *parrhesia* could be exhilarating and inspiring. But they tended also to be, on inspection, scrupulously qualified. Only some people might speak freely, and they might do so on only a limited range of topics, at carefully-defined times, in specified places and to selected audiences. For example, consider the phrasing of statements relating to free speech (*parrhesia*) in three plays by Euripides.[5] The first is spoken by Phaedra, in *Hippolytus*:

> I want my two sons to go back and live in glorious Athens, hold their heads high there, and speak their minds there like free men.[6]

Here, the right of free speech is available only to some (free men – not women, slaves or children), and only in a certain place ('speak their minds *there*'). The second is spoken by Ion:

> I pray my mother is Athenian, so that through her I may have rights of speech [*parrhesia*]. For when a stranger comes into the city of pure blood, though in name a citizen, his mouth remains a slave: he has no right of speech [*parrhesia*].[7]

Here, only those born of an Athenian can claim a right of free speech in Athens. The third is spoken by Theseus, in *The Suppliant Woman*:

> Freedom lives in this formula: 'Who has good counsel which he would offer to the city?' He who desires to speak wins fame; he who does not is silent. What can be more just than this?[8]

And finally here free speech is limited by its end or intention, namely that of doing good to the city. By implication it is not available to those who might wish to speak to a different purpose, no matter who they were, and where and to whom they were speaking.

Leaping forward into seventeenth-century England, Milton's *Areopagitica* (1644) is often described by contemporary defenders of free speech, such as Timothy Garton Ash, as 'an appeal for freedom from censorship' and as a 'great broadside against the English authorities restricting what printed matter can be read in their realm'.[9] It must then be surprising and disappointing for Garton Ash's readers who turn to *Areopagitica* expecting 'a great broadside' to find that in fact Milton's text is, when you look at the detail, much more a matter of precise sniping. Milton is clear that unlicensed publishing is not an end in itself, but rather is merely an instrument capable of serving the real end, namely knowledge of God's truth. But because Milton's goal is to serve God's truth rather than truth more generally conceived, the benefit of unlicensed printing is not to be extended universally. Jews, Muslims, atheists, and of course Roman Catholics, are excluded. Notwithstanding the occasional tremendousness of his rhetoric, the freedoms Milton seeks are in fact closely restricted, as to both purpose and those who can exercise them. Nor does Milton rule out – indeed, he explicitly calls for – post-publication prosecution of books found to be scandalous, seditious or libellous.[10]

It was during the century and a half following the publication of *Areopagitica* that statements of the right to freedom of speech began, at least in Western Europe, to expand their scope and to lose or mask their consequentialism. At the end of that period, around 1790, justifications of free speech become much more unconditional. Important examples include the French 'Declaration of the Rights of Man and of the Citizen' (1789);[11] the First Amendment to the Constitution of the United States (1791);[12] and Wilhelm von Humboldt's *The Limits of State Action* (composed in 1791),[13] which would exert such a strong influence during the next century on J. S. Mill.[14] These texts are the harbingers of the truly comprehensive and unqualified statements of the right to free speech that were composed in the mid-twentieth century, such as the UN Declaration of Human Rights (1948)[15] and the International Covenant on Civil and Political Rights (1966).[16]

Swift died in 1745, and so did not live to see even the first buds of what would grow into these expansive blossomings of the right to free speech. But if we review the century and a half between the publication of *Areopagitica* in 1644 and the French 'Declaration of the Rights of Man and of the Citizen' in 1789, it is clear that Swift had ample opportunity to judge the direction in which the tide was flowing. For example, in his sermon 'On the Testimony of Conscience' (first printed 1744, but composed and delivered long before that date), Swift put his finger on the modern trend:

> *Liberty of Conscience* ... properly speaking, is no more than a Liberty of knowing our own Thoughts; which Liberty no one can take from us. But those Words have obtained quite different Meanings: Liberty of Conscience is now-a-days not only understood to be the Liberty of believing what Men please, but also of endeavouring to propagate the Belief as much as they can, and to overthrow the

Faith which the Laws have already established, to be rewarded by the Publick for those wicked Endeavours: And this is the Liberty of Conscience which the Fanaticks are now openly in the Face of the World endeavouring at with their utmost Application.[17]

And the same insight about modernity is a cause of satisfaction to the speaker of the ironic *Argument Against Abolishing Christianity* (1708): 'Is not every Body freely allowed to believe whatever he pleaseth; and to publish his Belief to the World whenever he thinks fit; especially if it serve to strengthen the Party which is in the Right?'[18]

For over the course of the later seventeenth and eighteenth centuries the Christian liberty for which the sects had fought during the English civil war came to include also a liberty of free-thinking and free expression, to the point where those who argued for a right of free judgement in religion tended also to claim such rights in the civil sphere.[19]

The entanglement of those two kinds of liberty, originally so distinct, is a recurrent feature in the writings of the time. In 1701 John Toland followed James Harrington in asserting that 'where there is no liberty of conscience, there can be no civil liberty'.[20] In 1721 Trenchard and Gordon gave *Cato's Letters* the significant subtitle 'Essays on Liberty, Civil and Religious'. In 1776 Richard Price took religious liberty to comprise 'the power of exercising, without molestation, that mode of religion which we think best', the phrase 'without molestation' associating religious liberty closely with civil freedoms.[21] When William Paley said in 1785 that he wrote on behalf of 'the general cause of intellectual and religious liberty', his words crystallised and encapsulated this current in English thought.[22]

It was a current which Swift could not by himself hope to dam, still less reverse; but nevertheless it was a current which he certainly did his best to disrupt.

SWIFT AND THE RESISTANCE TO FREE SPEECH

Swift's ideas on the connected questions of freedom of conscience and freedom of expression were strongly conditioned by his views of the English Civil Wars. He seems never to have tired of reflecting on that great crisis of state, for instance reading Clarendon's *History of the Rebellion* no fewer than four separate times (as he tells us in the annotations he made in his copy).[23]

For Swift, the English Civil Wars illustrated the bitter political truth that anarchy was the parent of despotism. Given a straight choice between those evils, Swift preferred anarchy to arbitrary government, as he made clear in the *Sentiments of a Church of England Man* (1708):

> arbitrary Power ... which, notwithstanding all that *Hobbes, Filmer*, and others have said to its Advantage, I look upon as a greater Evil than *Anarchy* it self; as much as a *Savage* is in a happier State of Life, than a *Slave* at the Oar.[24]

Yet Swift also realised that anarchy might pave the way to arbitrary power: savages, it seemed, might easily be converted into slaves. According to Swift, the sects which had flourished in England during the 1640s and 1650s had been merely convenient tools to serve the nefarious ends of a small group of ambitious men:

> Thus was the whole Body of *Puritans* in *England*, drawn to be the Instruments, or Abettors of all Manner of Villany, by the artifices of a *few Men*, whose Designs, from the first, were levelled to destroy the Constitution, both of Religion and Government.[25]

But that political corruption had been the Trojan horse that had introduced linguistic licentiousness: 'During the Usurpation, such an Infusion of Enthusiastick Jargon prevailed in every Writing, as was not shook off in many Years after.'[26]

The consequences of this political and linguistic irresponsibility had not been extinguished by the Restoration. Indeed, rather the reverse. The habits of irresponsible thought and speech which had sprouted amongst the lower orders in the mid-seventeenth century had, after 1660 (so Swift believed) migrated towards and tainted the higher fractions of society, up to and including even the court itself:

> I cannot indeed, controvert the lawfulness of Free-Thinking, because it hath been universally allowed, that Thought is free. But however, although it may afford a large Field of Matter, yet, in my poor Opinion, it seems to contain very little, either of Wit or Humour; because, it hath not been antient enough among us, to furnish established authentick Expressions; I mean such as must receive a Sanction from the polite World, before their Authority can be allowed; neither, was the Art of Blasphemy or Free-Thinking, invented by the Court, or by Persons of great Quality, who properly speaking were Patrons, rather than Inventors of it, but first brought in by the Fanatick Faction, towards the End of their Power; and, after the Restoration, carried to Whitehall, by the converted Rumpers, with very good Reason; because, they knew, that King Charles the Second, from a wrong Education, occasioned by the Troubles of his Father, had Time enough to observe, that Fanatick Enthusiasm directly led to Atheism; which agreed with the dissolute Inclinations of his Youth.[27]

Whether or not this is a tenable interpretation of what happened in England between 1642 and 1685, Swift's conviction that those who had asserted freedom of conscience and freedom of expression most vehemently had been duped by others who were playing a deeper game decisively shaped his characterisations of free-thinkers and religious nonconformists. Whereas the Cromwellian insider Sir Charles Wolseley had held that to refuse a man the right to judge for himself in questions of religion was 'to change him from a rational man to a bruit', for Swift it was precisely the other way round. It was when individuals rashly embraced freedoms of thought and expression in their largest extent that they ran the risk of ceasing to be rational, ceasing to exercise judgement, and therefore ceasing to be fully human.

In the middle decades of the seventeenth century two powerful thinkers had adopted opposed stances on the question of freedom of belief and freedom of expression. In chapter 18 of *Leviathan* (1651) Hobbes had asserted that, although it was impossible to control what people thought, the sovereign could and should control the opinions that individuals disseminated in speech and print:

> it is annexed to the Soveraignty, to be Judge of what Opinions and Doctrines are averse, and what conducing to Peace; and consequently, on what occasions, how farre, and what, men are to be trusted withal, in speaking to Multitudes of people; and who shall examine the Doctrines of all bookes before they be published ... It belongeth therefore to him that hath the Soveraign Power, to be Judge, or constitute all Judges of Opinions and Doctrines, as a thing necessary to Peace; therby to prevent Discord and Civill Warre.[28]

Some twenty years later, in the *Tractatus Theologico-Politicus*, Spinoza had taken the directly opposite view: 'if no man, then, can give up his freedom to judge and think as he pleases, and everyone is by absolute natural right master of his own thoughts, it follows that utter failure will attend any attempt in a state to force men to speak only as prescribed by the sovereign despite their different and opposing opinions'.[29]

Swift lumped Spinoza and Hobbes together as enemies of Christianity,[30] but there is no doubt that on the particular point of the subject's duty to comply with the dictates of the magistrate he was at one with Hobbes, whom he liked noisily to denounce and decry, but on whose insights he frequently and silently drew. It was, after all, exactly Hobbes's position which Swift would put into the mouth of the King of Brobdingnag in Part II of *Gulliver's Travels*:

> He said, he knew no Reason, why those who entertain Opinions prejudicial to the Publick, should be obliged to change, or should not be obliged to conceal them. And, as it was Tyranny in any Government to require the first, so it was Weakness not to enforce the second: For, a Man may be allowed to keep Poisons in his Closet, but not to vend them about as Cordials.[31]

The King of Brobdingnag's views coincided precisely with those of Swift himself. The manuscript 'Thoughts on Religion', discovered in Swift's study after his death by the Dublin printer George Faulkner, and so far as we know composed by Swift simply for his own benefit and without thought of publication, includes this longer expression of exactly the same point:

> Liberty of conscience, properly speaking, is no more than the liberty of possessing our own thoughts and opinions, which every man enjoys without fear of the magistrate: But how far he shall publicly act in pursuance of those opinions, is to be regulated by the laws of the country. Perhaps, in my own thoughts, I prefer

a well-instituted commonwealth before a monarchy; and I know several others of the same opinion. Now, if, upon this pretence, I should insist upon liberty of conscience, form conventicles of republicans, and print books, preferring that government, and condemning what is established, the magistrate would, with great justice, hang me and my disciples. It is the same case in religion, although not so avowed, where liberty of conscience, under the present acceptation, equally produces revolutions, or at least convulsions and disturbances in a state; which politicians would see well enough, if their eyes were not blinded by faction, and of which these kingdoms, as well as France, Sweden, and other countries, are flaming instances. Cromwell's notion upon this article, was natural and right; when, upon the surrender of a town in Ireland, the Popish governor insisted upon an article for liberty of conscience, Cromwell said, he meddled with no man's conscience; but, if by liberty of conscience, the governor meant the liberty of the Mass, he had express orders from the parliament of England against admitting any such liberty at all.[32]

For Swift, the expression of religious nonconformity was to be suppressed on the Hobbesian grounds that it endangered public peace and order. It is no accident that the King of Brobdingnag in Part II of *Gulliver's Travels* can see no merit in the multiplication of opinion and rules over a state in which, although the art of printing has been long known, there has been no explosion of 'print culture'.[33] Similarly the society of the Houyhnhnms described by Swift in Part IV exhibits an austere and extreme verbal discipline.[34] These two 'remote nations' visited by Gulliver form a pointed contrast with the verbal excessiveness which characterises the oppressive kingdoms of Lilliput and Laputa.

Swift recognised that the state had neither right nor power to compel people to change their convictions. Provided that any heterodox opinions remained strictly private they did not – and could not – fall under the jurisdiction of the magistrate.[35] But even so, Swift was far from smiling indulgently on such opinions, even when privately held. Just as sects were to be suppressed by public authority, so individuals were obliged, so far as they could, to stifle and eradicate the heterodoxies which might bubble up in the privacy of their own mind. Once again, the entries in 'Thoughts on Religion' are revealing. Three are especially relevant to this question:

> Every man, as a member of the commonwealth, ought to be content with the possession of his own opinion in private, without perplexing his neighbour or disturbing the public.
>
> The want of belief is a defect that ought to be concealed when it cannot be overcome.
>
> I am not answerable to God for the doubts that arise in my own breast, since they are the consequence of that reason which he hath planted in me, if I take care to conceal those doubts from others, if I use my best endeavours to subdue them, and if they have no influence on the conduct of my life.[36]

The reasons for this rigid self-discipline are twofold. On the one hand, to indulge such thoughts makes their suppression more difficult, and thus it becomes more likely that you will bring down on yourself the legitimate wrath of the secular power. On the other, to surrender to them is not (*pace* those later optimists Wilhelm von Humboldt and J. S. Mill) to advance down the path towards *Eigentümlichkeit* and self-realisation. Rather, for Swift to indulge recklessly in free-thinking is to subvert and undermine your own identity. Another posthumously published manuscript, 'Some Thoughts on Free-thinking', makes the point:

> He ['a prelate of the kingdom of Ireland'] said, that the difference betwixt a mad-man and one in his wits, in what related to speech, consisted in this: That the former spoke out whatever came into his mind, and just in the confused manner as his imagination presented the ideas. The latter only expressed such thoughts, as his judgment directed him to chuse, leaving the rest to die away in his memory. And that if the wisest man would at any time utter his thoughts, in the crude indigested manner, as they come into his head, he would be looked upon as raving mad. And indeed, when we consider our thoughts, as they are the seeds of words and actions, we cannot but agree, that they ought to be kept under the strictest regulation.[37]

To indulge in free-thinking is to exchange the truly valuable birthright of being free-minded for the mess of pottage of a chaotic, insane alternative.

So the freedom promised by free-thinkers was a snare. It was the bait that drew you in to a maze of nonsense and self-contradiction. Swift's fullest and most wildly amusing anatomising of the fatuities of free-thinking is found in his *Mr. C—ns's Discourse of Free-Thinking, Put Into Plain English, by Way of Abstract, for the Use of the Poor* (1713). In this pamphlet Swift adopts the *persona* of Collins; but this is an unguarded 'Collins' unable to avoid betraying the confusion and deformity of his thought.

In the first place, 'Collins' reveals that free-thinking is not a benefit that, in Kantian terms, can be universalised:

> *Free Thinking* signifies nothing, without *Free Speaking* and *Free Writing*. It is the indispensable Duty of a *Free Thinker*, to endeavour *forcing* all the World to think as he does, and by that means to make them *Free Thinkers* too.[38]

But why do free-thinkers, in defiance of their declared principles, try to convert others to their position? Here Swift has an unsympathetic, but not unshrewd, answer, which he had explained in a work written a few years beforehand, the *Remarks Upon Tindall's Rights of the Christian Church* (1708):

> It is an Imputation often charged on these Sort of Men, that by their Invectives against Religion, they can possibly propose no other End than that of fortifying themselves and others against the Reproaches of a vicious Life; it being necessary for Men of libertine Practices to embrace libertine Principles, or else they cannot act in Consistence with any Reason, or preserve any Peace of Mind.[39]

Swift's free-thinkers are, notwithstanding their pretensions to independence of mind, in fact Yahoo-like herd animals, comfortable only when surrounded by their fellows. And in pursuit of this craving for like-minded company, they are prepared to run the gravest risks with public peace and order, as 'Collins' blithely confesses. Although 'Collins' is ludicrously sure that free-thinking, if only it were sufficiently indulged, would produce unanimity –

> a great deal of *Free-thinking* will at last set us all right, and every one will adhere to the *Scripture* he likes best; by which means Religion, Peace, and Wealth, will be for ever secured in Her Majesty's Realms.[40]

– even if that were somehow not to come about, free-thinking is still harmless and right and our bounden duty:

> There is not the least hurt in the wickedest Thoughts, provided they be free; nor in telling those Thoughts to every Body, and endeavouring to convince the World of them; for all this is included in the Doctrine of *Free-thinking*, as I shall plainly shew you in what follows; and therefore you are all along to understand the Word *Free-thinking* in this Sense.
>
> I affirm, that if Ten thousand Free Thinkers thought differently from the received Doctrine, and from each other, they would be all in Duty bound to publish their Thoughts (provided they were all sure of being in the right) though it broke the Peace of the Church and State, Ten thousand times.[41]

Not only do free-thinkers coerce their fellow men and endanger public peace and order. They also entangle themselves in the contradictions of their own position:

> But to this it may be objected, that the Bulk of Mankind is as well qualified for *flying* as *thinking*, and if every Man thought it his Duty to *think freely*, and trouble his Neighbour with his Thoughts (which is an essential Part of *Free-thinking*,) it would make wild work in the World. I answer; whoever cannot *think freely*, may let it alone if he pleases, by virtue of his Right to *think freely*; that is to say, if such a Man *freely thinks* that he cannot *think freely*, of which every Man is a sufficient Judge, why then he may not *think freely*, unless he *thinks* fit.[42]

Here the repetitions and circularities dramatise the undignified posture of the free-thinker, wriggling to no avail in the web of confusions in which he has enmeshed himself. 'Collins' shuffles and repeats his verbal counters, for instance inverting 'think freely' to 'freely thinks', in the desperate hope that with one of these almost random arrangements of words something identifiable as a reasonable and persuasive proposition will loom up through the mist.

Swift's free-thinkers are not merely ludicrous. They are also infectious. Here Swift draws on one of the common early modern arguments against religious toleration, namely that heretical beliefs had a polluting effect on the societies in which they were not suppressed and persecuted. To shoulder the task of engaging with and opposing the free-thinkers, Swift had to immerse himself in their writings, and in doing so he ran a mortal risk. 'Who can dwell upon a tedious Piece of insipid Thinking, and false Reasoning, so long as I am likely to do, without sharing the Infection?' he said of Tindal's *Rights of the Christian Church*.⁴³ The language here hovers between metaphor and literalness. Throughout his life Swift was mortally afraid of the plague, and he would frequently speak of ethical vulnerability in somatic terms, with language being both the infective agent and the symptom. Writing to Stella in 1712, he complained about the effect that working as Harley's *chef de propagande* was having on his prose style:

> See how my Stile is altered by living & thinking & talking among these People [i.e. the ministry].⁴⁴

Swift was contemptuous of free-thinkers and those who argued for untrammelled freedom of expression, but his morbidly acute sense of the susceptibility of the human personality to literal and metaphorical infections meant that his scorn was laced with fear. People like Collins and Tindal were both ridiculous and dangerous.

SWIFT AND SATIRIC OUTSPOKENNESS AS CONSTRAINED SPEECH

But if Swift was a secret sharer with Hobbes in the matters of those two very separable freedoms, the freedom of opinion and the freedom of expression, so too was he a secret sharer with Spinoza on the matter of the futility and unnaturalness of suppression, at least in some circumstances. Such unlikely, one might even say contradictory, alliances were characteristic of Swift, whose intellectual identity can be likened to sedimentary layers of divergent materials. It was such an image that Swift himself gave to his *persona* in the *Drapier's Letters*, when evoking his political commitments and affinities:

> I have likewise buried, at the bottom of a strong Chest, your Lordship's [i.e. the commonwealth Whig Robert Molesworth's] Writings, under a Heap of others that treat of *Liberty*; and spread over a *Layer* or two of *Hobbs*, *Filmer*, *Bodin*, and many more Authors of that Stamp, to be readiest at Hand, whenever I shall be disposed to take up a *new* Set of Principles in Government.⁴⁵

Swift, whose politics could encompass spasms of both Jacobite and commonwealth Whig feeling, was himself the model for the Drapier's buried box of books.

However, the outspokenness that Swift is prepared to defend as natural and irrepressible is sharply distinguished from the self-regarding garrulousness he associated with free speech. Again, the *Drapier's Letters* provides the illuminating quotation, when the Drapier notes the steepening intolerance of authority for expressions of disagreement or disaffection:

> For those who have used *Power* to cramp *Liberty*, have gone so far as to resent even the *Liberty* of *Complaining*; although a Man upon the Rack, was never known to be refused the Liberty of *roaring* as loud as he thought fit.⁴⁶

For Swift, satiric outspokenness is not free speech, but rather a special kind of constrained speech; namely, the truth that erupts when all capacity for restraint or forbearance has been eroded. It is a position with a lengthy genealogy, extending back to Juvenal:

> quem patitur dormire nurus corruptor avarae,
> quem sponsae turpes et praetextatus adulter?
> si natura negat, facit indignatio versum
> qualemcumque potest, quales ego vel Cluvienus.[47]

– lines which of course would be echoed by Swift's friend Pope:

> Not write? but then I *think*,
> And for my Soul I cannot sleep a wink.
> I nod in Company, I wake at Night,
> Fools rush into my Head, and so I write.[48]

Perhaps the most vivid Swiftian example of satire as exasperated and defeated tact is to be found in that late, great, wild poem, 'A Character, Panegyric, and Description of the Legion Club' (1736)[49] – a poem on which I have written at some length elsewhere.[50] But other examples come readily to hand. In 'The Lady's Dressing Room' Strephon, having made his lengthy and meticulous inventory of the contents of Celia's room, cannot suppress the famous, truthful cry:

> Thus finishing his grand Survey,
> Disgusted Strephon stole away
> Repeating in his amorous Fits,
> Oh! Celia, Celia, Celia shits!

– where 'Fits' plays brilliantly on the technical literary sense of the word as well as on its somatic meaning.[51] Literary conventions and truth are often at variance, and satire is sometimes the involuntary expostulation which erupts when the tension between the two grows too great. Or again, in the imitation of Horace that Swift wrote in 1713 to anatomise his relationship with Robert Harley, the Secretary of State who had selected Swift to be his *chef de propagande*, the climax of the poem is once more a dramatisation of that paradigmatic Swiftian moment when nature has been tried too sorely and plain resentful truth breaks out. Swift's preferment had not turned out well, and he resolves to be done with it:

> Poor S—t, with all his Losses vext,
> Not knowing where to turn him next;
> Above a Thousand Pounds in Debt,
> Takes Horse, and in a mighty Fret
> Rides Day and Night at such a Rate,
> He soon arrives at *HARLEY*'s Gate;
> But was so dirty, pale and thin,
> Old Read would hardly let him in.

Harley's welcoming blandishments do nothing to soothe Swift's troubled mind, and the poem ends with this memorable example of *parrhesia* – of, that is to say, plain, free speech addressed to mischievous power:

> Truce, good MY LORD, I beg a Truce!
> The Doctor in a Passion cry'd;
> Your Raillery is misapply'd:
> I have Experience dearly bought,
> You know I am not worth a Groat:
> But you resolv'd to have your Jest,
> And 'twas a Folly to Contest:
> Then since you now have done your worst,
> Pray leave me where you found me first.[52]

Such was the free speech Swift admired, and which on occasion he was himself ready to employ.

CONCLUSION

The movement from the control of speech to freedom of speech is not a simple passage from black to white, from a negative to a positive. Each position in the line running from absolute repression to absolute liberty contains a mixture of benefits and penalties. Reasonable people can differ about the desirable point of balance between those benefits and penalties. In particular, current fashionable arguments for restricting free speech, grounded on the bestowing or receiving of offence, are perhaps not the strongest available arguments for that position. Such arguments bring the position of resistance to free speech into disrepute. They are easily countered by assertions of the need for robustness. But is that necessary robustness always within the grasp of all those who are exposed to free speech? James Fitzjames Stephen argued that the radical weakness in J. S. Mill's arguments for freedom of expression was his exaggeration of the resilience of human nature when exposed to the conditions of perpetual unsettledness and the atmosphere of relentless solicitation which freedom of expression is liable to create in the realm of public opinion:

> Civil war, legal persecution, the Inquisition, with all their train of horrors, form a less searching and effective conflict than that intellectual warfare from which no institution, no family, no individual man is free when discussion is free from legal punishment ... The result of such a warfare is that the weaker opinion – the less robust and deep seated feeling – is rooted out to the last fibre, the place where it grew being seared as with a hot iron; whereas the prison, the stake, and the sword only strike it down, and leave it to grow again in better circumstances.[53]

For Swift, too, the problem of free speech turned on his conviction of the vulnerability and fragility of the human personality. Swift subscribed to a traditional, classical idea of the human personality as in need of protection, training, support and restriction. Hence his sustained interest over the course of his life in education – this was not so much to do with the dissemination of learning as with the proper disciplining, pruning and rigidifying of the personality of the child by the imposition of structure from outside. We might call this view of the human personality repressive, or paternalistic, or condescending, or realistic.

At the end of the eighteenth century that classical idea of the human personality would lose ground to a romantic alternative, in which the human personality, in order to flourish, needed only to be unconstrained and to exercise its own freedom in a process of organic blossoming so as to realise the unique principle of individuality buried like a seed within it. This change in the conceptualising of the human personality moved free speech from possibly a valuable, but also certainly a dangerous thing, permitted only to some, on certain occasions and in certain places, and in relation only to certain subjects, to being on the contrary one of the chief instruments of the individual's precious self-realisation, and therefore something that in principle should be available to all, at any time and in any place, and on any subject.[54]

Attending to the resistance to free speech mounted by Swift, and to the corollary of his representation of satiric outspokenness as a special kind of constrained speech, reminds us of different, now largely forgotten or ignored, ways of viewing the problem of *parrhesia*. Those forgotten ways warn us not to be too sanguine about the likely outcomes of an unrestricted liberty of thought and expression.

NOTES

1. The frequent mistranslation of 'virili' as 'human' obscures an important implication in the epitaph.
2. On which see T. Keymer, *Poetics of the Pillory: English Literature and Seditious Libel 1660–1820* (Oxford, 2019).
3. D. Woolley (ed.), *The Correspondence of Jonathan Swift, D.D.* (Frankfurt am Main, 1999–2014), II, 606.
4. Woolley (ed.), *Correspondence*, IV, 513.
5. These examples were all discussed by M. Foucault in his *Fearless Speech* (Los Angeles, 2001).
6. *Hippolytus*, ll. 420–5.
7. *Ion*, ll. 670–5.
8. *The Suppliant Woman*, ll. 438–42.
9. T. Garton Ash, *Free Speech: Ten Principles for a Connected World* (2016), 8, 26.
10. Relevant quotations from J. Milton, *Selected Prose*, ed. C. Patrides (Harmondsworth, 1974), include: 'I deny not, but that it is of greatest concernment in the Church and Commonwealth, to have a vigilant eye how Bookes demeane themselves as well as men; and thereafter to confine, imprison, and do sharpest justice on them as malefactors' (200); 'no envious Juno sate cros-leg'd over the nativity of any mans intellectuall off-spring; but if it prov'd a Monster, who denies, but that it

was justly burnt, or sunk into the Sea' (208); 'Had any one writt'n | and divulg'd erroneous things & scandalous to honest life, misusing and forfeiting the esteem had of his reason among men, if after conviction this only censure were adjudg'd him, that he should never henceforth write, but what were first examin'd by an appointed officer, whose hand should be annext to passe his credit for him, that now he might be safely read, it could not be apprehended less then a disgraceful punishment' (226–7); 'Give me liberty to know, to utter, and to argue freely according to conscience, above all other liberties' (241); 'Yet if all cannot be of one mind, as who looks they should be? this doubtless is more wholsome, more prudent, and more Christian that many be tolerated, rather then all compell'd. I mean not tolerated Popery, and open superstition, which as it extirpats all religions and civill supremacies, so it self should be extirpat ... that also which is impious or evil absolutely either against faith or manners no law can possibly permit, that intends not to unlaw it self' (244); 'that no book be Printed, | unlesse the Printers and the Authors name, or at least the Printers be register'd. Those which otherwise come forth, if they be found mischievous and libellous, the fire and the executioner will be the timeliest and the most effectuall remedy, that man's prevention can use' (246–7).

11 'Declaration of the Rights of Man and of the Citizen' (1789), article 11: 'The free communication of thoughts and of opinions is one of the most precious rights of man: any citizen thus may speak, write, print freely, except to respond to the abuse of this liberty, in the cases determined by the law.'

12 First Amendment (1791): 'Congress shall make no law respecting an establishment of religion, or prohibiting the free exercise thereof; or abridging the freedom of speech, or of the press; or the right of the people peaceably to assemble, and to petition the Government for a redress of grievances.'

13 W. von Humboldt, *The Limits of State Action* (composed 1791), ed. J. Burrow (Indianapolis, 1993): importance of 'Eigentümlichkeit', individuality (chapter 2); 'The highest ideal, therefore, of the co-existence of human beings seems to me to consist in a union in which each strives to develop himself from his own inmost nature, and for his own sake' (chapter 2, 13); 'The importance of free inquiry extends to our whole manner of thinking, and even acting. The man who is accustomed to judge of truth and error for himself, and to hear them similarly discussed by others, without fear of the consequences, weighs the principles of action more calmly and consistently, and from a higher point of view, than one whose inquiries are constantly influenced by a variety of circumstances not properly part of the inquiry itself' (chapter 7, 66); 'the beneficial results of complete liberty of thought on the mind and character of the entire nation extend their influence even to its humblest individuals' (chapter 7, 68).

14 E.g. 'The liberty of expressing and publishing opinions ... [is] almost of as much importance as the liberty of thought itself, and resting in great part on the same reasons, is practically inseparable from it' (*On Liberty*, chapter 1 (Buffalo, 1986), 19).

15 UN Declaration of Human Rights (1948), Article 19: 'Everyone has the right to freedom of opinion and expression: this right includes freedom to hold opinions without interference and to seek, receive and impart information and ideas through any media and regardless of frontiers.'

16 International Covenant on Civil and Political Rights (1966), Article 19: 'Everyone shall have the right to freedom of expression; this right shall include freedom to seek, receive and impart information and ideas of all kinds, regardless of frontiers, either orally, in writing, or in print, in the form of art, or through any other media of his choice.'
17 *PW*, IX, 151.
18 Ibid., II, 29.
19 The following two paragraphs are deeply indebted to the work of Blair Worden; see particularly *God's Instruments: Political Conduct in the England of Oliver Cromwell* (Oxford, 2012), 313–54.
20 J. Toland, *Anglia Libera* (1701), 100.
21 R. Price, *Observations on the Nature of Civil Liberty*, second edition (1776), 3.
22 W. Paley, *The Principles of Moral and Political Philosophy* (1785), vi.
23 'Finished the 4TH time, April 18, 1741' (*PW*, V, 295; on the authority of Scott).
24 *PW*, II, 15.
25 Ibid., II, 12.
26 J. Swift, *Parodies, Hoaxes, Mock Treatises: Polite Conversation, Directions to Servants and Other Works*, ed. V. Rumbold (Cambridge, 2013), 138.
27 Swift, *Parodies*, 280.
28 T. Hobbes, *Leviathan*, ed. R. Tuck (Cambridge, 1996), 124–5.
29 B. Spinoza, *Tractatus Theologico-Politicus*, trans. S. Shirley (Leiden, 1989), 292.
30 'Enemies to Christianity, such as *Socinus, Hobbes,* and *Spinosa*' (*Remarks on Tindall's Rights of the Christian Church*, in *PW*, II, 72).
31 Jonathan Swift, *Gulliver's Travels*, ed. D. Womersley (Cambridge, 2012), 187; hereafter cited as *GT*.
32 *PW*, IX, 263.
33 'when I happened to say, there were several thousand Books among us written upon the *Art of Government*; it gave him (directly contrary to my Intention) a very mean Opinion of our Understandings'; 'They have had the Art of Printing, as well as the *Chinese*, Time out of Mind. But their Libraries are not very large; for that of the King's, which is reckoned the largest, doth not amount to above a thousand Volumes' (*GT*, 194 and 196–7).
34 E.g.: 'he [*the Houyhnhnm master*] would laugh that a Creature pretending to Reason, should value itself upon the Knowledge of other Peoples Conjectures, and in Things, where that Knowledge, if it were certain, could be of no Use' (*GT*, 402–3); Houyhnhnm conversation: 'nothing passed but what was useful, expressed in the fewest and most significant Words'; 'no Difference of Sentiments' (*GT*, 418–19); accordingly when Gulliver is sentenced to leave the land of the Houyhnhnms, he does not think of trying to employ free speech: 'I knew too well upon what solid Reasons all the Determinations of the wise Houyhnhnms were founded, not to be shaken by Arguments of mine' (*GT*, 423).
35 Cf. 'Some Thoughts on Free-thinking': 'if such thinkers keep their thoughts within their own breasts, they can be of no consequence, further than to themselves. If they publish them to the world, they ought to be answerable for the effects their thoughts produce upon others' (*PW*, IV, 49); *Remarks Upon Tindall's Rights of the Christian Church*: 'if the Public be not disturbed with atheistical Principles preached, nor Immoralities, all is well' (*PW*, II, 89).

36 *PW*, IX, 261 and 262.
37 Ibid., IV, 49.
38 Ibid., IV, 36.
39 Ibid., II, 70.
40 Ibid., IV, 32–3.
41 Ibid., IV, 30 and 36.
42 Ibid., IV, 38.
43 Ibid., II, 73.
44 J. Swift, *Journal to Stella*, ed. A. Williams (Cambridge, 2013), 444 (15 September 1712).
45 *PW*, X, 93–4.
46 Ibid., X, 63.
47 Juvenal, satire I, ll. 77–80. 'Who can sleep for thinking of an avaricious daughter-in-law seduced, or of brides that have lost their virtue, or of stripling adulterers? Though it may be unnatural, indignation dictates my satire, of whatsoever kind it may be – such poetry as I or Cluvienus can write.' These lines may have prompted the phrase 'saeva indignatio' in Swift's epitaph.
48 'The First Satire of the Second Book of Horace Imitated', ll. 11–14.
49 H. Williams (ed.), *Swift's Poems* (Oxford, 1937), 827–39.
50 D. Womersley, '"Now deaf 1740": Entrapment, Foreboding, and Exorcism in Late Swift', in C. Rawson (ed.), *Politics and Literature in the Age of Swift: English and Irish Perspectives* (Cambridge, 2010), 162–84.
51 *fit*: a part or section of a poem (*OED*, 'fit' n. 1, 1); a sudden seizure accompanied by involuntary movements or cries (*OED*, 'fit' n. 2, c).
52 'Part of the Seventh Epistle of the First Book of Horace Imitated', ll. 113–20 and 130–8, Williams (ed.), *Swift's Poems*, 174–5.
53 J. Stephen, *Liberty, Equality, Fraternity*, ed. S. Warner (Indianapolis, 1993), 69.
54 This is the plain meaning of the UN declaration.

Chapter 7

Defending the truth: arguments for free speech and their limits in early eighteenth-century Britain and France

Ann Thomson

The title of this chapter may seem surprising in an age when the notion of the truth is a very contested one. However, after a long period in which doubt was cast on the very idea of truth and its existence, with emphasis on the way it was constructed and used by the powerful, one might argue that now, with the appearance of alternative facts and fake news, the notion is due for rehabilitation. This chapter therefore approaches the question of eighteenth-century discussions of the freedom of speech from the angle of the truth. The debate on censorship and the freedom of expression in the seventeenth and eighteenth centuries has been frequently studied, often in the context of a teleological history of the development of our freedoms. But if we wish to abandon a Whig perspective and look at the contradictions in this history, the question of the truth is an enlightening strand on which to focus. It is true that many of the questions raised in what follows became more acute in the later eighteenth century, and of course during the revolutionary period, particularly but not only in France.[1] However, it is worth going back earlier to see the tensions running through these issues and the debate around the freedom of the press. Although the focus here will mainly be on England, there are some excursions across the Channel, because the way the English situation and discussions were received, particularly in the very different French climate, helps to throw light on what was at stake in the English debates.

SEEKING THE TRUTH

The starting-point for this study is the period of official toleration and party strife in England after the 'Glorious Revolution' when some of these questions were particularly acute. In this period, as later, we find many echoes of the Protestant notion of the right to seek the truth, as defended in particular by Milton in *Areopagitica*. Without the right to think freely and to question the views of others, truth, in particular true religion, could not be found. Even the expression of erroneous views, if part of an honest pursuit of the truth, was an important step on the path to discover it. For this, God has accorded reason to humans. Even if eighteenth-century protagonists are not always defending the same type of truth, their debates are clearly predicated on the belief that the truth exists and can be discovered.

For many who defended the freedom of speech, the enemy was the church hierarchy, who imposed the official version of religious truth, which some critics considered to be mistaken or a corruption of the original revelation of the truth. Those who opposed church doctrine were not necessarily non-believers who wished to do away with religion, or 'secularisers', or those who believed that science was opposed to religious teaching (although those existed, as we shall see below). Many were simply opposed to the intolerance of the church authorities – whether Catholic or Protestant – who imposed a doctrine which some honest Christians believed to be a corruption of the true faith; these Christians wished to return to a 'purer' Christianity and believed that what the official church defended was not necessarily the truth. Such questions were particularly acute in the 1690s, when different factions were jostling for power against the background of the fear of Catholic plotters, nonconformist 'fanatics' and free-thinkers.

With the lapsing of the Licensing Act (which allowed prior censorship of publications) in 1695,[2] there was felt to be a free-for-all, in which there was total licence to print whatever one wanted, and there were attempts to have licentious books condemned and banned. In other words, the emphasis was on punishment after the fact, while attempts to reimpose preliminary censorship seem to have been abandoned. Although there were some, like Humphrey Prideaux and other High Church clergymen, who blamed the situation on toleration, as a result of which 'a great part of the nation ... are degenerated into perfect atheisme',[3] and probably many clergyman who would have liked to have the Toleration Act repealed, the main argument was not about toleration as such. It concerned rather, on the one hand, limitation of the political rights of nonconformists – as the High Church campaigned to abolish occasional conformity which allowed nonconformists to hold public office if they took Anglican communion – and on the other freedom of speech and the press, seen by many to have gone too far and to be endangering both religion and government. When the Convocation of the Church of England finally met in early 1701, the lower House immediately set about examining books considered to be directed against the Christian religion, which included not only John Toland's *Christianity not Mysterious* (considered to be a Socinian work) but also the Whig Bishop of Salisbury Gilbert Burnet's *Exposition of the Thirty-Nine Articles*. The lower House attempted, unsuccessfully, to have these books condemned as part of the High Church campaign against what they saw as heretical views inside the Church of England. This attitude was behind the 1698 Blasphemy Act, passed due to what was said to be the need to suppress 'pernicious books and pamphlets' containing 'impious doctrines against the Holy Trinity, and other fundamental articles of our faith',[4] by which they meant Socinianism and Unitarianism. Offences were to be punished with fines and imprisonment, sanctions which were apparently rarely applied. The latitudinarian Archbishop of Canterbury Thomas Tenison (the bête noire of the High Church clergymen) – who had in fact proposed a Bill against blasphemy directed more against atheism than antitrinitarianism, but who hesitated to act against books seen as heterodox – said he preferred prior 'restraint of the press' (preliminary censorship) but had not succeeded in getting his Bills to this effect passed.[5] Tenison himself was the object of violent vilification from the High Church faction, who accused him of Socinianism, deism and even atheism. His concern to repress atheism rather than Socinianism, which may have encouraged such accusations, was perhaps also a reaction to the latter, by showing where the main enemies were.

It was in this context that a pamphlet attributed to the free-thinker John Toland was published in 1698 condemning censorship and defending a free press. Its arguments concerning the need for freedom to search for the truth in religion and to follow God-given reason largely echo those of Milton, which leads the author to conclude:

> that Men, if they regard the employing their rational Faculties as God requires, and (the Consequence of it) the discovery of Truth in Religion, and their being influenced by it as they ought to be are obliged to allow one another an entire liberty in communicating their Thoughts, which was never forbidden but where Interest supplanted Religion.[6]

The pamphlet also reflects the Whig hostility to 'priestcraft' and the excessive power of the clergy of all denominations; the author writes: 'The Discovery of Printing seems to have been design'd by Providence to free Men from that Tyranny of the Clergy they then groan'd under.'[7] But he also points out the *political* dangers of restraint of the press:

> 'tis no wonder if all that make an ill use of their Power, especially those who have cheated the Government as well as abused the People, do endeavor with all their might to have the Press regulated, lest their Crimes being exposed in Print, may not only render them odious to the People, but to the Government. In a word, all sorts of Men whose interest it is not to have their Actions exposed to the Publick (which I am afraid are no small number) will be for restraining the Press, and perhaps will add Iniquity to Iniquity, by pretending they do it out of Conscience to suppress Immorality and Profaneness.[8]

At the same time, an arbitrary ruler will want censorship, as the press would be used to extend his power 'and to extol the Promoters of Arbitrary Power as the chief Patriots of their Country, and to expose and traduce those that were really so'.[9] The author provided examples from the past to support his argument. He was therefore defending the right to seek the truth by exercising one's reason, but also opposing attempts, whether by factions (in this period when party division ran deep) or authoritarian rulers, to impose their truth or to hide inconvenient truths.

Despite frequent High Church demands to proceed against immoral and irreligious works, prior censorship was not re-established. This does not mean, as we have seen, that there were no laws establishing what could and could not be said or printed (as in the Blasphemy Act). Occasionally there were even proceedings against individual publications, which were condemned to be burnt, and sometimes their authors were even imprisoned; this was what happened to Alberto Radicati di Passerano, who was briefly imprisoned, together with his translator and bookseller, for publishing *A Philosophical Dissertation on Death* in 1732.[10] Such cases reveal the continuing worries of churchmen in particular about the freedom of both subject and tone in published works.

Due to this liberty and the absence of prior censorship, England was the example for writers elsewhere, and particularly in France, of a free country enjoying freedom of speech and of the press, despite the public condemnation of defamatory and subversive pamphlets. As the Academician abbé Jean-Paul Bignon wrote from Paris to the Huguenot exile and hub of the republic of letters, Pierre Des Maizeaux, in London, in 1711:

> We live in a country in which licence does not predominate as in some of our neighbours. Authors' whims or passions are not given freedom to spread among the public whatever they like. We are careful to prevent printers putting into the hands of impressionable and unruly people anything that might hurt the principles of faith, moral teaching, the laws of the state or individual reputations.[11]

Interestingly, this letter concerned the publication not of an irreligious work but of the poet Boileau's *Satire des équivoques*, and the problem was one of morality.

Des Maizeaux was a leading member of the network of exiled Huguenot journalists, translators and booksellers who were responsible for publishing, mainly in the Dutch republic, many works that were then smuggled into France, where there was strict censorship despite the practice of 'permissions tacites' (which basically meant that the authorities guaranteed that they would close their eyes and not act against certain publications, which did not, however, have official permission). Among the translated works were not only free-thinking or 'philosophical' texts but also tracts by latitudinarian theologians. The freedom enjoyed in the Dutch republic was proverbial, but had its limitations, as the official church did keep a wary eye, and printers and editors of journals exercised some self-censorship to avoid giving offence to the theologians. The editor of the *Nouvelles de la république des lettres*, Jean-François Bernard, wrote to Des Maizeaux from the Dutch republic in 1700, to say that he could not use the latter's extract from Gilbert Burnet's book (the one that the High Church wanted to have banned in England):

> We dare not speak in this country as one can where you are, and it is very probable that after such an extract I would never publish another,[12]

and later:

> We live in a country where we are not as libertine as you are in England, so I beg you to be careful not to include innocently in the news you write for me anything that, if I used it, might cause me problems.[13]

According to the theologian and journalist Jean Le Clerc in Amsterdam,

> Here the theologians are as violent and ignorant as they have always been. Those who govern are afraid of them and care for neither truth nor virtue, but only want to take advantage of their offices and advance their families.[14]

Thus the bookseller du Sauzet hesitated to publish a translation of Anthony Collins's *Philosophical Inquiry concerning Human Liberty* in 1717 for fear of the theologians' reaction to an irreligious work, explaining 'I must not antagonize those gentlemen'.[15] Michel de La Roche, another Huguenot who settled in London and edited periodicals in both French and English, was removed from the direction of the journal he had founded, *La Bibliothèque angloise*, by its publisher Marret, because he had criticised the Dutch Calvinist church as much as the Catholics. He was therefore accused of being a heretic.[16] In his journals La Roche condemned intolerance and violent language from whatever quarter, and he defended the expression of all views, refusing to toe any party line. Without the freedom of thought and expression, he writes, truth is impossible.[17]

It would be a mistake to believe that these writers' demands for total freedom to publish, based on the argument that freedom of expression was vital in order to discover the truth, meant that they were necessarily 'libertines' or irreligious. It was often because they themselves were the victims of an intolerant church and state. Which does not mean that the same arguments were not also used with those who had a different agenda. When Locke's friend the English free-thinker Anthony Collins published in 1713 his *Discourse of Free Thinking*, in which he adopted the Protestant argument concerning the need to think freely in order to discover the truth, his aim was to defend a much more sweeping freedom of thought, questioning any religious doctrine. The truth here was not revealed truth but the truth discovered by reason, truth about the world. As a result, the expressions 'free-thinker' and 'free-thinking' became synonymous in both England and France with irreligion. Collins's basic argument was:

> if the Knowledge of some Truths be requir'd of us by God: if the Knowledge of others be useful to Society; if the Knowledge of no Truth be forbidden us by God, or hurtful to us; then we have a *right* to know, or may lawfully know, any Truth whatsoever. And if we have a *right* to know any Truth whatsoever, we have a *right to think freely* ... because there is no other way to discover the Truth.[18]

This implied of course an honest search for truth, and supposed that both the authors and the readers should be using their God-given reason in this honest search. This in turn had implications both for the arguments used to defend the freedom of speech and for reflection on its possible limitation.

LIMITING THE FREEDOM OF SPEECH

These were questions broached by Voltaire in his *Lettres anglaises*, better known as *Lettres philosophiques*, which lavishly praises English toleration and freedom of the press. In the famous thirteenth Letter, on Locke (also called 'On the soul'), he insists that public disorder is not caused by philosophers writing freely (the list of names he provides – Montaigne, Locke, Bayle, Spinoza, Hobbes, Lord Shaftesbury, Collins, Toland – includes free-thinkers); but this is to a large extent because 'their writings are not calculated for the Vulgar, and they themselves are free from Enthusiasm'.[19] The danger comes from theologians and religious fanatics or 'enthusiasts', not thinkers. This is therefore a defence of the freedom for philosophers to seek the truth and publish arguments and truths which go against established doctrine, particularly that of the church. It is in fact a defence of the intellectual elite, who should be free to express their opinions and unauthorised truths, which have no effect on the uneducated masses who cannot understand them; disinterested thinkers who follow their reason are not dangerous and need to be free. Thus the defence of free speech founded on the need to seek the truth entails its limitation to those who are capable of exercising their reason in this search, and this excludes the mass of the population. This elite attitude is famously expressed in a remark attributed to Fontenelle that if his hand were full of truths he would certainly not open it ('s'il avait la main pleine de vérités, il se garderait bien de l'ouvrir').[20]

A long discussion defending precisely the freedom of speech or publication on the basis of the limited probable audience is found in Julien Offray de La Mettrie's presentation of his scandalous atheistic and materialistic writings, placed at the beginning of his *Oeuvres philosophiques* published in Berlin in 1750; this defence was made necessary by his dependence on the favour of Frederick II of Prussia, whose laxity concerning the Frenchmen at his court was under attack.[21] La Mettrie himself had already had to leave France after the condemnation of his *Histoire naturelle de l'âme* (1745) and then to flee the Dutch republic because *L'Homme machine* (1747) was condemned by the authorities. He distinguishes the sphere of philosophy from that of politics and religion, and quotes Voltaire, insisting that the arguments of philosophers are so far above the heads of ordinary people that they could not possibly have an effect on the people's behaviour, or undermine religion and society. Interestingly, a similar limitation is found in the defence of freedom of the press published by the Huguenot bookseller Elie Luzac after he had been attacked for publishing La Mettrie's *Homme machine*, despite the fact that his *Essai sur la liberté de produire ses sentiments* (1749) went much further in defence of the freedom of the press than most contemporary works on the subject.[22] La Mettrie also appeals to rulers to encourage philosophy, and defends the need for philosophers to publish freely what they consider to be the truth, as he had done, whatever the consequences; he writes: 'Let us be free in our writings as in our behaviour; let us show the proud independence of republicans ... A philosopher must write with noble daring or expect to crawl like those who are not philosophers.'[23]

La Mettrie cites with approval a 'jeune et célèbre savant' – by which he means Denis Diderot – who had recently ended up in a dungeon in Vincennes for publishing the *Lettre sur les aveugles*. As a result of this unpleasant experience, Diderot kept to his promise not to publish openly subversive works, contenting himself with allusions or more often satire and humour. He was mainly writing for the intellectual elite and those in the know, and indeed his most daring works were known only to a small circle, being published sometimes long after his death. However, his belief in the need to educate and inform more widely is obvious from the huge amount of time he devoted to editing the *Encyclopédie*, in which he managed to include subversive ideas, although in a way that was probably obvious only to the more intellectual readers. The *Encyclopédie* is in fact an expression of the belief in the need to publish the truth, even if it was often in a hidden way; in fact, the diversity of voices found within the work needs careful deciphering. On occasion, however, Diderot went too far, and the printer of the later volumes that appeared (dated 1765) after the first interruption of publication due to the banning of the work, censored his text by removing certain passages considered dangerous. Thus, in the article PYRRHONIENS, a long passage on Bayle was removed. Here Diderot had defended the publication of the truth, however dangerous it seemed to be:

> if all truths cannot be told, it can only be the result of bad laws, by an inappropriate linkage between the political system and the religious system. Wherever the civil power supports religion or seeks support in religion, the progress of reason will be necessarily delayed and there will be useless persecution, because minds can never be effectively constrained, and toleration will be non-existent or limited; these two suppositions are almost equally unwelcome ... Truth, whatever it is, if harmful for the moment, is necessarily useful in the future. A lie, whatever it is, if perhaps advantageous for the moment, is necessarily harmful in the long term.[24]

However, in the same volume of the *Encyclopédie*, Jaucourt did manage to publish an uncompromising defence of the freedom of the press and its lack of danger for the government, but using slightly different arguments. For him the freedom of the press was vital:

> It is of the greatest importance to preserve this use in all states founded on liberty; I would go even further: the disadvantages of this liberty are so small compared to

its advantages that it should be the common law of the universe and it is suitable to authorise it under all governments.[25]

He claims that unlike unrestrained speech, which can incite riots, a man reading alone at home will not be moved to violent action; according to him, it is more dangerous to forbid printing, as this will encourage rumours, much more likely to foment sedition, including 'in countries where people are not used to thinking aloud and distinguishing truth from falsehood'. He refers to the liberty in Britain, which is based on the freedom of the press.

So Jaucourt differentiates here between printing and speech; the latter seems more dangerous as it is directed at a wider public. We see here a fainter echo of the suspicion voiced by Voltaire and La Mettrie of the ordinary uneducated people who are variously incapable of understanding the truth or are moved by passions excited by unscrupulous people, often using religion. For Jaucourt, the person who is not dangerous is the individual 'dans son cabinet', in other words probably a man and once again a member of the intellectual elite reading in his study (this idea is probably taken from David Hume). But there is also implied the distinction between freedom of thinking and reading, and actions, such as speech, which incite to behaviour such as riots and sedition. I shall come back to this distinction below. For the moment, it is clear that Jaucourt believes that freedom of the press will enable more people to distinguish truth from falsehood.

A similar view was expressed around the same time by Claude-Adrien Helvétius in his *De l'esprit*, published with official permission but then condemned for irreligion; as a result of the scandal created, his subsequent *De l'homme* was published only posthumously. In the Preface to *De l'esprit*, Helvétius also insists that the truth is useful to humans and that it is often discovered by daring speculation; echoing Milton's argument about the usefulness of error, he claims that we should not be afraid to make mistakes in the search for truth. He continues:

> In vain will vile cowardly men want to proscribe it and sometimes give it the odious name of licentiousness; in vain do they repeat that truths are often dangerous. Supposing that they were sometimes dangerous, what greater danger would a nation not risk if it agreed to stagnate in ignorance? ... From the very moment the knowledge of some truths was forbidden, it would no longer be allowed to utter any truth. A thousand powerful and often even evil people would ban it entirely from the universe on the pretext that it is sometimes wise not to speak the truth.[26]

Once again, the freedom of speech is based on the need to discover the truth, without which no progress is possible and humans cannot realise their potential; but, unlike Voltaire, Helvétius claims that it is for everyone without exception.

This supposes that people are reasonable and will use this freedom responsibly if they are educated to do so; and Helvétius insists on the importance of education, including for women. However, many thinkers were aware that this was not always the case. There was thus an important discussion to be had about licentious or untruthful works, or those written by the ignorant – who were the first to want to publish, as Spinoza wryly remarked after his *Theological-Political Treatise*, which defended freedom of speech, had attracted criticism.[27] Such works cannot be defended on the basis that they help to discover the truth, however one defines it. Thus there was widespread hostility towards scurrilous works whose purpose was simply to attack or defame other people and which spread lies. Pierre Bayle, who defended toleration and the freedom of speech vigorously and believed in a Republic of Letters governed by truth and reason, limited freedom of the press to those defending truth. While he accepted the validity of criticism denouncing errors in the works of others, he approved censorship of satires, lampoons and defamatory pamphlets attacking both the government and individuals. Satires 'tendent à dépouiller un homme de son honneur, ce qui est une espèce d'homicide civil' (tend to deprive a man of his honour, which is a sort of civil homicide), and such an author 'hides, in order not to be obliged to prove what he publishes and to be able to do harm without taking responsibility for it'.[28] In his essay against 'libelles diffamatoires', he says they can destroy the honour and reputation of whole families, based on 'the smallest suspicions, rumours, and inn and barrack-room gossip'.[29] Bayle thus makes a clear distinction between the freedom of thought and expression in the pursuit of truth, and personal attacks and satires which spread lies and discredit blameless individuals.[30] These must be punished (at least in the case of calumny), although Bayle hesitates between admitting the intervention of the state authorities and leaving it up to the tribunal of the Republic of Letters.[31]

In a similar vein, the 1698 pamphlet attributed to John Toland claimed that those who published or spoke from the pulpit 'Atheism, Profaneness, and Immorality, as well as Sedition and Treason' should be punished as they are dangerous to society. This was no reason to introduce censorship in advance, but the author did not believe that one could allow anything to be published with impunity. As for pamphlets, he claimed that it was enough to make printers or booksellers put their names on them, which would prevent people publishing such books.[32] Here he is explicitly not only condemning personal attacks, satires and immorality but also apparently denying that those who defend atheism could be motivated by a sincere search for the truth. It is difficult to know how to interpret this, if it is indeed by Toland, as his own views are not always easy to decipher and was himself accused of spreading atheism.[33]

The same argument was made by Daniel Defoe, who strenuously opposed prior censorship but at the same time called for a regulation of the press 'to restrain the licentious extravagance of authors' and works 'tending to Atheism, Heresie, and Irreligion', some of which he named; his list included authors who had recently contested certain doctrines of the Church of England, but who can plausibly be said to have been sincerely seeking the truth and providing reasoned arguments.[34] Defoe stated clearly that 'Licentiousness of all sorts ought to be Restrain'd whether of the Tongue, the Pen, the Press or any thing else',[35] but to prevent publication by means of prior licensing would put arbitrary power in the hands of a few and decide who (in other words, which party) had the right to speak and who did not. Instead, the limitations on what can be defended or criticised should be clearly indicated by law and the punishments specified for those who knowingly break this law. Here we can see the effects of Defoe's own unhappy experience. His position seems driven more by a concern to guard against arbitrary punishment for publication (to which he felt he had been subjected) than a defence of complete freedom of speech.

These examples show the difficulty, in the early eighteenth century as today, of defending total freedom of the press. There seems to have been a general acceptance that certain works, not only scurrilous pamphlets but also those arguing against doctrinal 'truths' proclaimed by the official church, should not be published with impunity, and that those who infringed the law should be punished. But the consensus in Britain was also against prior censorship; hence the press freedom enjoyed in Britain that was admired by many others, as we have seen. As David Hume wrote in 1742:

> Nothing is more apt to surprise a foreigner, than the extreme liberty, which we enjoy in this country, of communicating whatever we please to the public, and of openly censuring every measure, entered into by the king or his ministers.[36]

And he considered this liberty to criticise the government to be a 'common right of mankind', claiming that the mass of ordinary people can be governed like rational creatures.[37] However, not everyone, as we have seen, was so sanguine, and later Hume himself came to consider the 'unbounded liberty of the press' as an 'evil'.[38]

It is interesting to note that the deistic free-thinker the marquis d'Argens, who criticised the restraint on free-thinking and the freedom of the press exercised by the Catholic Church and press censorship in France, considered also that the authorities should exercise some sort of restraint on the scurrilous press. He put in the mouth of one of his imaginary Jewish travellers a criticism of the bad authors in Amsterdam who are destroying good taste and human understanding, and the excessive freedom given to them by the authorities:

> In Paris they prevent a book from being printed because it does not spare the court of Rome, because it speaks too freely about indulgences, because it says that Arnaud was a great man. What! surely it is more essential to stop the circulation of thirty writings which ruin taste, destroy good sense and offend reason?[39]

One of the few whose defence of the freedom of the press included allowing scurrilous pamphlets and lampoons was Louis de Jaucourt in his *Encyclopédie* article 'LIBELLE (*Gouvern. politiq.*)'. While echoing Bayle and using some of the same examples, Jaucourt's position is not the same, and it is not clear that he is restricting his remarks to Bayle's Republic of Letters. He defends complete liberty, arguing that restriction is more dangerous than the abuse some people make of it. He refers specifically to the practice across the Channel:

> In enlightened monarchies, lampoons are seen less as a crime than as an object of police. The English leave them to their fate and see them as a disadvantage of a free government which it is not in the nature of human affairs to avoid. They think one should allow, not the unbridled licence of satire, but the freedom of speech and writing, as guarantees of a state's civil and political freedom, because it is less dangerous for a few honourable people to be unfortunately libelled than if people did not dare enlighten their country about the behaviour of powerful people in positions of authority.[40]

According to him, when the behaviour of those who govern gives no occasion for criticism, then they have nothing to fear from calumny and lies. Honest people follow virtue and despise calumny. As for opinions rather than calumny:

> Lampoons are even less dangerous in relation to speculative opinions. Truth is so powerfully victorious over error! Once she shows herself she attracts esteem and admiration. We see her every day destroying the chains of fraud and tyranny or breaking through the clouds of superstition and ignorance. What could she not do if we removed all the barriers to her progress![41]

This article represents a conviction that the truth will show through, and that lies and superstition will be ignored. Here again the underlying belief seems to be in the reasonable nature of humans, who will naturally accept the truth when it is expressed. This does not mean that calumny should go unpunished but this should be done by wise laws which do not destroy liberty – although Jaucourt also quotes Helvétius's claim that flattery can be more dangerous for a prince than a scurrilous pamphlet, which may bring a tyrant back to the path of virtue. But even Helvétius admitted that most people, being lazy, prefer ideas similar to those they already know and that it is difficult for new truths to be accepted.[42]

Which brings us to the question of publishing 'lies' (or alternative facts). Helvétius's opinion seems more realistic than that of Jaucourt, who claimed, as we have just seen, that truth always overcomes error and that, presumably, 'new truths' would be recognised for what they are. A similar scepticism to that of Helvétius about recognition of the truth had been expressed in a different way by Anthony Collins in the preface to his *Discourse of Free Thinking*. He admitted his despair that those who denied self-evident truths (in this case the right to free-thinking) could ever agree to be informed or open to reason: they must have principles 'inconsistent with the Principles of knowledge, and consistent with the greatest absurdities. And under that distemper'd state of mind, it remains only for them to take up with some disorder'd fancies of their own; or which is much more common, with the dictates of artificial designing men or crack brain'd enthusiasts.'[43] Unreason, fanaticism or credulous acceptance of lies spread by dishonest people are difficult to overcome.

But there is another aspect of Jaucourt's defence of unrestricted freedom of the press that I would like to highlight here. His argument in favour of it is based not on the need to seek the truth but on the claim that free speech is a vital aspect of a free government and the basis of civil and political liberty. He writes in his article 'LIBELLE', 'In general, any country in which it is forbidden to think and write what one thinks must necessarily fall into stupidity, superstition and barbarism'.[44] The same argument was, as we have seen earlier, used in his article on the press. This emphasis on freedom of thought and the press as the basis of a free state and society had been found much earlier in Spinoza's defence of the freedom of speech in the last chapter of his *Tractatus Theologico-politicus*. Spinoza's argument is based not on Milton's postulate of the need to seek the truth but on natural right. For Spinoza 'it is impossible to deprive men of the liberty of saying what they think' and it is 'destructive of the common good of the republic' to try to limit it.[45] The state can punish only opinions that imply an action against the foundation of the state; here he is making a distinction between thought and action, which seems to lie behind Jaucourt's distinction between freedom of the press and that of speech in his *Encyclopédie* article 'PRESSE' quoted above. Like Spinoza, Jaucourt apparently has no illusions about the ease with which unscrupulous (for Spinoza often religious) people can incite the uneducated to action by inflammatory speech. This led Spinoza to use an elitist argument similar to that invoked later by Voltaire (seen above), namely that the intolerant who stir up the uneducated people against writers are more dangerous than the authors themselves, who write mainly for the learned and appeal only to reason. Like Spinoza, Jaucourt nevertheless defends the unlimited freedom of the press and of the use of reason, and he has a much more optimistic view concerning the victory of the truth.

CONCLUSION

What conclusions can we draw from this admittedly partial but, I believe, representative review of the opinions of eighteenth-century British and French defenders of the freedom to seek and speak the truth? Firstly, despite the differences in the arguments, all these authors share an underlying belief that for those who sincerely seek the truth – understood generally not as religious truth, or God's revealed word, but as an objective entity discoverable by reason – freedom of the press should in no way be curtailed, and that attempts to censor it can result only in evils for society and hand the power over to arbitrary government. For society to progress, freedom of both thought and expression is vital. But these authors accept in general a certain number of limitations. The first concerns the type of expression. The danger of freedom of expression is generally seen to come from rabble-rousers or fanatics, who can stir up the uneducated people and endanger society, and from unscrupulous peddlers of lies and calumny. Such people should therefore not be able to publish with impunity, which means, in general, not that they should be censored but that they should be punished for breaking the law, although here it is not clear whether the punishment should come from state authorities or public opinion. This limitation implies a distinction, not always formally developed, on the one hand between speech and print, and, on the other, between reasoned works seeking the truth and lampoons and libels. Speech is often seen as more dangerous because it can be used to stir up ordinary uneducated people and appeal to their emotions rather than their reason, whereas print is directed towards the educated élite, ideally scholars in their studies, who know how to use their reason. As for lampoons and libels, those who defend opinions contrary to the accepted orthodoxy are above all keen to dissociate themselves from the authors of such unacceptable scurrilous works.

But there is also uncertainty about arguments which go against doctrinal 'truths', in particular arguments seen to be defending 'atheism', an accusation that could cover a variety of heterodox opinions and not necessarily strict denial of the existence of the divinity. Even in Britain there were few in the early eighteenth century who openly countenanced such publications, as these writings were thought to undermine society and government. So, while the unfettered search for truth by the use of reason is an ideal, in practice most people are more hesitant.

The second question, inherent in the distinction between speech and print, as we have seen, concerns the public to which these writings are addressed. The claim that no printed opinions are dangerous often depends on the assertion that they are read only by reasonable educated people. Many believe that the majority do not use their reason, either because they are incapable of it (an opinion that contradicts the claim that reason is a gift of God to all or the Cartesian statement about common sense) or because they have not been educated to do so. Thus, behind even the broad claims for the freedom of speech there is nearly always an overt or implied restriction of its extent and the target readership, and an assumption that the argument concerns the educated elite, not the mass of the people. This again reveals the underlying tension between arguments about the freedom to seek the truth and recognition that certain opinions cannot be circulated without restrictions and must be punished. It is thus the commitment to the truth which is behind these limitations: on the one hand, works which are not committed to an impartial search for truth do not in general (despite a few exceptions) merit impunity; on the other, people who are incapable (whether congenitally or through lack of education) of using their reason in this impartial search are excluded from this conversation. It is therefore interesting to note that the few defences of completely unrestricted freedom of the press that we have seen abandon the argument based on the need for the individual to seek the truth and ground it in rights and/or the interest of society and the state.

The fragility of arguments for the freedom of speech is clear, particularly when a large part of the public is unable to use its reason to distinguish truth from lies. We are, I think, today far from the certainty about the truth that characterised its eighteenth-century defenders. The belief that the truth existed and could be discovered, and that it was vital for society, is expressed in the passage removed from the *Encyclopédie* article 'PYRRHONIENS':

> It is ignorance and lies that cause trouble amongst men; ignorance which confuses everything, is against everything, which makes one neither reject nor choose; lies which are never firmly enough established in people's minds for them not to be suspected, disturbed, contested; man is only at peace with the truth.[46]

We are left with the unresolved question of who can decide on the truth when it is contested. The tribunal of the Republic of Letters or public opinion implies a domain in which truth can be demonstrated to reasonable people. Once the truth is a contested notion, in which 'alternative truths' vie for a hearing and reason does not prevail, the decision rests with the more powerful. Secondly, deriving from the first question, is the problem of how to police a public space in which each individual can give free rein to his or her passions, spleen or desire to do mischief or, in eighteenth-century language, 'licentiousness'. As we have seen, even the defenders of unrestricted freedom of the press agreed that thought or speech which implied or incited action subversive of the foundations of society or the state should not go unpunished. Similar arguments are currently being voiced in reaction to the excesses of social media. It is doubtless time to revisit the basis for arguments in defence of free speech.

NOTES

1 See C. Walton, *Policing Public Opinion in the French Revolution* (Oxford, 2009).
2 On the background to this, see E. Tortarolo, *The Invention of Free Press* (Dordrecht, 2016), 25–33.
3 Humphrey Prideaux to his sister, 21 August 1692, HMC, *Fifth Report* (1876), 376.
4 *Journals of the House of Commons*, XII, 102–3.
5 LPL, MSS Conv., Proceedings of the Lower House 1/2/5A, fol. 296; Proceedings of Upper House 1/1/13, fol. 38.
6 [J. Toland,] *Letter to a Member of Parliament showing, that a Restraint on the Press is inconsistent with the Protestant Religion, and dangerous to the Liberties of the Nation* (1698), 9.
7 Ibid., 22.
8 Ibid., 25
9 Ibid., 26.

10 See F. Venturi, *Saggi sull'Europa illuminista I: Alberto Radicati di Passerano* (Turin, 1954), 209–15.
11 BL, Add. MS 4281, fol. 215v: 14 juin 1711.
12 Ibid., fol. 82.
13 Ibid., fol. 86.
14 Le Clerc to J. Turretini in Geneva, 5 June 1710 (J. Le Clerc, *Epistolario*, ed. M. Grazia and M. Sina (Florence, 1994), III, 275).
15 BL, Add. MS 4287, fol. 350.
16 *Mémoires littéraires de la Grande-Bretagne*, 16 (1724), 337ff.
17 Ibid., 2 (1720), 495. See A. Thomson, 'In Defence of Toleration. La Roche's *Bibliothèque angloise* and *Mémoires littéraires de la Grande-Bretagne*', in A. Thomson, S. Burrows and E. Dziembowski (eds), *Cultural Transfers: France and Britain in the Long Eighteenth Century* (Oxford, 2010), 161–74.
18 *A Discourse of Free Thinking, Occasion'd by the Rise and Growth of a Sect called Free Thinkers* (1713), 5. On Jonathan Swift's reactions to this argument, see David Womersley, Chapter 6 above.
19 *Letters concerning the English Nation* (1733), 107.
20 See R. Mortier, *Clartés et ombres du siècle des Lumières* (Geneva, 1969), 63–9.
21 A. Thomson, *Materialism and Society in the Mid-eighteenth Century* (Geneva, 1981), 12–15.
22 See W. Velema, 'Introduction to Elie Luzac, *An Address on Freedom of Expression* (1749)', in J. Laursen and J. van der Zande (eds), *Early French and German Defenses of the Freedom of the Press* (Leiden, 2003), 11–33.
23 J. La Mettrie, *Machine Man and Other Writings*, ed. A. Thomson (Cambridge, 1996), 171.
24 D. Gordon and N. Torrey, *The Censoring of Diderot's* Encyclopédie *and the Re-established Text* (New York, 1947), 76–7.
25 'PRESSE (*Droit polit.*)', in *Encyclopédie, ou Dictionnaire raisonné des sciences, des arts et des métiers* (Neufchâtel, 1765), XIII, 320.
26 *De l'esprit* (Paris, 1758), v.
27 Letter to Jelles, quoted in W. Klever, 'Spinoza's Life and Works', in G. Lloyd (ed.), *Spinoza. Critical Assessments* (2001), I, 30.
28 P. Bayle, *Dictionnaire historique et critique* (Amsterdam, Leiden, The Hague, Utrecht, 1740), art. 'Catius', Rem. D (II, 102); see Mara Van der Lugt, *Bayle, Jurieu, and the Dictionnaire historique et critique* (Oxford, 2016), 80.
29 'Dissertation sur les libelles diffamatoires', *Dictionnaire historique*, IV, 580–1.
30 See Van der Lugt, *Bayle*, 97–102 (which also discusses Bayle's earlier 'Digression concernant les libelles diffamatoires').
31 Ibid., 110–14. Similarly, Elie Luzac excluded from his defence of the free press 'des romans, des Libelles, et autres productions de cette nature', *Essai sur la liberté de produire ses sentiments* ('Au pays libre, pour le Bien public' [Leiden], 1749), 9.
32 [Toland,] *Letter*, 18.
33 For one interpretation, see T. Dagron, 'Toland and the Censorship of Atheism', in M. Laerke (ed.), *The Use of Censorship in the Enlightenment* (Leiden, 2009), 137–53.
34 *An Essay on the Regulation of the Press* (1704), 3–4. He mentions Asgil, Coward, '___ against the Trinity' and Burnet's *Sacred Theory of the Earth*.
35 Ibid., 11.

36 D. Hume, 'Of the Liberty of the Press', in Hume, *Political Essays*, ed. K. Haakonssen (Cambridge, 1994), 1.
37 This was the version in the first editions of the essay, removed in 1777; see *Political Essays*, 261–2.
38 Ibid., 3.
39 D'Argens, *Lettres juives* (The Hague, 1737), IV, 84.
40 *Encyclopédie*, IX, 459.
41 Ibid., 460.
42 See Helvétius, *De l'esprit*, 78–9; 68.
43 Collins, *Discourse of Free Thinking*, 3–4.
44 *Encyclopédie*, IX, 459.
45 Spinoza, *Theological-Political Treatise*, ed. J. Israel (Cambridge, 2007), 258–9. See J. Steinberg, 'Spinoza's Curious Defense of Toleration', in Y. Melamed and M. Rosenthal (eds), *Spinoza's Theological-Political Treatise* (Cambridge, 2010), 210–30; M. Rosenthal, 'Spinoza's Republican Argument for Toleration', *Journal of Political Philosophy* 11 (2003), 320–37.
46 Gordon and Torrey, *The Censoring of Diderot's* Encyclopédie, 77.

Chapter 8

'The warr ... against heaven by blasphemors and infidels': prosecuting heresy in Enlightenment England

Robert G. Ingram and Alex W. Barber

On Saturday 29 April 1721, George Verney, Dean of Windsor and Lord Willoughby of Broke, presented in the House of Lords a 'Bill for the more effectual suppressing of Blasphemy and Profaneness'.[1] That bill replicated the title of a 1698 piece of legislation commonly referred to as the Blasphemy Act (9 William c. 35); indeed, it addressed problems that many saw in that earlier legislation.[2] The 1698 act's preamble contended that 'many Persons have of late Years openly and avowedly published many blasphemous and impious Opinions contrary to the Doctrines, and Principles of the Christian Religion'. After the Restoration, judges identified blasphemy as a common-law crime, where once it had been the preserve of church courts.[3] In *Rex* v. *Taylor* (1676), Matthew Hale famously held that 'wicked and blasphemous words were not only an offence to God and religion, but a crime against the laws, State and Government and therefore punishable in this court'. The reason for this was that 'to say religion is a cheat, is to dissolve all those obligations whereby the civil societies are preserved, and that Christianity is a parcel of the laws of England; and therefore to reproach the Christian religion is to speak in subversion of the law'.[4] The civil magistrate needed to suppress blasphemy to preserve the civil peace. As Hale explained it, 'the reasonableness and indeed necessity of this coercion in matters of religion is apparent for the concerns of religion and the civil state are so twisted with one another that confusion and disorder an[d] anarchy in the former must necessarily introduce confusion and dissolution in the latter'.[5] What legally constituted blasphemy resisted precise definition, though the courts judged it to involve heterodox expressions regarding or attacks against God, the Bible or religion more generally.[6] But Hale and other judges were explicit that public expressions of blasphemy threatened the civil order.

In the 1698 Blasphemy Act, the English Parliament legislated what constituted 'blasphemous and impious Opinions'. In particular, Parliament proscribed public attempts to 'deny any one of the Persons in the Holy Trinity to be God or ... assert or maintain there to be more Gods than One or ... deny the Christian Religion to be true or the Holy Scriptures of the Old and New Testament to be of Divine Authority'. These propositions concerned truth's content (the nature of the Christian God) and truth's foundation (the revealed sources of Christian belief). Professing legally proscribed untruths ran one afoul of the civil authorities, for those found guilty of 'writing, printing, teaching or advised speaking' them were barred from any 'Ecclesiastical, Civil or Military' employment. Second offences merited three years' imprisonment. Safeguards ensured that the new law was not used to settle old scores. None the less, the fact remained that the 1698 Parliament legislated what was and was not true and imposed civil penalties upon those convicted of writing, publishing or teaching what it had deemed to be untrue. Why? Here the act was unambiguously clear and parroted Hale's *Rex* v. *Taylor* rationale: blasphemy 'greatly tend[ed] to the Dishonour of Almighty God and may prove distructive to the Peace and Welfare of this Kingdom'. Truth was worth protecting not simply because it was true but because untruth threatened the civil peace.[7] Truth's fate and the state's fate were, then, bound up together.

In 1698, anti-blasphemy legislation passed into law; in 1721, it did not. In 1698, a decided parliamentary majority supported legally defining blasphemy and prosecuting blasphemers in civil courts; in 1721, two-thirds of the Lords – and more bishops than not – refused to accept a more precise definition of blasphemy or a more expansive prosecution of blasphemers and their publishers. Explanations for the 1721 bill's failure to pass into law differ. Some cite declining zeal for moral reform.[8] Others reckon that the 1721 bill's supporters made a Cnut-like attempt to turn back the liberalising and secularising tide of history.[9] Others adduce the weakening hold of providence as an explanation for the bill's parliamentary defeat.[10] Still others contend that the nation's political class actually remained interested in moral reform into the 1720s and 1730s, but the Whig schism of the late 1710s and early 1720s 'prevented parliamentary action against sin'.[11]

This chapter offers a fuller explanation. More importantly than simply explaining why Parliament successfully scuttled the 1721 Blasphemy Bill, though, it uses the rich evidence regarding the bill's parliamentary failure to consider how early Georgian England differed from late Williamite England regarding freedom of speech in general and freedom of religious speech more particularly. So, what had changed between 1698 and 1721? Parliament's resolute determination to maintain the civil peace had not. What had changed, instead, was what most in Parliament thought constituted civil peace; what most in Parliament thought threatened civil peace; and what most in Parliament thought should be done to deal with perceived threats to civil peace. Moreover, what had changed in the two decades after the Blasphemy Act's passage in 1698 was that the established church itself was riven even more deeply not simply about how to deal with public expressions of untruth but about what even constituted truth and untruth. Indeed,

'The warr ... against heaven by blasphemors and infidels'

one of the striking things about the 1721 Blasphemy Bill was that some of its chief opponents were clerics; were clerics who believed that heresy and blasphemy were real; were clerics who believed that early eighteenth-century England abounded with heretics and blasphemers; and were clerics who would later prove willing to act on that belief. And yet they voted down a piece of legislation that promised to punish heretics and blasphemers. Put another way, they voted against the Blasphemy Bill not because they thought heretics and blasphemers did not need restraining but because they thought they should be restrained only under certain conditions. Principled support of free speech did not drive clerical opposition to the bill; something else did.

The 1721 Blasphemy Bill had three architects: Thomas Trevor, Baron Trevor; Daniel Finch, Earl of Nottingham; and William Wake, Archbishop of Canterbury. Trevor, a lawyer, had begun his parliamentary life in 1692 as a reliable Court Whig before drifting into the moderate Tory orbit by the end of the decade. Raised to the peerage in 1711 as part of Harley's Lords-packing scheme, he none the less was courted by the Whigs in 1717 and again in 1721 to come into the government.[12] Trevor drafted the Blasphemy Bill, a measure for which he was 'very zealous'.[13] Nottingham insisted that he was for 'Things, and Propositions, not men and Parties'; and the things and propositions he supported above all were the established Church of England and the Crown. So, during the 1680s when it looked as if Roman Catholics might pose the greatest threat to the church, Nottingham pressed schemes for toleration and comprehension of Protestant dissenters.[14] When, in turn, it seemed to him during the early 1700s that Protestant dissenters most put the 'Church in danger', he supported legislation to ban occasional conformity.[15] After the Hanoverian succession, the Tory Nottingham involved himself less in parliamentary affairs, but still concerned himself with religious debates and refused to 'concur in any measures ... destructive of our Constitution in Church and State'.[16] By the early 1720s, Archbishop Wake was also something of a peripheral political figure. A resolute opponent of Francis Atterbury during the Convocation crisis, Wake's appointment to the see of Canterbury in 1715 initially had met with Whig clerical approval.[17] For reasons both temperamental and ideological, though, he never fitted easily with the post-1714 Whig political leaders, especially with the Stanhope–Sunderland ministry.[18] This meant he sometimes defied the nation's secular leaders to protect what he took to be the church's interests. The 1721 Blasphemy Bill was one such instance.

The Lords debate over the bill highlighted the salient issues. The three most important concerned morality, truth and the state's role in securing both. Both the 1689 Blasphemy Act and the 1721 Blasphemy Bill got drawn up during perceived periods of moral crisis. The 1721 bill's presentment, the parliamentary record notes, came during the midst of deliberations about how the government should deal with the South Sea Bubble. The speculative bubble's popping occasioned broad agreement across the political spectrum that something had gone terribly wrong and that what had gone wrong had some moral dimension to it.[19] As Trevor put it in the Lords, 'he verily believed, the present calamity, occasioned by the South-Sea project, was a judgment of God on the blasphemy and profaneness the nation was guilty of!'[20]

This sort of providentialism undergirded the December 1720 national day of fasting.[21] The fast day's purpose was to avert the plague's spread, but most also related it to the South Sea Bubble. The fast-day prayers correlated human actions in the here and now with divine responses in the here and now. And those prayers evinced anxiety that Britons had not merited divine reward: 'We were brought to the brink of ruin, and ... were almost given up as prey to Arbitrary power, Idolatry, and Superstition'. Britons, though, had shown God neither 'a due Thankfulness for thy Mercy, [n]or a religious Fear of thy Judgments', a neglect that opened up the nation to divine retribution. The fast prayer, as such, pleaded with God to '[p]ardon the many and great Offences of us thy servants, and the crying sins of the whole Nation'.[22] Yet some fretted that fasting alone could not protect Britain from divine punishment; an active reformation of manners was needed. As the *London Journal* put it, 'let us reform before we fast; let Vice and Debauchery, Whoring, Swearing, Perjury, Blasphemy, Drunkenness, Adultery, Masquerading, the notorious Crimes of the Times, be discountenanced and suppressed in our Streets'.[23] Only changed behaviours could secure God's temporal blessings upon the nation. And that change might require coercion.

Moral reform, then, paid out civic dividends. This conviction informed the Societies for the Reformation of Manners (SRM).[24] The SRM argued that their private prosecution of vice had both individual and corporate benefits.[25] In his 1720 SRM anniversary sermon, for instance, John Heylyn advised his audience to pursue a 'Reformation' with two dimensions: 'self amendment' and 'Publick Reformation'. Heylyn focused on the reformation of the self not for its own sake but as it related to the reformation of society. As he put it, the SRM's members had 'combined your strength, and have listed your selves into regular Troops, to beat down the strong Holds of Satan, and Fight the Cause of Religion under the Banners of Publick Justice'.[26] The SRM's 'great Work of Reformation' was 'National Justice'.[27] On Heylyn's accounting, then, the SRM's chief task was social and political, not soteriological. And to achieve those social and political tasks, the civil magistrate needed to 'put the Laws in Execution' so that 'the contagion of evil Examples' might be stopped by way of 'exemplary Punishments'.[28] This was possible, Heylyn reckoned, because England's 'Laws are constituted for the Support and Maintenance of Religion; since the Sword of the Civil Magistracy is drawn and wielded in the Defence of Christianity'.[29] Heylyn's arguments echoed earlier anniversary sermons, including Wake's from 1705.[30] For Heylyn, Wake and most others at the time, the reformation of manners campaign was about changing individual immoral behaviours for both soteriological and providential ends.

In the House of Lords sat a notorious example of immorality in early Georgian England, the Duke of Wharton.³¹ Wharton, the parliamentary record notes, was one of the '[s]everal persons of quality' who were rumoured to be members of 'a scandalous society at London, with the shocking name of the Hell-Fire Club'.³² That club was an inversion of the Societies for the Reformation of Manners: where the SRM aimed for moral reform, the Hell-Fire Club aimed for moral depravity.³³ '[T]heir whole discourse is Blasphemy', complained one correspondent to Wake.³⁴ In particular, the club mocked the Christian God. In 'monstrously impious' fashion, the three leading club members reputedly referred to 'themselves as Father, Son and Holy Spirit' and 'ridicule[d] the Trinity'.³⁵ In this, the Hell-Fire Club succeeded the putative Calves-Head Club, whose critics accused its members of republicanism, libertinism and atheism.³⁶ Evidently the government thought it needed to take some public stance on the matter.³⁷ So, the day before the Blasphemy Bill got presented in the Lords, George I issued an order to royal officials and to the Middlesex Justices of the Peace and Quarter Sessions to ferret out the 'scandalous Clubs or Societies ... who meet together, and in the most impious and blasphemous Manner, insult the most sacred Principles of our Holy Religion, affront Almighty God himself, and corrupt the Minds and Morals of one another'. The king promised 'to make use of all the Authority committed to Him by almighty God, to punish such enormous Offenders, and to crush such shocking Impieties before they Increase and draw down the Vengeance of God upon this Nation'.³⁸ The royal injunction did little, but it was notable for linking truth, behaviour and providence.³⁹

Truth was central both to the 1698 Blasphemy Act and to the 1721 Blasphemy Bill. A perceived sense of national moral crisis might have given salience to concerns about truth, but in the end public debates about a central Christian truth claim – the Son's eternity, begottenness and consubstantiality – made anti-blasphemy legislation necessary in the eyes of its architects. Both the 1698 act and the 1721 bill were legislative measures designed to resolve a debate about the Christian God's nature by preventing debates about the Christian God's nature. The Church of England's official self-conception committed it to the formulation of God's nature as expressed in the Nicene Creed. The English state's alliance with the church, in turn, obliged it to defend Nicene orthodoxy.⁴⁰ The Trinitarian debates during the three decades after the Glorious Revolution covered no new intellectual ground: indeed, defenders of Nicene orthodoxy would have argued that there was no true innovative position to be had regarding God's nature and that any innovative position was necessarily untrue since the Nicene Creed was the primitively pure articulation of God's nature. Instead, the Trinitarian debates that continued without abatement from the early 1690s to the early 1730s were debates over scholarship and discipline, ones, firstly, about which scholarly methods and sources could confirm or re-prove the Nicene articulation of God's nature and ones, secondly, about who had authority to defend the Nicene articulation against doubters and to what lengths that defence might go. The 1721 Blasphemy Bill was part of those debates.[41]

Wake's agitation for the Blasphemy Bill is perhaps surprising given that, at the start of the Trinitarian crisis during the 1690s, he purposefully stayed out of the matter, protesting that he was not 'qualified for such an Undertaking'.[42] It seems, though, that what really troubled him was the lengths to which anti-Socinians went in that controversy. 'I thank God I am so far from being engaged in favour of Socinus, that I think a worser Heretick never troubled the Church', he assured a friend. 'Yet ... as in the Popish, so in this Controversy, men have run things to an Extreme: and for my part though I detest Socinianism, yet I cannot subscribe to the other Extreme.'[43] Three decades later, though, the debate raged on, and Wake fretted about the irresolution's consequences: '60 tracts have been printed ... upon the Great Controversy of our Saviours Divinity', he reported in early 1720 to William King in Dublin.[44] Samuel Clarke's Christologically heterodox acolytes within the Church of England had taken up his mantle publicly during Clarke's enforced silence.[45] In addition, the Christological divisions among the Exeter dissenters in 1716 spilled over into more general dissenting Christological divisions in the Salters' Hall debates of 1719.[46] The heart of the matter in all of these debates, Wake reckoned, was 'the Authority of men to impose upon their Brethren human forms of Subscription to the truth of [the Nicene Creed]'. The casuitical manner in which some who denied Christ's divinity none the less subscribed to the Thirty-Nine Articles irked Wake and was, to his way of thinking, symptomatic of an age in which '[o]ur morals have long been corrupted'. But the civil magistrate's evident reluctance to prosecute heretics also troubled him. 'The Judges have declared that our Law is very expresse both in the description, and punishment of Blasphemy', he groused to King. 'Yet in despight of all this, men go on every day to oppose our Lords divinity; and no prosecution is made of this crime, though confessed to be within the Laws force.'[47] Wake thought more needed to be done to strengthen the state's coercive powers to punish blasphemers. The 1721 Blasphemy Bill was part of that effort.

The Blasphemy Bill's crafting coincided with a pamphlet by the Earl of Nottingham which retorted William Whiston's recent public criticism of Nicene and Athanasian Creeds.[48] In that 1719 work, Whiston deployed patristic sources to prove that 'the Son was not an underiv'd, unoriginated, independent and, in that sense, an Eternal Being'.[49] Instead, Christ had been 'voluntarily begotten by the power of the Father ... a little before the Creation of the World'.[50] Whiston argued nothing new, and, indeed, his heterodox Christology (what his contemporaries called Arianism) had earlier got him ejected from the Lucasian mathematics chair at Cambridge.[51] That Whiston singled out one of the Toleration Act's chief architects as being persecutory *was* slightly surprising. Nottingham, Whiston asserted, had wanted to impose 'a new Athanasian Test' on clergy when, in the Lords, he had recently 'opposed for the Toleration of the Christian Religion itself, or all that believed the Holy Scriptures and the Common Creed'.[52]

Whiston was right that Nottingham was committed to Nicene orthodoxy, or what Whiston and others called 'the Athanasian doctrine'.[53] During the December 1718 debates over the Bill for Strengthening the Protestant Interest, Nottingham had put forward a clause that those obliged to make oaths of supremacy, allegiance and abjuration should also swear an oath in which they did 'Profess Faith in God the Father and in Jesus Christ his Eternall Son the true God, And in the Holy Spirit One Blessed for Evermore. And do acknowledge the Holy Scriptures of the Old and New Testament to be given by Divine Inspiration.'[54] Nottingham's published defence of the Trinity a few years later similarly affirmed the Nicene conception of the Son.[55] What is relevant in the context of the Blasphemy Bill is what damage Nottingham thought flowed from public espousals of Christological heterodoxy. Firstly, there were individual soteriological consequences. 'If the Lord Jesus be a Creature, and you worship him 'tis Idolatry: If he be God, and you deny him, 'tis Blasphemy', Nottingham reckoned. 'And what Punishment Almighty God ordain'd for both of these sorts of Offenders you know.'[56] Worse still were the corporate consequences attending public expressions of Christological heresy. Arianism had, for instance, 'laid the Foundation of Mahometism'. It had produced 'as ill an Effect upon the Jews, by hardening them into their Infidelity and Blasphemy'. More recently Arians had encouraged 'the Scepticks of this Age, who deny all reveal'd Religion'.[57] All of these were religious innovators, and religious innovators had rent English society within living memory. As Nottingham put it, 'what Disturbances, what Miseries, Innovations in Religion have caus'd this Nation, the History of the last Age informs us sufficiently; and how fatal the Feuds and Animosities, occasion'd by the Pretenders to Religion, in this may be, no Man can fortel [*sic*], every good Man fears'.[58]

Civil peace, then, required restraining public expressions of untruth. Ideally, Convocation ('a Part of the Parliament') would be allowed 'to sit and act in taking Care of that Flock of Christ, of which the Holy Ghost has made them Overseers, and which the laws of the Land have committed to them; especially at a Time when the Doctrines of our most holy Faith, and the Apostolical Institution of the Government of our Church, are so virulently attack'd, and in so open and insolent a Manner'.[59] But England's secular rulers blocked Convocation from conducting meaningful business after 1717 precisely because they believed that the clergy's public deliberations in Convocation threatened the civil peace.[60] If the Christologically heterodox were to be disciplined, the civil magistrate would have to do it. The common law courts offered one option, and the Court of King's Bench tried nineteen cases for blasphemous libel between 1689 and 1720, reaching seven guilty verdicts.[61] Yet after Joseph Hall's 1720 guilty verdict for his *Sober Reply to Mr. Higg's Merry Arguments ... for the Tritheistick Doctrine of the Trinity*, only Thomas Woolston (1729) and Peter Annett (1763) were charged for writing blasphemous works.[62] As everyone recognised, these were not the only – or perhaps even the most egregious – Christologically heterodox authors to publish during the first two-thirds of the eighteenth century. The conclusion that exemplary punishments had been ineffective drove the 1721 legislative effort to clamp down on public expressions of anti-Trinitarianism.

The Blasphemy Bill was crafted over months in a process that Wake himself acknowledged was messy. None the less, the bill got revised in light of comments from the Earl of Sunderland, one of the Whig ministry's leaders.[63] Those revisions failed to satisfy Sunderland, for he spoke out against the bill in the Lords – saying that it 'tends to an Inquisition' and 'frustrates the Toleration Act' – and voted to kill it.[64] Sunderland and fifty-nine others voted against a bill with two main features, both of which dealt with perceived failures in the 1698 Blasphemy Act. Firstly, the original Blasphemy Act had not 'been sufficient to restrain' the many authors who had recently 'denied the Divinity of our Saviour Jesus Christ, the Doctrine of the Holy Trinity, and the Truth of the Christian Religion' and thus measures needed to be devised 'for the more effectual suppressing of such detestable Practices'.[65] As such, the 1721 bill targeted printers and clerics, those supposedly insufficiently restrained by the original 1698 act. A printer or bookseller who published or sold a blasphemous book would be imprisoned 'unless he make Proof who was the Author of such Book'. This provision aimed to remove the protection of anonymity and pseudonymity. In addition, the archbishops and bishops of the established Church of England, the Justices of the Peace and the various dissenting congregations also were enjoined actively to promote the prosecution of any clergy who published or publicly propagated blasphemous views. The second failure of the 1698 Blasphemy Act which the 1721 bill's architects identified concerned truth. The bill's architects were convinced that the 1698 act had not precisely enough specified what constituted truth. The 1721 bill thus stipulated that those convicted of blasphemy could renounce their errors with an oath that recapitulated the Nicene Creed: 'I do believe that there is but One Living and True God Everlasting, the Maker and Preserver of all Things both visible and invisible; and that in the Unity of the Godhead there be Three Persons of one Substance, Power and Eternity, the Father, Son and Holy Ghost.' The 1721 bill, then, proposed new ways to prevent the public dissemination of blasphemous ideas and sharpened its definition of what constituted blasphemy.

The parliamentary record of the debate over the bill focuses on the opposition speeches, but both Wake and Nottingham made notes of speeches they at least planned to give during those debates.[66] Wake offered a history of its growth in England and a Hobbesian rationale for suppressing blasphemy. The history highlighted coercion's effectiveness. English anti-Trinitarianism,

Wake argued, 'began in our Civil Wars' with John Biddle.⁶⁷ The Socinian Biddle was imprisoned in 1652 and the Racovian Catechism burnt, which Wake thought explained why Biddle's following remained so small. 'Nor', he continued, 'did they openly show themselves, till after the revolution'. The Glorious Revolution, on Wake's reading, catalysed the production of so much anti-Trinitarian work that William III issued *Directions ... for Preserving the Unity of the Christian Church and the Purity of the Christian Faith concerning the Trinity* (1695), and Parliament passed the 1698 Blasphemy Act. Yet neither these measures; nor Convocation's 'zeal to put some stop to it' under Anne; nor George I's instructions for suppressing blasphemy had worked sufficiently. '[S]till the Controversy goes on', Wake bemoaned. 'And the result has been a general inclination to Infidelity, or libertinism of principle [and] Horrid lewdness in morals'. Some measure needed to be taken to put an 'effectual stop' to the Trinitarian controversy: the Blasphemy Bill was that effort.

Wake's rationale for the bill was Hobbesian to the core. Firstly, the Toleration Act had expressly not tolerated anyone who expressed views 'to the prejudice of these fundamental doctrines of the Trinity': anti-Trinitarians, by implication, were fair game. Secondly, he professed concern only with outward expression. 'I desire not to enquire into any Man's private Opinions', he insisted. 'But then let them not disturb, nor infect others with them.' Thirdly, as the nation's established church, the Church of England deserved the state's protection: 'Establishments whether in things sacred, or Civil, are to be supported, not attacked by private persons. Much less should it be done, where so much liberty is allow'd in matters of Religion, would men be content to be quiet, and Enjoy their own Opinions, without disturbing the public.' This, he insisted was not persecution but prosecution. 'The controversy here is not with the weakness, but wickedness of men', he pleaded. 'I am willing to allow as much to men's errors, innocent errors, as any; [I] hate persecution; but am not willing to be frightened with the cry of persecution where there is no ground for it. Here is none; unless it be persecution to bring malefactors to judgment.' Because blasphemy was a crime of volition – a crime of deliberate and active choice – it merited deliberate and active punishment. The Blasphemy Bill, as such, was proposed merely to 'strengthen the laws already in force: not to look back but forward; not to restrain men's opinions, but the attempts and actions'. That restraint, Wake argued, would 'preserve the peace of religion'. Wake, surely no fan of the 'monster of Malmesbury', could hardly have done a better job of ventriloquising Hobbes's prescriptions for maintaining the civil peace.

Why did the 1721 Blasphemy Bill get voted down by the Lords? Wake's diary offers circumstantial evidence that the Privy Council had cut him out of its discussions regarding the bill, and he complained afterwards that the ministry had, in fact, greenlighted the version that contained Sunderland's revisions.⁶⁸ Publicly, the bill's opponents, both lay and clerical, argued that the bill was persecutory. Neither support nor opposition to the bill conforms neatly to historiographical expectations. Tories and High Churchmen should have been the bill's chief supporters, while Whigs should have been opposed to it. Reality proved muddier, especially within the church, as the bill ended up pitting some Church Whigs against other Church Whigs.

No one in the parliamentary debates openly denied Christ's divinity. Instead, every opposing speaker claimed the bill would make church and state persecutors. The Whig Baron Onslow set the tone. He assured the Lords that he 'was as much as against blasphemy, and for promoting religion, as it is professed in the Church of England, as any body; but he could not be for any law that was for persecution, of which nature he took this bill to be'.⁶⁹ Prosecuting untruth, on Onslow's view, was not prosecution but persecution. Moreover, Onslow questioned whether Christological heterodoxy was 'prejudicial to the state' and wondered why the House was debating 'nice points of faith & neglect[ing] our trade'.⁷⁰

The Duke of Wharton – a sometime Jacobite, sometime opposition Whig – picked up Onslow's argument. Acknowledging the public rumours about his behaviour in the Hell-Fire Club and 'declaring, he was far from being a patron of blasphemy, or an enemy to religion', Wharton brandished the family Bible during his speech. Reading from it, 'he quoted ... several passages from the Epistles of St Peter and St Paul' to support his contention that the bill was 'repugnant to the holy Scripture'.⁷¹ Presumably Wharton did not read from 1 Timothy 5:22, upon which Henry Sacheverell had expounded in *The Communication of Sin* (1709) and on the basis of which Sacheverell had advocated actively restraining sin on both soteriological and providential grounds.⁷² None the less other lay lords echoed Wharton's claims about the biblical prohibition against prosecuting blasphemers. He and the Earl of Sunderland also proclaimed that the Blasphemy Bill 'impugns the Toleration Act'.⁷³ Some echoing Wharton were ministry Whigs; others were Whigs and Tories drawn from the Cowper-led parliamentary opposition.⁷⁴ All agreed, though, that prosecuting blasphemers was immoral. The last lay lord to oppose the bill was the venerable Whig Earl of Peterborough, who declared that '[t]hough he was for a parliamentary king, yet he did not desire to have a parliamentary God, or a parliamentary religion; and, if the House was for such a one, he would go to Rome and endeavor to be chosen a cardinal; for he had rather sit in the conclave, than with their lordships upon those terms'.⁷⁵

Peterborough made the commonplace case about the inherent connection between persecution and popery, one which had been made since the sixteenth century and one which provided the intellectual foundation of Whig anticlericalism.⁷⁶ *Coercion* made persecution possible and coercion's opposite was *liberty*, which Whigs valorised.⁷⁷ Implicit in Peterborough's speech was that the Blasphemy Bill's supporters favoured coercion, while its opponents favoured liberty: state-imposed religious beliefs resulted from coercion, while allowing people freedom to discern the truth resulted from liberty. And yet it was the case that England did have a 'parliamentary God' and a 'parliamentary religion': the Church of England, after all, had been established by sixteenth-century parliamentary statutes and full civil and political rights depended on publicly adhering to religious views stipulated by seventeenth-century parliamentary statutes. The Whig lay lords who opposed the Blasphemy Bill, then, could hardly have done so because of some principled commitment to religious liberty. More likely, they aimed above all to preserve the civil peace and reckoned that prosecuting blasphemers was more disruptive than simply letting them alone. Perhaps they even doubted that what Wake and Nottingham thought was blasphemy actually was blasphemous. Certainly the Lords' treatment of Nathaniel Mist in 1720 showed that they were perfectly willing to prosecute those who espoused political heresies like Jacobitism.[78]

Yet the opposition to the 1721 Blasphemy Bill came not just from the lay lords but from within the established church itself: only four bishops supported the legislation, while eight voted against it.[79] White Kennett, the Bishop of Peterborough and Wake's old friend, was the only bishop recorded as having spoken out against the bill. Kennett picked up Peterborough's anti-popish analogy and 'said that neither himself, nor, he hoped, any of that bench, would be executioners of such a Law, which seemed to tend to the setting up of an inquisition'.[80] A few years before, Kennett had explained to the Bishop of Meath, though, that he and a majority of the bishops had not supported repealing the Occasional Conformity and the Schism Acts on the principled grounds of not leaving dissenters 'to the cry of Persecution or to the Arbitrary Humour of Princes, who had sometimes made Church Men the Tools of Persecution, and that at other times without Law indulg'd the Dissenters only to Cover the Papists'. Instead, prudential reasons dictated support for repeal, that is to say 'really to unite the Protestant Interest against Jacobites & Papists & Tories of all Sorts'. And he reassured the Bishop of Meath that 'they had never once thought of repealing the Test Act or affecting the Act of Uniformity'. The point was that if one wanted the established church 'effectually secur'd' against Protestant dissenters, 'you must allow for their Civil Interests, and consistently secure, your own Ecclesiastical Establishment'.[81] Kennett's ultimate strategic aim was to safeguard the established church. So too was that the strategic aim of other Church Whigs who opposed the Blasphemy Bill. And that defence required sometimes unpalatable compromises, especially during the first decade after the Hanoverian succession.[82]

Put another way, the post-revolutionary religious settlement had been one in which Whig churchman had made a deal, one which protected the church's establishment status but one which also highlighted perennial post-Reformation questions about the proper relationship of church to state. Was the church an independent, equal or subordinate partner to the state? Did the church enjoy its establishment status by grace or by right? Most argued the latter, but suspected the former. And that meant that protecting the church's interests required delicacy. Against this background, the bishops thought about the 1721 Blasphemy Bill.

The figure who would soon eclipse William Wake as the leading Church Whig was Wake's old friend and ally, Edmund Gibson. Part of their break had to do with how best to superintend the church under the post-revolutionary circumstances, something which Gibson's opposition to the Blasphemy Bill highlights. In an anonymous pamphlet, published in late May 1721, Gibson zeroed in on the bill's clause regarding episcopal responsibilities for ferreting out and prosecuting blasphemers within their dioceses. Not once did Gibson forswear persecution, but instead he focused on the bill's enforcement mechanisms and their potential to damage the church. Gibson complained, firstly, that bishops had no room for discretion to discern whether someone accused of espousing Christological heterodoxy actually was doing so or whether he even understood what he was espousing. The bill, Gibson argued, made a bishop 'a mere Ministerial Executioner, without either Knowledge, or Judgment, or Enquiry, to be used or made on his part'.[83] Secondly, even a false accusation of Christological heterodoxy would sully a clergyman's name with his parishioners.[84] Moreover, there was a danger that the Blasphemy Bill might be used to settle political party scores.[85] Most importantly, though, Gibson worried about the problems of casuitical subscription. The Blasphemy Bill, he noted, presupposed that Arian clergy like Samuel Clarke or John Jackson would willingly choose to be deprived of their livings rather than falsely subscribe to the Thirty-Nine Articles; and, indeed, Gibson pointedly reminded his readers that Clarke had long advocated for subscribing to the articles with a sense of latitude.[86] Moreover, Gibson noted that Jackson had recently made the necessary subscription to become the head of the Leicester Hospital, his Arianism notwithstanding.[87] '[T]he Consequence is, that such a Bill, if pass'd into a Law', Gibson concluded, 'would be of no manner of Use, in order to the End which it mainly aims at, nor prove the least Difficulty upon the Persons who are design'd to be reach'd and punish'd by it'.[88] Gibson's pamphlet on the Blasphemy Bill focused not on the injustice of coercion but on the bill's inefficacy and what damage that inefficacy might do to the church and its leaders. Gibson also fretted about dragging theological wrangling into the public.

That concern about publicity is evident in Gibson's response to the various clerical addresses to the Earl of Nottingham in the spring of 1721 for defending Nicene orthodoxy. Nottingham received at least sixteen clerical addresses, including ones thanking him for 'his affectionate concern for the Legal sitting' of Convocation and for his 'most excellent Defence of our Blessed Saviour's Divinity'.[89] It is unclear how those addresses originated and no evidence exists of active co-ordination with Wake or Nottingham. But the addresses first appeared just before the Blasphemy Bill came under parliamentary consideration, and it looked like a co-ordinated public campaign on the bill's behalf.

Gibson responded both anonymously in print and directly to the clergy of his diocese who had orchestrated the address. In an anonymous pamphlet on the addresses to Nottingham, Gibson praised the earl's orthodoxy, but noted that he also loved the 'Peace, Order and Unity of the Church'.[90] The rest of the pamphlet accused the clergy who had praised Nottingham's defence of Christological orthodoxy of being religious innovators, turning the typical orthodox case on its head. In the Church of England, all priests within a diocese had sworn oaths of loyalty, duty and obedience to their bishops, and within the Church of England bishops had final authority regarding collective clerical actions. Any clergyman who had drafted or signed on to the addresses to Nottingham, as a result, had acted like a 'Presbyterian, or Independent'.[91] And, like the Presbyterians and independents of the previous century, they risked unleashing zeal that that could threaten the civil order. As such there needed to be 'a Check on all such Innovations'.[92] Moreover, Gibson insisted that making public arguments showed that one actually distrusted one's own case.[93] In sum, Gibson counselled quiet and subordination.

To the clergy of his own diocese who had organised the Lincoln address to Nottingham, Gibson was more threatening.[94] Firstly, their behaviour was 'inconsistent with the oath of canonical duty' which they had sworn to their bishop (Gibson). Worse still, they had behaved like latter-day Cardinal Wolseys. '[B]y making a publick declaration of your opinion on a matter of doctrine', Gibson claimed, 'which 'tis a matter wholly foreign to the work of Visitations ... as the Law now stands, it cannot be done without danger of a praemunire, by any assembly of the Clergy whatsoever, except by a Convocation of the Bishops & Clergy legally assembl'd by the King's Writ & the Mandate of the Metropolitan'. Even if the clerical address were legal, 'it will prove highly prejudicial to the order and government of the Church'. This response left the clergy of Gibson's own diocese unsatisfied because his 1720 visitation charge had defended Nicene orthodoxy. In refusing to fortify the laws to squelch public expressions of Christological heterodoxies, Gibson risked looking like a leader who lacked the courage of his conviction.[95]

Gibson's 1720 visitation charge to which some of his diocesan clergy pointed was a mixture of clarity and equivocation. On matters of doctrine, Gibson was forthright. He had inveighed 'against those among us who ... out of a love of Novelty, and under pretence of Thinking with Freedom, are become zealous Advocates for such Doctrines and Principles, as Subvert the Christian Faith, and destroy the divine mission and authority of a Christian Church'.[96] The charge's first half methodically addressed the issues regarding reason, revelation, the primitive Church and the philosophical questions regarding divine attributes raised by those who rejected Nicene Christology, before concluding that 'there is no cause to leave the Divinity of Christ out of the Christian Scheme, as a Point doubtful and not sufficiently revealed. And as we need not leave it out as a point doubtful, so neither may we leave it out as a point Speculative.'[97] The visitation charge's second half, which addressed 'the Authority, Government and Discipline of the Church', was a fudge. In that second section, Gibson set out to refute the arguments of 'Erastians, who own no power in the Church, but that of the Civil Magistrate'; of 'Papists, who assert greater Powers to the Church, than Christ has given'; and of some 'Protestants ... concerning the particular Forms of Government which the Apostles instituted in the Church'.[98] To these Gibson added a fourth erroneous conception of the church's authority and discipline, a latecomer voluntarist one. This 'new Scheme', Gibson contended,

> is equally against the three; excluding the Civil Magistrate from any Concern whatsoever in matters of Religion as such; and denying at the same time, that Christ has any Government or Governours in his Church upon earth; and affirming, that no more is needful to become a Christian, than for every particular person, in his own mind, to believe Christ to be the Messiah.[99]

Gibson surely had in mind someone like Benjamin Hoadly. Against Hoadleian voluntarism, Erastianism, popery and anti-episcopalian Protestants, Gibson defended what he thought was 'the true ancient Apostolical Scheme', one in which Christ intended his Church to be a 'Visible Society, under Governours and Pastors, duly sent and regularly appointed ... [T]he Catholick Church is made up of such particular Visible Societies, that therefore every Christian is bound to be a member of such particular Society; That being a member he is also bound to conform himself to the Rules and Orders of it, so far as they are agreeable to the Rules and Orders left by Christ and his Apostles'. Furthermore, if a church member is excommunicated, he is 'bound to submit and to make Satisfaction, and to seek to be reconciled to the Church; the Governours of which are the proper Judges of the fitness of person is to be admitted into the Society of the Church or excluded out of it'.[100] His was a robust view of clerical authority within its proper sphere. But what was the proper sphere of clerical authority was the nub of the matter. In his defence of this primitive understanding of the church, Gibson focused his fire on the voluntarist, popish and dissenting conceptions of church authority and discipline, while leaving the Erastian one untouched. His silence was telling and damning in the eyes of anti-Erastian clergy. Gibson would surely have responded that discretion was the better part of valour; that the nature of the post-revolutionary relationship between church and state required the church to pick and choose its spots to act; and that co-operation with the state might yield the best results under the circumstances.

Put another way, Edmund Gibson believed that that there were blasphemers in the England of his day and that they needed to be prosecuted. But, he also recognised that the church needed the state to prosecute blasphemers and those who helped them to propagate their blasphemy. As he reported put it to Wake during the run-up to Thomas Woolston's trial, he had 'delivered to the person on whose judgment they depend in criminal Prosecutions, a large Extract of blasphemous passages out of Wolston's Books; in order to consider of the most proper and effectual methods to do justice upon Printers, Publishers &c agreeably to the usual practice in the State, for the discouraging of seditious Pamphlets'.[101] The key phrase is 'agreeably to the usual practice of the State', for blasphemy could remain a common law crime only if the state continued to recognise it as one and was, furthermore, willing to prosecute it in the courts. Some have quipped that there is no blasphemy without the law. In post-revolutionary England, it would be more precise to say that there was no blasphemy without the state.

The Glorious Revolution had set in train a series of events which confirmed the Church of England as England's civil religion. William Wake would have liked to manage the relationship between church and state on terms which acknowledged the church's status as an independent corporate body. But by the 1720s he recognised that the 'Erastian notions, and an Indifference in all thing that concern the State of the Church and Religion' made that impracticable.[102] Edmund Gibson, for his part, increasingly recognised that, if the Church of England hoped to continue as the nation's civil religion, it would need at times to place the state's interests before its own. In 1721, that meant letting blasphemy go unpunished.

NOTES

1 N. Sykes, *William Wake* (Cambridge, 1959), II, 135–9.
2 E. Davies, 'The Blasphemy Act of 1698' (Cambridge University BA dissertation, 2016); D. Hayton, 'Moral Reform and Country Politics in the Late Seventeenth-century House of Commons', *P&P* 128 (1990), esp. 59, 69–70, 73. We thank Ms Davies for sharing her thesis with us.
3 G. Nokes, *A History of the Crime of Blasphemy* (1928), 1–64.
4 M. Robertson and G. Ellis (eds), *English Reports: King's Bench: Volume 86* (1908), 189. See also E. Visconsi, 'The Invention of Criminal Blasphemy: *Rex v. Taylor* (1697)', *Representations* 103 (2008), 30–52.
5 M. Hale, 'Of policy ... in matters of religion', quoted in A. Cromartie, *Sir Matthew Hale, 1609–1676: Law, Religion and Natural Philosophy* (Cambridge, 1995), 177.
6 Nokes, *History*, 107–17. See also J. Spurr, 'The Manner of English Blasphemy, 1676–2008', in S. Brown, F. Knight and J. Morgan-Guy (eds), *Religion, Identity and Conflict in Britain* (Farnham, 2013), 27–46; D. Manning, 'Blasphemy in England, c.1660–1730' (Cambridge University PhD, 2008)
7 W. Bulman, *Anglican Enlightenment: Orientalism, Religion and Politics in England and Its Empire, 1648–1715* (Cambridge, 2015); R. Ingram, *Reformation without End: Religion, Politics and the Past in Post-Revolutionary England* (Manchester, 2018).
8 Hayton, 'Moral Reform', 88.
9 R. Stromberg, *Religious Liberalism in Eighteenth-century England* (Oxford, 1954), 49; A. Starkie, *The Church of England and the Bangorian Controversy, 1716–1721*

(Woodbridge, 2007), 47; D. Wykes, 'Religious Dissent, the Church, and the Repeal of the Occasional Conformity and Schism Acts, 1714–19', in R. Cornwall and W. Gibson (eds), *Religion, Politics and Dissent, 1660–1832* (Aldershot, 2010), 183.

10 D. Nash, *Blasphemy in the Christian World* (Oxford, 2007), 191.

11 T. Isaacs, 'The Anglican Hierarchy and the Reformation of Manners, 1688–1738', *JEH* 33 (1982), 404; G. Townend, 'Religious Radicalism and Conservatism in the Whig Party under George I: The Repeal of the Occasional Conformity and Schism Acts', *PH* 7 (1988), 39–40. Cf. G. Townend, 'The Political Career of Charles Spencer, Third Earl of Sunderland, 1695–1722' (Edinburgh University PhD, 1984), 290.

12 R. Frankle, 'Thomas Trevor, First Baron Trevor (bap. 1658, d. 1730)', *ODNB*; W. Wynne, 'Sir Thomas Trevor (1658–1730)', in E. Cruickshanks, S. Handley and D.W. Hayton (eds), *House of Commons, 1690–1715* (Cambridge, 2002), V, 687–90.

13 Edward Harley to Robert Harley, 17 February 1721, 20 April 1721 (*HMC Portland*, V, 614–15; BL, Add. 70236); William Wake to Charles Spencer, third Earl of Sunderland, 22 April 1721 (CCO, Wake 9, no. 46); Edward Harley to Abigail Harley, 21 May 1721 (BL, Add. 70145).

14 J. Spurr, 'The Church of England, Comprehension and the Toleration Act of 1689', *EHR* 104 (1989), 927–46; H. Horwitz, *Revolution Politicks: The Career of Daniel Finch, Second Earl of Nottingham, 1647–1730* (Cambridge, 1968), 87–93.

15 White Kennett to [William Nicolson], 6 December 1705 (BL, Lansdowne 1034, fols 4–5); G. Holmes, *British Politics in the Age of Anne* (1967), 101. Nottingham, though, opposed the Schism Act (1714), which he thought undermined the Toleration Act: Horwitz, *Revolution Politicks*, 244.

16 Nottingham to Thomas Coningsby, Earl of Coningsby, 24 July 1721 (BL, Add. 57861, fol. 184).

17 N. Sykes, 'Archbishop Wake and the Whig Party, 1716–1723: A Study in Incompatibility of Temperament', *Cambridge Historical Journal* 8 (1945), 97.

18 S. Taylor, '"Dr. Codex" and the Whig "Pope": Edmund Gibson, Bishop of Lincoln and London, 1716–1748', in R. Davis (ed.), *Lords of Parliament: Studies, 1714–1914* (Stanford, 1995), 9–27.

19 J. Sheehan and D. Wahrman, *Invisible Hands: Self-organization and the Eighteenth Century* (Chicago, 2015), 99–123; J. Champion, '"Anglia Libera": Commonwealth Politics in the Early Years of George I', in D. Womersley (ed.), *'Cultures of Whiggism': New Essays on English Literature and Culture in the Long Eighteenth Century* (Newark, DE, 2005), 86–107; J. Hoppit, 'The Myths of the South Sea Bubble', *TRHS* 12 (2002), 141–65.

20 W. Cobbett, *Parliamentary History of England* (1811), VII, 893.

21 Nicolson to Wake, 6 December 1720 (BL, Add. 6116, no. 129) credits Wake with having originally pressed for the fast. On providence, see Sheehan and Wahrman, *Invisible Hands*, esp. 11–46.

22 P. Williamson, A. Raffe, S. Taylor and N. Mears (eds), *National Prayers: Special Worship since the Reformation. Volume 2: General Fasts, Thanksgivings and Special Prayers in the British Isles, 1689–1870* (Woodbridge, 2017), 389, 390. This was an argument repeated in the published fast sermons, including ones in given in the

Lords and in the Commons: H. Boulter, *Sermon preach'd ... On, Friday, December the 16th, 1720* (1720); J. Wilcocks, *Increase of Righteousness* (1720).
23 *London Journal*, LXXIV (17–20 December 1720), 3.
24 A. Craig, 'The Movement for the Reformation of Manners, 1688–1715' (Edinburgh University PhD, 1980); J. Spurr, 'The Church, the Societies and the Moral Revolution of 1688', in J. Walsh, C. Haydon and S. Taylor (eds), *The Church of England, c.1689–c.1833: From Toleration to Tractarianism* (Cambridge, 1993), 127–42.
25 S. Burtt, *Virtue Transformed: Political Argument in England, 1688–1740* (Cambridge, 1992), 39–63.
26 J. Heylyn, *Sermon Preached to the SRM* (1721), 14.
27 Ibid., 19.
28 Ibid., 14–15.
29 Ibid., 20.
30 W. Wake, *Sermon Preached before the SRM* (1706).
31 L. Smith, 'Philip James Wharton, Duke of Wharton (1698–1731)', *ODNB*.
32 Cobbett, *Parliamentary History*, 893.
33 E. Lord, *The Hell-Fire Clubs: Sex, Satanism and Secret Societies* (New Haven, 2011), esp. 45–61.
34 Anonymous to Wake, [1721] (CCO, Wake 9, no. 38).
35 Anonymous to Wake, [c. February–May 1721] (CCO, Wake 9, no. 37); Anonymous, *The Hell-Fire Club: kept by a society of blasphemers* (1721), 20.
36 [E. Ward,] *Secret History of the Calves-Head Club* (1704); R. Lund, 'Guilt by Association: The Atheist Cabal and the Rise of the Public Sphere in Augustan England', *Albion* 34 (2002), 391–421. Cf. Kennett to Arthur Charlett, 3 June 1721 (Bodleian, Ballard 7, fol. 158).
37 W. Whiston, *Memoirs* (1749), I, 155.
38 *London Gazette*, 5958 (25–9 April 1721), 1.
39 Mary Wortley Montagu to Lady Mar, [March 1724] (R. Halsband (ed.), *The Complete Letters of Lady Mary Wortley Montagu* (Oxford, 1966), II, 38).
40 Ingram, *Reformation without end*, 44–6.
41 Bulman, *Anglican Enlightenment*, 261–76; B. Sirota, 'The Trinitarian Crisis in Church and State: Religious Controversy and the Making of the Postrevolutionary Church of England, 1687–1702', *JBS* 52 (2013), 26–54.
42 Wake to Arthur Charlett, 2 April [1691] (Bodleian, Ballard 3, no. 29).
43 Wake to Charlett, 5 February 1692 (Bodleian, Ballard 3, no. 26).
44 Wake to King, 24 March 1720 (TCD, 1995–2008/1947).
45 Ingram, *Reformation without end*, 44–63; B. Young, 'Newtonianism and the Enthusiasm of Enlightenment', *Studies in History and Philosophy of Science: Part A* 35 (2004), 645–63.
46 D. Wykes, 'Subscribers and Non-subscribers at the Salters' Hall Debate', *ODNB*; Edward Harley to Abigail Harley, 25 December 1718 (BL, Add. 70034).
47 Wake to King, 24 March 1720 (TCD, 1995–2008/1947). See also B. Young, *Religion and Enlightenment in Eighteenth-century England* (Oxford, 1998), 19–44.
48 Edward Harley to Robert Harley, 17 February 1721 (*HMC Portland*, V, 614–15); Nottingham to Humphrey Prideaux, 10 February 1721 (Cornwall Record Office, PB/8/4/427).

49 [W. Whiston,] *Mr. Whiston's letter to ... the earl of Nottingham* (1719), 28–9.
50 Ibid., 29–30.
51 S. Snobelen, 'William Whiston (1667–1752)', *ODNB*; P. Gilliam, 'William Whiston: No Longer an Arian', *JEH* 66 (2015), 755–71.
52 [Whiston,] *Mr. Whiston's letter*, 1.
53 W. Whiston, *The true origin of the Sabellian and Athanasian doctrines of the trinity* (1720).
54 'Lord Nottingham's Clause', 22 December 1718, in S. Taylor and C. Jones (eds), *Tory and Whig: The Parliamentary Papers of Edward Harley, Third Earl of Oxford, and William Hay* (Woodbridge, 1998), 206–7. Wake and thirteen other bishops voted for the clause; twelve bishops joined a majority in the Lords to defeat the clause's adoption.
55 D. Finch, *Answer of the earl of Nottingham to Mr. Whiston's letter* (1721). See also Whiston to Wake, 18 May 1721 (CCO, Wake 9, no. 64).
56 Finch, *Answer*, 77.
57 Ibid., 7, 8.
58 Ibid., 76.
59 Ibid., 76.
60 N. Sykes, *From Sheldon to Secker: Aspects of English Church History, 1660–1768* (Cambridge, 1958), 36–67.
61 Nokes, *History*, 147–52.
62 A House of Lords committee had recommended that Hall be tried at King's Bench and that Hall's *Sober Reply* be 'burnt by the Common hangman' because the pamphlet was 'a mixture of the most scandalous Blasphemy, Profaneness and Obscenity; [which] does, in a most daring, impious Manner, ridicule the Doctrine of the Trinity, of all Revealed Religion': C. Gillett, *Burned Books: Neglected Chapters in British History and Literature* (New York, 1932), II, 588–90.
63 Edward Jennings to Wake, 27 Mach 1721 (CCO, Wake 9, nos 39–40); Wake to Sunderland, 22 April 1721 (ibid., no. 46); Edward Harley to Robert Harley, 25 April 1721 (BL, Add. 70237); Wake to Sunderland, 29 April 1721 (BL, Add. 61612, fol. 196); Edward Harley to Robert Harley, 29 April 1721 (BL, Add. 70236). See also Wake notes and draft speech regarding Blasphemy Bill, [1721] (CCO, Wake 9, nos 49–50): 'The bill as it was drawn was very imperfect; nor did I like it as it was brought into the House. I was for amending many things in it, & particularly that part which concerned the Bishop, which I never approved, and would have opposed.'
64 Wake to Sunderland, 11 May 1721 (CCO, Wake 9, no. 52); Sunderland to Wake, 12 May 1721 (ibid., no. 53); Nottingham's notes on the Blasphemy Bill debate, 1721 (LRO, DG7, Box 4960, PP 154).
65 Bill for the more effectual suppressing of Blasphemy and Profaneness, 1721 [engrossment] (LRO, PP 177). Unless otherwise noted, all quotations in this paragraph draw from this source.
66 Wake notes and draft speech regarding Blasphemy Bill, [1721] (Wake 9, nos 49–50). Unless otherwise noted, all quotations in this and the next paragraph draw from this source.
67 Cf. S. Mortimer, *Reason and Religion in the English Revolution: The Challenge of Socinianism* (Cambridge, 2010).

68 William Wake's diary, 1705–1725 (LPL, 1770, fol. 239v): 'A Councill at St. James: The Order to my Lord Chancellor for suppressing Wickedness & Profanesse: I was there a Quarter before One, yet the Council was over'. Wake notes and draft speech regarding Blasphemy Bill, [1721] (Wake 9, nos 49–50): 'This was a new Cause offence given to the Ministers tho' I had a meeting with them about this bill, and their Consent to appear for it: And here I was again deserted by my Brethren, as in the Other bill for Repealing the Act against Occasional Conformity.'
69 Cobbett, *Parliamentary History*, 893. P. Gauci, 'Thomas Onslow (1679–1740)', in Cruickshanks et al. (eds), *House of Commons, 1690–1715*, V, 37–40.
70 Nottingham's notes on the Blasphemy Bill debate, 1721 (LRO, DG7, Box 4960, PP 154).
71 Cobbett, *Parliamentary History*, 893.
72 H. Sacheverell, *Communication of sin* (1709), 16.
73 Nottingham's notes on the Blasphemy Bill debate, 1721 (LRO, DG7, Box 4960, PP 154).
74 C. Jones, 'The New Opposition in the House of Lords, 1720–1723', *HJ* 36 (1993), 309–29; C. Jones, 'Jacobitism and the Historian: The Case of William, 1st Earl Cowper', *Albion* 23 (1991), 681–96. Wake was on friendly terms with Cowper and his wife, Mary: Hertfordshire Archives, D/EP/F62.
75 Nottingham's notes on the Blasphemy Bill debate, 1721 (LRO, DG7, Box 4960, PP 154). J. Hattendorf, 'Charles Mourdant, Third Earl of Peterborough and First Earl of Monmouth (1658?–1735)', *ODNB*.
76 On anti-popery, see P. Lake, 'Antipopery: The Structure of a Prejudice', in R. Cust and A. Hughes (eds), *Conflict in Stuart England* (1989), 72–106; J. Collins, 'Restoration Anti-Catholicism: A Prejudice in Motion', in C. Prior and G. Burgess (eds), *England's Wars of Religion, Revisited* (Aldershot, 2013), 281–306. On Whig anticlericalism, see J. Champion, '"Religion's Safe, with Priestcraft is the War": Augustan Anticlericalism and the Legacy of the English Revolution, 1660–1720', *The European Legacy* 5 (2000), 547–61; M. Goldie, 'Priestcraft and the Birth of Whiggism', in N. Philipson and Q. Skinner (eds), *Political Discourse in Early Modern Britain* (Cambridge, 1993), 209–31.
77 M. Goldie, 'The English System of Liberty', in M. Goldie and R. Wokler (eds), *The Cambridge History of Eighteenth-century Political Thought* (Cambridge, 2006), 40–78, surveys the scene.
78 P. Chapman, 'Nathaniel Mist (d. 1737)', *ODNB*. See also Edward Harley to Abigail Harley, 30 May 1721 (*Tory and Whig*, 234).
79 No extant division list for this bill is extant, but the bishops who joined Wake to support the bill included John Robinson (London), Jonathan Trelawney (Winchester), Edward Chandler (Lichfield and Coventry). Those opposing the bill included Edmund Gibson (Lincoln) and White Kennett (Peterborough).
80 Cobbett, *Parliamentary History*, 894.
81 Kennett to John Evans, 30 December 1718 (BL, Lansdowne 1034, fols 10–11).
82 R. Ingram, 'The Church of England, 1714–1783', in J. Gregory (ed.), *The Oxford History of Anglicanism. Volume II* (Oxford, 2017), esp. 49–56.
83 [E. Gibson,] *Remarks on part of a bill lately brought into the House of Lords* (1721), 4.
84 Ibid., 4–5, 10

85 Ibid., 11.
86 Ibid., 6.
87 Ibid., 7–9.
88 Ibid., 9.
89 Addresses from the clergy, 1721 (LRO, DG7, Box 4976, Lit.10); Canterbury Clergy to Nottingham, July 1721 (BL, Add. 29589, fols 503–4); Papers relating to the thanks of the clergy of the diocese of Peterborough to the Earl of Nottingham, 1721 (BL, Lansdowne 989, fols 160–1). Clerical addresses to Nottingham came from the universities of Oxford and Cambridge and from London, Middlesex, Berkshire, Peterborough, Ossory, Oxford, Burcester, Chester, Buckinghamshire, Hereford, Salop, Doncaster, Wiltshire and Essex.
90 [E. Gibson,] *The case of addressing consider'd* (1721), 3.
91 Ibid., 8.
92 Ibid., 10.
93 Ibid., 14.
94 Gibson to Matthew Tate, 11 May 1721 (Bodleian, Eng.d.2405, fols 27–8). Unless otherwise noted, all quotations in this paragraph draw from this letter. White Kennett also wanted to ensure 'that the clergy might not make a Separate and independent Application to a Lay Lord, but in subordination to the Bishop and through his hands, as Head of Ecclesiastical Unity among them': BL, Lansdowne 989, fol. 162.
95 Cf. Thomas Frank to Wake, 10 June 1721 (CCO, Wake 9, no. 72).
96 Edmund Gibson's visitation charges to the dioceses of Lincoln and London, 1720–24 (BL, Egerton 2073, fol. 1).
97 Ibid., 7.
98 Ibid., 14.
99 Ibid., 14.
100 Ibid., 14–15.
101 Gibson to Wake, 22 April 1728 (Cornwall Record Office, PB8/6/348–350).
102 Wake to King, 16 August 1723 (TCD, 1995–2008/2035).

Chapter 9

David Hume and 'Of the Liberty of the Press' (1741) in its original contexts[1]

Max Skjönsberg

David Hume (1711–76) famously said that humankind was governed by opinion, and has in this regard been followed by political writers from James Madison and William Godwin to Hannah Arendt.[2] Considering the importance Hume placed on public opinion, the burgeoning British press was naturally of great interest to him. Most discussions of his dedicated contribution to the subject, his 1741 essay 'Of the Liberty of the Press', concentrate on the context of the final version of the text.[3] The essay was heavily edited in 1770 in response to what Hume perceived as the threat to political stability posed by the radical 'Wilkes and Liberty' movement.[4] When editing the essay, Hume removed his initial and more positive conclusion about press freedom and instead called it one of the inconveniences of mixed governments. According to what is arguably the most important book on Hume's politics ever written, these revisions represent 'perhaps the most striking example of a retreat in the later Hume from a liberal to a less liberal position'.[5] While Hume's change of heart has often been discussed and debated by historians and political theorists, little has been said about what prompted the essay in the first place. The aim of the present chapter is to focus on the original contexts of the essay.[6] I will not concentrate either on Hume's revisions or on 'Wilkes and Liberty' since this has already been done by many others at great length. When situating the essay in its original political and intellectual contexts, we can be more precise than to simply describe it as a 'liberal' position. To achieve this, we must consider sources which most historians of political thought tend to stay well clear of, including all too often neglected parliamentary debates.[7] When discussing and contextualising Hume's first edition, it will become evident that it was written with a specific target in mind, namely Walpole's Whig administration (1721–42). This is not to say that Hume unequivocally sided with the opposition. Importantly, he appears to have supported conciliation rather than confrontation with Spain in 1739, and in that policy he agreed with Walpole's government. As usual, Hume's argument was distinctive and relied on his understanding of independence, that is to say, not meaning never taking sides but rather never siding with one party consistently.

Jürgen Habermas singled out the expiry of the Licensing Act (1662) in 1695 as one of the most important catalysts for the development of a 'bourgeois' public sphere in Britain.[8] Habermas's thesis inspired and provoked important historical research, especially in the wake of its English translation in 1989, but many aspects of the original thesis have been rightly criticised, including the public sphere's alleged inclusivity, 'bourgeois' nature and anti-court bias.[9] For one thing, Habermas's protagonist Bolingbroke was not 'bourgeois' in any meaningful sense but a viscount and Secretary of State to Queen Anne and briefly to the Stuart Pretender. His opposition to Walpole's 'Court Whigs' had more to do with his exclusion from court circles after his Jacobite adventure in 1715–16 as opposed to any principled hostility to court culture as such. If the Marxian teleology and terminology are removed from Habermas's thesis we are left with the uncontested, and indeed previously known, fact that print culture – including pamphlets, journals, newspapers, books, prints, and printed sermons, ballads and plays – expanded enormously in the eighteenth century. London in particular had already had a mass market for periodicals in the turbulent seventeenth century, and the period also saw the publication of an attack on censorship in the shape of John Milton's *Areopagitica* (1644). After 1695, however, when pre-publication censorship in England and Wales ended, print culture exploded and became more regular.[10] Around mid-century, London had eighteen newspapers and the provinces had forty.[11] Annual sales of newspapers have been estimated at 7.3 million in 1750, a significant increase from 2.5 million in 1713.[12] These figures are even more astonishing if we consider the fact that these papers generally had multiple readers as they were available in coffee houses. Moreover, as the non-juror hack Charles Leslie observed, even the illiterate were consumers of journalism, since they would gather around someone who could read in the streets.[13]

The lapse of the Licensing Act had to do very little with any intention to increase press freedom but rather with the inability of the political parties to agree on how to regulate the press because of mutual suspicion.[14] Most newspapers and periodicals in the eighteenth century were 'party papers' with unmistaken political agendas.[15] Nevertheless, as a result of its lapse, and the many failures to reintroduce licensing,[16] England (and Britain after 1707) developed a press culture that was unmatched by any major power on the Continent.[17] Pre-publication censorship remained in force in Hume's native Scotland, but it was rarely enforced after 1710.[18] We also have to remember that Hume was writing about English politics in his first collections of *Essays: Moral and Political* (1741–42), sometimes with a Scottish perspective, but with focus on political debates and events in London and Westminster. The importance of the press for British politics at this point in time can hardly be exaggerated. Sir Joseph Danvers, independent MP for Totnes, said in 1738 that 'the people of Great Britain are governed by a power that was never heard of as a supreme authority in any age or country before ... [that is] the government of the press'.[19]

It would be a mistake, however, to view the Walpole era as a time when the British press became 'increasingly free', as has fairly recently been suggested.[20] First of all we have to note that the press had never been completely free, despite the end of pre-publication censorship in 1695. The Blasphemy Act of 1697 (introduced at least in part in response to John Toland's scandalous *Christianity Not Mysterious*)[21] restricted religious criticism, and perceived attacks on the Glorious Revolution were treated as sedition, as can be seen in the (in)famous trial of Dr Sacheverell in 1710.[22] The method of prosecuting anti-government propaganda for seditious libel, one of Hume's specific targets, began properly around the turn of the eighteenth century under Lord Chief Justice John Holt. There were of course exceptional cases previously, notably the trial of the seven bishops in 1688, but in the seventeenth century licensing had done most of the censorship work. Prolific writers such as Daniel Defoe and John Tutchin fell victim to this practice in the early years of the century.[23] Charles Leslie defended the libel laws in his High Church *Rehearsal* on the basis that it 'wou'd confound all government' if 'private men are ... the judges of their superiors'.[24] As a consequence, it became common for government-critical publications to resort to irony and innuendo, paving the way for the age of Swift and Defoe. Moreover, outright Jacobite propaganda was for evident reasons treated as high treason. The young printer John Matthews was executed on these grounds in 1719, the last printer to be put to death in Britain.[25] A less dramatic way to restrict the press was to tax it. At the end of Queen Anne's reign, the Tory ministry, well-supported at the time by the sharp pens of Swift and Defoe, introduced the Stamp Act (1712) in an attempt to both monetise the growing press and curb opposition publications.[26] At the end of the century, in the wake of the French Revolution, the stamp duty was increased in order to suppress the distribution of newspapers among the poor.

Walpole also increased this levy, but there is a sense that his ministry was perceived as making a more direct onslaught on the liberty of the press.[27] The main targets were Jacobite publications such as the *True Briton*, *Mist's Weekly Journal* and *Fog's Weekly Journal*. The ironically entitled *Fog's* was set up after Nathaniel Mist, who had been arrested on several occasions, was impelled to flee to France after being tried for libel of the king.[28] The offensive print had been the so-called 'Persian Letter', published in August 1728, written by the Duke of Wharton, a Jacobite with a Whig family background, under the pen name of 'Amos Drudge'. In an apologia justifying his exile and Jacobitism, and defending Mist, Wharton denounced 'The Barbarity & Severity which the present ministers illegally exercise to destroy the liberty of the Press'.[29]

Opposition journalists were continuously arrested during the period, although there were few convictions.[30] For example, repeated but failed attempts were made to arrest and try Nicholas Amhurst, editor-writer of the *Craftsman*, the leading opposition journal, set up by Bolingbroke and the opposition Whig William Pulteney in 1726.[31] It was easier to target printers, if they could be identified, but it could also be risky; the libel trial against the *Craftsman*'s printer, Richard Francklin, in 1731, was followed by public outcry.[32] When the ministerial writer William Arnall ('Walsingham') defended the Whig credentials of Walpole's administration in 1731 by saying that unlike the Tory administration of 1710–14 it had not restrained the press, the opposition press responded that 'taking up the *Printers* and *Publishers*, and harassing their *Persons* and *Pockets* with *Imprisonment* and *Prosecutions*, will as effectually restrain the Press, as any *Grand Committee* in *England*'.[33] Paul Whitehead and his publisher were ordered into custody by the House of Lords following the anti-Walpole satire *Manners* (1739). In the event, only the publisher showed up.[34] In a speech relating to the affair, Lord Chancellor Hardwicke called the liberty of the press 'sacred to every Englishman', but a poorly understood concept: the English laws and constitution did not recognise any right to publish defamatory statements, he stressed.[35]

Papers without the high sales and financial backing of the *Craftsman* were vulnerable to government action. The *Universal Spy*, the *Alchymist* and the *National Journal* all went bankrupt in the 1730s and 1740s because of official prosecutions.[36] The *Craftsman* fought its most distinguished campaign against Walpole during the Excise Crisis of 1733, when Walpole's ministry sought to extend the excise duty to wine and tobacco. The campaign was a success in the sense that Walpole gave up the excise scheme, but for Bolingbroke it was a failure since the first minister managed to cling on to power in the general election of 1734, albeit with a smaller majority.

In May 1737, just a few months before Hume arrived in London for an eighteen-month stint, the Walpole ministry introduced pre-performance censorship of stage plays. The government had earlier been able to ban John Gay's *Polly*, the sequel to the *Beggar's Opera*, in 1728. The move to introduce formal censorship of plays nine years later was prompted by an anti-government play called *The Golden Rump*, based on a series of satirical articles published in the opposition journal *Common Sense*, and Henry Fielding's *Historical Register for the Year 1736*.[37] *The Golden Rump* is also often attributed to Fielding – although people speculated that it had been written either by Walpole himself or by one of his hirelings, in order to build a case for censorship of the theatre – or alternatively to William King, the known Oxford Jacobite.[38] Although censorship of the stage had no direct impact on the printed word, opponents of the so-called Playhouse Bill often compared the two.[39] It seems clear that many at the time saw print culture and the theatre as belonging to the same or at least a comparable bundle of rights: that of communicating one's sentiments freely to one's fellow men and women.

For example, when the bill was debated in the Lords, the Earl of Chesterfield[40] argued that it 'seems designed not only as a restraint on the licentiousness of the stage, but it will prove a most arbitrary restraint on the liberty of the stage; and, I fear, it looks yet farther, I fear it tends towards a restraint on the liberty of the press, which will be a long stride towards the destruction of liberty itself'.[41] The *Craftsman* protested against the censorship with a similar slippery-slope argument: 'There is not one Argument for restraining the *one* [the stage], which will not equally extend to the *other*' [the press], it wrote on 25 June.[42] The first play to be proscribed under the Licensing Act of 1737 was Henry Brooke's *Gustavus Vasa* (1739), which was about the sixteenth-century eponymous king who liberated Sweden from Denmark.[43] It was hard for anyone to be blind to the potential Jacobite allegory of Brooke's play, although it might have been an exhortation to Frederick, the Prince of Wales, who was a figurehead of the opposition at the time, as was common in Hanoverian Britain.[44] Hume was most likely familiar with the play since he referred to the Swedish king twice in his early essays.[45]

The Licensing Act of 1737 sparked a public debate about the liberty of the press, led by the *Craftsman*, whose new printer after Francklin's 1731 conviction, Henry Haines, was prosecuted for seditious libel after having compared George II to King John in Shakespeare's play.[46] The following year, Milton's *Areopagitica* was republished with a new preface by the opposition poet James Thomson. Press freedom continued to be at the centre of parliamentary debates in the next parliamentary session, as when the size of the standing army was discussed at the beginning of 1738. The Walpolean Whig William Hay spoke against a reduction in the size of the army, effectively as a defence against the 'liberty of the press', which protected scribblers who were 'spirit[ing] up the people against their governors'.[47] In response to this rather hyperbolic suggestion, Hay was mocked by the Tory-Jacobite John Hynde Cotton and the City MP John Barnard. As we shall see, Hume would also ridicule such suggestions, and agree with Chesterfield that further restrictions of the press would lead to an end of liberty.

The Walpole ministry also sought to crack down on parliamentary reporting. It is often mistakenly believed that reporting of parliamentary debates began in the late 1760s if not the early 1770s.[48] Reporting of parliamentary proceedings, albeit during recess, was not a new phenomenon in the second half of the century, as can be seen from Abel Boyer's *Political State of Great Britain* (1711–29) and Walpole's own *Short History of the Parliament* (1713).[49] The printing of parliamentary business was such a common practice and became such a headache for the Walpole ministry that, in April 1738, it introduced a resolution prohibiting the publication of debates and other proceedings in Parliament. One of the first to question the resolution was Bolingbroke's close friend and Tory ally Sir William Wyndham, who expressed his apprehension on the grounds that 'it is a question so nearby connected with the Liberty of the Press, that it will require a great deal of tenderness to form a Resolution which may preserve gentlemen from having their sense misrepresented to the public, and at the same time guard against all encroachment upon the Liberty of the Press'.[50] Wyndham's main complaint was that the resolution would prevent parliamentary reporting when Parliament was sitting as well as in recess. While being concerned about the danger of misrepresentations in the press, Wyndham believed that a knowledge of parliamentary proceedings was 'necessary for their [the people out of doors] being able to judge of the merits of their representatives within doors'.[51] Despite the objections expressed by Wyndham as well as Pulteney, the resolution passed unanimously. As a result, the press had to resort to allegory when reporting parliamentary business. Samuel Johnson wrote of the Senate of Lilliput in the *Gentlemen's Magazine*, and the *London Magazine* of debates in a political club with Roman names.[52]

Clamping down on press freedom was not the only way that Walpole sought to counter Bolingbroke, Pulteney and the other writers in the disparate opposition.[53] Walpole's Court Whig party also tried to build up a powerful counterweight to the illustrious opposition writers by employing government hacks such as James Pitt, William Arnall and Ralph Courteville.[54] It is not inconceivable that Samuel Richardson, printer of the ministerial *Daily Gazetteer*, wrote occasionally for the government.[55] On exceptional occasions, the ministerial case was formulated in pamphlets by bigw(h)igs such as Benjamin Hoadly, Lord Hervey, Walpole's brother Horatio and Walpole himself.[56] Although much exaggerated, the opposition's caricature of Walpole as the chief corrupter, whose greatest talent consisted in knowing every person's price, was not entirely false.[57] After the death of his collaborator John Trenchard in 1723, Walpole managed to neutralise the independent Whig Thomas Gordon by giving him the sinecure of first commissioner of the wine licences.[58] In the process, Gordon's *London Journal* – which had published *Cato's Letters* from 1720 to 1723 – was turned into a propaganda organ for Walpole's administration. Gordon was often identified as one of the people supervising Walpole's 'media strategy', along with the treasury solicitor Nicholas Paxton.[59]

A general sense remained that the sharpest pens were employed by the opposition as Walpole failed to patronise the greatest wits of the age. Jonathan Swift, Alexander Pope, John Gay and John Arbuthnot were some of those wits periodically involved in the loose literary opposition to Walpole.[60] The edge the opposition had over the ministry in this regard was acknowledged by the Court Whigs themselves, as when Lord Hervey wrote in his *Memoirs* that the *Craftsman* was 'a much better written paper than any of that sort that were published on the side of the Court'.[61] This together with the superior sales of the *Craftsman* compared with the government press may have prompted Walpole to turn to more draconian measures in the second half of the 1730s, as outlined above.[62] When Walpole himself referred to 'the warmest advocates for the Liberty of the Press' in Parliament, no one would have doubted that he referred to the opposition.[63]

The most immediate context for Hume's essay was undoubtedly what later became known as the War of Jenkins's Ear, the Anglo-Spanish conflict starting in 1739, soon to be incorporated into the War of the Austrian Succession (1740–48). As Tim Blanning has argued, and Edmund Burke before him, the war demonstrated the power of public opinion in Britain as Walpole was pressurised into declaring a war he had preferred, and indeed tried, to avoid.[64] The case for war was summarised in the opera *Alfred* (1740), the libretto of which was written by the opposition poets James Thomson and David Mallet, the latter being Bolingbroke's future literary executor. The closing chorus contained the immortal lines 'Rule, Britannia, Britannia rules the waves; Britain never will be slaves', embodying the opposition's preference for naval warfare.[65] Whitehead's aforementioned *Manners* was part of an earlier stage of the literary campaign for a naval war against Spain:

> Wrap'd into Thought, Lo! I *Brittania* see
> Rising superior o'er the subject Sea;
> View her gay Pendants spread their silken Wings,
> Big with the Fate of Empires and of Kings:
> The tow'ring Barks dance lightly o'er the Main,
> And roll their Thunder thro' the Realms of *Spain*.
> *Peace*, violated Maid, they ask no more,
> But waft her back triumphant to our Shore;
> While buxom *Plenty*, laughing in her Train,
> Glads ev'ry Heart, and crowns the Warriour's Pain.[66]

The war against Spain was clearly what Hume had on his mind when he opened 'Of the Liberty of the Press' by saying that '[i]f the administration resolve upon war, it is affirmed, that ... peace ... is infinitely preferable. If the passion of the ministers lie towards peace, our political writers breathe nothing but war and devastation, and represent the pacific conduct of the government as mean and pusillanimous.'[67] Hume's statement proved prophetic for the remaining of the 1740s: the ministerial Whigs who pursued the war after the fall of Walpole in 1742 sought to associate themselves with the interventionism of William III and Marlborough in the Nine Years War (1688–97) and the War of the Spanish Succession (1701–14). On their part, the opposition, including Patriots with both Tory and Whig backgrounds, argued against continental entanglements and pushed for a so-called 'bluewater strategy'.[68]

Despite the Walpolean pushback, it can be and has been argued that the vigorous press was one of the most important aspects that differentiated eighteenth-century Britain from other European societies at the time, notably France.[69] One of Hume's key claims was that it also differentiated Britain from republics such as the United Provinces and Venice.[70] As a matter of fact, the relative press freedom of eighteenth-century Britain was not surpassed by any European country until Sweden ended its censorship laws towards the end of the Age of Liberty (*frihetstiden*) in 1766.[71] In the wake of the *coup d'état* of Gustav III (1772), however, press freedom was curtailed, and by the time of his assassination in 1792 the liberty of the press had effectively been extinguished in Sweden.[72] The first question Hume announced that he was going to investigate in his essay was '*How it happens that* GREAT BRITAIN *alone enjoys this peculiar privilege?*'[73] In the original edition he added that he was also keen to test 'whether the unlimited exercise of this liberty be advantageous or prejudicial to the public?'[74]

His answer to the first question was straightforward: Britain's mixed constitution, neither entirely monarchical nor republican, was a form of government which naturally 'beg[o]t a mutual watchfulness and jealousy'.[75] In absolute monarchies, the monarch can have no jealousy of the people because they have no power, and, in pure republics, the people can have none of the magistrates, since no magistrate would be eminent enough to merit jealousy in such a regime. Because they were unmixed, the pure monarchy of France and the pure republic of the United Provinces were closer to each other than either was to Britain.[76] The British government, or the English government as Hume here calls it, shared characteristics with Rome under the emperors, with the difference that despotism had prevailed over liberty in the Roman Empire and liberty over despotism in Britain.[77] For the republican part of the constitution to stay dominant in Britain, Hume argued that the liberty of the press was a necessary institution:

> The spirit of the people must frequently be rouzed, in order to curb the ambition of the court; and the dread of rouzing this spirit must be employed to prevent that ambition. Nothing so effectual to this purpose as the liberty of the press, by which *all the learning, wit, and genius of the nation* may *be employed on the side of freedom*, and every one animated to its defence.[78]

Although Hume in other essays sought to tread a middle path between the arguments of Court and Country, or government and opposition – as in the final pages of 'That Politics May be Reduced to a Science' – it is difficult to read the preceding paragraph as anything other than a panegyric to the Country opposition writers. Although Hume was often critical of Bolingbroke's opportunistic opposition to the government, it is significant that he was prepared to moderately praise Bolingbroke's literary skills in his early essays, before he grew much more critical and tweaked some of his earlier claims.[79] In the original edition of 'Of the Independency of Parliament' (1741), Hume had said that the hired scribblers of the Court party had no advantage over the Country party writers. On the contrary, they were often 'scurrilous', even though they wrote for the government, in other words, 'the least popular side', which, according to Hume, 'shou'd be defended with most Moderation'.[80] Hume singled out the Walpolean pamphlet *The False Accusers Accus'd* as particularly poor. By contrast, '[w]hen L[or]d B[olingbrok]e,

L[ord] M[archmon]t, Mr. L[yttelto]n take the Pen in Hand, tho' they write with Warmth, they presume not upon their Popularity so far as to transgress the Bounds of Decency'.[81] The third Earl of Marchmont, earlier Lord Polwarth, was an opposition Whig and author of *The State of the Rise and Progress of the Difference with Spain* (1739). Hume was himself distantly related to the influential Scottish Marchmont family, in opposition to Walpole since 1733 and, while Whig, well-acquainted with Bolingbroke.[82] During his stay in London in 1737–39, Hume was in touch with its members, including the third earl and his twin brother, Alexander Hume-Campbell.[83] Interestingly for our present purposes, the third Earl of Marchmont had defended the 'Freedom of the Press' in an election pamphlet from 1740 entitled *A Serious Exhortation to the Electors of Great Britain*.[84]

As has been shown, that the 'Liberty of the Press' was an opposition slogan is evident from the parliamentary debates of the time, and all debates here cited took place either when Hume stayed in London or immediately before or after. Protecting the liberty of the press was quintessentially an opposition activity, whether Whig, Tory, a coalition of both or Jacobite. As Laurence Hanson pointed out, '[t]o appeal to public opinion was the only hope of the parliamentary opposition if it was deprived of royal favour or the expectation of a victory at the polls'.[85] This explains why Bolingbroke could go from being a 'gagger' of the press in government in 1710–14 to a proponent of press freedom when writing for the *Craftsman*.[86] Hume's essay raises questions about his political allegiance at this particular point in time. Commonly described as a court or establishment Whig,[87] what he often did in his early essays was to juxtapose conflicting arguments. It is thus possible to find plenty of evidence for him being pro-ministerial as well as in favour of the opposition.[88] This is what objectivity meant for Hume. It did not mean never taking sides, but rather meant never espousing one side consistently, which is at the heart of Hume's critique of political parties and the type of dogmatic behaviour he complained about in the conclusion of his essay 'That Politics May be Reduced to a Science' and elsewhere.

Hume's character sketch of Walpole (1742) has recently been described as the best example of his general aim to reach a balanced assessment not by suspending judgement but by weighing different partisan considerations against each other.[89] This may be an exaggeration, as Hume among other things in this essay says that, while trade had flourished under Walpole, liberty had declined and learning destroyed. While David Armitage has rightly pointed out that Hume here *implicitly* argues in favour of conciliation rather than war with Spain in 1739 by placing emphasis on Walpole's pacific legacy,[90] Hume goes on to write that Walpole was better suited to the second place rather than the first in government, and, while he loves Walpole as a man, he hates him as a scholar, and, as a Briton, wishes for his rapid retirement. '[W]ere I a member of either house, I would give my vote for removing him from ST. JAMES'S [i.e. the court]', he concludes.[91] As might be suspected, this was generally not seen as an impartial assessment at the time but opposition propaganda dressed as moderation.[92]

In a short conclusion of the essay, added in 1770 in the midst of the 'Wilkes and Liberty' panic, Hume said that 'the unbounded liberty of the press, though it is difficult, perhaps impossible, to propose a suitable remedy for it, is one of the evils, attending those mixt forms of government'.[93] As set out in the introduction, Hume's revisions have been discussed at length elsewhere and are not my main concern in the present chapter. By sharp contrast to this later, pessimistic ending of the essay, Hume had originally included a much longer conclusion in which he went beyond saying that the liberty of the press was necessary under Britain's mixed constitution. Indeed, his original assessment was that it 'is attended with so few inconveniences, that it may be claimed as the common right of mankind'.[94] The choice of terminology here is noteworthy since Hume usually shunned natural-rights language and arguments, and it is hard to escape the conclusion that Hume is here simply being rhetorical. We should also note that, even if this may sound close to natural-rights language, it is clear from the discussion that Hume is thinking about civil rights, that is to say, rights granted by governments rather than such that could be upheld *against* governments.

The only form of government in which press freedom would be fatal would be ecclesiastical forms (such as the papacy), Hume contended in one of his many swipes at religion. Ridiculing the idea that the press would foster dangerous popular discontent, Hume argued that the British press was a far cry from the demagogues of Athens and the tribunes of Rome. Reading was mainly a solitary and calm occupation and could 'scarce[ly] ever excite popular tumults or rebellion', which Hume was as keen to avoid in 1741 as in 1770.[95] Experience had shown, moreover, 'that the *people* are no such dangerous monsters as they have been represented, and that it is in every respect better to guide them, like rational creatures, than to lead them or drive them, like brute beasts'.[96] As people grew more accustomed to 'free discussion of public affairs', they were less likely to be seduced by popular clamour.

A recent historian has argued that Hume's essay was the first time anyone had called freedom of speech a human right.[97] This is not quite true. For one thing, it is probable that Hume was thinking about a civil right that he thought government should grant people rather than a natural or human right that people could claim against governments. Moreover, many of Hume's contemporaries were using human-rights arguments in very different ways. Only a few years earlier, his fellow Scot James Thomson had called it *'the best of human Rights'* in his preface to a republication of Milton's *Areopagitica*.[98] Gordon had called freedom of speech 'the Right of every man' in *Cato's Letters*, even though his discussion was entirely concerned with people living in 'free governments'.[99] Matthew Tindal, the religious freethinker with whose work Hume was acquainted,[100] had called it a 'natural Right' for all Protestants, as restrictions on the press could only be consistent with Catholicism, which for him was the same as slavery.[101] Joseph Addison, one of the 'polite' writers that Hume sought to emulate with his *Essays*, had written in 1712 that '[t]here never was a good government that stood in fear of Freedom of Speech, which is the natural Liberty of Mankind'.[102]

Other writers of Addison's generation such as Defoe had supported some 'restraints' on press freedom in the shape of post-publication prosecution, although Defoe thought that this could be done in a less arbitrary way than the enforcement of the seditious libel legislation.[103] Echoing the opposition of his day and disputing Court Whigs such as Hardwicke, Hume said that the 'laws against sedition and libelling are at present as strong as they possibly can be made'.[104] At the beginning of 1738 the libel laws had been discussed in British press, with a series of pamphlets and commentary on the *Crown* v. *J.P. Zenger* case in New York (1735).[105] This is most likely the case that Hume had on his mind when he referred to a libel case in a letter to Montesquieu in 1749.[106] The key for Hume was that Britain should not revert back to a system of press licensing. Such an attempt would equal 'the last efforts of a despotic government', and, if it succeeded, Hume believed it would mean that 'the liberty of *Britain* is gone for ever'.[107] Hume was thus sending a warning to the Walpole ministry, sharing the suspicion of the opposition that the government was aiming at curtailing the press further.[108] The fact that Hume was speaking in hypotheticals should not confuse us too much, as it was a standard technique in the opposition literature discussing press regulation and other threats.[109]

Hume's defence of the free press differed from the earlier championing of Thomson, Addison and Tindal, however. In fact, most arguments against censorship before Hume were repetitions and elaborations of themes discussed in Milton's *Areopagitica*. Although Hume believed that free discussion made the people more accustomed to 'distinguish between truth and falsehood', this was not one of his key arguments, and the word 'truth' occurs only this once in the essay.[110] By contrast, for Thomson, Addison and Tindal, the discovery of truth was all-important, as they appeared more confident than Hume that the free press really did aid the search for certainty. Simply put, Hume's defence was a sceptical one and needs to be distinguished from these earlier Protestant expressions. Thomson's preface to Milton described the freedom of the press as that which 'spreads Light, [and] diffuses Knowledge through the World'.[111] According to Tindal, human beings are rational creatures capable of discovering truth and whose 'chief Happiness as well as Dignity ... consists in having the liberty of thinking on what Subjects they please, and of as freely communing their Thoughts'.[112] Thomson agreed: in order for people to be either virtuous or religious, free use of reason was a precondition.[113] Restricting the liberty of writing and publishing meant limiting the means of promoting knowledge, virtue and religion, according to Thomson.[114]

In contrast to this optimism, Hume was highly sceptical about the ability of the press to approximate political truths, although many of his own essays on politics must have been intended as a form of myth-explosion and truth-seeking.[115] In general, it is evident that Hume did not think that the benefit of the British press was that it led to any increase in knowledge or cultural improvement. *Pace* Addison and the third Earl of Shaftesbury, he argued that it was the French, without press freedom, who had 'carried the arts and sciences as near perfection as any other nation' and were 'the only people, except the GREEKS, who have been at once philosophers, poets, orators, historians, painters, architects, sculptors, and musicians'.[116] The reason was that subjects of absolute monarchies in general and the French in particular pursued what was honourable, and the British what was profitable.[117] Even though a free government was a prerequisite for the *initial* rise of the arts and sciences, absolute monarchies may be better at cultivating such findings, at least in the polite arts, once they had been discovered.[118] What distinguished Britain from France was the British party press and political criticism; France was already publishing works in the arts and sciences.[119] This line of thinking was diametrically opposite to that of *Cato's Letters*, which had claimed that without freedom of expression there could be 'neither liberty, property, true religion, art, sciences, learning, or knowledge [sic]'.[120] A similar line of argument could be found in Thomson: what distinguished human beings from brutes was the flourishing of arts and sciences, and that was entirely dependent on 'the free Exercise of Wit and Reason'.[121] If read in conjunction with Hume's assertion that 'learning [had] gone to ruin' under Walpole, his point about France's success in letters and the arts could be read as criticism of Walpole's failure to support people of wit and genius, like his favourite writers Pope and Swift.[122] 'Bob, the Poet's Foe' was a common complaint in opposition literature and propaganda in the 1730s.[123] Hume was prepared to take this criticism further than most of the opposition writers, however, by acknowledging that France was perhaps beating Britain in the arts and sciences, and in particular in the liberal arts.

This did not mean that the free press was redundant; indeed, far from it. Hume's main argument was that, even if the party press was usually mistaken and could do with a lot more humility and moderation, the partisan scribblers, especially of the opposition as the court had political power on its side, helped to sustain the delicate balance of Britain's mixed constitution. Complete victory of either side would have meant an end to the constitutional equilibrium. What is more, press freedom was valuable not just for the British but for humankind. Public debate in its modern, written form had the potential to soften manners and decrease the risk of popular tumult.[124] This larger perspective distinguished Hume from many of his contemporaries who preferred to speak of the liberty of the press as 'the privilege of an Englishman'.[125] His argument is not only distinctive in a national context, however. Hume's defence of freedom of expression as primarily a defensive institution set him apart from later famous Continental thinkers, including Kant and Diderot, for whom it was an instrument of 'enlightenment'.[126]

Few who read 'Of the Liberty of the Press' when it was first published in 1741 would have read it as a non-partisan essay. The original essay has strong traces of anti-Walpole propaganda, although it is clear from Hume's other essays, importantly the conclusion of 'That Politics May be Reduced to a Science', that Hume cannot be firmly categorised as either Court or Country. Be that as it may, none of the caveats from the ministerial papers about press freedom can be found in the first edition of Hume's essay on the subject. Although not all members of the broad literary opposition to Walpole were in favour of unbridled press freedom (see David Womersley, Chapter 6 above), the 'Liberty of the Press' was an opposition slogan in the late 1730s. At this time, Hume spent a year and a half in London, seeking to publish his *Treatise on Human Nature* which he had written in France earlier, but also studying and thinking about *English* politics.[127]

As usual, however, Hume approached the subject in a somewhat idiosyncratic way. Whilst he was clear that Britain was different from other European powers, he did not take its uniqueness for granted, nor did he regard it as an unmixed blessing. Britain's mixed constitution was a product of a series of unintended consequences, and Hume sought to diagnose its merits as well as demerits. Although he leaned towards a more optimistic verdict on the liberty of the press in the original version of the essay, he was no starry-eyed admirer. The free press could be 'abused' and was indeed often 'licentious' and 'scurrilous', but it was all the same a crucial bulwark for preserving the precarious balance of Britain's mixed constitution, one with a high degree of monarchy but which inclined firmly towards liberty. The press was thus necessary to sustain Britain's 'ancient constitution',[128] as Hume here referred to it, which is something all states should do, he stressed, although he added that this was especially important in free states.[129] While his rhetoric was unmistakably of the kind found in the opposition press, by preserving the ancient constitution Hume probably meant little more than upholding stability and avoiding revolution. This was as important in Britain as in the equally legitimate civilised monarchy of France. For this reason, the liberty of the press was not the birthright of English people or Protestants but 'the common right of mankind', since it was so harmless for governments to allow such a right. Indeed, it might even help to stave off popular turbulence by giving a civilised outlet, or a 'vent in words', to discontent.[130]

NOTES

1 I have benefited from comments by Janet Chan, Tim Hochstrasser and Vanessa Lim, and conversations with James Harris. All the usual caveats apply.
2 D. Hume, 'Of the First Principles of Government' (1741), in *EDH*, 32; J. Madison,

'Federalist No. 49', in *The Federalists Papers*, ed. T. Ball (Cambridge, 2010), 245–8; W. Godwin, *An Enquiry Concerning Political Justice* (Oxford, 2013), 65; H. Arendt, *Crises of the Republic* (New York, 1972), 140.

3 M. Hanvelt, 'Politeness, a Plurality of Interests and the Public Realm: Hume on the Liberty of the Press', *HPT* 33 (2012), 629–31; B. Dew, '"Waving a Mouchoir à la Wilkes", Radicalism and the *North Briton*', *Modern Intellectual History* 6 (2009), 235–60; M. Baumstark, 'The End of Empire and the Death of Religion: A Reconsideration of Hume's Later Political Thought', in R. Savage (ed.), *Philosophy and Religion in Enlightenment Britain* (Oxford, 2012), 243–6; D. Livingston, *Philosophical Melancholy and Delirium: Hume's Pathology of Philosophy* (Chicago, 1998), 256–89.

4 Wilkes called the 'liberty of the press' the main bulwark of British liberty: P. Thomas, *John Wilkes: A Friend to Liberty* (Oxford, 1996), 19. Ironically, the *North Briton* often quoted from Hume's original essay when making the case for press freedom.

5 D. Forbes, *Hume's Philosophical Politics* (Cambridge, 1975), 184.

6 The different versions of the essay are discussed in Hanvelt, 'Politeness', which also seeks to connect it to other areas of Hume's thought. Hanvelt does not focus on the essay's immediate political context in 1741, however. Since this chapter was submitted, E. Hellmuth, 'Towards Hume – The Discourse on the Liberty of the Press in the Age of Walpole', *History of European Ideas* 44 (2018), 159–81, has been published, which provides useful and mostly complementary contexts.

7 See, however, R. Bourke, *Empire and Revolution: The Political Life of Edmund Burke* (Princeton, 2015).

8 J. Habermas, *The Structural Transformation of the Public Sphere*, trans. T. Burger (Cambridge, MA, 2016), 57–67.

9 See, for example, J. Melton, *The Rise of the Public in Enlightenment Europe* (Cambridge, 2001); T. Blanning, *The Culture of Power and the Power of Culture: Old Regime Europe 1660–1789* (Oxford, 2002); M. Knights, *Representation and Misrepresentation in Later Stuart Britain: Partisanship and Political Culture* (Oxford, 2005). For criticism of the applicability of Habermas's thesis to eighteenth-century England, see J. Downie, 'Public and Private: The Myth of the Bourgeois Public Sphere', in C. Wall (ed.), *Concise Companion to the Restoration and the Eighteenth Century* (Oxford, 2005), 58–79. In particular, the extent to which women could participate in the public sphere can be questioned.

10 It had lapsed earlier, between 1679 and 1685. See also M. Knights, *Politics and Opinion in Crisis, 1678–81* (Cambridge, 1994), esp. 153–92.

11 Melton, *Rise of the Public*, 29; B. Harris, *Politics and the Rise of the Press: Britain and France, 1620–1800* (1996), 12.

12 Harris, *Politics*, 12.

13 J. Downie, *Robert Harley and the Press* (Cambridge, 1979), 7.

14 R. Astbury, 'The Renewal of the Licensing Act in 1693 and its Lapse in 1695', *Library* 33 (1978), 296–322.

15 Professed 'impartiality', usually in the first issue of new publications, was conventional, however: J. Black, *The English Press in the Eighteenth Century* (1987), 13.

This should not be taken at face value since even the most partisan publications claimed to be impartial.
16 Ibid., 10.
17 Melton, *Rise of the Public*, 1–44.
18 Harris, *Politics*, 6.
19 Cited in ibid., 1. See also K. Wilson, *The Sense of the People: Politics, Culture, and Imperialism in England, 1715–1785* (Cambridge, 1995), 29–54.
20 L. Mitchell, *The Whig World, 1760–1837* (2005), xi.
21 This work (1696) argued that the doctrine of the trinity was nonsense and was condemned and burned for blasphemy in 1699.
22 G. Holmes, *The Trial of Doctor Sacheverell* (1973).
23 P. Hamburger, 'The Development of the Law of Seditious Libel and the Control of the Press', *Stanford Law Review* 37 (1985), 661–765. In *A Hymn to the Pillory* (1703), Defoe claimed that it was an honour to stand in the pillory, as he had been condemned to do for *The Shortest Way with Dissenters* (1703).
24 Cited in L. Hanson, *Government and the Press, 1695–1763* (Oxford, 1967), 1.
25 J. Nordin, 'Från uppfostrade undersåtar till upplysta medborgare: Censur och tryckfrihet från medeltiden till 1700-talet', in *Fritt ord 250 år: Tryckfrihet och offentlighet i Sverige och Finland – ett levande arv från 1766* (Stockholm, 2016), 44; P. Monod, *Jacobitism and the English People, 1688–1788* (Cambridge, 1989), 40.
26 Downie, *Robert Harley*, esp. chapter 7.
27 Cf. Black, *English Press*, 11–12, 165–8.
28 Mist moved in Jacobite circles in France; see Jeremy Black, 'An Underrated Journalist: Nathaniel Mist and the Opposition Press during the Whig Ascendency [sic]', *Journal for Eighteenth-Century Studies* 10 (1987), 27–41. Mist's was the most popular opposition journal before its demise; *Fog's* was overtaken by the *Craftsman*; see M. Harris, *London Newspapers in the Age of Walpole* (1987), 115.
29 *His Grace the Duke of Whartons Reasons for leaving his native Country & espousing the Cause of his Royal master K. J.3. in a Letter to his friends in G. Britain & Ireland* [c. 1728], Bodleian, MS Eng.hist.C 274, fol. 26.
30 Harris, *London Newspapers*, 189–97.
31 Ibid., 141. In the *Craftsman* 264 (24 July 1731), Bolingbroke named 'the liberty of the press' as perhaps the most important among 'the scared Liberties of *Britain*'; see Bolingbroke, *Contributions to the Craftsman*, ed. S. Varey (Oxford, 1982), 135.
32 Harris, *London Newspapers*, 143. Francklin was punished for having published the so-called 'Hague Letter' in January 1731, widely attributed to Bolingbroke, although this is denied by his biographer; see H. Dickinson, *Bolingbroke* (1970), 229.
33 P. Chamberlayne, *Full Answer to that Scandalous Libel, the Free Briton of July 1* (1731), 46.
34 The poem eulogised many prominent opposition members; see P. Whitehead, *Manners: A Satire* (1739), 10, 11, 17, 19, 20.
35 G. Harris, *Life of Lord Chancellor Hardwicke* (1843), I, 430.
36 Harris, *London Newspapers*, 148.
37 V. Liesenfeld, *The Licensing Act of 1737* (Madison, 1984), chapter 5.
38 *An Historical View of the Principles, Characters, Persons, &c. of the Political Writers*

in Great Britain (1740), 22. Another target of the legislation was Henry Fielding's *Historical Register for the Year 1736*; see E. Avery and A. Scouten, 'The Opposition to Sir Robert Walpole', *EHR* 83 (1968), 331.

39 Plays prohibited under the new legislation could still be printed and were often advertised as banned to boost sales.

40 As an opposition writer, Chesterfield is believed to have contributed to *Common Sense: or the Englishman's Journal*, edited by Charles Malloy, who had previously edited *Fog's Journal*. The Old Pretender was involved in the founding of the journal: G. Hilton Jones, 'The Jacobites, Charles Molloy, and *Common Sense*', *RES* 4 (1953), 144–7. Other opposition Whigs such as George Lyttelton also contributed to *Common Sense*. Chesterfield was also close to the *Old England Journal*: R. Harris, *A Patriot Press: National Politics and the London Press in the 1740s* (Oxford, 1993), 40.

41 W. Cobbett, *Parliamentary History*, X, col. 329.

42 Cited in Liesenfeld, *Licensing Act*, 152.

43 Brooke's play was defended by Samuel Johnson's ironical *Compleat Vindication of the Licensers of the Stage* (1739). Johnson's pamphlet contended that the only effective method of censorship was to abolish education and live in 'Ignorance and Peace' (31).

44 For example, Whitehead concluded his *Manners* (20) with the following lines: 'Such [glorious] Days, what *Briton* wishes not to see? / And such each *Briton*, FREDERICK, hopes from Thee.'

45 Hume, 'Of the Parties of Great Britain' (1741) and 'Of the Middle Station in Life' (1742), in *EDH*, 66, 549.

46 Liesenfeld, *Licensing Act*, chapter 7; Hanson, *Government*, 69–70.

47 Cobbett, *Parliamentary History*, X, col. 379.

48 Melton, *Rise of the Public*, 21, 32; P. Thomas, *George III: King and Politicians 1760–70* (Manchester, 2002), 16; Nordin, 'Från uppfostrade undersåtar till upplysta medborgare', 49. Moreover, Thomas argues that the printing of parliamentary speeches was a new phenomenon in George III's reign (see *George III*, 19), but this practice went back at least to Archibald Hutcheson in the reign of his great-grandfather; see, for example, [A. Hutcheson,] *Speech made in the House of Commons ... 24th of April 1716* (1716).

49 As has recently been shown, however, handwritten newsletters remained for many the key source about government and Parliament; see A. Barber, '"It is Not Easy What to Say of our Condition, Much Less to Write It": The Continued Importance of Scribal News in the Early 18th Century', *PH* 32 (2013), 293–316.

50 Cobbett, *Parliamentary History*, X, col. 802.

51 Ibid., X, col. 803.

52 After 1771, Parliament stopped prosecuting newspapers for parliamentary reporting, although the law was not changed.

53 To be clear, this article recognises the disunity of the opposition to Walpole. On this, see A. Pettit, *Illusory Consensus: Bolingbroke and the Polemical Response to Walpole, 1730–7* (Newark, NJ, 1997).

54 S. Targett, 'Government and Ideology during the Age of Whig Supremacy: The Political Argument of Sir Robert Walpole's Newspaper Propagandists', *HJ*

37 (1994), 289–311. The practice of using the press as a government tool had begun properly with Robert Harley/Oxford in the reign of Anne: Downie, *Robert Harley*. This challenges Habermas's suggestion that the eighteenth-century public sphere was 'oppositional' in nature, a suggestion questioned by Melton and Blanning.
55 J. Dussinger, '"Ciceronian Eloquence": The Politics of Virtue in Richardson's *Pamela*', in D. Blewett (ed.), *Passions and Virtue: Essays on the Novels of Samuel Richardson* (Toronto, 2001), 27–52.
56 H. Dickinson, *Walpole and the Whig Supremacy* (1973), 116.
57 It was also something the opposition genuinely believed; see Earl of Stair to second Earl of Marchmont, 10 December 1736 (*A Selection from the Papers of the Earls of Marchmont* (1831), II, 76–7).
58 C. Robbins, *The Eighteenth-century Commonwealthman* (Indianapolis, 2004), 111 downplays Gordon's apostasy. However, it is hard to explain away the fact that he dedicated his *Works of Tacitus* (1728–31) to Walpole.
59 Harris, *London Newspapers*, 103–4.
60 This is a key theme in B. Goldgar's *Walpole and the Wits: The Relation of Politics to Literature, 1722–1742* (Lincoln, NE, 1976). All of them were affiliated with the *Craftsman*, and some of them may even have contributed, although this is hard to prove.
61 J. Hervey, *Some Materials towards Memoirs of the Reign of King George II*, ed. R. Sedgwick (1931), I, 263.
62 This was certainly reflected in the sales figures; in 1730 the *Craftsman* is estimated to have sold up to twelve thousand copies per week, whereas the *London Journal* sold between two thousand and three thousand copies. On the other hand, the ministerial papers could make more effective use of the post office to distribute copies to provincial readers. Also, sales of the *Craftsman* varied greatly depending on the frequency of the contributions of Bolingbroke, its most popular writer. On this, see Harris, *London Newspapers*, 134–54.
63 Cobbett, *Parliamentary History*, X, col. 811.
64 Blanning, *Culture of Power*, 296; E. Burke, *Letters on a Regicide Peace*, ed. F. Canavan and E. Payne (Indianapolis, 1999), 108. Dickinson, *Walpole and the Whig Supremacy*, 129, describes Walpole's foreign policy as 'peace at almost any price'.
65 Cited in Blanning, *Culture of Power*, 298.
66 Whitehead, *Manners*, 20.
67 Hume, 'Of the Liberty of the Press', in *EDH*, 9. Cf. C. Gerrard, *The Patriot Opposition to Walpole: Politics, Poetry, and National Myth, 1725–42* (Cambridge, 1994), 6–10.
68 Harris, *Patriot Press*, 49–64. This division in foreign policy can be traced back to the post-revolutionary Whig–Tory dichotomy: S. Pincus, *1688: The First Modern Revolution* (New Haven, 2009), 305–65.
69 Harris, *Politics*.
70 Hume, 'Liberty of the Press', 9–10.
71 Before the 'TF 1766', discussion of the government's politics was essentially forbidden and was conducted almost entirely via illegal handwritten texts. See M.-C. Skuncke, 'Tryckfriheten i riksdagen 1760–2 and 1765–6', in *Fritt ord 250*

år, 109–44. Frederick the Great of Prussia abolished censorship in 1740, only to reimpose it three years later: Blanning, *Culture of Power*, 223–4.

72 Skuncke, 'Tryckfriheten i riksdagen 1760–2 and 1765–6', 138. Denmark-Norway also experienced an even shorter period of press freedom between 1770 and 1772; it began and ended with the rise and fall of the regent Johann Friedrich Struensee.
73 Hume, 'Liberty of the Press', 10.
74 Ibid., 604.
75 Ibid., 12.
76 However, the lack of jealousy had different effects in the two regimes: in France, it led to 'mutual confidence and trust', and in the Dutch republic to 'arbitrary power', since 'there is no danger in instructing the magistrates with large discretionary powers' there (ibid., 10–11). The press in the United Provinces was not as free as might be thought. For example, it was a capital offence to suggest that William of Orange aspired to sovereignty (Black, *The English Press*, 2).
77 Hume, 'Liberty of the Press', 11–12. My emphasis.
78 Ibid., 12.
79 Hume, 'Of Eloquence' (1742), in *EDH*, 108 (compare with variant readings, 622). Hume was very disparaging after the posthumous publication of Bolingbroke's collected *Works* (1754), but he later listed Bolingbroke as one of the 'eminent writers' to be used as an authority on spelling; see J. Greig (ed.), *The Letters of David Hume* (Oxford, 2011), I, 168, 208, 282. For the writing skills of Bolingbroke's friends and political brethren Swift and Pope, Hume had nothing but praise. He did send his *Treatise on Human Nature* (1739–40) to Pope, who at the time was active in opposition politics and corresponded with the Marchmont family on opposition tactics; see *Selection from the Papers*, II, 248; R. Sher, *The Enlightenment and the Book: Scottish Authors and Their Publishers in Eighteenth-century Britain, Ireland, and America* (Chicago, 2006), 60.
80 Hume, 'Independency of Parliament', in *EDH*, 609.
81 Ibid., 609.
82 Hume, *My Own Life*, in *EDH*, xxxii; Hume to George Carre of Nisbet, 12 November 1739 (*Letters of David Hume*, I, 36). The second Earl of Marchmont wrote in March 1739: 'I have for some time seen Lord Bolingbroke frequently; the more I know him, I esteem him more.' *Selection from the Papers*, II, 114.
83 Hume to Michael Ramsay, 22 February 1739 (*The Letters of David Hume*, I, 27–9).
84 Harris, *Patriot Press*, 31.
85 Hanson, *Government*, 3. After the Septennial Act of 1716, the City Elections Act 1725, and other measures, victory at the polls was not necessarily a reflection of public opinion.
86 For example, Bolingbroke arrested fourteen booksellers and printers in 1711. His antipathy to the printed word should not be exaggerated, however. Already in 1710–14, Bolingbroke had been a supporter and member of a famous writers' club, later to be known as the Scriblerus (or Scriblerian) Club, which included Swift, Pope, Gay and Arbuthnot. Although certainly not above the battle, many of these writers were fond of satirising political journalism, as when Pope

described a competition of Grub Street hacks in sewage diving in book two of the *Dunciad* (1728–43). However, the overwhelming majority of 'dunces' singled out by Pope were ministerial, and the *Craftsman* and its writers were let off the hook completely (Goldgar, *Walpole*, 76–7).

87 J. Pocock, *Virtue, Commerce, and History* (Cambridge, 1985), 138, 250; H. Dickinson, *Liberty and Property: Political Ideology in Eighteenth-century Britain* (1977), 132–3.
88 As soon as one finds enough evidence that points in one ideological direction, evidence pointing in the opposite direction, from the same chronological phase, can be found (Forbes, *Hume's Philosophical Politics*, 135).
89 J. Harris, *Hume: An Intellectual Biography* (Cambridge, 2015), 196–7.
90 D. Armitage, *The Ideological Origins of the British Empire* (Cambridge, 2000), 189.
91 Hume, 'A Character of Sir Robert Walpole' (1742), in *EDH*, 576. The publication of this essay for the second edition of the *Essays* at the beginning of 1742 accidentally coincided with the downfall of Walpole, although it had been written months earlier when the minister was at the 'zenith' of his power, as Hume clarified. There is little doubt that the quoted sentence was a reference to the failed vote to remove Walpole at the beginning of 1741. Due to the context, it was widely reprinted, e.g. in the *Newcastle Journal*; see J. Fieser (ed.), *Early Responses to Hume* (Bristol, 2005), II, 9–12. In later editions, Hume moved the essay to a footnote to 'Politics a Science', and eventually removed it entirely from his essay collections.
92 On this, see M. Goldsmith, 'Faction Detected: Ideological Consequences of Robert Walpole's Decline and Fall', *History* 64 (1979), 16–18.
93 Hume, 'Liberty of the Press', 13.
94 Ibid., 604.
95 Ibid., 604.
96 Ibid., 604–5.
97 Nordin, 'Från uppfostrade undersåtar till upplysta medborgare', 45.
98 [J. Thomson,] *Areopagitica: A speech of John Milton ... With a Preface by Another Hand* (1738), iii.
99 *Cato's Letters*, 15 (4 February 1721): 'Of Freedom of Speech: That the same is inseparable from publick Liberty'.
100 Hume, 'Of the Independency of Parliament', in *EDH*, 608.
101 [M. Tindal,] *Reasons Against Restraining the Press* (1704), 8. See also [M. Tindal,] *A Discourse for the Liberty of the Press* (1698), in *Four Discourses* (1709), 291–329. Thomson agreed, calling restrictions on the liberty of the press in a Protestant country 'a Contradiction in Terms', since Protestantism meant 'a Resolution to steadfastly and undauntedly ... oppose all Encroachments upon rational Liberty' (preface to *Areopagitica*, vi–vii).
102 [J. Addison,] *Thoughts of a Tory Author Concerning the Press* (1712), 13. Needless to say, the title of the pamphlet is ironic.
103 Hamburger, 'Seditious Libel', 744. Indeed, Defoe encouraged his patron Harley to prosecute the notorious High Church Tory-scribbler John Dyer; see Barber, '"It is Not Easy to Say of our Condition"', 314.
104 Hume, 'Liberty of the Press', 605.

105 *Tryal of John Peter Zenger, of New-York, Printer* (1738); *Remarks on the Trial of John-Peter Zenger* (1738); *Craftsman* 602 (21 January 1738).
106 *Letters of David Hume*, I, 135. Hanson, *Government*, 22, has suggested that it is also possible that Hume could have referred to a misreading of a trial against Francklin in 1729, but that is unlikely seeing that Hume spoke about a trial '[i]l y a douze ou quatorze ans', and his description fits so neatly with Zenger's trial, which was debated in London when Hume was staying there.
107 Hume, 'Liberty of the Press', 605.
108 [Johnson,] *Compleat Vindication of the Licensers of the Stage*, 28; [Thomson,] *Areopagitica*, preface; Lord Cobham to Alexander, second Earl of Marchmont, 30 December 1734 (*Selection from the Papers*, II, 57). Hardwicke suggested a more general suppression of opposition propaganda in an interview with George II at the start of 1745, in the same interview as the king famously said that 'Ministers are the king, in this country'; see W. Coxe, *Memoirs of the Administration of ... Henry Pelham* (1829), I, 202–3. It would probably be wrong to think that Hardwicke was referring to pre-publication censorship, however, and no major legislative actions with regards to the press were taken under the Pelhams (Hanson, *Government*, 70).
109 Goldgar, *Walpole*, 180.
110 Hume, 'Liberty of the Press', 604.
111 [Thomson,] *Areopagitica*, iii.
112 [Tindal,] *Reasons Against Restraining the Press*, 13. Tindal called Locke's *Essay Concerning Human Understanding* 'the most rational that ever was writ' (p. 9).
113 [Thomson,] *Areopagitica*, iv.
114 Ibid., viii.
115 For example, in 'Politics a Science', Hume contends that we can identify scientific rules in politics – both *a priori* and based on experience.
116 Hume, 'Of Civil Liberty' (1741) (originally entitled 'Of Liberty and Despotism'), in *EDH*, 91. Defoe had anticipated this unusual argument about France in *An Essay on the Regulation of the Press* (1704), 9.
117 See also Hume, *Enquiries Concerning Human Understanding and Concerning Principles of Morals*, ed. P. Nidditch (Oxford, 1998), 248–9.
118 Hume, 'Of the Rise of the Arts and the Sciences' (1742), in *EDH*, 111–37.
119 Political criticism would become more conspicuous and widespread in France in the second half of the eighteenth century; see R. Chartier, *The Cultural Origins of the French Revolution* (Durham, NC, 1991), chapters 3–4.
120 *Cato's Letters*, 100 (27 October 1722): 'Discourse upon Libels'. Trenchard's main example was Turkey (the Ottoman Empire), but his contemporaries would also have thought of France as a key example of an 'unfree' government.
121 [Thomson,] *Areopagitica*, iv.
122 The early Hanoverian court was arguably more successful in patronising scientific than literary endeavours; see H. Smith, *Georgian Monarchy: Politics and Culture, 1714–60* (Cambridge, 2006), 76–7, 83–92.
123 The phrase is from Swift's *Epistle to John Gay* (1731), but it was widely reflected in opposition propaganda, and Pulteney said that anyone wanting to cut a figure among 'the *gay*, the *polite*, the *witty Part of the World*' could not unite with

Walpole, in *An Humble Address to the Knights, Citizens, and Burgesses* (1734), 10. See also Goldgar, *Walpole*.

124 This is exactly what Hume began to doubt around 1770, in the wake of the 'Wilkes and Liberty' unrest.

125 See, for example, H. Fielding, *Jacobite's Journal* 26 (28 May 1747), cited in Hanson, *Government*, 2. Fielding went on to say that discussion of 'matters merely belonging to the royal prerogative, in print, is in the highest degree indecent, and a gross abuse of the liberty of the press'. No similar caveat is to be found in Hume's original essay.

126 I. Kant, *Beantwortung der Frage: Was ist Aufklärung?* [1784] *und andere kleine Schriften* (Berlin, 2016), 4–11; Raynal [and Diderot], *Histoire philosophique et politique des établissements et du commerce des Européens dans les deux Indes* (Geneva, 1780), III, 59–61.

127 This is a plausible assumption since he began composing his essays almost immediately on his return to Scotland; see Hume to Henry Home, 4 June and 1 July 1739 (R. Kilbansky and E. Mossner (eds), *New Letters of David Hume* (Oxford, 2011), 5, 6–7).

128 As a historian, Hume was later highly critical of this concept, but rather than abandoning the term completely he spoke of a series of ancient constitutions: D. Hume, *History of England*, ed. W. Todd (Indianapolis, 1983), IV, 355 n. l.

129 Hume, 'Liberty of the Press', 604.

130 Ibid., 604.

Chapter 10

The argument for freedom of speech and press during the ratification of the US Constitution, 1787–88

Patrick Peel

In his highly influential *Emergence of a Free Press*, Leonard Levy argued, 'If the Revolution produced any radical libertarians on the meaning of freedom of speech and press, they were not present at the Constitutional Convention or the First Congress, which drafted the Bill of Rights'.[1] Consequently, Levy believed that the First Amendment originally did not prohibit prosecution for the crime of seditious libel, but merely removed the limitation of prior restraint on speech and printing. In this view, Levy echoed the most influential legal commentator of the nineteenth century, Joseph Story, himself a Supreme Court Justice and Harvard Law professor, who had argued in his *Commentaries on the Constitution of the United States* (1833) that

> there is a good deal of loose reasoning on the subject of the liberty of the press, as if its inviolability were constitutionally such, that, like the king of England, it could do no wrong, and was free from every inquiry, and afforded a perfect sanctuary for every abuse; that, in short, it implied a despotic sovereignty to do every sort of wrong, without the slightest accountability to private or public justice. Such a notion is too extravagant to be held by any sound constitutional lawyer ... If it were admitted to be correct, it might be justly affirmed, that the liberty of the press was incompatible with the permanent existence of any free government.[2]

In this analysis, Story was explicitly following William Blackstone's *Commentaries on the Laws of England* (1765–69), and directly quoted Blackstone following the passage above:

> The liberty of the press is ... essential to the nature of a free state; but this consists in laying no previous restraints upon publications, and not in freedom from censure for criminal matter when published. Every freeman has an undoubted right to lay what sentiments he pleases before the public ... but if he publishes what is improper, mischievous, or illegal, he must take the consequences of his own temerity ... Thus the will of individuals is still left free, the abuse only of that free will is the object of legal punishment.

Hugely influential, Levy's adoption of the Story–Blackstone view of the freedom of speech and press in the early republic remains legal orthodoxy today.[3]

This interpretation of the early law surrounding freedom of speech and the press has not gone unchallenged, however. In fact, in response to the dominance of this view, some scholars have emphasised the difference between 'law on the books' and 'law in action'.[4] For example, Michael Kent Curtis in *Free Speech, 'The People's Darling Privilege'*, argues that at 'the time of the American Revolution, there were two American approaches to free speech – an orthodox legal view and a more popular free speech tradition' and furthermore that there was 'a chasm between the orthodox understanding of the right many judges would apply and the popular right many citizens exercised and thought they had'.[5] As recent scholarship on the Constitution outside the courts has demonstrated, this approach to freedom of speech and press has much to recommend it.[6]

Still, in framing their views of freedom of speech and press in the Founding Era, even scholars such as Curtis, who are aware of the larger political and legal context of American thinking about freedom of expression, have yet to fully excavate the debate over the ratification of the Constitution and mine it for insight into the meaning of freedom of speech and press.[7] This is regrettable since, in contrast to the debates within the Constitutional Convention or the First Congress, the ratification debates contain a robust set of arguments – arguments wholly at odds with the Story–Blackstone interpretation so influential today. Indeed, one aim of this chapter is to bring to the fore the fact that the Story–Blackstone interpretation was itself a conscious attack on the theory of freedom of speech contained in the ratification debates, an attack which, as the reigning influence of Levy's interpretation of the origin of the law of free speech shows, has been largely successful.

To see how and why Americans rejected the Story–Blackstone account of freedom of speech, two clusters of argument, each of which defined the dispute over free speech and press in the ratification debates, must be brought into focus.[8] First is a cultural struggle that represented the culmination of the revolution of 1776, which was waged between elite and middling social groups over the nature of acceptable public speech and the character of the emerging democratic public sphere. And second is a spectrum of moral and political arguments that linked together freedom of speech, press, liberty of conscience and the right to a jury trial as the means to promote the ends of republican self-government.

THE STRUGGLE FOR THE CHARACTER OF THE PUBLIC SPHERE

The ratification debate continued the profusion of public speech the revolution had ignited.[9] Yet the right to freedom of speech and press was not a factor in the revolutionary controversy between Great Britain and the colonies.[10] The list of grievances in the Declaration of Independence contains no mention of the suppression of printing or speech. Still, speech was everywhere in the Declaration. It was, after all, a speech act, a declaration of a shift from dependency to independence, one that *charged* imperial officials with an unwillingness to *listen* to the petitions of the people. The Declaration *reminded, appealed* and ended with its signatories pledging to each other their lives, fortunes and sacred honour. 'We do', the Declaration concluded, 'publish and declare, That these United Colonies are ... Free and Independent States.'

Mirroring the Declaration, the Constitution announced the performance of a further public act: 'We the People of the United States ... do ordain and establish this Constitution.' Unlike a simple referendum, in which the public merely gives or withholds its consent to a public proposal without agenda-setting power, the ratification debate laid the groundwork for a representative democracy with a provision for self-correction by amendment, a process begun immediately as flaws in the proposed constitution were highlighted and argued. As such, the ratification debate signalled that *the people* might no longer be conceived of as a mere multitude directed by a sovereign head, but rather might co-construct a constitution in dialogue with elites.[11] It was this sense of the significance of the opening words of the Constitution that led one of its leading theorists, James Wilson, to link the American Revolution and subsequent Constitution to the role of the people in ancient Britain under the Saxons prior to the Norman Conquest: 'the people held the helm of government in their own power' he said, citing Francis Bacon. This, Wilson tells us, meant that the Saxons were freemen, 'because they were born free from all yoke of arbitrary power', and stipulates how we ought to understand the way in which 'the people appear in the foreground of the national constitution ... We, the people of the United States, do ordain and establish this Constitution for the United States of America.'[12]

Elite Federalists and Anti-Federalists alike insisted that the debate over the ratification of the Constitution was to be conducted calmly and rationally, along the lines of polite literary conventions. '[A]fter a lapse of six thousand years,' Wilson concluded, 'America has now presented the first instance of a people assembled to weigh deliberatively, and calmly, and to decide leisurely, and peacefully, on a form of government by which they shall bind themselves and their posterity'.[13] Similarly, the Anti-Federalist Cato encouraged citizens to 'deliberate ... on this new national government with coolness; analyze it with criticism; and reflect on it with candor'.[14] Or, as another Anti-Federalist put it, 'Let them enjoy every light a free press can afford that they may judge for themselves, like rational creatures and freemen – Truth will shine the brighter when brought to the test'.[15]

And yet, throughout the ratification debates there is a forceful sense, in the wake of first the revolution, then the agrarian uprisings of the 1780s, and finally the proposal for a new Constitution issued from the secret conclave of the Constitutional Convention, that the very stability and character of American society were at stake in marking out the boundaries of legitimate and illegitimate public speech. Contained within the question of how fundamental public debate should be conducted was, participants suggested, the answer as to who was entitled to speak on behalf of the people and thus who exactly was to be in charge. Were those who opposed the Constitution, as a satirical Federalist piece entitled 'Wat Tyler, a Proclamation' would have it, no more than 'vagrants' who were 'requiring and commanding all and every of our subjects ... and more especially such of them as are *judges, counsellors ... constables,* and *public officers*' to preserve 'those rights and privileges which have ever been held sacred by the freest of all commonwealths, *a mob*'?[16] Or were elites simply trying to capture government by denigrating workaday blacksmiths, carpenters and millers, in short all middling and labouring people? 'It must be considered', the Anti-Federalist Honestus satirically noted,

> that government is a very abstruse science, and political disquisition a very arduous task, far beyond the reach of common capacities; and that no men, but those who have had a liberal education, and have time to study, can possibly be competent to such an important matter ... Whenever men of neither abilities or education, presume to meddle, with such matters as are above the reach of their knowledge or abilities, they will find themselves out of their proper sphere.[17]

Honestus then went on to document all the complex practical know-how being a blacksmith, carpenter, baker, miller, clock and watchmaker and mason entailed, thus implying that the public the Federalists represented was devoid of real content, pompous and false.

These disputes over who was entitled to speak for the public and in what way bled into debates about who controlled the press. Writing in 1788, for instance, Senex began from the premise that freedom of press was 'the surest defence of liberty; and those who have made attempts to controul it, have deservedly met with the indignation of every lover of his country'.[18] Indeed, it was rightly 'the channel through which the oppressed may utter their injuries, and the lowest innocent force the shafts of satire through the guards with which men in power are encompassed'. Still, there was a distinction to be made between 'rational language' and 'the roarings of a mad man' who might 'vent the poison of his heart, at those whom envy or blind party rage, has made the objects of his hate'. The 'manly' 'duty of every member of the community ... of freemen: To sound the alarm, and drag the servants of the public to a tribunal' via the press was ennobling and the use of satire edifying. But Senex condemned in language borrowed from Scottish common-sense philosophy what he called 'a lower denomination' of speech for being a wound to 'every benevolent mind', describing those who did not conform to polite literary conventions as 'these little things emulating the works, for which great minds alone are destined, [which] excite in us the emotions we feel at seeing children, in mock plays, acting the characters of heroes; or mad men swaggering with the fancied importance of princes'.[19]

The conflict between elite and middling definitions of appropriate public speech are ever-present throughout the ratification debates and suggest a society whose political institutions were fragile, one in which published attacks on government seem more like a reckless act of faith than the catty swipes we take for granted in the brawl of party politics today.[20] Yet the ratification debates comprise a massive outpouring of political writing and speech of every kind: accusations, diatribes, exaggerations, misstatements, insults, political pleadings, prayers, prophesies.[21] It was as if the type of speech unleashed by the Declaration of Independence had gone viral. One cannot read the ratification debates on freedom of speech and press without hearing a profound shift from a monarchical world characterised by public authority that confronts subjects who are private persons and thus not entitled to hold political power to a world in which a welter of competing deliberative publics struggle to compel government to legitimate itself before public opinion.[22]

MONARCHIES, FREE STATES AND SPEECH

Even more than over the nature of acceptable public speech and what the character of the emerging democratic public sphere was to be, debate over freedom of the press and speech centred on what it meant to be a free person, a member of a free society living in a free state, as opposed to in a monarchy. These debates formed the moral centre of disputes over the freedom of the press and speech. They echoed eighteenth-century commonwealth arguments in important details, but also inherited a deeper intellectual pedigree stretching back to the contributions made by Renaissance humanism to early modern political thought.[23]

The distinction between *free states* and *monarchies* was principally an argument about freedom, which contrasted with the contention that living in fear of prosecution for speech was compatible with political liberty, and an argument that the people were indeed capable of governing themselves – thus implying that the great body of the people would need free speech to call its agents to account.[24] Thus, an appreciation of the distinction writers drew between *free states* and *monarchies* is essential if one is to understand how the ratification debates represented a continuation of a wider European debate and repudiation of the Blackstone–Story theory of speech. Once that distinction is in place, the moral and political edge of American arguments becomes sharper, as do the arguments of eighteenth-century writers whom Americans so much admired, such as Montesquieu, Trenchard and Gordon.

Building on the classical republican tradition of political liberty and free states derived from Roman moral philosophy – including Livy, Sallust and Cicero – and most powerfully advanced in Machiavelli's *Discourses on Livy*

(1531), middle seventeenth-century critics of the Stuart monarchy developed the following argument: the great body of the people did not need a sovereign head (head of state) to function as a state; rather, the people themselves could be a state.[25] And even more to the point, for the people to rule themselves as a state was absolutely essential because only if they could do so could they truly be said to live in a personal condition of freedom.[26] Those who lived under a monarchy, according to this line of argument, were subject to the prerogative rights of a king and lived in a condition of dependence – a position on par with slavery, according to the *Digest* of Roman Law, which itself used the term '*liber homo*' (free-man or person) as a status in contrast to the status of a slave.[27] A common pun was this: if you (personally) wish to live in a free state (i.e. a free condition), you must live in a free state (i.e. political body).[28] Therefore, radical and parliamentary writers were led to describe self-governing polities not simply as *states* in contrast to monarchies but as *free states* in contrast to the dependence and slavery imposed by kingly rule.

According to this view, to have the status of a free person (a *liber homo* and free-man) was to live in a free state, such that one had a set of fundamental liberties secured from relationships of dependence, which in turn required some exercise of control over one's government so that the institutions necessary for one's political liberty (e.g. courts, legislatures, executives) did not themselves become sources of oppression.[29] It this context, discussion of political liberty was rooted in an analysis of what it meant to speak of being a free person – a member of a free society living in a free state.

Whilst the depth of the American reception of these views remains to be fully explored by scholars, Americans unquestionably inherited much of the English debate regarding the nature of free states as opposed to monarchies.[30] They inherited them, firstly, through the political language they spoke, which they used to conceptualise the dramatic events of 1776 and their aftermath; the Declaration of Independence, it will be recalled, concluded that these United States were not only to be independent states, but 'free states'.[31] A figure no less important than George Washington could, for instance, note in defence of Massachusetts during the revolution that 'none of them [the revolutionaries] will ever submit to the loss of those valuable rights and privileges which are essential to the happiness of every free state, and without which life, liberty and property are rendered totally insecure'.[32]

Secondly, Americans inherited the debate between *free states* and *monarchies* through the authors they read, including eighteenth-century publications of Roman historians and seventeenth-century parliamentarian thinkers such as Marchamont Nedham, whose *The Excellencie of a Free-State; Or, The Right Constitution of a Commonwealth* (1656) had been much discussed in the United States, according to John Adams in his *Defense of Constitutions* (1787).

However, still more influential were eighteenth-century critics of monarchy, such as Montesquieu, John Trenchard and Thomas Gordon, whose account of free states owed much to Machiavelli's *Discourses on Livy* and whose critiques of monarchical states presented an outlook similar to that of earlier writers.[33] Indeed, in their first collective statement on the significance of freedom of speech, Americans in their *Letters to Quebec* (1774) cited Montesquieu to the effect that 'in a free state everyman, who is supposed to be a free agent, ought to be concerned in his own government: therefore, the legislative should reside in the whole body of the people'. In referring to Montesquieu, Americans were emphasising republican conceptions of liberty that centred on living free from a condition of insecurity and dependency and hence not being forced to censor themselves, thereby emphasising the psychology of liberty, in contrast to servitude. Thus, quoting Montesquieu again in their *Letters to Quebec*, Americans argued, 'The political liberty of the subject' is 'a tranquility of the mind, arising from the opinion each person has of his safety', which, as they noted, was secured through a free of press whose 'importance consists, besides the advancement of truth, science, morality, and arts in general, in its diffusion of liberal sentiments on the administration of Government, its ready communication of thoughts between subjects, and its consequential promotion of union among them, whereby oppressive officers are shamed or intimidated to more honorable and just modes of conducting affairs'.[34]

American arguments for freedom of speech and press also paralleled the wildly influential eighteenth-century commonwealth arguments of John Trenchard and Thomas Gordon's *Cato's Letters*.[35] According to this view, 'freedom of speech is the great bulwark of liberty', a phrase that could be entrenched in revolutionary state constitutions for two reasons.[36] Firstly, since the 'administration of government is nothing else, but the attendance of the trustees of the people upon the interest and affairs of the people', freedom of speech and press liberated the people to call their governors to account. 'Power in a free state', Trenchard and Gordon said, 'is a trust committed by all to one or a few', but a trust that had to be continuously monitored, and executors of that trust censured when it was broken.

The price of freedom was, in short, eternal vigilance.[37] Freedom of speech and press institutionalised that vigilance. This sentiment implied that libels (written statements that damaged the good reputation of government officials, thus undermining their authority) were not in fact sedition and faction, but rather the endeavour to preserve the right of the people to criticise their governors. Libels were, Gordon said, 'liberties assumed by private men, to judge of and censure the actions of their superiors, or such as have possession of power and dignities'. Instead of speech inconsistent with the safety of government, libel was a way for citizens to contest those who 'took it into their heads to call themselves the government, and thought that others had nothing to do but to sit still, to act as they bade them, and to follow their motions'.[38] Along parallel lines, writing as 'One of the Common People', an author in the *Boston Gazette* argued that the idea of a bill of rights and, in particular, freedom of the press was 'so important and valuable [a] discovery' because it guarded 'the people against the increasing powers of artificial aristocracy, whose seeds are everywhere disseminated in free states'.[39] One satirical article asserted that, according to the 'Federalist's Political Creed', 'a libel is whatever may happen to give offence to any great man'.[40]

In addition, freedom of speech promoted the aims of public deliberation, virtue and human dignity, each of which could serve as a check on government. Written just three months before the debate on the ratification of the Constitution was to begin, David Ramsay's 1778 Fourth of July address entitled 'Oration on the Advantages of American Independence' put the point thus: 'In an oppressive regime "ignorance" was better than knowledge', whereas 'eloquence is the child of a free-state'. In contrast to kingly governments where the body of the people is overwhelmed by insincerity, pride and luxury, republics are favourable to 'truth, sincerity, frugality, industry, and the simplicity of manners'. Ramsay went further, suggesting that living in a free society promoted human dignity and self-worth. 'I appeal to the experience of all', he said,

> whether they do not feel an elevation of soul growing out of the emancipation of their country, while they recollect that they are no longer subject to lawless will, but possess the powers of self-government, and are called upon to bear an active part in supporting and perpetuating the sovereignty of the United States ... In this elevation of soul, consists true genius; which is cramped by kingly government, and can only flourish in free states.

To say, as Ramsay did, that to live in a free state facilitated the 'elevation of soul' was to appropriate for democratic purposes the central aristocratic virtue of magnanimity (literally great soulfulness); it was to highlight, as did authors throughout the ratification debates, how freedom of speech and press promoted the psychology and sociology of freedom, which they believed acted in turn as checks on the abuses of government.[41]

As the previous section of this chapter argued, the ratification debates were characterised by a profound struggle between elite and middling groups to define the scope of legitimate public speech after the revolution. In the context of that struggle, the contrast between a subject within a monarchy and a free person living within a free state amplified arguments for freedom of speech and press, bending them in directions largely unacceptable in the eighteenth-century Anglo-American world. In fact, as I suggested at the outset, the arguments Americans were advancing in the ratification debates contrasted sharply with the view of freedom of speech and press that had dominated that world. As noted, the premise of that theory had been established most forcefully by Blackstone's *Commentaries* (1765–69), which gave a clear exposition of a view at odds with the theory that flowed from republican free-state ideology, a view premised on a natural-rights-centred view of freedom of the press. In his *Commentaries*, Blackstone argued that 'where blasphemous, immoral, treasonable, schismatical, seditious, or scandalous libels are punished by the English law ... the liberty of the press, properly understood, is by no means infringed or violated'. 'The liberty of the press', he said, was

> essential to the nature of a free state; but this consists in laying no previous restraints upon publications, and not in freedom from censure for criminal matter when published. Every freeman has an undoubted right to lay what sentiments he pleases before the public; to forbid this is to destroy the freedom of the press, but if he published what is improper, mischievous, or illegal, he must take the consequence of his own temerity ... Thus the will of individuals is still left free, the abuse only of that free will is the object of legal punishment.[42]

Blackstone's account of the freedom of speech and press – as well as the definition he gave to the term 'free state' and 'freeman', arguing as he did that they were compatible with severe prosecution for speech, since to be free simply meant, as he previously defined the concept, not to be restrained – represented a powerful attack on the moral and political vocabulary whose intellectual pedigree we have been examining. In the ratification debates, Americans did not follow Blackstone. Quite the contrary, throughout the debates Americans repeatedly rejected that view, appealing to the 'free state' tradition they inherited, and asserting that 'the people' had a right to free speech and press and that in this context it was a right of 'free-men'.

Indeed, what is particularly striking about the arguments underlying the moral reasons for the right to freedom of speech and press is the marked lack of discussion of natural rights or the social contract as a basis for these rights. The entire framework of the Blackstone account is almost wholly absent. To the small extent that ideas of natural right and social contract circulate in the ratification debates, where speech is concerned they are largely, with one notable exception, a gloss placed on free-state arguments. For instance, in a piece published in the *Winchester Virginia Gazette* in 1788, the author offers a strongly republican interpretation of the proposition that 'the Freedom of the Press is the unalienable Right of a free Government particularly when matters of the greatest moment demand the serious attention, and free discussion of the citizens'.[43] Citing Milton, Addison and the history of Rome and its decline into slavery, the entire moral force of the essay is framed by the language of republicanism. In another strongly republican article, an author asks:

> What have we not a right to expect will be the fate of our natural rights – and what new species of tyranny may we not experience, when any one individual, by virtue of, and under the authority of office, shall dare, under the eye too of our rulers, to check or suppress an institution so highly necessary and beneficial as the establishment even in the bondage of monarchy, for the conveyance of letters, newspapers?[44]

Of the major figures in the ratification debates, Richard Henry Lee, a scion of the Virginia gentry and leading Anti-Federalist, was one of the few to make regular use of natural-rights language, which he at times borrowed from Blackstone without acknowledgement.[45] But even there his arguments retained a strongly republican quality. In his proposed amendments of 27 September 1787 to the Constitution, he argued that the purpose of a 'Bill of Rights' was to mark out the principles of the 'Social Contract':

> it having been found from Universal experience that the most express declarations and reservations to protect the just rights and liberty of Mankind from the Silent, powerful, and ever active conspiracy of those who govern – And it appearing to be the sense of the good people of the America by the various Bills or Declarations of rights whereon the governments of the greatest number of the state are founded, that such precautions are proper to restrain and regulate the exercise of the great powers necessarily given to Rulers.[46]

Despite his recourse to the idea of social contract, Lee thus strongly implied that, in order for the majority to keep the agents of government in check, bills of rights had been instituted. The emphasis here, as elsewhere, is on the need not to keep the sphere of the individual inviolable against the people themselves but to prohibit the agents of the people from overstepping their rightfully established boundaries.

However, one noteworthy and significant use of language touching on natural rights was not a gloss on republican themes.[47] Advocates for freedom of speech and press repeatedly expressed anxiety that the new constitution would undermine the principle of religious liberty. As such they linked the freedom of speech and press to freedom of conscience, seeing them as conjoined. Scholars Mark Noel and Nathan Hatch have done a great deal to show how Americans democratised Christianity during this period, leading, as Noel has argued, to a distinctive Christian republicanism. One cannot read the ratification debates without being struck by the blending of Christian and republican idioms. For instance, in a strongly republican attack on the proposed constitution, Philadelphiensis could proclaim: 'Every freeman of America ought to hold up this idea to himself, *that he has no superior but God and the laws.*'[48] Indeed, the ratification debates illustrate political partisans using the issue of religious liberty to mobilise religious denominations on one side or the other of the debate.[49]

In a powerful critique of Blackstone, one that distilled Anti-Federalist thinking of the late 1780s and 1790s, St George Tucker captured the essence of the argument implied throughout the ratification debates.[50] He said:

> The right of personal opinion is one of those absolute rights which man hath received from the immediate gift of his Creator, but which the policy of all governments ... hath endeavored to restrain, in some mode or other. The mind being created free by the author of our nature, in vain have the arts of man endeavored to shackle it ... This right of personal opinion, comprehends first, liberty of conscience in all matters relative to religion; and secondly, liberty of speech and of discussion in all speculative matters, whether religious, philosophical, or political.[51]

In advancing these arguments, Tucker drew on Richard Price's *Observations on the American Revolution* (1784), but it is clear he also drew on older lines of argument.[52] Linking the themes of individual conscience and freedom of speech and press, Tucker emphasised that government was merely the agent of the people and thus must be responsible to the people themselves for its conduct: 'that to enforce this responsibility' it was

> indispensably necessary that the people should inquire into the conduct of their agents; that in this inquiry, they must, or ought to scrutinise their motives, sift their intentions, and penetrate their designs; and that it was therefore, an unimpeachable right in them to censure as well as to applaud; to condemn or to acquit; and to reject, or employ them again, as the most severe scrutiny might advise.[53]

Nothing, he said, 'could more clearly evidence the inestimable value that the American people have set upon the liberty of press, than their uniting it in the same sentence ... with the right of conscience, and freedom of speech'.[54] Summing up the American position, Tucker concluded: 'The people, not government, possess the absolute sovereignty', and thus what was required was 'a freedom unlimited as the human mind; viewing all things, penetrating the recesses of the human heart, unfolding the motives of human actions; and estimating all things by one invaluable standard, truth; applauding those who deserve well; censuring the undeserving; and condemning the unworthy, according to the measure of their demerits'.[55]

Tucker did not dwell on the right to a jury trial here, mentioning the court of the Star Chamber only in passing.[56] But critics of the Constitution almost always linked freedom of conscience, speech and the press to the right to a trial by jury.[57] An article by Timoleon from 1787 shows how all these issues could come together, in addition to lawyerly worries about the broad language of the Constitution.[58] He asked his reader to suppose the following:

> [A] gentleman ... is appointed a *judge* of the supreme court under the new Constitution, and the *rulers*, finding that the rights of conscience and the freedom of the press were exercised in such a manner, by *preaching* and *printing* as to be troublesome to the new government – which event would probably happen, if the rulers finding themselves possessed of great power, should so use it as to oppress and injure the community. – In this state of things the *judge* is called upon, *in the line of his profession*, to give his opinion – whether the *new Constitution* admitted of a legislative act to *suppress the rights of conscience*, and *violate the liberty of the press?* The answer of the learned *judge* is conceived in didactic mode, and expressed in learned phrase; thus, – In the 8th section of the first article of the *new Constitution*, the Congress have power given *to lay and collect taxes for the general welfare of the United States*. By this power, the right of taxing is co-extensive with the *general welfare*, and the *general welfare* is as unlimited as actions and things are that may disturb or benefit that general welfare. A right being given to *tax* for the general welfare, necessarily includes the right of judging what is for the general welfare, and a right of judging what is for the general welfare, as *necessarily* includes a

power of protecting, defending, and promoting it by all such laws and means as are fitted to that end; for ... who gives the end gives the means necessary to obtain the end. The Constitution must be so construed as not to involve an absurdity, which would clearly follow from allowing the end and denying the means. A right of *taxing* for the general welfare being the highest and most important mode of providing for it, cannot be supposed to exclude inferior modes of effecting the same purpose, because the rule of law is ... From hence it clearly results, that, if *preachers* and *printers* are troublesome to the new government; and that in the opinion of its rulers, it shall be for the general welfare to restrain or suppress both the one and the other, it may be done consistently with the new Constitution.

Blending the concerns of republican self-government with the language of Christianity, Timoleon concluded by quoting a Bible passage favoured by the Anti-Federalists, Joshua 9:12: 'if agreed to [the Constitution], must inevitably convert the people of this free country into hewers of wood and drawers of water for the few great ones, into whose hands all power will be thereby unwarily delivered'.[59]

CONCLUSION

Public debate surrounding freedom of press and speech, and in addition liberty of conscience and trial by jury, centred on concerns more politically and morally substantive than lawyerly debates over the inclusion or exclusion of freedom of speech and press within the Constitution. Contrary to the standard story within legal casebooks, the insistence by the public on the right to free speech and press represented a deep moral commitment to building a society in which human beings might live in full possession of their liberty. The critics of Levy's thesis thus have a point: while strong proponents of an extensive right to freedom of speech and press may not have been present at the Constitutional Convention or the First Congress, such views were present in the larger public debate over the ratification of the Constitution. For these participants, to live as a free person required living in a free society within a free state and this required the people themselves, not as a heedless and headless multitude, but as that great self-governing body of the people, to hold their agents to account. In advancing these arguments, Americans were participating in a profound quarrel regarding the nature of free states that stretched back to at least the middle of the seventeenth century, but they were doing so in a distinctively late eighteenth-century American context, in the aftermath of independence and against the backdrop of a fretful, anxious debate over the nature of acceptable public speech and what the character of the emerging democratic public sphere would be.[60]

The collision of these two debates manifested less in the articulation of novel political arguments than in the encouragement of a shift in the terms of what was to count as publicly justifiable speech. Speech used for the purposes of organised political opposition, or what today would be called a political party, became acceptable in this period, and in no small part because of the momentum behind the two profound quarrels we have been examining. Who, after all, was to speak for the public? Might multiple, conflicting, deliberative publics each claim legitimate title to public speech? And did not the free-state arguments on behalf of freedom of expression decidedly authorise the profusion of public speech? Various, competing publics were, as participants in the ratification debates clearly understood, *speaking*; however, the free-state, free-speech ideology implied that no principled ground could be supplied to deny one or the other of clashing deliberative publics the right to speech.

Put simply, with the expansion of public argument unleashed by the Declaration of Independence, and then propelled forward in the context of the ratification debates, the moral and political arguments of the free-state ideology that Americans embraced established for them the premise necessary to justify ongoing, organised, oppositional political speech – speech they had already begun to experience in the ratification debates. Where political parties and the speech of factious men were once viewed as antithetical to responsible republican self-government, the legitimating of constitutional opposition and the speech that went with it marked a new turn in the history of American political thought.[61]

Further attempts to delegitimise speech used for organised political opposition would later surface, as the passage of the Sedition Act in 1798 attests. And, in fact, the arguments used to justify the Sedition Act relied heavily on Blackstone's assertion that 'freemen' who live in a 'free-state' have the right to lay their sentiments before the public, but the aggressive prosecution of such speech none the less leaves 'the will of individuals ... free, the abuse only of that free will is the object of legal punishment'. However, by the end of the ratification debates that position, as the failed Sedition Act of 1798 and the collapse of the Federalist Party following the election of Thomas Jefferson underscored, had lost public and thus political legitimacy.

In his First Inaugural Address, Jefferson captured this shift in public sentiment towards the nature of political parties and the organised oppositional political speech that it implied when he famously sought to unify the country in the aftermath of its first democratic transfer of political power from the Federalist administration of Adams to his own Republican administration:

> During the contest of opinion through which we have passed the animation of discussions and of exertions has sometimes worn an aspect which might impose on strangers unused to think freely and to speak and write what they think ... [But] let us reflect that, having banished from our land that religious intolerance under which mankind so long bled and suffered, we have yet gained little if we countenance a political intolerance as despotic as wicked and capable of as bitter and bloody persecutions ... We have called by different names brethren of the same principle. We are all Republicans, we are all Federalists.[62]

If a plurality of competing, proselytising organised religious denominations could coexist within one republic, then, as Jefferson suggests here, so, too, should there be toleration of competing organised political parties.

Still, other momentous political events hovered on the horizon that would help to eclipse the republican, free-state argument of freedom of speech and the press despite its contribution to the legitimating of oppositional political speech; the populist uprisings of the 1840s, the secession crisis of 1861, the passage of the Fifteenth Amendment (legalising African American males' right to vote), the push to roll back Reconstruction, and the introduction of Jim Crow each pushed American free-speech doctrine away from the arguments advanced in the ratification debates and towards the acceptance of the view found in Story and Blackstone. Proponents of this view held that if speech had a bad tendency, if its consequences were harmful as judged by government officials, then it could be rightfully prosecuted without any harm to the principle of free speech, since to live as a free person within a free state meant only that one was not interfered with in speaking.

Modern-day First Amendment jurisprudence has done away with the crime of seditious libel.[63] By doing so, it is often supposed, the Supreme Court's modern free-expression doctrine represents a radical departure from its historical origin in the doctrine of Blackstone and Story. However, the robust debate regarding freedom of speech and press contained in the ratification debates and its contribution to justifying the idea of legitimate party opposition within a constitutional democracy indicates that modern freedom-of-expression jurisprudence holds more continuity with the past than is generally appreciated.

NOTES

1 L. Levy, *Emergence of a Free Press* (Oxford, 1985), xii–xv.
2 J. Story, *Commentaries on the Constitution of the United States* (1833), section 1878.
3 C. Sunstein, *Democracy and the Problem of Free Speech* (New York, 1993), xii–xvi; A. Bhagwat, 'Posner, Blackstone and Prior Restraints on Speech', *Brigham Young University Law Review*, 5 (2015), 1151–3. Indeed, the Story–Blackstone theory of freedom of speech operated in American constitutional law as late as Justice Oliver Wendell Holmes's decision in *Patterson* v. *Colorado* (1907). However, Holmes famously repudiated the view that government could ban political speech because it was dangerous in *Abrams* v. *United States* (1919). The change in Holmes's thinking is documented in T. Healy, *The Great Dissent: How Oliver Wendell Holmes Changed His Mind – and Changed the History of Free Speech in America* (New York, 2013). On the larger shift to the modern doctrine of free speech, see V. Blasi, 'Rights Skepticism and Majority Rule at the Birth of the Modern First Amendment', in L. Bollinger and G. Stone (eds), *The Free Speech Century* (Oxford, 2019), 13–32. Cf. D. Rabban, 'The Ahistorical Historian: Leonard Levy on Freedom of Expression in Early American History', *Stanford Law Review* 37 (1985), 795–856.

4 N. Rosenberg, *Protecting the Best Men: An Interpretative History of the Law of Libel* (Chapel Hill, 1986), 3–12.
5 M. Curtis, *Free Speech, 'The People's Darling Privilege': Struggles for Freedom of Expression in American History* (Durham, NC, 2000), 3–4.
6 B. Ackerman, *We the People: Foundations* (Cambridge, MA, 1993); L. Kramer, *The People Themselves: Popular Constitutionalism and Judicial Review* (Oxford, 2004); C. Fritz, *American Sovereigns: The People and America's Constitutional Tradition before the Civil War* (Cambridge, 2008).
7 Curtis's excellent book contains no discussion of the ratification debates, but rather skips from the English and colonial background of free speech and press to the debate over the Sedition Act of 1798. Similarly, Norman Rosenberg's superb piece of legal history, *Protecting the Best Men*, while discussing in detail the early American debate, does not draw on the ratification debates. See, however, S. Solomon's *Revolutionary Dissent: How the Founding Generation Created the Freedom of Speech* (New York, 2016), 219–54, which contains a chapter making use of the ratification debates. Akhil Reed Amar is one of the few legal scholars to take seriously the implications of the ratification debates for the meaning of the First Amendment: A. Amar, *America's Unwritten Constitution* (New York, 2012); A. Amar, 'How America's Constitution Affirmed Freedom of Speech Even before the First Amendment', *Capital University Law Rview* 38 (2000), 503–15. On the ratification debates generally, see P. Maier, *Ratification: The People Debate the Constitution 1787–1788* (New York, 2010); J. Heideking, *The Constitution before the Judgement Seat: The Prehistory and Ratification of the American Constitution, 1787–1791*, eds. J. Kaminski and R. Leffler (Charlottesville, 2012).
8 Since participants in the ratification debates made no distinction between freedom of speech and press, I do not distinguish those categories in this chapter. As Solomon says: 'The founding generation made no distinction between speech and press in the way they actually engaged in protests ... They used every mode of communication available to them to make their points. One means of protest merged into another. They read newspapers and gathered in taverns to argue about the articles': Solomon, *Revolutionary Dissent*, 11. The modern Supreme Court does not distinguish freedom of speech and press either: Bhagwat, 'Posner, Blackstone and Prior Restraints on Speech', 1156.
9 For scholarship that explores the impact of the political and cultural developments of the 1780s for a vastly enlarged public sphere, see M. Warner, *The Letters of the Republic: Publication and the Public Sphere in Eighteenth Century America* (Cambridge, MA, 1990); W. Holton, *Unruly Americans and the Origins of the Constitution* (New York, 2007); S. Cornell, *The Other Founders: Anti-Federalism & the Dissenting Tradition in America, 1788–1828* (Chapel Hill, 2012); J. Kloppenberg, *Toward Democracy: The Struggle for Self-Rule in European and American Thought* (Oxford, 2016).
10 J. Reid, *Constitutional History of the American Revolution: The Authority of Rights* (Madison, 1986), 8. Colonial Whigs controlled the juries, making it impossible for the British government to indict or convict its critics. The 1735 trial of John Peter Zenger famously illustrates the American situation: R. Kluger, *Indelible Ink: The Trials of John Peter Zenger and the Birth of America's Free Press* (New York, 2016). The state of affairs was very different in Ireland: Reid, *Constitutional History*, 8.

11 The 1689 English Bill of Rights gave MPs the right to be free from prosecution for speech. Americans followed their lead, including a similar right within the Articles of Confederation (1781) and within Article I, Section 6 of the US Constitution (1789). However, revolutionary state constitutions began to include provisions for the protection of freedom of speech and press that extended to the people themselves. The logic of that assertion followed from the premise of popular sovereignty that Americans were beginning to work with. As James Wilson put it in the context of the ratification debates, 'Power is with the body of the people ... Under the practical influence of this great truth, we can ... change a constitution as a legislature can sit and deliberate under the power of a constitution in order to amend a law' (*DHRC*, II, 473). Thus, whereas Parliament as the sovereign entailed the right to speak without prosecution, so, too, did the people themselves as sovereign enjoy the right to freedom of speech and press. After all, without that right, how could the sovereign people exercise their sovereignty?

12 J. Wilson, *Collected Works of James Wilson* (Indianapolis, 2007), II, 830–1. Ancient constitutionalist theories of the Norman Yoke were heavily used during the early period of American political development, emphasising as they could historical arguments in favour of republican conceptions of political liberty against oligarchy.

13 *DHRC*, II, 342.

14 Ibid., XIII, 257.

15 Ibid., XIII, 386.

16 Ibid., II, 202. Walter 'Wat' Tyler led the 1381 Peasants' Revolt in England.

17 Ibid., XXI, 1507–9.

18 Ibid., XX, 809.

19 Ibid., XX, 810.

20 J. Waldron, *The Harm in Hate Speech* (Cambridge, MA, 2011), 20–2.

21 A. Amar, *America's Unwritten Constitution* (New York, 2012), 51.

22 This is a theme of J. Habermas's *The Structural Transformation of the Public Sphere: An Inquiry into a Category of Bourgeois Society*, trans. T. Burger (Cambridge, MA, 2015). Scholars have noted the similarity of this period in American history with dynamics described by Habermas: Solomon, *Revolutionary Dissent*, 59–62; Cornell, *The Other Founders*.

23 Q. Skinner, *Visions of Politics, Volume II: Renaissance Virtues* (Cambridge, 2002), 6. Cf. B. Worden, 'Factory of the Revolution', *London Review of Books* 20 (1998), 13–15. Nevertheless, Worden notes: 'What *is* true is that in the English-speaking world there existed, at least from the early 17th century, a loose but enduring vocabulary which connected liberty not, or not only, with individual rights but with particular forms of government ... We see it, for example, in the common usage of the term "free state" to describe kingless commonwealths ... Skinner's book alerts us to that tradition and opens it to investigation.'

24 See Smith's important essay on popular republicanism, including his comments on John Streater's views on freedom of speech and free states: N. Smith, 'Popular Republicanism in the 1650s: John Streater's "Heroik Mechanicks"', in D. Armitage, A. Himy and Q. Skinner (eds), *Milton and Republicanism* (Cambridge, 1995), 140–2, 149–51, 154.

25 Q. Skinner, *Hobbes and Republican Liberty* (Cambridge, 2008), 211–16.

26 Q. Skinner, 'Introduction', in Q. Skinner and M. van Gelderen (eds), *Freedom and the Construction of Europe. Volume II: Free Persons and Free States* (Cambridge, 2013), 1–6.
27 Skinner, *Hobbes and Republican Liberty*.
28 Q. Skinner, 'A Genealogy of the Modern State', *PBA* 162 (2009), 334.
29 P. Pettit, *Just Freedom* (New York, 2014), 1–27.
30 See, however, the insightful remarks of W. Adams, *The First American Constitutions: Republican Ideology and the Making of the State Constitutions in the Revolutionary Era* (New York, 2001), 94–125.
31 Similar sentiments could be echoed in the ratification debates. As a Georgian said, 'It is my heart's wish to see a federal constitution established agreeable to the principles of republican liberty and independence, and on the basis of a democratical government, meaning that of the people, being that very government intended by our glorious Declaration of Independence' (*DHRC*, III, 236).
32 G. Washington, *The Writings of George Washington* (New York, 1889), 441.
33 Q. Skinner, *Liberty before Liberalism* (New York, 1998), 26; Skinner, *Visions of Politics*, 344–67.
34 See too Gordon: 'The good of the governed being the sole end of government, they must be the greatest and best governors, who make their people great and happy; and they the worst, who make their people little, wicked, and miserable. Power in a free state, is a trust committed by all to one or a few, to watch for the security, and pursue the interest, of all: And, when that security is not sought, nor that interest obtained, we know what opinion the people will have of their governors': J. Trenchard and T. Gordon, *Cato's Letters*, ed. R. Hamowy (Indianapolis, 1995), I, 127.
35 On the influence of Trenchard and Gordon on American thinking in the eighteenth century, see B. Bailyn, *The Ideological Origins of the American Revolution* (Cambridge, MA, 1992). Levy, by contrast, minimised the significance of Trenchard and Gordon: 'Cato did not, however, initiate a break-through in libertarian thought. He was a flashing star in an orthodox sky that exponents of intellectual and political liberty occasionally but dimly lit': Levy, *Emergence of a Free Press*, 115. Cf. Rabban, 'The Ahistorical Historian', and Solomon, *Revolutionary Dissent*, 43–5.
36 Trenchard and Gordon, *Cato's Letters*, I, 114.
37 Ibid., I, 127.
38 Ibid., II, 712–13.
39 *DHRC*, IV, 368. Echoing the concern over the basic character of the public sphere and who was entitled to engage in public speech, 'One of the Common People' argued that basic rights needed to be written down. If they were not, he argued, then the rights of the people would depend as they did in England on the 'mere opinion of the learned and contradictory authors'. Our rights, he said, will depend on 'volumes of contradictory reports of the learned' (*DHRC*, IV, 367–9).
40 *DHRC*, XVIII, 6.
41 See too the claim that a free press in a 'free state' gave 'all the people an opportunity to learn and be wise, to choose or refuse, in an important affair: indeed it is the noblest exhibition, the new world has yet witnessed. Let us therefore seek after truth, no matter where, or from whom' (*DHRC*, X, 1638).

42 W. Blackstone, *Commentaries on the Laws of England: Book I: Of Public Wrongs* (Oxford, 2016), section 122. In saying this, Blackstone was building on the definition of political liberty he had previously put forth in Book I of the *Commentaries*. There he said 'Political ... or civil liberty, which is that of a member of society, is no other than natural liberty so far restrained by human laws ... as is necessary and expedient for the general advantage of the public' (W. Blackstone, *Commentaries on the Laws of England: Book I: Of the Rights of Persons* (Oxford, 2016), section 122). On Blackstone's rejection of the republican tradition of political liberty as rooted in security, making liberty simply a matter of the absence of interference, see Skinner, *Liberty efore Liberalism*, 97.
43 *DHRC*, VIII, 469–70.
44 Ibid., IX, 699.
45 Lee says, for instance, 'The corrupting nature of power, and its insatiable appetite for increase, hath proved the necessity, and procurement of the strongest and most express declarations of the Residuum of natural rights, which is not intended to be given up to Society; and which indeed is not necessary to be given for any good social purpose' (*DHRC*, VIII, 36). This claim borrows without acknowledging from Blackstone the phraseology that there is 'a Residuum of natural rights which no individual can give up to society'. Patrick Henry also associated the freedom of press with a right of human nature (*DHRC*, X, 1299).
46 *DHRC*, I, 33.
47 On the blending of republican, liberal and Christian idioms in early American political thought, see J. Kloppenberg, 'The Virtues of Liberalism: Christianity, Republicanism and Ethics in Early American Political Discourse', *Journal of American History* 74 (1987), 9–33. On Locke's influence and social-contract language in the eighteenth century Anglo-American context, see M. Goldie, 'The English System of Liberty', in M. Goldie and R. Bokler (eds), *The Cambridge History of Eightenth-century Thought* (Cambridge, 2006), 47–50.
48 *DHRC*, XVI, 58.
49 To cite but one interesting example, historical evidence indicates that Baptists in Virginia were particularly concerned about the issue of religious freedom and were of critical importance to James Madison winning a seat in the First Congress, and, perhaps, to changing his mind about the need for a bill of rights.
50 On the importance and influence of Tucker, in addition to his connection to Anti-Federalism, see Cornell, *The Other Founders*, 263–73: 'One of the most important points Tucker made regarding freedom of the press in America was that it rested on entirely different grounds from the common law understanding enshrined in Blackstone ... Tucker drew extensively on the Virginia ratification convention to demonstrate that the promise of an explicit provision ensuring freedom of the press was instrumental in securing the ratification of the Constitution' (264).
51 St George Tucker, *View of the Constitution of the United States*, ed. C. Wilson (Indianapolis, 1999), 371–2.
52 Citing Price, Tucker rejected the idea that 'a bad tendency' could be used as the standard to censure speech as is the case in the Story–Blackstone theory, since 'were this a right opinion, all the persecution that has ever been practiced, would be justified' (Tucker, *View*, 377).
53 Tucker, *View*, 380.

54 Ibid., 382. See Solomon, *Revolutionary Dissent*, 255–92, and B. Neuborne, *Madison's Music: On Reading the First Amendment* (New York, 2015), on the integrated nature of the First Amendment's forty-five words, linking the issue of religion, freedom of thought, speech, press, assembly and petition.
55 Tucker, *View*, 328.
56 Ibid., 381.
57 J. De Lolme, *Constitution of England; Or An Account of the English Constitution* (1784), ed. D. Lieberman (Indianapolis, 2007), 280, argued that the two most important rights in England were trial by jury and the liberty of the press: 'If we consider the great advantages to public liberty which result from the institution of the Trial by Jury, and from the Liberty of the Press, we shall find England to be in reality a more Democratical State than any other we are acquainted with. The Judicial power, and the Censorial power, are vested in the People.' De Lome was deeply aware of the problem of democratic aristocracy (that is, a democratic state, where power is in the people, but whose administration is oligarchic, such that it is democratic only in appearance). According to De Lome, both trial by jury and liberty of the press help moderate that problem by making government accountable. Republican authors, such as Marchamont Nedham's *The Excellencie of a Free-State: Or, The Right Constitution of a Commonwealth*, could also be concerned with the problem of democratic oligarchy, the 'multiplied monarchy': B. Worden, 'English Republicanism', in J. Burns and M. Goldie (eds), *The Cambridge History of Political Thought, 1450–1700* (Cambridge, 1991), 449; Worden, 'Introduction', in M. Nedham, *The Excellencie of a Free-State, or the Right Constitution of a Commonwealth*, ed. B. Worden (Indianapolis, 2011), xxxiv–xlii.
58 Timoleon was a Greek statesman and general who won the Syracusans their freedom by defeating the tyrant Dionysius II. Plutarch's *Lives* contains a chapter on Timoleon. In *The Commonwealth of Oceana* (1656), James Harrington says: 'Timoleon ... gave the gods thanks for their return unto his frequent prayers, that he might but live to see the Syracusans so free that they might question whom they pleased': J. Harrington, *The Commonwealth of Oceana and A System of Politics*, ed. J. Pocock (Cambridge, 1992), 265. See, too, Smith, 'Popular Republicanism', 149, for the Leveller John Lilburne's populist republican use of Timoleon.
59 DHRC, XIX, 166–70.
60 In support of this conclusion, in contrast to Levy's thesis, see Solomon, *Revolutionary Dissent*, 293–302. While I agree with Solomon, contrary to the current legal consensus, that 'the founding generation created the freedom of speech', I would emphasise that they did so in profound dialogue with early modern European political thought. On the intertwining of early American and European thought, see J. Ratner-Rosenhagen, *The Ideas that Made America: A Brief History* (Oxford, 2019); Kloppenberg, *Toward Democracy*.
61 R. Hoffstadter, *The Idea of a Party-system: The Rise of Legitimate Opposition in the United States, 1780–1840* (Berkeley, CA, 1969), xii; S. Elkins and E. McKitrick, *The Age of Federalism: The Early American Republic, 1788–1800* (Oxford, 1993), 592–3, 691–714.
62 M. Peterson (ed.), *The Portable Thomas Jefferson* (New York, 1975), 291.
63 The Supreme Court finally rejected seditious libel in American law in *New York Times* v. *Sullivan* (1964).

Chapter 11

Before – and beyond – *On Liberty*: Samuel Bailey and the nineteenth-century theory of free speech

Greg Conti

An 1829 article for the *Westminster Review*, the official journal of philosophic-radical principles with which Bentham and both Mills were involved, described a book 'so finished in its parts and so perfect in their union' that 'like one of the great statues of antiquity, it might have been broken into fragments, and each separated limb would have pointed to the existence of some interesting whole, of which the value might be surmised from the beauty of the specimen'. The object of this bizarre hyperbole was, Thompson did not hesitate to say, the second most important of all 'comparatively modern books', surpassed only by *The Wealth of Nations*.[1] Such exorbitant praise was, surely, intended for a seminal philosophic-radical production such as Bentham's *Rationale of Judicial Evidence* or James Mill's *History of British India*, or for a great Enlightenment tract from a Hume or Voltaire.

In fact, Thompson's accolades were directed at a work first published earlier in the decade, *Essays on the Formation and Publication of Opinions* by one Samuel Bailey. Bailey was born almost exactly mid-way between James and John Stuart Mill, and so he straddles the intellectual cultures of the late Enlightenment and high Victorian period.

If intellectually Bailey seemed to sit between eras, biographically he was a representative figure of nineteenth-century liberalism.[2] Like myriad writers of that time he was both (*a*) swept up in the philanthropic enterprises and discussion societies that marked the 'age of improvement' and (*b*) enticed to stand for parliamentary election – although in Bailey's case his two attempts were not only unsuccessful but also apparently undertaken with little enthusiasm. Finally, Bailey's literary output was characteristic of the extraordinary energy of the nineteenth-century liberal mind. The 'Bentham of Hallamshire', as he was nicknamed, wrote on an astonishing panoply of subjects in what we now call the social sciences, with particular emphasis on economics and politics – as well as on 'mental philosophy' and metaphysics, educational methods, the natural sciences and the theory of morals. Sadly, he did not stop even there: a piece of poetry in middle age and two volumes at the end of his life *On the Received Text of Shakespeare's Dramatic Writings* found few sympathetic readers.[3]

Amid this varied slate of subjects, however, Bailey's greatest impact came on toleration and free speech. In keeping with the philosophic-radical prioritisation of the cause under the repressive governments of the century's early decades,[4] the liberty of discussion was the earliest topic to which Bailey devoted himself. His first book, the aforementioned *Formation and Publication of Opinions*, was 'a vigorous argument on behalf of the widest possible toleration'.[5] This very successful text would be joined by a sequel, *Essays on the Pursuit of Truth and the Progress of Knowledge*.[6] In the following decade Bailey completed his trilogy on the liberties of speech and thought in unexpected fashion: with an epistolary novel in which an apostate from Islam writes from England back to a friend in Egypt describing the intellectual journey that has led him to abandon their native religion and become an advocate for toleration.[7] And Bailey continued to comment on the subject off and on until his death in 1870. Beyond being a persistent concern for Bailey, it was also the issue by which his legacy would be defined for the Victorians themselves. 'We have never had a more earnest or strenuous advocate of intellectual liberty and free discussion than Samuel Bailey', concluded one author; in the 'Apostolate' who had fought for 'free thought and fair discussion', judged another, 'no living man exerted so large an amount of directly formative influence' as Bailey – an influence so potent, this journalist hyperbolically claimed, that it prompted Bentham, the Mills and their allies to found the *Westminster Review* in the first place.[8] So great was James Mill's enthusiasm for the *Formation and Publication* that John Stuart considered it a fitting tribute after James's death to republish the review essay that his father had written on the occasion of its second edition, accompanied by selected quotations from Bailey, as a pamphlet entitled *The Principles of Toleration*.[9]

Sadly, despite his remarkable corpus and these testimonials to his influence, Bailey has vanished from the historiography of political thought.[10] But for all of these plaudits and achievements the neglect of Bailey would really be just a failure of inventory were it not for the fact that his treatment of toleration possessed certain distinctive features. A comprehensive account of Bailey's self-confessedly multifaceted defence of free speech would exceed the space of a single essay.[11] I want, accordingly, to home in on four particularly interesting aspects of his thought: his notions of social intolerance; of duty in matters of belief; of the involuntariness of belief; and of the marketplace of ideas.

SOCIAL INTOLERANCE

The aforementioned facts about the notice which the Mills and their milieu took of Bailey are not mere curiosities of reception history. They are theoretically significant because the *Formation and Publication* is astonishingly similar to *On Liberty*.[12] For one thing, Bailey articulates nearly the full range of arguments to which Mill would appeal in showing the benefits of free expression.[13] Furthermore, Bailey gave a picture-perfect statement of the consequentialist basis of his reasoning that rivalled the famous declaration at the outset of *On Liberty* that Mill would 'forego [sic] any advantage which could be derived ... from the idea of abstract right, as a thing independent of utility'.[14]

Striking as these similarities are, even more notable was that Bailey anticipated Mill at exactly the point to which Mill attributed greatest novelty. What Mill believed was most original about *On Liberty* was not the set of benefits which he showed free thought and discussion to produce but the application of these more-or-less timeless considerations to a situation in which social, rather than legal or political, intolerance had become primary.[15] In this light what is truly remarkable is that already in 1821 – a decade and a half before Tocqueville would publish the passages from which Mill would claim to have learned this lesson – Bailey was voicing worries about extralegal, social constraints on thought and expression.

Bailey's writing is replete with warnings about what Mill would later decry as the 'tyranny of opinion'.[16] A clearer statement of the continuity between state-directed violence against subscribers to unlawful beliefs and the constriction of debate via social pressure would be difficult to find in any Tocqueville- or Mill-inspired text of high Victorianism:

> Although the advanced civilization of the age rejects the palpably absurd application of torture and death, it is not to be concealed, that, amongst a numerous class, there is an analogous, though less barbarous persecution, of all who depart from received doctrines – the persecution of private antipathy and public odium. They are looked upon as a species of criminals, and their deviations from established opinions ... are regarded by many with as much horror as flagrant violations of morality.[17]

Importantly, like his more famous successors Bailey considered 'the practice of what has been expressively termed "casting odium" upon others for differences of opinion' – 'the mischievous interference' and 'indulgence of hatred and malignity against other people because they hold different opinions from [one's] own' – not merely an evil but an *equivalent* evil to punishment through formal legal-political channels: 'the persecution inflicted by society itself' could be 'equal in atrocity to any which proceeds from the hand of power'.[18] A major thread throughout Bailey's writings on free discussion was that the distinction between state-driven penalisation of certain opinions and the more diffuse arts by which 'society' reinforced conformity to a narrow rung of beliefs was solely one of *means* or *technique*, rather than a normatively differentiated hierarchy of worse and better kinds of coercion:

> In every age persecution has destroyed the happiness of mankind, either by public torture, or ... by that scarcely perceptible oppression which is almost equally felt at the heart's core.
>
> Nor must it be supposed that these remarks are applicable only to the grosser arts of persecution. Threats and insults, obloquy and proscription, reproaches and sneers, the malice of looks and whispers and innuendos, are as real violations of right in this matter as the sack or the bowstring.[19]

Tocqueville himself was hardly more eloquent in depicting the possibility of an 'intellectual' 'violence' that 'goes straight for the soul'.[20]

For Bailey, the tragedy of social intolerance lay not just in the suffering it wrought in dissenters' lives and the epistemic costs of inhibiting 'unshackled and reiterated discussion' in favour of 'prevailing opinions'.[21] An added layer of tragedy emerged from reflection upon its causes. Social intolerance originated not just in obviously malign instincts but also in some 'positive' features of the human personality. Of course, many obviously 'sinister' considerations, paradigmatically the interests of the clergy in a state church, drove people to 'intolerance and persecution'.[22] But in a manner reminiscent of Hume's observation that the principles underlying 'factions' were not just selfish ones but also 'affection' and 'good nature',[23] Bailey acknowledged melancholically that among the 'mingled' 'causes' of these ills were sympathy and fellow-feeling:

> There seems to be a principle inherent in the nature of man, that leads him to seek for the approbation of his fellow-creatures, not only in his actions, but in his modes of thinking. He covets the concurrence of others, and is uneasy under dissent and disagreement. Objections to his opinions seem to place a disagreeable impediment in the way of his imagination; they disturb his self-complacency, and render him restless and uneasy. This, of itself, is sufficient to make him regard with displeasure and resentment all those who are of a different opinion from his-own.[24]

Put simply, our very sociability and desire to be in accord with those around us contributed to the prickliness which led us to ostracise or bully holders of opinions at variance with our own. If human beings had been isolated Leibnizian monads, indifferent to others, then they would not have bothered to employ 'severities ... against mere differences of opinion'.[25]

A similar observation explained another obstacle to true intellectual liberty, which was the mirror image of the problem of extralegal pressure being brought to bear on the heretic: the impulse simply to conform in the face of an apparent consensus of our compatriots or coreligionists.[26] It was because people were 'lovers of sympathy' that they were so hesitant to give serious consideration to any but 'received or established opinions'. Hence for all but a few individuals of 'bolder dispositions' sympathy and sociability constituted major hindrances to the disinterested investigation and open discussion of ideas.[27]

There was a similar pathos to other portions of Bailey's diagnosis of the roots of intolerance. For instance, while his texts ring with denunciations of those who 'assum[ed] themselves to be unerringly in the right',[28] Bailey ultimately concluded that it was less the assumption of one's own infallibility that fed the urge to heap 'odium and persecution' on proponents of unpopular ideas than a justified intuition on the part of many people of the weak basis on which their views were founded.[29] Bailey showed, in one reviewer's words, that 'those men in general are the least hurt at opposition who, having a clear discernment of the foundation of their tenets, least require the support of other people's approbation'.[30] It was thus not because people were overconfident in their reason, but because they could never truly suppress the 'latent apprehension' of the flimsy reasoning on which their beliefs rested, that they were so inclined to shun and harass 'every one who dissents from their traditional dogmas'.[31] Individuals of 'narrow views and confused notions' were more easily discomfited than those of more 'thorough conviction' by confronting spokespeople of an 'opposite persuasion'. Such encounters threw them instantly into a 'state of doubt', which Bailey conceived of as a 'state of trouble' so disagreeable that lashing out at others was inevitable.[32]

Alongside the role played by arrogance, therefore, an irrepressible inkling of intellectual deficiency contributed to the pervasiveness of intolerance and persecution. In parallel fashion, while 'self-love' was assigned a healthy share of the blame for the 'contumely' directed at exponents of 'different sentiments', it was possible to recast this in a more pathetic light, as the understandable preference for what is dear and familiar to what is alien and strange.[33] Although in a perfect world ideas would be valued only for their approximation to truth, the pitiable fact was that people formed sentimental attachments to ideas just as they did to possessions or persons.[34]

Bailey's account of the psychological principles underlying social intolerance was, then, quite a subtle mélange of factors that avoided Voltairean caricatures of the benightedness or malignity of persecutors – although he did in good Enlightenment fashion believe that education could diminish intolerance and that priestcraft needed a more definitive defeat.[35] Whilst it was indisputable that different societies attained different degrees of tolerance and intellectual openness,[36] Bailey's analysis placed much of the responsibility for persecution in 'deeply rooted and tenacious' facets of the human psyche.[37] Since many of the 'causes of intolerance' were 'discoverable in the passions of mankind', a 'mitigation' could be hoped for but not, Bailey suggested, an eradication.[38]

Such were the keystones of Bailey's theory of social intolerance. A perceptive reader, however, might have noticed something missing: Bailey did not include any reference to 'democracy' or the 'tyranny of the majority'. This absence, we must stress, was not an artefact of his having preceded Tocqueville and thus having lacked the conceptual apparatus to analyse the relationship between social intolerance and regime types. Editions of the *Pursuit of Truth* and the *Formation and Publication* appeared after the publication of *Democracy in America*, as did the *Letters of an Egyptian Kafir*, yet none incorporated these Tocquevillian themes. Bailey was aware of and appreciated Tocqueville: he added notes on *Democracy in America* to the second edition of the *Pursuit of Truth*, including a long citation from the section 'On the power that the majority in America exercises over thought'. Tellingly, the gloss which Bailey put on the passage scrubbed anything specifically *democratic* from the picture; his enthusiasm resided, rather, in finding an author who treated the 'atrocious spirit' of 'social proscription' as seriously as he did. To Bailey, Tocqueville's merit did not lie in pointing out a truth about a political form – what Tocqueville 'described is much more prevalent in England ... than philosophers seem to be generally aware of, and is dependent on causes not peculiar to republics' – but instead lay in identifying 'the powerful influence of public opinion, independently of positive institution, in seducing and deterring individuals from the fearless and manly pursuit of truth'.[39] Since Bailey emphatically did not judge his native land to be (either before or after the Reform Act) a democracy, it is clear that he meant to reject the thesis that there was a special level of intolerance reserved for democracies.[40]

In thus severing the social realisation of free speech from the question of democracy, Bailey had distinguished company: J. S. Mill. Many scholars, perhaps from perceiving the laudatory tone that marks Mill's lifelong reflections on Tocqueville, fail to note that Mill's initial response to *Democracy in America* disagreed forthrightly with the claim that the 'daily persecution' dissenters faced in 'democratic republics' amounted to a uniquely 'formidable barrier around thought'.[41] Although the route which Mill's argument took was not identical to Bailey's, he wound up in substantially the same place, namely, that the potential for a 'tyranny of opinions' stemmed from 'human nature itself': 'in any government', 'whatever the ruling power be', ways to temper 'the despotic yoke of public opinion' had to be sought.[42] The just-shy-of-thirty-year-old Mill refused to follow Tocqueville in seeing social constraints on intellectual independence and diversity of opinion as a hallmark of *democracy*. Well into the mid-1830s, when the 'measure of celebrity' Bailey had earned with the *Formation and Publication* was at its height,[43] Mill remained with Bailey in being sceptical that the 'tyranny of the majority' was the proper lens through which to understand threats to intellectual-expressive liberty.

Mill, of course, would change his tune on the relationship between social intolerance, majorities and democracy, adopting the vocabulary of majority tyranny and drawing upon Tocqueville in *On Liberty*.[44] This way of framing the problem, to which Bailey never came around, put Mill solidly within the mainstream of the mid-Victorian conversation about tolerance and freedom, and I suspect that Bailey's lack of impact on Victorian liberalism relative to what he had on the earlier philosophic-radical tradition derived in part from his mode of thought never having been 'updated' to the then-current Tocqueville-saturated concerns.

This shift in approach, however, did not shield Mill's account of *social intolerance* from criticism. The criticism just tended to come from another direction. Specifically, what drew objections was the *equivalence* he posited between 'social stigma' and 'legal persecution';[45] J. F. Stephen, J. A. Froude, D. G. Ritchie, Herbert Cowell and others all considered themselves some sort of intellectual-expressive libertarians while at the same time denying that there was a meaningful continuity between social intolerance and legal censorship or coercion.[46] For someone like Stephen, Mill's condemnations of the former amounted to trying to hem in the freedoms of others in favour of the dissenter – if many people sincerely felt revulsion towards an advocate of what they believed to be immoral views, why should the latter not be able to behave in accordance with and to fully express that revulsion? And ought not the champions of unpopular positions to expect an unpleasant welcome, since it was implied in the very fact of their positions being unpopular that they ran counter to sentiments cherished by their fellows?[47] What, exactly, was it about that diffuse set of 'practices and expedients' that went under the heading of 'social intolerance' that warranted being treated as on a par with the 'pains and penalties' dispensed by the state?[48]

Bailey believed that he had an answer to this question. To understand it, we need to turn to a second theme in his theory: the 'duty of investigation' or 'duty of inquiry'.[49]

DUTY

Bailey understood unfettered thought and speech to be not only a matter of *right* but also a matter of *duty*. The primacy of duty in Bailey's account of toleration was noted and celebrated. As one appreciative estimate of his career put it, what distinguished Bailey was that he advocated not just free thought but '*dutiful* free thought';[50] another wrote that 'no author of this century has written with greater force and clearness, or with more powerful reasoning, on the right *and duty* of free inquiry in every department of human thought'.[51] These judgements fit nicely with Bailey's own self-understanding: one of his goals was to spell out the 'duties of mankind in the collection and examination of evidence'.[52]

By 'duty', Bailey in fact intended a package of interrelated obligations that ranged from requirements for assessing evidence to practices of introspection to standards for communicating with others. Reconstructing in detail Bailey's ethics of belief would require a great deal of space; it suffices to indicate a few of its principal elements.

To begin with the issue of scope: special responsibilities obtained for those whose profession was to instruct others and for those with the ability and resources to contribute to science (broadly understood).[53] Yet many onerous requirements applied universally. Everyone – scholarly or illiterate, rich or poor – was obligated to inquire into the correctness of (*a*) their practical maxims, those ideas which had an 'important and direct effect on his conduct in life', and (*b*) their religious and 'moral sentiments'. Generally, people avoided examining their beliefs in these areas out of fear that doing so would lead them into doubt or falsehood.[54] These fears, Bailey was adamant, had no moral or epistemic standing.[55]

It was, further, not enough that we set out to discern the truth; we also had to pursue our inquiry in the correct ways. Our obligations in the course of inquiry were intricate, but essentially boiled down to two: thoroughness and impartiality, or what he called 'adequate diligence and rigorous impartiality'.[56] Between these two, impartiality was the more important, for without impartiality even the most diligent intellectual undertaking was liable to lead one astray.[57] This liability resulted from the pertinacity of bias in the mind of even the most upright person.[58] The pertinacity of bias, in turn, rendered impartiality itself more of a regulative ideal than a moral dictate as such: we had to strive for it even if we could never fully realise it. What we were obliged to was the cultivation of a set of dispositions that together approximated the unattainable epistemic virtue of impartiality: self-knowledge, control of one's emotions, humility. Self-knowledge and emotional control were needed to mitigate, as far as possible, the impact of the passions and habits which skewed us toward those beliefs which we cherished or which served our interests;[59] humility was needed because complete achievement of the former was impossible and hence our 'intellectual condition' would always be imperfect.[60]

If we were bound to observe these norms in our own deliberations and investigations, we were equally required to help others down the same path. The golden rule of the other-regarding side of Bailey's morality of belief was that 'honesty of investigation and fairness of statement should be greeted with eager and hearty commendation', and 'all attempts on the part of any one to excite odium against others for differences of thought should be unsparingly reprobated'.[61] These principles, it is worth reiterating, were not simply best practices, but true *moral imperatives.*

Two features of this outline of Bailey's morality of opinion merit highlighting. The first recalls our previous subject: social intolerance. From a solely rights-based perspective, it is not obvious why social restrictions on speech should be treated as on a par with legal ones. For, it is often said, a constitutionally guaranteed right to free speech cannot also be a right insulating one from the *consequences* of speech; the law cannot mandate that, say, your neighbours continue to keep your company after you make statements they find abhorrent, or that they continue to shop at your store despite your criticising their church. However, from a duty-based perspective, the line between legal and extralegal forms of intolerance looks less stark. For the infliction of 'pain' or bestowing of 'advantage' on the basis of the 'conclusions' of a 'fellow creature' equally constituted 'a mischievous meddling with' our duties as opinion-holders whether it came through the 'positive institution' of law or through 'custom or modes of feeling'.[62] A social climate of intolerance interfered with the fulfilment of duties more directly than it diminished the content of rights. Given that sociability figured so largely in Bailey's political philosophy, a culture of intolerance could be seen as tantamount to legal persecution because we were so liable to neglect our duties if faced with disapprobation from others. Especially given our psychological aversion to these claims of duty,[63] the wrong 'application of *moral* approbation and censure' seriously threatened the integrity of intellectual life.[64]

Conceiving of freedom of thought as anchored in a set of intellectual duties thus permitted an extension of the area of concern from the state's laws and punishments to social mores. It also extended the reach of the theory in another way: Bailey condemned not only negative repercussions for holding unwelcome ideas but also positive enticements for espousing desired ones. Both *'bribing* and terrifying the poor human creature' were inconsistent with the obligation to 'examine fully and freely' and encouraged him 'to hide his internal convictions, and to profess what he does not feel'. 'The annexation of emoluments, honours, and other advantages, to the profession of the chosen doctrines' existed on the same continuum of means for 'preventing or impairing' dutiful inquiry as 'the infliction of punishment'.[65]

Bailey's stance against 'honesty of inquiry' being 'subverted' whether by 'disgrace and persecution' or 'temptation' was demanding. Institutionally it set him in opposition even to other fervent supporters of liberty of speech and religion who did not wish the Anglican Church to be disestablished; for these figures, from Burke to J. F. Stephen and others, liberty did not require the neutrality of public powers but required merely their restraint from penalising belief and expression. The upshot of Bailey's argument was that disestablishment was a moral necessity, since the perks which belonging to a state church conferred distorted the cultural-intellectual climate in which the truth was pursued. More nebulously but no less importantly, scrupulous abstention from bestowing any favour on others for the 'doctrine' they held was required in order that we not 'seduce' them from 'performing that duty of inquiry which is equally incumbent on them as it is on ourselves'. Instead, we had to regulate 'our moral sentiments' solely according to the degree of 'diligence and fairness' by which they investigated issues.[66] These injunctions against favouritism Bailey called a 'high ground' vantage on intellectual liberty; they were deliberately intended to counter a minimalist conception of free thought as simply the absence of state coercion. Such minimalism, he believed, disregarded the sacredness of the duties that underlay our desire that thought be free in the first place.[67]

I stated above that Bailey's elevation of duty left his equation of state coercion and social intolerance less exposed to criticism than Mill's view that 'the despotism of society' was equivalent 'whether exercised by governments or by public opinion'.[68] But is it accurate to characterise Mill as indifferent to intellectual duties? It depends on our scope of reference. Viewing the totality of his corpus, it is indisputable that Mill was an ethicist of the intellect after Bailey's own heart.[69] His personal impartiality was legendary and his call for us to understand the positions of our opponents better than they did themselves was crucial to his break with dogmatic Benthamism.[70] Yet it is true that his most famous text did not present the liberties of thought and discussion as the counterparts of an integral set of duties to seek and speak the truth. The 'duty of inquiry', in anything like the elaborate form in which Bailey presented it, is absent from *On Liberty*. For this reason *On Liberty*'s denunciation of social intolerance was easier to dismiss by those disposed to see a chasm separating state action from the social harms incurred by heterodoxy.

Bailey's notion of duty, then, was essential to what was, in his milieu, the most bracing side of his work, namely, the extension of the theory of intellectual-expressive liberty beyond the legal-governmental to the social-cultural realm. It was also distinctive in another respect: the relationship that Bailey's epistemic duties had to religion. For Bailey, religion was not a privileged site.[71] Precisely the same rules about apportioning belief to evidence; considering the range of arguments *pro* and *contra*; taking the measure of one's own biases as part of ensuring the impartiality of inquiry; encouraging others to investigate questions for themselves rather than trying to steer them to particular results – all of these applied to religion as to 'all other subjects of investigation'.[72] This employment of an identical ethics of belief to non-religious and religious questions distinguished Bailey's view from the epistemological moralities at both ends of the religious spectrum. It differed from the 'Protestant' position in not setting up religion as a sphere of special epistemic duties where the exercise of 'private judgment' was of vastly more (because of eternal, salvific) significance than elsewhere. It differed equally from the 'fideist' position (most common among but not exclusive to Catholics) which presented faith and reason as incommensurable and which therefore prescribed a suspension of the normal canons of evidence where religion was concerned. What Bailey offered, in contrast to most Christian thought of his day and before,[73] was a seamless set of duties covering all fields of knowledge, and this feature generated much of the excitement about his work from radicals like James Mill.

Beyond the elements hitherto covered, perhaps the most significant part of Bailey's notion of duty was the sharp *limit* which he set on it. Bailey placed heavy burdens on us with respect to forming and disseminating our beliefs. But there was one demand that he resolutely refused to impose. This stopping-point was intimately tied to another great pillar of Bailey's reputation as a philosopher of liberty.

THE INVOLUNTARINESS OF BELIEF

The duty that Bailey put at the heart of his theory of toleration was two-pronged: to pursue the truth oneself, and to assist (or at least refrain from impeding) others in their pursuit. It was *not* a duty to find the truth.[74] The failure to include the latter was not an oversight – instead, it was fundamental to Bailey's libertarian architectonic. Understanding the reason for this absence foregrounds some particularly dicey material for supporters of toleration, as well as indicating one way in which Bailey's theory fizzled as the conditions of the debate over free speech shifted over the course of the century.

Bailey did not uphold a duty to reach the truth because he was committed to the idea that belief was not a function of will. Having an erroneous belief was not itself a matter of culpability; these were 'involuntary and innocent mistakes'.[75] Belief was the 'necessary and involuntary consequence of the views presented to his understanding without the slightest interference of choice'. It followed from beliefs not being 'the result of any exertion of the will' that they 'imply neither merit nor demerit in him who is the subject of them'.[76] Possessing erroneous views could therefore not be considered 'criminal' or 'sinful', but was only 'unfortunate', and not liable to penalties social or legal.[77]

Like the arguments for toleration from duty, Bailey's espousal of the involuntary character of belief was treated, by both himself and his contemporaries, as a major innovation which would permanently liberate discussions of toleration from the grip of this 'common error'.[78] Although 'many of the actions, as well as many of the moral judgments of mankind, proceed on an assumption of the voluntary nature of belief', Bailey rued that 'the subject has [n]ever been examined with that closeness of attention which its importance deserves'.[79]

Bailey was insistent that the involuntariness of belief was the core of his argumentation, and he was much lauded for this piece of the *Formation*. It was, however, not sturdy enough ground on which to erect such an ambitious edifice of liberty. Several problems bedevil Bailey's attempt to make this tenet the centrepiece of a defence of toleration or free expression.

First, and least important: it was hardly as radical or original an argument as Bailey and some of his interlocutors made out. Although he claimed and received credit for a breakthrough, in truth the involuntariness of belief was already one of the venerable strains in the history of toleration. This appears particularly evidently in one American theologian's 1870s survey of the 'proposition ... that *all belief is involuntary*', where Bailey was slotted into a list of supporters running from the Church Fathers through Locke up to William Hamilton.[80] And indeed, Bailey was really restating the point most famously made in the *Letter Concerning Toleration* that the will and the understanding were categorically separate. If Bailey downplayed this lineage and his contemporaries did not consider it to have minimised the striking quality of his demonstration, this was likely due to two factors (beyond the carelessness about acknowledging one's sources and intellectual debts typical of many nineteenth-century thinkers). Firstly, Bailey offered quite a 'secularised' version of the thought, neither privileging religion as a realm of belief which the will was impotent to affect nor employing religious terminology. Secondly, Bailey's aspiration towards a mental science unpolluted by the 'extraordinary and even extravagant doctrines' of the 'personification' of the 'faculties' of *conscience, will,* etc. led him to treat the question of the causes of belief in a manner that seemed more scientifically respectable.[81] But the simple truth is that Bailey was hardly conquering new territory here.

More substantive difficulties attended the placement of the involuntariness thesis at the heart of the case for free speech, as well.[82]

Trouble arises first of all from the fact that, even if Bailey were correct that belief is in the end a response to the 'the nature of the considerations present to the mind' over which the will has no control,[83] it would not follow that censorship or sanctions were inefficacious. For these practices are employed precisely to alter the *condition of the evidence* that one encounters. Censorship is a means of controlling the sorts of evidence available. Further, even punishment of those with undesired beliefs can be justified on this score. For example, Locke's antagonist, Jonas Proast, did not dispute the premise that 'Belief is to be wrought in men by Reason and Argument' alone. Rather, he sidestepped it. To his mind, the involuntariness thesis simply did not serve as an objection to his preferred policy, which was to use 'moderate Penalties' to ensure 'a due consideration of things', 'to balance the weight of those Prejudices' which disinclined men from their responsibility 'thoroughly and impartially to examine a Religion'.[84] Bailey's proofs of involuntariness do not defeat a proposal such as Proast's.

A related problem with relying on this view about the nature of belief to support a theory of toleration can also be glimpsed in Proast's rejoinder to Locke: that it does not securely insulate the heretic from the anger of the true believer. For the true believer is often characterised by such great certainty that his religion or ideology is true that he does not hesitate to impute a deficiency in the ethics of belief to those on the other side. From his perspective, it seems that interest or prejudice or 'self-love' must have prevented dissenters from giving the issue a 'fair Tryal', for how else could they have arrived at such abhorrent views?[85] Note that this is not in conflict with the stance that beliefs are involuntary – after all, Bailey warned against the vice of partiality at length, without thinking that these warnings undermined his point about belief's involuntariness. Proast was simply observing that downstream moral failings reduced our likelihood to be able to appreciate evidence in a way conducive to reaching the truth. All that being confronted with the message of involuntariness accomplishes, when presented to the fanatic or the ideologue, is to move back the site of the infraction from holding the opinion itself to having the *moral failings that alone could account for holding such an obviously incorrect opinion*. Ultimately, then, to break the tendency of 'imputing guilt' or 'moral turpitude' to those who disagree with us, what was required was to show that however 'firmly convinced of the truth of our creed' we might be it was still wrong to imagine 'ourselves as infallible'.[86] Like Mill, Bailey had arguments against the 'arrogant presumption' of our infallibility.[87] But he seems not to have seen that these latter – and not any tenets about the irrelevance of the will in forming beliefs – were really bearing the brunt of his argumentative work for toleration.

Similarly, Bailey seems not to have recognised a problem with the substance of his conception of the distance between will and belief that arose from his conceding a great deal of ground at a key point. If this 'single error' were widespread enough to have had such 'pernicious influence' throughout all societies, then Bailey needed some kind of error theory to explain how it could have appeared true for so long. His answer to this question invoked psychological facts that weakened the force of the involuntariness claim. 'The error of regarding belief as voluntary'

> may have arisen ... from the circumstance of many people having no real conception of the truth or falsehood of those opinions which they profess. They adopt an opinion according to their interest or their passions; or, in other words, they undertake to assert some particular doctrine, and regard as adversaries all who oppose it ... In this sense, and with such people, *opinions may be said to be voluntary*, and being mere professions, forming a sort of party badge, and having no dependence on the understanding, they may be assumed and discarded at pleasure.[88]

Because people were, in general, so little scrupulous about forming their beliefs in an ethical manner, they were able to arrive at opinions almost *at will*. Pascalian 'fake it 'til you make it'-style modifications of belief were rife; most people, Bailey admitted, came to at least some of their views through this process of letting their opinions flow into the most convenient channels. At the end of the day, belief, like so much in human life,[89] involved a delicate interplay of the willed and the un-willed. With this acknowledgement, though, it begins to look as if there was merely a semantic difference between Bailey and writers who held that 'since our opinions are notoriously influenced in a high degree by our passions and our character, it follows that we are morally responsible for our opinions also'.[90] The involuntariness thesis was therefore far from the impenetrable shield for the dissenter against society's hostility that Bailey made it out to be.

Even if we consider the preceding challenges somehow defeasible, it is unlikely that any improved account of the involuntary nature of belief would get us to a convincing vindication of free expression. For one thing, the involuntariness of opinion shows that it is irrational to persecute only in so far as the object is to convert the person targeted. If the goal, however, is as a later Victorian put it, 'not cure but prevention', then the involuntariness point no longer obtains; that is, if the would-be censor or persecutor claims that they are acting not to reform the heretic or mete out justice against the heretic but to keep the contagion of the latter's errors from spreading to other citizens, then all the proofs of involuntariness in the world are irrelevant.[91] The involuntariness point puts up a barrier against inquisition-like programmes, given that an inquisition does not wait on heretics to proselytise before penalising them but punishes on the basis of what it understands their beliefs to be. But precisely because the involuntariness thesis concerns itself solely with the *nature of belief*, it does not itself provide reasons why allowing an unrestricted right to express beliefs is the correct policy.

In light of these limitations, the postulate of the 'independence of belief on the will' could not anchor a full-fledged theory of intellectual-expressive liberty.[92] J. S. Mill, for one, seems to have recognied this shortcoming. Hence, although the *Logic* glances at the involuntariness thesis,[93] in *On Liberty* it plays no role. Quite rightly, Mill perceived that propositions about the relationship between will and belief were too thin a reed on which to hang a robust argument for 'liberty of thought *and* discussion'.[94]

To what extent Bailey appreciated these difficulties is hard to ascertain. On the one hand, he advanced several lines of argument, so knocking out any one in particular was not a decisive blow. Further, the fact that he addressed the 'formation of opinions' and the 'publication of opinions' in distinct essays suggests that he understood that claims about the nature of belief were not directly transferable to the realm of expression.[95] On the other hand, readers were not off-base in responding to Bailey's work as if his proof of involuntariness was its be-all-and-end-all. Bailey did often write as if the involuntariness of belief was the *sine qua non* of his case for liberty, and when in his later epistemological writings he looked back on his earlier work it was the independence of opinion from the will that he highlighted.[96] This fixation on the topic was due not just to its (fraught) place in the structure of his normative argument for free discussion but also to his empirical treatment of the 'doctrine' that beliefs are 'voluntary' as a root *cause* of censorship and persecution: 'neither the virtue nor the happiness of man will ever be placed on a perfectly firm basis, till this fundamental error has been extirpated from the human mind'.[97] Because of this investment in the precept of the voluntariness of belief as an *explanation* for the prevalence of intolerance – an investment that sat uneasily with his view that natural and institutional factors made some degree of intolerance a permanent prospect – the truth that combated this 'terrible error' was accorded a rhetorical primacy which its conceptual place in the theory of free discussion did not warrant.[98]

A final substantive problem is also worth noting, although it involves indulging in a bit of anachronism. This is that the conjunction between his commitments to the involuntariness of belief *and* to the duty to pursue truth in fact did not produce an indefeasible objection *in principle* to penalisation in intellectual matters. This weakness emerges in a few remarkable passages:

Now, the *only proper principle* on which [interfering with another in matters of opinion] could be done ... is to bestow commendation and rewards in proportion as the duty of inquiry has been fulfilled, and to administer censure and punishment in proportion as the duty has been neglected ... But, in order to be able to act upon this principle towards any persons whatever, it is obviously indispensable that the agent or judge should be capable of appreciating their conduct in the business of inquiry, with tolerable exactness; and this human beings are totally incapable of doing.

Unless we could see into men's minds ... it would be rash in us to pass judgment in a matter where the justness of the sentence must depend on so many subtle and secret considerations.[99]

To Bailey, of course, these truisms about our incapacity to gain the appropriate knowledge to evaluate – and hence to 'punish or persecute'[100] – another's intellectual performance in light of the rules of ethical inquiry must have looked like an impassable barrier. However, in the present day it is not clear that we can treat this as quite the airtight argument that Bailey thought it was. Are we certain that, through brain scanning and other technologies, some agency could not plausibly claim to be able to monitor 'with tolerable exactness' the quality of our conduct in inquiry? The confidence that psychologists can accurately identify 'bias' is already prevalent. The involuntariness of belief, as Bailey conceived it, supplied an argument against penalising the sphere of thought and opinion because it could be combined with confidence in the *inscrutability of other people's mental lives.* Whether we should place quite as much faith in the latter principle any longer is, at least, dubious.

To sum up: the involuntariness of belief was a crucial plank of Bailey's platform, and one which earned him considerable recognition. But it was also one of his most suspect and overstretched arguments. Perhaps for this reason – from a sense that it was less relevant and less sound than Bailey had supposed it – it would go on to fade from prominence as the Victorian era wore on. Or perhaps its significance diminished because it had done its work too well, and so the debate naturally progressed to other issues.[101] Whatever the explanation for the fading of the involuntariness of belief in debates over free expression, the fact is that those discussions have for a long time centred on quite other topics. It is the opposite with the final area of his thought which I want to consider, which retains much resonance today – maybe deceivingly so.

THE ECONOMY OF IDEAS[102]

Although it may come as a surprise to readers today who are accustomed to associating this rationale for free speech with the author of *On Liberty*, Mill did not in fact invoke the 'free market of ideas'. Nor did his early comrades among the *Westminster Review* set.[103] Bailey, on the other hand, was struck by the analogy. Notice how Bailey couched the promise of the *Formation and Publication*; he would prove that the extrication of mankind from error will be most readily and effectually accomplished by perfect freedom of discussion; that to check inquiry and attempt to regulate the progress and direction of opinions, by proscriptions and penalties, is to disturb the order of nature, and is analogous, in its mischievous tendency, to the system of forcing the capital and industry of the community into channels, which they would never spontaneously seek.[104]

Opinions, no less certainly than prices, must be allowed to 'find [their] level'.[105]

Several lessons about the nature of the appeal to liberal political economy in the defence of free speech can be drawn from its appearance in Bailey. Firstly, much discussion of this trope understandably assumes that the economic side was prior: that is, that advocates for intellectual freedom imported an independently existing proposition of economic theory to add lustre to their cause. This assumption, however, is often misleading. For example, in the imaginary of deeply religious Protestant communities, from seventeenth-century Puritans to nineteenth-century dissenting evangelicals, prior convictions about the necessity of intellectual-religious liberty suggested that economic freedom might be beneficial as well.[106] With Bailey, who fits the label of 'classical liberal' if anyone does, it is probably fairest to say that the freedoms of capital and of ideas were coeval pieces of a single overarching truth about the wrongfulness of state interference and 'protection' in the fundamental concerns of life.[107] His libertarianism at its broadest level drew from both the economic and the intellectual wells.[108] The flipside of this outlook was that, as an admirer of Bailey and Mill put it, champions of the free trade in goods and in ideas were contending against the same 'protective spirit'.[109]

Secondly, Bailey's notion of the marketplace of ideas was not a one-note song. Due perhaps most of all to Justice Holmes's popularisation of the marketplace of ideas as the 'best test of truth',[110] the analogy of freedom of opinion with the competition of goods in the market is usually considered a way of explaining intellectual progress – the triumph of truths over falsehoods.[111] And this epistemic logic was very prominent in Bailey. But the analogy was also intimately linked to another crucial argument for free speech in Bailey's corpus: namely, that it was necessary for the achievement of civic peace and social stability. Penalising certain opinions or incentivising others disrupted what was otherwise a peaceful process of creative destruction by which worse ideas were slowly supplanted by better ones and new links between far-flung domains of thought were forged.[112] Thus prohibition and persecution were at once an attack on intellectual progress and on societal stability:

> Now all restraints on the free examination of any subject are an interference with the natural and regular process here described, and produce mischievous irregularities ... Under a system of restraint and coercion, we see apparently sudden revolutions in public sentiment ... Such ebullitions are to be feared only where the

natural operation of inquiry has been obstructed. As in the physical so in the moral world, it is repression which produces violence ... When novel doctrines are kept down by force, they naturally resort to force to free themselves from restraints. Their advocates would seldom pursue violent measures, if such measures had not been first directed against them.[113]

Not only truth, but peace, cried out for a free market of ideas.

A final point about Bailey's conception of the relationship between free speech and free markets is more difficult to articulate, but none the less important. Bailey had a profoundly holistic notion of the market – something which was far from a matter of course in an age and within a movement commonly judged 'individualistic'. Bailey's vision of the economy was not reducible to an agglomeration of atomised actors each pursuing their self-interest, though that kind of analysis played a part.[114] It was also a vision of a *system*, that is, of a complex whole in which small distortions in one part could reverberate in larger ways in another.[115] In this respect I think his economic texts read more like those of a Hayekian 'neoliberal' than do most nineteenth-century liberals'.

A parallel conviction about the connectedness of thought was fundamental to his treatment of intellectual-expressive freedom. Though not quite 'whatever is, is right', Bailey was none the less putting forth something reminiscent of this notorious Leibnizian claim, for he argued that whatever the distribution of opinions in a society was, was what it ought to be, and was, moreover, unalterable by such blunt methods as the coercive intervention of the state. The views current in a society necessarily and unavoidably reflected an underlying matrix of social and intellectual conditions for which the instruments of authority were ill-suited. 'The interference of power cannot obviate this necessity [for the 'regular process' of the contestation of views to take place], nor can it prevent the operation of those general causes, which are constantly at work on the understandings of men, and produce certain opinions in certain states of society and stages of civilization.' 'The various branches of knowledge' were 'so intimately connected' that it would be absurd to try to stifle only that small subset of opinions which society deemed harmful. The 'general causes' that governed the 'natural progress' of opinions were deeper, stronger, and (in a sense) more just than society's efforts to stall or direct this movement could ever be.[116]

In the sphere of ideas, this interlocking quality meant that interference with the 'natural course' of opinions portended ills not just of an epistemic but also of a civil kind. It followed from the deep link between all branches of thought – the unity of the 'general improvement of science' – that persecution and prohibition could not but be myopic, either falling inert before the natural laws that determined the movement of belief or generating political or ideological consequences that rippled out in devastating ways.[117]

Due to this element of systematicity whereby he refused to see either economic or intellectual life as a bundle of unrelated phenomena, Bailey's work arguably bears a closer resemblance to the theories of free speech that emerged later in the nineteenth century than does Mill's. For by the final third of the century evolutionary theory had come to dominate political philosophy, and this shift did not miss our subject. Theories of the *evolution of thought* and *natural selection* of ideas proliferated.[118] But Mill was never interested in evolution,[119] and his reputation as a philosopher of toleration and liberty of discussion correspondingly dipped among many late Victorian thinkers. Even if they agreed in the practical result, enthusiasts for the application of the evolutionary outlook to politics such as Leslie Stephen (who knew Bailey's work well) came to see *On Liberty* as outdated. To these post-Darwinian thinkers, what needed stressing as the true basis of toleration was the interconnectedness of thought, the unity of its development. This is what proved the incoherence of the project of intolerance:

> The only choice ... is not between permitting or suppressing 'an opinion', but between permitting or suppressing scientific inquiry in general ... This familiar example may illustrate the extreme difficulty of catching, isolating, and suppressing so subtle an essence as an opinion ... The philosophy of a people is the central core of thought, which is affected by every change taking place on the remotest confines of the organism. It is sensitive to every chance in every department of inquiry. Every new principle discovered anywhere has to find its place in the central truths; and unless you are prepared to superintend and therefore to stifle thought in general, you may as well let it alone altogether. Superintendence means stifling. That is not the less true, even if the doctrine suppressed be erroneous ... We may have to pass beyond it; but in any case we have to pass through it ... The conclusion is, briefly, that ... you have to choose between tolerating error and suppressing all intellectual activity ... We are becoming daily more fully aware of the unity of knowledge; of the impossibility of preserving, isolating, and impounding bits of truth, of protecting orthodoxy by the most elaborate quarantine.[120]

There is a striking resemblance, even down to the wording, between Stephen's 'evolutionary' update of toleration theory and Bailey's pre-Millian notion of an economy of interlinked ideas which could not accurately be treated in separation from one another and which, if their natural path of development was disturbed, would just move, like capital, into 'pernicious' or 'unproductive channel[s]'.[121] Though Bailey would not make the lasting imprint on political thought that Mill would, even the most 'scientific' of late Victorians (as Leslie Stephen fashioned himself) never really got beyond the substance of his defence of toleration.

NOTES

1 T. Thompson, 'Essays on the Pursuit of Truth, &c.', *Westminster Review* 11 (1829), 477–8.

2 On Bailey's biography, see: [T.S.,] 'Introduction', to S. Bailey, *Letters of an Egyptian Kafir on a Visit to England in Search of a Religion* (Bury, 1881), v–xii; T. Corley, 'Bailey, Samuel (*bap.* 1791, *d.* 1870)', *ODNB*. Scant information on Bailey's life has come down to us.
3 For instance, the *Encyclopaedia Britannica* entry on Bailey summed up his researches on Shakespeare as 'more fantastic than felicitous': *Encyclopaedia Britannica* (New York, 1878), III, 242.
4 E.g. K. O'Rourke, *John Stuart Mill and Freedom of Expression: The Genesis of a Theory* (2001), 2–10; S. Collini, 'Introduction' in *CWJSM*, XXI, xl–xli.
5 L. Stephen, *The English Utilitarians* (1900), II, 339.
6 For both the *Pursuit of Truth* and the *Formation and Publication*, citations will be to the latest edition except where otherwise indicated. Editions of the *Formation and Publication* appeared in 1821, 1826 and 1837, and of the *Pursuit of Truth* in 1829 and 1844.
7 Bailey, *Egyptian Kafir*. The original was privately printed in London in 1839.
8 A. Ireland, 'Samuel Bailey of Sheffield', *Notes and Queries*, fifth series 9 (9 March 1978), 182–5; Anon., 'The Works of Samuel Bailey, of Sheffield', *The British Controversialist, and Literary Magazine*, third series 20 (1868), 1–25. And A. Bain, *John Stuart Mill, A Criticism with Personal Recollections* (1882), 47.
9 J. Mill, *The Principles of Toleration* (1837). The editorship of the *Principles* was anonymous, but Keith Quincy has made a persuasive case that J. S. Mill was the editor: K. Quincy, 'Samuel Bailey and Mill's Defence of Freedom of Discussion', *The Mill Newsletter* 21 (1986), 4–18.
10 The extent to which Bailey has been forgotten is attested by his exclusion from such comprehensive works as G. Stedman-Jones and G. Claeys (eds), *The Cambridge History of Nineteenth-century Political Thought* (Cambridge, 2011), and J. Crimmins (ed.), *Bloomsbury Encyclopedia of Utilitarianism* (New York, 2013). The mid-twentieth century saw a brief flurry of interest in his economic writings, of which a few traces have lingered in the historiography of economic thought; Joseph Schumpeter in particular had a very high estimation of Bailey. See, for instance, J. Schumpeter, *History of Economic Analysis*, ed. E. Schumpeter (1954); R. Rauner, *Samuel Bailey and the Classical Theory of Value* (Cambridge, MA, 1961).
11 S. Bailey, *Questions in Political Economy, Politics, Morals, Metaphysics, Polite Literature, and Other Branches of Knowledge* (1828), 158.
12 In the lone article on Bailey and toleration in relatively modern scholarship, Quincy points out some resemblances between *Formation and Publication* and *On Liberty*: Quincy, 'Bailey and Mill's Defence', 10–16.
13 The four arguments were that: a silenced opinion might be true; if not wholly true, it might still contribute to the production of truth through the process of the interchange of opinions; silencing contestation of even true views renders the latter mere prejudices in the minds of their believers; and eliminating the possibility of opposition causes even true doctrines to lose their force and meaning; Mill, *On Liberty*, in *CWJSM*, XVIII, 258.
14 Mill, *On Liberty*, 224. Cf. Bailey, *Formation and Publication*, 95: 'A society has a perfect right to adopt such regulations, for its own government, as have a preponderance of advantages. Utility, therefore, in the most comprehensive

15 For instance, Mill to Pasquale Villari, 30 June 1857 (*CWJSM*, XV, 534).
16 Mill, *On Liberty*, 269.
17 Bailey, *Formation and Publication*, 87 (at 92 in the first edition).
18 Bailey, *Pursuit of Truth*, 150, 181.
19 Bailey, *Egyptian Kafir*, 119.
20 Tocqueville, *Democracy in America*, trans. A. Goldhammer (New York, 2004), I, 294.
21 S. Bailey, *The Rationale of Political Representation* (1835), 372.
22 'There is an inseparable connection between the lucrativeness of opinions and persecution'; Bailey, *Egyptian Kafir*, 114–15.
23 *EDH*, 63.
24 Bailey, *Formation and Publication*, 80–1. He quoted Hume explicitly: '"Our opinions of all kinds", says Hume, "are strongly affected by society and sympathy, and it is almost impossible for us to support any principle or sentiment against the universal consent of every one, with whom we have any friendship or correspondence"'; ibid., 55.
25 Bailey, *Egyptian Kafir*, 118.
26 S. Bailey, *Letters on the Philosophy of the Human Mind* (1855–63), III, 220.
27 Bailey, *Pursuit of Truth*, 183, 52.
28 Ibid., 96.
29 Bailey, *Pursuit of Truth*, first edition, 10.
30 Anon., 'Review: Essays on the Formation and Publication of Opinions', *Monthly Repository* 17 (1822), 553–8.
31 Bailey, *Pursuit of Truth*, 44; Bailey, *Egyptian Kafir*, 80.
32 Bailey, *Formation and Publication*, 82–3, 32. In this pessimistic moral psychology – whereby the experience of doubt caused by encountering views different from one's own was disagreeable enough to cause the average person to behave intolerantly – Bailey was in accord with a long tradition in English thought which included such figures as Hume; e.g. G. Conti, 'Hume's Low Road to Toleration', *HPT* 36 (2015), 165–91.
33 Bailey, *Formation and Publication*, 77.
34 'Our affections attach themselves to a doctrine as well as to any external object'; 'such opinions are sometimes really objects of affection, and things of habit. We are accustomed to regard them as true; we love them as the rallying points of pleasant ideas and cherished feelings, and we are troubled and even pained when they are presented to us in a different light.' Bailey, *Formation and Publication*, 286; Bailey, *Pursuit of Truth*, 62–3.
35 Although he did in good Enlightenment fashion believe that education could diminish intolerance; Bailey, *Egyptian Kafir*, esp. letters 8, 12.
36 Ibid., 2; Bailey, *Formation and Publication*, 85–6.
37 Bailey, *Pursuit of Truth*, 227.
38 Bailey, *Formation and Publication*, 85.
39 Bailey, *Pursuit of Truth*, 266–8, 169.
40 Bailey himself was sceptical of universal suffrage He fell between the most democratic (Bentham) and the most restrictive (Austin) members of the

Benthamite camp on the suffrage question. For instance, S. Bailey, *A Discussion of Parliamentary Reform* (1831), 12.
41 Tocqueville, *Democracy in America*, I, 293. Alan Ryan and J.H. Burns are among the more nuanced readers who acknowledge the young Mill's defensiveness about democracy in the face of Tocqueville's strictures: A. Ryan, *J.S. Mill* (1974), 29–58; J. Burns, 'J.S. Mill and Democracy, 1829–61 (II)', in G. Smith (ed.), *John Stuart Mill's Social and Political Thought, Critical Assessments* (1998), III, 53–68.
42 Mill, 'De Tocqueville on Democracy in America [I]', in *CWJSM*, XVIII, 81–3.
43 P. Connell, *Romanticism, Economics, and the Question of Culture* (Oxford, 2005), 107. In addition to the first review of *Democracy in America*, 1835 saw Mill review Bailey's *Rational of Political Representation*. The essay began with high praise of Bailey; Mill, 'Rationale of Representation', in *CWJSM*, XVIII, 17.
44 Whether Mill actually changed his *mind*, though, is a more open question than is generally realised. While there is a distinct overlay of Tocquevillian language in *On Liberty*, much of the treatment of the sources of intolerance relies on the kinds of more or less atemporal psychological principles that are resolvable into a framework like Bailey's. While he was not approaching the matter from this angle, John Rees's points about the persistence into *On Liberty* of Benthamite psychological analysis as an explanation of intolerance pushes in the direction of my suggestion in this note: J. Rees, *John Stuart Mill's* On Liberty (Oxford, 1985), chapter 1.
45 Mill, *On Liberty*, 240.
46 For a reconstruction of this debate, see G. Conti, 'James Fitzjames Stephen, John Stuart Mill, and the Victorian Theory of Toleration', *History of European Ideas* 42 (2016), 364–98, section 3.2.
47 For example D. Ritchie, *Natural Rights: A Criticism of Some Ethical and Political Conceptions* (1895): 'Every new idea with regard to matters of religion, or matters of morality, must offend a great mass of prevalent opinion, and must struggle for existence among the ideas already in possession of the ground. This is inevitable; and it need not be a matter of regret. A great many new ideas are not true or valuable, and it is well that they should not survive. A general willingness to take up every idea, simply because it is new, is not a healthy sign either of a society or of an individual mind.'
48 Bailey, *Egyptian Kafir*, 92.
49 Bailey, *Pursuit of Truth*, 37, 107.
50 Anon., 'The Works of Samuel Bailey', 1.
51 Ireland, 'Samuel Bailey of Sheffield', 183. My italics.
52 Bailey, *Pursuit of Truth*, first edition, iv.
53 Bailey, *Pursuit of Truth*, 19.
54 Ibid., 19, 26, 42–50.
55 'As a fear of this sort, while it is totally discordant with that spirit of candour and fairness which every one must acknowledge to be the proper disposition for the attainment of truth, is at variance with the positive duty of the occasion, no man should suffer it to prevent him from boldly engaging in the requisite inquiry'; ibid., 44. Bailey's claim that overcoming this fear of examination was the true condition for confidence in one's beliefs would become a hallmark of Victorian

liberalism; G.J. Holyoake's citations to Bailey in *English Secularism: A Confession of Belief* (1896), 12, 90.
56 Bailey, *Pursuit of Truth*, 77.
57 'Impartiality of examination is, if possible, of still higher value than care and diligence. It is of little importance what industry we exert on any subject, if we make all our exertions in one direction, if we sedulously close our minds against all considerations which we dislike, and seek with eagerness for any evidence or argument which will confirm our established or favourite views'; ibid., 81.
58 'His prejudices, his passions, his interests, the sentiments and actions of those of his fellow creatures around him ... all would exercise a control over his conclusions not to be resisted but by a mind of extraordinary force and perspicacity, and not, perhaps, even by such a mind': Bailey, *Egyptian Kafir*, 72.
59 Ibid., 74–5, 61; Bailey, *Formation and Publication*, 54–8. The American social theorist D.G. Thompson cited Bailey's dicta on emotional control in ranking him with Mill as one of the two greatest defenders of 'liberty of expression'; D. Thompson, *Social Progress* (1889), 120, 138–9.
60 Bailey, *Pursuit of Truth*, 74–5.
61 Ibid., 146.
62 Bailey, *Egyptian Kafir*, 115, 119.
63 'Indolence, ignorance, misapprehension, prejudice, or fearfulness' posed formidable obstacles to carrying out our 'duty of investigation': Bailey, *Pursuit of Truth*, 37.
64 Ibid., 146.
65 Bailey, *Egyptian Kafir*, 88, 90.
66 Bailey, *Pursuit of Truth*, 190, 171–7, 106–7.
67 Bailey, *Egyptian Kafir*, 132–3. This line of objection to a state church shared much with the tradition of 'rational dissent' as it had developed in the late eighteenth century under the influence of thinkers such as Joseph Priestley; e.g. J. Seed, 'Gentlemen Dissenters: The Social and Political Meanings of Rational Dissent in the 1770s and 1780s', *HJ* 28 (1985), 299–325.
68 Mill to Theodor Gomperz, 4 December 1858 (*CWJSM*, XV, 481).
69 E.g. H. Jones, 'John Stuart Mill as Moralist', *JHI* 53 (1992), 287–308.
70 E.g. Mill, 'Bentham', in *CWJSM*, X, 91: 'The hardiest assertor, therefore, of the freedom of private judgment – the keenest detector of the errors of his predecessors, and of the inaccuracies of current modes of thought – is the very person who most needs to fortify the weak side of his own intellect, by study of the opinions of mankind in all ages and nations, and of the speculations of philosophers of the modes of thought most opposite to his own.'
71 For example, Bailey, *Letters on the Philosophy*, III, 54–5.
72 Bailey, *Egyptian Kafir*, 31.
73 Milton might be seen as the greatest English exponent of the Protestant account of the duty of inquiry and its relationship to the freedom of discussion; e.g. I. Samuel, 'Milton on Learning and Wisdom', *PMLA* 64 (1949), 708–23. While, as we have seen, Bailey was not particularly open about his intellectual debts, he was evidently admiring of Milton the political mind and not just the poet: see Bailey, *Rationale of Representation*, 97–8; Bailey, *Pursuit of Truth*, 206.
74 For example Bailey, *Egyptian Kafir*, 39: 'it is manifestly not incumbent upon us

... to succeed in discovering the truth ... it is incumbent upon us only to do all in our power to discover it.'

75 Ibid., 43.
76 Bailey, *Formation and Publication*, 63, 61.
77 Bailey, *Egyptian Kafir*, 40.
78 Bailey, *Formation and Publication*, 26. James Mill's review of Bailey principally centred on this point; J. Mill, 'Formation of Opinions', *Westminster Review* 6 (1826), 1–23.
79 Bailey, *Formation and Publication*, 9.
80 'This position is not new, having received the sanction of some of the best minds in every age'; D. Olmstead, *A Lecture on the Protestant Faith* (New York, 1874), 33–6.
81 E.g. these aspersions: 'Thus the intelligent being, like a constitutional monarch, transacts all regular business through his ministers; as if the Understanding were Secretary of State, for the Home Department; the faculty of Judgment, Chief Justice of the Common Pleas; and Reason, First Lord of the Treasury': Bailey, *Letters on the Philosophy*, I, 26.
82 For a related assessment of the difficulties such an account faces, J. Waldron 'Locke: Toleration and the Rationality of Persecution', in S. Mendes (ed.), *Justifying Toleration: Conceptual and Historical Perspectives* (Cambridge, 1988), 61–86.
83 Bailey, *Formation and Publication*, 12.
84 J. Proast, *A Third Letter Concerning Toleration* (Oxford, 1691), 2–3, 10–11. And see A. Wolfson, *Persecution or Toleration: An Explication of the Locke-Proast Quarrel, 1689–1704* (Lanham, MD, 2010).
85 Proast, *A Third Letter*, 11.
86 Bailey, *Formation and Publication*, 87, 288, 130.
87 Bailey, *Pursuit of Truth*, 76.
88 Bailey, *Formation and Publication*, 30–1.
89 On this front Bailey found a surprising analogy for belief: sleep. 'Sleep is involuntary, but it may, to a certain extent, be prevented or induced according to our pleasure; and in a similar manner, although we have no power to believe or disbelieve as we choose, yet there are cases in which we may imperfectly modify our belief, by subjecting our minds to the operation of such evidence as promises to gratify our inclination in its result': ibid., 34.
90 T. Arnold, 'Mill on Liberty', in A. Pyle (ed.), *Liberty: Contemporary Responses to John Stuart Mill* (South Bend, IN, 1994), 159–83, at 177.
91 'A disease may be incurable as to the individual it has once fastened on, and yet the infection may be cut off by sanitary police or stamped out by slaughter. If heretical opinions are damnable, and the infection of them dangerous to the soul, the best thing the prince can do is to contrive, as far as in him lies, that his faithful subjects shall have no opportunity of hearing them ... Even if his own soul is stubborn beyond saving, the souls of his innocent neighbours are in constant danger because of him': F. Pollock, *Essays in Jurisprudence and Ethics* (1882), 154.
92 Bailey, *Formation and Publication*, 9.
93 Mill, *Logic*, in *CWJSM*, VIII, 738.

94 Mill, *On Liberty*, 228. My italics.
95 Bailey, *Formation and Publication*, 93. And U. Henriques, *Religious Toleration in England, 1787–1833* (Toronto, 1961), 252.
96 S. Bailey, *The Theory of Reasoning*, second edition (1852) 182; Bailey, *Letters on the Philosophy*, I, 89–91; III, 239–40.
97 Bailey, *Formation and Publication*, 89. Also Bailey, *Letters on the Philosophy*, I, 90–1. For a valuable explication of how this 'fundamental error' operated in an earlier epoch, see M. Goldie, 'The Theory of Religious Intolerance in Restoration England', in O. Grell, J. Israel and N. Tyacke (eds), *From Persecution to Toleration: The Glorious Revolution and Religion in England* (Oxford, 1991), 339. Goldie's reconstruction of the argument for the voluntariness of belief and the way in which this was deployed to justify intolerance holds true for many opponents of toleration in subsequent periods as well, down to Bailey's day and beyond; consult, for instance, an interesting text that appeared between the first and second editions of the *Formation and Publication*: R. Wardlaw, *Man Responsible For His Belief, Two Sermons* (Glasgow, 1825).
98 Bailey, *Egyptian Kafir*, 106.
99 Ibid., 64–5, 69. My italics. Elsewhere he clinched the argument with a quotation from Locke's *Third Letter on Toleration* that only 'the Searcher of hearts, the great and righteous Judge of all men' was fit to judge 'whether another has done his duty in examining the evidence on both sides': Bailey, *Pursuit of Truth*, 110.
100 Bailey, *Pursuit of Truth*, 110.
101 This was the verdict of the mid-Victorian historian H.T. Buckle, who saw the 'diffusion' of this view as having already contributed to the 'increasing spirit of toleration' around the mid-century and gave Bailey credit for this change: T. Buckle, 'Mill on Liberty', *Fraser's Magazine* 59 (1859) 509–42, at 529.
102 This section expands on ideas in G. Conti, 'What's Not in *On Liberty*: The Pacific Theory of Freedom of Discussion in the Early Nineteenth Century', *JBS* 55 (2016), 57–75.
103 Quincy goes so far as to claim that 'Bailey was the only Benthamite utilitarian openly to have suggested the analogy'; Quincy, 'Bailey and Mill', 15–16. And see J. Gordon, 'Mill and the "Marketplace of Ideas"', *Social Theory and Practice* 23 (1997), 235–49.
104 Bailey, *Formation and Publication*, 97–8.
105 S. Bailey, *Money and Its Vicissitudes in Value* (1837), 74.
106 E.g. E. Barker, 'Puritanism', in *Church, State, and Study* (1930), 109–30; T. Larsen, *Friends of Religious Equality: Nonconformist Politics in Mid-Victorian England* (Rochester, NY, 1999), 110–36.
107 'The truth' was too frequently ignored 'that the functions of government are properly of a supplementary character': Bailey, *Rationale of Representation*, 54.
108 'It will be enough to remind the reader of the mischiefs which have resulted from this erroneous supposition, in the two cases of religion and commerce'; ibid., 54–5.
109 T. Buckle, *History of Civilization in England* (1857), I, 557. For a characteristic treatment of these as the two faces of the same error by another 'classical liberal', see the magnificent passage at J. Russell, *An Essay on the History of the*

English Government and Constitution from the Reign of Henry VII, to the Present Time (1866), 272.
110 Holmes, 'Dissent in Abrams v. United States', in R. Posner (ed.), *The Essential Holmes: Selections from the Letters, Speeches, Judicial Opinions, and Other Writings of Oliver Wendell Holmes, Jr.* (Chicago, 1992), 316–20.
111 E.g. A. Goldman and J. Cox, 'Speech, Truth, and the Free Market for Ideas', *Legal Theory* 2 (1996), 1–32.
112 This process was, paradoxically, aided by our very intellectual deficiencies: 'The reluctance of the human mind to receive ideas contrary to its usual habits of thinking would be a sufficient security from violent transitions, did we not already possess another in the slowness with which the understanding makes its discoveries. Arguments, by which prescriptive error is overturned, however plain and forcible they may be, are found out with difficulty, and in the first instance can be entered into only by enlarged and liberal minds, by whom they are subsequently familiarized and disseminated by others.' Bailey, *Formation and Publication*, 152–3.
113 Ibid., 153–4.
114 Hence Albert Schatz, a French academic influential in constructing the category of nineteenth-century individualism, had no problem treating Bailey as just another author in the school: A. Schatz, *L'individualisme économique et social* (Paris, 1907).
115 See, for instance, the analysis at S. Bailey, *Defence of Joint-stock Banks and Country Issues* (1840), 1–13.
116 Bailey, *Formation and Publication*, 149–51.
117 Ibid., 149.
118 For example, F. Montague, *The Limits of Individual Liberty* (1885), chapter 7
119 For example, J. MacCunn, *Six Radical Thinkers* (1907), 53.
120 L. Stephen, 'The Suppression of Poisonous Opinions [I]', *The Nineteenth Century* 13 (1883), 493–508, at 498–500.
121 Bailey, *Questions*, 103.

Chapter 12

Unfree, unequal, unempirical: press freedom, British India and Mill's theory of the public

Christopher Barker

Mill's *On Liberty* (1859) offers one of the most powerful arguments for the progressive effects of liberty of speech and of the press. When interpreted within the contexts of his other writings, Mill's approach is notable for three exceptions to its general liberty-defending rule. Mill appears to exempt defamatory speech from protection; he does not defend speech that incites violence; and, most importantly, Mill argues that the liberty principle – including freedom of speech and of the press – does not apply in precisely the democratising places where progressive liberty of speech and press promise the greatest short-term benefits. This chapter focuses attention on the oddity of this last claim by making the first sustained analysis of Mill's theory of free speech in the context of his published and unpublished writings on India. Below, I argue that Mill's theory is a near-absolutist yet *conditional* theory of free speech. By interpreting defamation and incitement narrowly, Mill's theory of free speech becomes nearly absolutist. However, Mill's comparative experience with British India, coupled with an unempirical philosophy of history borrowed from Auguste Comte, makes Mill's theory conditional. In my conclusion, I argue that Mill's theory of free speech remains defensible if it is released from its straitened conception of (British Indian) publics. Publics were very much in existence in English, in Continental Europe and in Mill's India, even if they were not recognised by Mill, whose argument in *On Liberty* annuls them. The risk in making the argument of this chapter is to imply that the liberty principle can be applied to all societies indiscriminately, at any place or time. A truly utilitarian theory of the useful effects of free speech and freedom of the press should, instead, be theorised relative to its historical and political circumstances.

THEORY OF PUBLIC ENGAGEMENT

Readers are familiar with John Stuart Mill as perhaps the most uncompromising late modern proponent of liberty of discussion and debate. But close readers of Mill must do a surprising amount of double-entry bookkeeping to tally the merits and demerits of free speech and a free press. As a philosophical radical, the very young Mill authors a series of newspaper articles in 1823 which defend 'unlimited toleration' of religious doctrines. Two years later, Mill writes an essay on press freedom defending unlimited discussion and debate.[1] Mill's commitment to free thought and expression is sustained throughout the twists and turns of his intellectual life, most notably of course in *On Liberty* (1859).[2] However, Mill argues for three limitations on liberty of speech and press: Mill does not necessarily protect public speech about private lives, even if speech concerns the private lives of public figures; he does not protect speech causing political violence; and Mill consistently supports East India Company (EIC) policy restricting publicity and debate in British India.

The current chapter is primarily about the third exception, which is particularly relevant for Mill during the thirty-five years that he worked in the India House (1823–58). The exception, and Mill's thoughts on empire, remain relevant in an era of democratisation and globalisation, and they provide a context for the interpretation of *On Liberty* that has not been sufficiently theorised. Then as now, it is easy to say that homogeneous populations with shared commitments deserve absolute liberty of speech and press. It is more difficult to defend freedom for distant and different persons in alien circumstances, especially if they use this freedom to disseminate repugnant ideas about social hierarchies and exclusions. It is this context of conflict between ideas and cultures that provides the crucial and understudied frame of Mill's argument in *On Liberty*.

To anticipate the conclusion of this chapter, complete *unity* of opinion in a future organic age is the European (dangerous) 'not-yet'. As Mill explains, 'unity of opinion ... is not desirable ... until mankind are much more capable than at present of recognizing all sides of the truth'.[3] *Diversity* of opinion and true pluralism, in contrast, is India's dangerous 'not-yet' and uniformity is its current, flawed state.[4] For Mill, these contexts are different enough that a different theory of liberty of speech and of the press is required for each social state. I ultimately disagree, but it is crucial to trace Mill's complex argument rather than simply reject his view as culturally hegemonic or racist. Below, I offer a brief introduction to the first two exceptions to what *On Liberty* calls 'absolute freedom of opinion and sentiment'. I then provide a contextually rich examination of publics, speech and press in British India during Mill's early years in the Examiner's office. My conclusion offers a convergent theory of speech and press for both India and England that corrects Mill where he is (surprisingly) at his most unempirical, namely in his cancellation of 'the public' in British India and his rather optimistic identification of a liberal public in England.

THE FIRST EXCEPTION: GOSSIP

The first exception to absolute freedom of speech and press is one that could be called the gossip sanction.[5] Mill argues that English libel law is deeply flawed, judge-made law.[6] According to Mill, the term libel includes 'a number of acts, of a very heterogeneous nature, resembling one another scarcely at all'.[7] Uncertainty in libel law weakens the rule of law and makes truth-telling costly, but Mill avoids simplifying things by making truth an absolute defence in all cases of private libel, as an absolutist might. An article in *The Spectator*, for example, approves the truth defence for libels about private lives in the following terms: 'in calling the character of a bad man by its right name, [a speaker] was doing good service to the cause of public morals'.[8] Mill disagrees with this type of narrow reasoning.[9] Mill's position is instead in line with his explanation of the sphere of liberty in the *Principles of Political Economy*. There, liberty is affirmed about speech and action that affects the life of the individual and 'does not affect the interest of others'.[10] For Mill, reputation-destroying gossip clearly affects the interests of others.

As Jonathan Riley notes, Mill may change his mind about libel: in 1825, Mill supports suppressing private libels so long as we do not rely on coercive law to do so. In 1834, he argues that we should suppress private libel by public censure or by law. In 1859, it is not clear whether we should use law or not.[11] If there is a change of emphasis in these years, it may be because Mill, having met Harriet Taylor in 1830, becomes increasingly aware of gossip's reputational implications for women. Harriet Taylor's reputation was damaged by Mill's relationship with her, and, perhaps reflecting this concern, one of the essay topics the Mills jointly planned to write in the mid-1850s was an article on slander.[12] Since the essay was not written, though, we have no stand-alone statement on defamation outside of what we find in *On Liberty* and scattered observations on the 'dominion of public authority', which undermines the 'development of individual character and individual preferences'.[13]

About the airing of dangerous doctrines as opposed to the airing of dirty personal laundry, in contrast, Mill has no similar reservations. In the aforementioned 1834 article on Daniel O'Connell's libel reform bill, Mill contends that reformers should begin by affirming the freedom 'to controvert any political doctrine, or attack any law or institution, without exception; in any manner and in any terms not constituting a direct instigation to an act of treason, or to some other specific act to which penalities [sic] are attached by the law'.[14] This broad freedom scoops up all doctrine, religious or political. Here we find evidence for the traditional and now somewhat tired image of J.S. Mill, James Mill and the philosophical radicals, namely that they are intransigent and unapologetic in their defence of the 'utmost possible publicity and liberty of discussion'.[15]

Mill repeats the argument against private libel laws in his article on Thomas Babington Macaulay's draft Indian Penal Code of 1838. In 1838, Mill argues that truth should be a defence in criminal cases, but, in cases where the private lives of persons are the subject of discussion, he argues that no court can competently judge what is defamatory. This, Mill writes, is 'the principal reason for leaving any immoralities whatever exempt from legal punishment'.[16]

THE SECOND EXCEPTION: POLITICAL VIOLENCE

The second exception to the general defence of free speech and the free press concerns cases where speech acts incite violent acts. Here, Mill finds a delicate line. If government 'could suppress all censure, its dominion, to whatever degree it might pillage and oppress the people, would be for ever secured'.[17] This would be disastrous. Mill argues that English law misconstrues speech against government as a threat to safety. Instead, Mill asserts with uncertain empirical justification, free speech and a free press *are* safety.

J.S. Mill's long quotation from James Mill's 'Liberty of the Press' gives pride of place to James Mill's argument against criminalising mere speech. Criminal codes should criminalise inchoate offences (attempt, conspiracy) and completed offences. There is no need to make a duplicate criminal code that criminalises these acts specifically as they occur through the medium of the press. In this vein, Mill also cites Montesquieu's *Spirit of the Laws*, Book 12, Chapter 12, which narrows the definition of treason so that it requires an *actus reus*. However, to be subject to criminal penalty, the treasonous words must prepare, accompany or follow a criminal act; words alone cannot be punished.[18]

James Mill and J.S. Mill both argued that the usual outcome of sustained discussion and debate was not violence but engagement. Citing the example of the French Revolution, both the Mills argue that the discussion of extreme political opinions did not lead to the Terror. It is instead repression that causes violence.[19] Explaining, then, the situations where spoken arguments or actual incitement lead to imminent political violence, Mill argues that violent reactions to speech are analogous to temporary conditions of infancy of reason, rendering free and equal discussion no longer possible. The hearers of rhetoric inciting violence are transformed by speech in a manner that is different from an argumentative presentation of doctrines. Thus, Mill famously uses the example of the corn dealer endangered by a demagogic speaker in *On Liberty* as an example of the need to prohibit incitement to violence, which, again, is a *deed* and not an example of free speech.[20]

The incitement exception to the general rule of absolutely free discussion and debate is best understood as a narrow times-and-places exception. Mill does not prohibit offensive speech except 'in grave cases'.[21] As Mill observes in *On Liberty*, one may need to discourage 'offensive attacks on infidelity' but he still insists that it is 'obvious that law and authority have no business with restraining either orthodoxy or infidelity'.[22] This judgement reflects Mill's lifelong dislike for the imposition of rules of civility, and this (in conjunction with his theory of representation, which permits the representation of adverse and even low-value views) should remind us that Mill's theory of free speech does not come with epistemic restrictions on what counts as useful speech.[23] The same holds for one's manner of speaking. In 1825, largely on public safety grounds, Mill calls it wrong to say that 'calm and fair discussion should be permitted, but that ridicule and invective ought to be chastised'. Ridicule and invective merely amuse the already converted, and are therefore typically without power to corrupt the public.[24] There is also a time where impassioned invective is appropriate; for example, it is a moral duty to speak indignantly against indignities.[25] An ugly and ridiculous public sphere is not a threat to liberty, as Mill understands it, and dispassionate speech is not always a sign of one's reasonableness.

THE THIRD EXCEPTION: INAPPLICABILITY OF LIBERTY TO SOME ENVIRONMENTS

If the preceding interpretation is correct, Mill's two exceptions for gossip and violence can and probably should be interpreted very narrowly. The third exception concerns contexts where Mill's support of absolute-ish freedom of speech and of the press simply does not apply, and does not apply for more than temporary reasons. How does Mill develop his argument?

Readers of Mill's *Considerations on Representative Government* know him as a thinker who tries to reconcile principles of order and progress. Order, or the demands of public safety, may either favour or oppose liberty of speech and of the press. The liberal version of order, sometimes identified as the 'vent' or 'safety-valve' argument, holds that it is safer to air criticisms, even if they are noxious.[26] The conservative interpretation of the demands of order highlights the dangers of a free press, manipulated by disaffected EIC officers, which pollutes Company rule, infects Indian allies with a spirit of independence, and encourages elites to rouse peasant cultivators into mutiny. Progress, or development, as Mill sometimes calls it, is similarly ambivalent about the value of free speech and the free press. Some progressives argue that the EIC's despotic rule over India is justified by its 'higher purposes, one of which is to pour the enlightened knowledge and civilization, the arts and sciences of Europe over the land', as Governor General Charles Metcalfe argues while defending a free press.[27] Others who are opposed to free speech argue that the Indian community cannot (for reasons of language and culture) profit from free speech or a free press.

All the arguments against freedom of speech and of the press for these environments reduce, as Mill argues in 1825, to an argument from the hearer's *incapacity* to be improved by discussion and debate.[28] Mill's argument will cause many readers to clench their teeth. It sounds racist, although it should be noted that Mill refers here and elsewhere in *On Liberty* to 'the [human] race', not to Indians as a specific racial group.[29] If not racist, as the scholarly consensus seems to think that it is not, then at the very least Mill's argument is culturally insensitive or obtuse, if not hegemonic in the Gramscian sense; or, if neither of these things, then simply wrong as an empirical matter of fact. We must therefore seek for the theory, and, we hope, develop the resources to decide whether the theory is the problem, or whether the problem is merely the application of the theory in India.

Mill's argument on behalf of free speech is made to defend the right of hearers to hear the widest range of opinions on a diversity of subjects.[30] If a community is incapable of being improved by discussion and debate, then the liberty principle is irrelevant and does not apply. In such cases, as Mill dourly points out in *On Liberty*, the best that the community can hope for is the benevolent superintendence of an Akbar or a Charlemagne, on analogy to the paternalistic rule over children for their own sake.

If history's children are in an age of infancy ('nonage', according to *On Liberty*), speech should be as harmless to them as political harangues are to toddlers. There is a worrisome implication here for really retrograde states, which, for this alleged reason, deserve paternalistic rule. India, however, is described as 'semi-barbarous', meaning that disaffected and badly intentioned EIC officers and merchants *can* corrupt the judgement of Anglo-Indians and India's educated elites. To ensure public safety, the EIC policy restricted the English press during the time when Mill first began writing dispatches from the India House to India. At nearly the time when J. S. Mill, following in his father's footsteps, wrote blistering defences of absolute freedom of speech and of the press, he also wrote approvingly about Tory-sponsored press restrictions in India. What can one make of this apparent inconsistency?

Some scholars argue or rather explain Mill's dispatches away by claiming that, as a functionary of the Company, he had no independent opinions; or that he did not develop his own voice; or that, if he had a voice, he developed it only in 1836, after the death of his father.[31] There is also Mill's philosophy of history to consider. Mill proudly synthesises a 'philosophy of history' from the Germano-Coleridgian school, from the stadial intellectual history of Auguste Comte and from Mill's Scottish Enlightenment forebears.[32] Mill's theory of history explains his view that 'different stages of human progress not only *will* have, but *ought* to have, different institutions'.[33] In this vein, one can also point to (alleged) structural problems with Indian publics: their use of vernacular languages, their education and socialisation within a certain form of despotic political rule (or misrule) and, perhaps most importantly, the effects of the Hindu caste system. Significantly, Mill thinks that the earliest and most primitive stage of human history is 'founded on caste, and in which the speculative, necessarily identical with the priestly caste, has the temporal government in its hands or under its control'.[34] India is the 'typical specimen of the institution of caste' and (in Mill's view) the only clear historical example of a rigid, theologically inspired caste system.[35] This is complicated: whilst only semi-barbarous, India is also the paradigmatic caste society. Finally, Mill's criticisms of semi-barbarous India may be racist.[36]

THE DISPATCHES ON THE PRESS RESTRICTIONS

Greater clarity on these questions can be achieved by a granular look at Mill's dispatches to British India in the context of British Indian press restrictions. There are roughly two epochs in the limitation of the press in India. The first period stretches from Governor-General Wellesley's pre-publication censorship, instituted in 1799, to the 1818 change from pre-publication censorship to post-publication responsibility under Governor-General Hastings. Included in this first period are the 'more general and more stringent' rules instituted by Hastings in 1813.

Although it is common to view Hastings as the liberator of the press in India, the moniker is misapplied. Hastings did not establish a free press by abolishing censorship. Instead, he shifted responsibility from pre-publication censors, who were charged with the nearly impossible task of catching offensive material prior to publication, to a system where editors became personally responsible for everything that appeared in their papers. Under the former system, when something offensive appeared everyone could justly blame the overworked censors (or no one); under the latter system, the emphasis was shifted to self-censorship. The proximate cause of the change was not an administrative change of heart regarding the value of press freedom, but to close a loophole. (Transmission, or deportation to England, which was the punishment typically employed by Wellesley and his successors, was not appropriate for editors of mixed or Indian heritage, and another schedule of punishments was required.) More importantly, the content that was prohibited by Hastings was expansive.[37]

The process of censorship and restriction was, it must be noted, more lenient than English libel laws, in so far as transmission was preferred to fines or imprisonment, and the British system in India was far more lenient than Dutch or French colonial laws which simply prohibited press freedom. However, transmission involved significant monetary losses to editors who were sent back to England. In one of the first cases of transmission, Charles Maclean was sent back to England in 1798 by Wellesley, allegedly suffering a loss of £700 in income and an investment of £2,000 in his paper.[38] The most famous case was that of James Silk Buckingham, who was transmitted in 1823 after numerous warnings. He was forced to sell his interest in the *Calcutta Journal*, which then closed.[39] In an apologetic pamphlet of 1823, Buckingham defended his criticisms as 'harmless raillery', and, more importantly, characterised his journal as the 'only zealous and determined Advocate of Free Discussion, and the only channel for the full, fair, and free exercise of Public Opinion'.[40]

The British MP and past EIC chairman James Hogg, reacting to Buckingham's self-characterisation during a parliamentary session concerning possible compensation for Buckingham's losses, accused him of usurping the traditional right of parliamentary petition by positioning the free press as the arbiter of political authority:

> As editor of The Calcutta Journal, Mr. Buckingham arrogated to himself the right of arraigning all the measures of Government, and all public officers before the tribunal of what he was pleased to call 'public opinion'. He inculcated the doctrine, that it was vain and idle to apply for redress to the Government or constituted authorities, and invited all persons to appeal to him as the supreme arbiter.[41]

Whichever man was right as to theory – and the question is, of course, an important one – Charles Metcalfe, in rescinding the prevailing press restrictions in 1835, was right in practice to argue that a 'continual expostulatory and inculpatory correspondence' between the Company and newspaper editors was 'much more likely to bring [the government] into disrepute than any freedom of discussion'.[42] Simply put, press restrictions are not worth the candle.

Mill's dispatches on press restrictions in the late 1820s mirror the Company's official position. Although he is very young when he writes in support of them – merely an apprentice on his way to becoming an Assistant to the Examiner in 1828 – the dispatches provide some evidence as to what Mill is willing to write, and (one must assume) to endorse.[43] Writing on 5 September 1827, for example, he has 'no doubt whatsoever of the expediency of the enactment' against the free press.[44] Replying on 23 July 1828, to letters on the abuses of the press in Calcutta from 6 August 1827, 29 August 1827 and 27 September 1827, Mill expresses regret at government's having been 'calumniously misrepresented by two Calcutta newspapers'. Mill writes:

> We learn with great displeasure from the proceedings here transmitted, that officers in our service are in the habit of attacking the official acts of one another, and defending their own, through the medium of the public Press, even to the extent of virtual, if not direct censure, of the Supreme Government, or the government under whose orders they are acting.[45]

Mill's displeasure is clearly not one that a free-speech absolutist would take. It is that of a utilitarian who is convinced of the merely conditional value of press freedom, and of the likely harmful effects of press freedom on the Company's presence in India.

These youthful dispatches conducting company business may not tell us much about Mill's theory of speech and press freedom. However, much later, when Mill summarises the contribution of the press in India to the

Select Committee of the House of Lords on India Affairs in 1852, as a mature thinker, he makes a surprisingly dismissive nod to the English and vernacular press:

> the English newspapers in India are of very little use to good government, except in promoting inquiry, and drawing the attention of the Government to facts which they might have overlooked. From the little knowledge I have of the Indian newspaper press, I should say that its comments are seldom of any value.[46]

For Mill, the great arguments in favour of the free press are unpersuasive in the Indian context, although it is perhaps precisely because Mill expects so much from expression and governmental oversight that he is disappointed by happenings in India.

THE FLAWED PUBLICS IN INDIA

The main point is that Mill thinks that liberty does not exist in India. To address the crucial and puzzling claim made in *On Liberty*, it is helpful to adapt a framework used in John Malcolm's *Political History of India*, which makes explicit Mill's implicit comparison between three differing communities: (1) the Indian population, which company officials often subdivide into (*a*) the 'infant society' of educated and English-speaking 'half-caste' (also, 'Indo-Briton' or Anglo-Indian) persons, and (*b*) 'superstitious' and uneducated peasant cultivators; (2) the English population in British India, which is largely composed of EIC officers and (after 1813) uncovenanted tradesmen; and (3) the British public at home, which provides restraint and oversight on the EIC through parliamentary publicity and the free press in England.[47]

It is plausible that Mill defends press restrictions in British India primarily because he thinks that there is no public in India. Thus, James Hogg, in India from 1822 to 1833 (and twice elected chairman of the EIC), argues against press freedom in India in a Select Committee meeting of 1834, when he was an MP:

> Where, I ask, was 'the public' in India ... It is mockery to talk of 'a public', and 'public opinion', in India. There is no public in India. There, every man is in office, civil or military, controlling those below him, and owing obedience to those above him. It is a society of public functionaries, but there are no elements to form a public.[48]

Despite the partial truth of this observation – the EIC's military had expanded massively, amounting to 250,000 soldiers in 1814, and military subscriptions made up the largest single group of subscribers to the four main English-language daily newspapers in 1834 – British India was no longer a military outpost in the period under discussion.[49] It was instead a thriving and variegated community by the late 1820s, and it clearly included a variety of English voices, progressive Indian voices and a thriving vernacular press.

Sir John Malcolm, later Governor-General of Bombay (1827–30), also criticises the suggestion that a free press can be transplanted to India. Malcolm affirms that the value of a free press lies in its ability to inform an 'independent public' in order to 'check misrule'. However, Malcolm asserts, 'no part of this description of an independent public applies to our empire in India'. Publics are not created by the mere presence of English people abroad, and neither are traditional English rights; only a 'portion' of the 'free constitution' travels with the English wherever they go.[50]

In a speech of 9 July 1824, to the Court of Proprietors, Malcolm further considers whether the free press of England can be transplanted to India.[51] First, Malcolm compares the community in British India to 'the Public' in England. The 'essential component part' of the British public, 'that which gives gravity and steadiness to the whole', is 'the numerous class who occupy the middle ranks of life'.[52] Without 'moderation' and 'good sense' of the 'middle class', the free press is a curse. Is there, one might ask, an English middle class in India?[53] Not according to Malcolm. Thus, it would be incorrect to conclude that Malcolm denies the importance of publics. Instead, he concludes that the English public *at home* is sufficient to oversee the EIC's activity in India. He explains:

> Government in India ought to be, and is, under the control of public opinion, but that public is in England ... the appeal from injustice in India is to this House, and through this House to the people of England, – and not to the editor of a paper in Calcutta, and a discontented faction, by whom he may be supported, and which he may dignify with the name of 'a public'.[54]

In sum, for Malcolm, 'the English community in India neither are, nor ever can be, a body resembling the public in England'.[55]

But is it really the case that no native public exists in British India? The countervailing argument in favour of complete freedom of speech and of the press in India is made by figures such as Charles Metcalfe and Leicester Stanhope, and they presumably believe either that a reading public already exists in India or that one can soon be created. Metcalfe, later a Tory MP, was acting Governor-General from 1835 and a member of the 'empire of opinion' school. Drawing sustenance from Burke and Hume, this school (in Lynn Zastoupil's characterisation) believed that public opinion and even prejudice 'were necessary in a stable civil society'.[56] For Metcalfe, whose Act XI of 1835 liberated the press in India by repealing the 5 April 1823 licensing act of John Adam, press freedom was a positive good and among the tools of the EIC's 'higher purposes' in enlightening India.[57] Although Mill certainly agrees with Metcalfe's evaluative standard – that is, that rule of dependencies should work to the benefit of the dependent nation – there is no evidence from any of his unpublished or published writings that Mill agrees with Metcalfe's argument about the centrality of the press in India, or that its 'promethean spark' will spread enlightenment.

In a Miltonian pamphlet of 1823 defending free speech, Leicester Stanhope, a soldier and administrator in British India and a peer (Earl of Harrington), asserts that there *is* a public in British India, and he memorably complains that this oppressed native public enjoyed greater liberty to speak and educate under the Mughal emperor Akbar than under English rule.[58] Stanhope reassures his reader that 'all history demonstrates that nothing tends so much to avert revolutions, as those timely and temperate reforms which result from free discussion'.[59] Thus, the EIC's soldiers' grievances about inequalities of compensation, slowness of promotion and preferential treatment in some presidencies versus others are all grievances that should be aired so as to achieve 'favourable reform without ... awful convulsions'.[60] The alternative to hearing complaints from the army and honouring the opinions of native subjects, argues the abovementioned surgeon and editor Charles Maclean, is 'Colonial alienation'.[61]

It is surprising, on its surface, that Mill makes the Stanhopian argument about England but not about India.[62] Thus, in an August 1857 pamphlet on the free press, Mill endorses a 12 April 1822 minute by Thomas Munro (Governor of Madras from 1820 to 1826).[63] This pamphlet cannot indicate a continuity of position in Mill's thinking from the 1820s to his retirement from the EIC – and, to be sure, it does not illuminate what Mill thought about the utility of Governor-General Charles Canning's notorious temporary Gag law targeting the vernacular press in British India after the 1857 'rebellion' – but it does display Mill's thinking at a key inflection point in EIC history. Mill calls attention to Munro's 'remarkable and prophetic' observation that '[t]he native troops are the only body of natives who are always mixed with Europeans, and they will therefore be the first to learn the doctrines circulated among them by the newspapers'. About the possibility of corruption by the English influence, Mill observes: 'this no doubt is the case, and the results we are, I believe, now witnessing'. Thus, Mill is clearly worried about the consequences of translating seditious articles into native languages, and he asks: 'amongst whom do these papers circulate first? Undoubtedly among the Sepoys.' This is an example where Mill's concern for public safety leads him to favour press restrictions rather than press freedom.

Having said all this in favour of order, Mill also emphasises that the need for order is justified by the aim of progress: 'our empire in India, consisting of a few hundred Europeans holding 100 millions of natives in obedience by an army composed of those very natives, will not exist for a day after we shall lose the character of being more just and more disinterested than the native rulers and of being united among ourselves'.[64] Press restrictions are justified by the Company's civilising improvements in British India. However, it is not at all clear – it is perhaps even unlikely, given the admissions regarding the avowedly commercial aims of the EIC's administrative despotism in British India – that the Company actually lives up to Mill's standard.

THE THEORY OF PUBLIC ENGAGEMENT REFINED

As the reader of *On Liberty* and of Mill's reviews of Tocqueville is well aware, Mill worries that the power of the public will be used to stifle individuality.[65] In his India writings and dispatches, Mill writes very critically of proto-publics and, at least in India, he clearly does not think that freeing the 'salt of the earth' to complain about misrule will help India from becoming a 'stagnant pool'.[66] His point is not clear. England and India require different political projects because of their differing social and political conditions; this much is clear. For England, Mill recommends bootstrapping: liberal discussion and debate will elevate the country to a higher and more reflective freedom. In India, Mill blames two related flaws in the public: local or small-scale despotisms, and what he calls 'native despotism'. It is an empirical question that Mill may answer incorrectly, but for him, both of these types of despotic rule are worse than foreign despotism, and it is this that justifies the EIC's intervention in India.[67]

Orderly, administrative despotism can improve upon the deeper despotism of thoughtless conventionalism, where one is 'the slave of the vulgar prejudices, the cramped, distorted and short-sighted views, of the public of a small town or a group of villages'.[68] Native despotism similarly deifies tradition and habit and can also be broken by foreigners.[69] However, in order to break the despotic bond of custom, Mill somewhat exaggeratedly rejects incremental bootstrapping.[70] In England and in Continental Europe, localities can also be stupid and backwards; but only in native despotism, so Mill thinks, is there an ugly ditch that degrees of discussion and debate cannot cross. Given Mill's generally low opinion of English character, it is frankly puzzling that Mill thinks that England and India are so different. The press is an agent of 'collective mediocrity', he writes in *On Liberty*, presumably including England in that judgement.[71] The family is a 'school of despotism', as he observes in *The Subjection of Women*.[72] If he rejects liberty in India, why does he not see that his criticism of the subjection of women in England justifies authoritative governmental intervention at home? Or, to turn the question around in a more positive light, why does he not recommend bootstrapping in native dependencies that can use their own press and speech freedoms to criticise their own customs, caste and religion?

One answer is that the young Mill grew up steeped in his father's teachings. James Mill's 1823 essay 'Liberty of the Press' offers a largely absolutist argument in defence of free speech, as noted above. James Mill's support for the free press in India is more qualified. Thus, in his 1818 *History of British India*, James Mill saw that '[s]olid objections may indeed be started to the institution as yet of a free press in India, though objections of much less weight than is generally imagined'.[73] For James Mill, and for absolutists and quasi-absolutists, free speech and a free press should create a public if one does not already exist. Not only must there be the 'greatest freedom' to publish on governmental action, the elder Mill writes, 'but measures ought to be taken to *make* a public, and to *produce publication*, where there is any chance that a *voluntary* public, and voluntary publication, would be wanting'.[74]

While the *History of British India* is at least as pessimistic about native despotism as J. S. Mill's writings on India, James Mill is thus *more* optimistic about the incremental contribution that press and speech can make, even in communities that are not prepared for freedom. James Mill writes,

> Considering the mental state of the people of India, it is possible that among them, at the present moment, the unrestrained use of the press might be attended with inconveniences of a serious nature, and such as would surpass the evils it would remove. *There is no people, however, among whom it may not be introduced by degrees.* The people of India, it is certain, ought to receive, as one of the indispensable instruments of improvement, as much of it as they can bear; and this would soon prepare them, if properly encouraged, for the receipt of more, and hence, by rapid steps, for the enjoyment of it, in all its fullness, and all its efficiency.[75]

John Stuart clearly thinks that the introduction of discussion and debate by degrees will not help India. Why? In addition to the influence of James Mill's utilitarianism, John Stuart also believes in the basic correctness of the Simonian and Comtist stadial history, which assumes something like a 'paradigm shift' between distinct epochs of history. Working out the consequences of his view, John Stuart argues that the EIC's elaborate system of 'recordation' (the so-called paper empire) is as close to diverse, informed discussion that one can get in India.[76]

Comparing India to Ireland, a European country, may help to further clarify Mill's position, both in order to clear Mill of the charge of racism and to do more than simply write Mill off as a Comtist. 'India is now governed', Mill writes, 'if with a large share of the ordinary imperfections of rulers, yet with a full perception and recognition of its differences from England. What has been done for India has now to be done for Ireland'.[77] That is, India should be ruled despotically for its own benefit! As in the case of the peasant cultivators (*ryots*) of India, Mill was an advocate of the rights of Irish cultivators.[78] More to the point, however, Mill thought that Ireland was not ready for governmental accountability through publicity. In Ireland, the key problem was the oppressive, structural inequalities between landlord and tenant, the latter of whom had (almost uniquely in Europe) no rights in the soil. In order to break the bonds of local despotism, and specifically the land tenure system that creates extreme structural poverty among peasant farmers – largely, it must be observed, through England's own pernicious influence – Mill remarks in a private letter of 1837 that his preference for Ireland and India is despotism: 'There is much to be said about Ireland. I myself have always been for a good stout Despotism – for governing Ireland like India. But it cannot be done. The spirit of Democracy has got too much head there, too prematurely.'[79] So, rather than advocate a 'simple, straightforward military despotism' over Ireland (as he did in India), Mill advocates a change in the economic system as a next-best solution.[80] In both India and Ireland, hierarchical land tenure systems were imposed by the English; in the Irish case, Mill is literally arguing that two wrongs make a right.

By way of further comparison across different publics, Mill observes that public opinion is relatively absent in Restoration France. Although it is too difficult and broad a topic to address in this chapter, Mill's broader comparison of European publics helps to provide crucial context concerning Mill's thoroughgoing incrementalism in Europe.[81] In an 1832 *Examiner* article comparing the revolutionary contexts of 1789 and 1830, Mill argues that the French public is capable of exerting a counterweight to royal power only in the domain of one issue: hereditary rule.[82] Otherwise, there is discontented public clamour for instruction but no actual public instruction in the press.[83] It seems, once again, that in practice Mill sees Europe and Britain with the same jaundiced eye as he sees India. The rather perverse-sounding inference is that, except in the domain of monarchy, France is fit for benevolent despotism; Ireland is suited for benevolent despotism *tout court*; and the Anglo-American common law of family suggests that gender hierarchies prohibit the existence of free and equal discussion. Mill does not draw these inferences, and it is interesting to ask why he does not.

The answer is that the relation between publics and instructive discussion is dialectical. In the context of French politics in this period, Mill offers two necessary condition of progress: freedom of thought and utterance, which is 'the sole and indispensable instrument of all other political good', and 'exemption from the iron yoke of a caste-oligarchy over the body, and of a retrograde priesthood over the soul'.[84] A public must be somewhat equal to be free. In India, caste and land tenure destroy the nascent Indian public. In Ireland, Catholicism may impede equality, but the true problem is the land tenure system. Finally, in France, Catholicism and aristocratic social hierarchies stifle the public. None of these countries, properly speaking, has a public, but only India's yoke is (it seems) truly iron.

Writing on empire, Fitzjames Stephen takes this to mean that people everywhere needs guardians to rule them for their own good.[85] That is the inference Mill does not draw. For Mill, the opposite holds true of *civilised* countries. However, if Mill is consistent, it is unlikely that empire in India and Ireland is defensible. In fact, Mill's understanding of the value of free speech and of a free press is not only highly contextual but even more contingent than he lets on. In India, structural inequality, combined with the structural self-interest of an oligarchic English commercial population, renders a free press almost useless. The situation of India is similar to Ireland's; there, what is needed is not the freedom to criticise government – after all, anyone with eyes correctly apprehends the basic problem – but either a revolution or structural changes in land tenure. In contrast, Mill's solution for France or England involves neither revolution nor structural change, except in the area of gender. Mill's theory of publicity is therefore more contingent than he lets on. Structural hierarchies *sometimes* render discussion and debate useless in the face of deep-set inequalities, and the only means sufficient to break the ties of custom are revolution or foreign conquest; but, in other contexts, Mill embraces incrementalism without explaining his optimism about the one case or his pessimism about the other.

CONCLUSION

Mill's argument about the relation between multiple publics in the areas of press and speech freedoms does not carve out an 'exception to his general principles of government'.[86] Mill's criticism of the flawed English community composed of EIC functionaries and tradespeople, his criticism of the Anglo-Indian and Indian elites and his dismissal of democratic self-government of peasant cultivators are instead nearer to the core of his social and political theory than is often imagined. Mill's India writings underline the fact that the liberty principle is not context-independent. It is fragile and not appropriate to all places and times. However, if the above interpretation is correct, the theory may need to be changed, and not only to shed the vestiges of company loyalty and biographical baggage that Mill carries from his thirty-five years' employment by the East India Company. The theory may be tainted by a theory of stadial and developmental history, and it may suffer from an unempirical blindness to the developed and sophisticated Indian public for other reasons, including Mill's lack of contact with Indians and his valorisation of the paper empire, which, for all its merits (oversight, deliberateness), was transacted at more than arm's length from India. How can Mill's theory of free speech be improved?

Firstly, Mill's theory can be improved by paying heed to the rights of hearers at various stages of development. While covenanted EIC servants and non-covenanted Englishmen *may* form a corporate body rather than a public, this is simply not true of the Indian populace. Given the tension within Mill's theory of representation between 'numbers' and competence, one cannot prove that a public exists simply by looking at subscription numbers, but the several thousand Indians reading vernacular newspapers in 1825, joining debates on British politics and reacting to changes in Continental liberties makes it nearly impossible to say that no nascent public existed in British India.[87] In fact, it is more accurate to infer that the EIC itself is suppressive of existing, liberal reading publics in India. Admitting as much, for example, John Malcolm concludes that native newspaper editors must not be allowed to advocate for Indian independence, because, as he revealingly admits, 'it would be their duty, if worthy of the task, to disseminate [independence] amongst their countrymen'.[88] Escaping the leading-strings of colonial government and achieving self-government is precisely the goal of the Millian EIC's presence in India, but Mill does not theorise the incremental beginnings of independence.

Mill holds throughout his life that India is not yet ready for discussion, debate and diversity. India is mired in custom and superstition, and the most obvious lubricant, 'free and equal discussion', cannot help Indians out of this allegedly stationary state. Mill never explains exactly what he means in *On Liberty*'s Chapter One when he explains that India lacks free and equal discussion. But, reconstructing his view, a crucial problem is the caste system, along with religio-cultural practices such as *sati* (widow-burning) and the subjection of women, which present near-absolute, short-term bars to social equality. Consistently with Mill's understanding of structural inequality's gross effects on discussion and exchange, Mill holds that both Ireland and India would be served by the imposition of external, non-political (despotic) administration.

Mill clearly understands that some flawed publics *can* become sovereign publics by their own bootstrapping. The problem is that India's caste system is a tailor-made example of the theological epoch of stadial history: the paradigmatic stationary state. This exaggerated view can be chalked up to Mill's Comtist and reductive historical sociology, which is a theory about religion and science, not race, but one that is less than helpful in analysing India as a complicated, living state. Mill also never visits India; in this mistake, he follows his father's example. To the extent, then, that Mill mechanically understands India as the product of a Hindu caste system, and thus as a country stuck in a theological age, he fails to make even a pragmatic case for press and speech liberties, and he rejects the developmental argument for a free press in India that his father accepts.

As other writers in this volume have argued, full freedoms of speech and press are most defensible and safe in organic ages of mutually reinforcing social norms. However, since an age of complete consensus and unity is always 'not-yet' in relation to the present moment, Mill's defence of 'free and equal discussion' never becomes what it is often thought to be, namely the absolute freedom to say anything. It is a pragmatic argument about extending to speakers and hearers the degree of liberty that suits a particular time and place. What it *should* have been is an even more pragmatic and empirical theory. In this way, Mill could have avoided the reformer's trap of cancelling existing publics in order to lay the foundations for future publics which do not yet exist, and may never exist so long as the heavy hand of intervention shapes institutions.

NOTES

1 J. S. Mill, 'Free Discussion, Letter I', 'Free Discussion, Letter II', 'Free Discussion, Letter III', in *CWJSM*, XXII, 9–18 at 10; J. S. Mill, 'Law of Libel and Liberty of the Press', *CWJSM*, XXI, 1–34.
2 An important caveat is offered by Mill's essays and letters of the 1830s, a period during which his increased attention to tradition, custom and prevailing opinion

muted his regard for the transformative power of discussion. See A. Brady, 'Introduction' in *CWJSM*, XVIII, lv.
3. Mill, 'On Liberty', *CWJSM*, XVIII, 260. However, Mill foresees a 'future which shall unite the best qualities of the critical with the best qualities of the organic periods; unchecked liberty of thought, unbounded freedom of individual action in all modes not hurtful to others; but also, convictions as to what is right and wrong, useful and pernicious, deeply engraven on the feelings by early education and general unanimity of sentiment ('Autobiography', *CWJSM*, I, 109).
4. For a related interpretation of universality as liberalism's not-yet, see K. Mantena, 'Mill and the Imperial Predicament', in N. Urbinati and Z. Zakaras (eds), *J.S. Mill's Thought: A Bicentennial Reassessment* (Cambridge, 2007), 307.
5. The gossip exception is explored at length by Jonathan Riley, who argues that Mill is not particularly absolutist about speech, in contrast to K.C. O'Rourke, who argues that Mill makes no content-based restrictions on free speech. See J. Riley, 'J. S. Mill's Doctrine of Freedom of Expression', *Utilitas* 17 (2005), 147–79, and K. O'Rourke, *John Stuart Mill and Freedom of Expression* (2001), 20, 135, 138.
6. J. S. Mill, 'Law of Libel', 20.
7. Ibid., 5, 23–6; J. Mill, 'Jurisprudence', in J. Mill, *Political Writings*, ed. T. Ball (Cambridge, 1992), 88–9.
8. 'O'Connell's Amendment of the Libel Law', *Spectator* (22 February 1834).
9. J. S. Mill, 'Notes on the Newspapers', *CWJSM*, VI, 167.
10. See J. S. Mill, 'Principles of Political Economy', *CWJSM*, III, 938 and D. Jacobson, 'Mill on Freedom of Speech', in C. Macleod and D. Miller (eds), *A Companion to Mill* (Malden, MA, 2017), 445.
11. Riley, 'J. S. Mill's Doctrine of Freedom of Expression', 169–71.
12. See F. Priestley, 'Textual Introduction', *CWJSM*, X, cxxii–cxxiii.
13. J. S. Mill, 'Chapters on Socialism', *CWJSM*, V, 746.
14. Mill, 'Notes on the Newspapers', 166.
15. J. S. Mill, 'Considerations on Representative Government', *CWJSM*, XIX, 436.
16. J. S. Mill, 'Penal Code for India', *CWJSM*, XXX, 29.
17. J. S. Mill, 'Law of Libel', 6.
18. Montesquieu, *The Spirit of the Laws*, trans. A. Cohler, B. Carolyn Miller and S. Stone (Cambridge, 1989), 198–9 (Mill appears to make his own translation rather than use the imperfect Thomas Nugent translation); Mill, 'Law of Libel', 5. Solicitation and pornography are marginal cases. See C. McGlynn, 'John Stuart Mill on Prostitution: Radical Sentiments, Liberal Proscriptions', *Nineteenth-century Gender Studies* 8 (2012), and C. McGlynn and I. Ward, 'Would John Stuart Mill Have Regulated Pornography?', *Journal of Law and Society* 41 (2014), 518.
19. J. S. Mill, 'Law of Libel', 11; James Mill is quoted in O'Rourke, *John Stuart Mill*, 10.
20. J. S. Mill, 'On Liberty', 260; Mill, 'Liberty of the Press', 112. Even the advocacy of tyrannicide is permissible unless an 'overt act' can be tied to the instigation by a 'probable connexion'. See Mill, 'On Liberty', 228n.
21. Mill, 'On Liberty', 279; B. McElwee, 'Mill and Virtue', in Macleod and Miller (eds), *Companion to Mill*, 390–406 at 399.
22. Mill, 'On Liberty', 259.
23. The extent of Mill's restrictions is contested. For the position that Mill would

prohibit autonomy-reducing hate speech, see D. Brink, *Mill's Progressive Principles* (Oxford, 2013), 166ff.
24 Mill, 'Law of Libel', 15.
25 O'Rourke, *John Stuart Mill*, 136–7.
26 The EIC historian John Kaye praises the free press as a new Cloacina, the Roman goddess of the sewers. See J. Kaye, *The Life and Correspondence of Major-General Sir John Malcolm* (1856), I, 462.
27 Quoted in ibid., II, 149.
28 Mill, 'Law of Libel', 10: 'The objections which have been urged against the principle of free discussion, though infinitely diversified in shape, are at bottom only one assertion: the incapacity of the people to form correct opinions'.
29 Mill, 'On Liberty', 224.
30 The right to hear is the basic insight propelling K.C. O'Rourke's absolutist interpretation of Mill on speech. O'Rourke, *John Stuart Mill*, 4, 78–84. For epistemic diversity, see Mill, 'On Liberty', 260.
31 See M. Moir, 'John Stuart Mill's Draft Despatches to India and the Problem of Bureaucratic Authorship', in M. Moir, D. Peers and L. Zastoupil (eds), *J.S. Mill's Encounter with India* (Toronto, 1999), 72–86.
32 For Mill's support of the 'law of stages' see Mill, 'Auguste Comte and Positivism', *CWJSM*, X, 269–79. For an example in comparative political history (analogising 'Hindoos' and archaic Greeks), see 'Grote's History of Greece [I]', *CWJSM*, XI, 288.
33 J.S. Mill, 'Autobiography', *CWJSM*, I, 169. See D. Thompson, *John Stuart Mill and Representative Government* (Princeton, 1976), 136–73 and 153–4.
34 Mill, 'Auguste Comte and Positivism', 319.
35 Ibid., 320–1.
36 See responses by N. Urbinati, 'The Many Heads of the Hydra', in N. Urbinati and Z. Zakaras (eds), *J.S. Mill's Thought: A Bicentennial Reassessment* (Cambridge, 2007), 76, 94; Mantena, 'Mill and the Imperial Predicament', 309; and J. Pitts, *A Turn to Empire: The Rise of Imperial Liberalism in Britain and France* (Princeton, 2005), 123–62. It is worth noting that Mill could be racist about so-called *barbarous* communities, even if his opinions about semi-barbarous communities are tempered, but his essay on African-Americans and Southern chattel slavery ('The Contest in America') does not support this interpretation, in my view.
37 The 1818 prohibition includes the following: 'Animadversions' or 'offensive remarks at the Company or the British government'; anything 'having a tendency to create alarm or suspicion among the native population, or any intended interference with their religious opinions or observances'; and 'private scandal and personal remarks on individuals, tending to excite dissension in society'.
38 Maclean's crime was to criticise a judge in Gauzepore in print on 28 April 1798. He wrote: 'I am happy to add that the only disagreeable effects of the rencontre have arisen from the interference of the magistrate of Gauzepore, whose conduct upon this occasion I will take a due opportunity of appreciating'. Maclean was sent to England after refusing to apologise. Maclean's career is described in M. Harrison, 'Networks of Knowledge', in D. Peers and N. Gooptu (eds), *India and the British Empire* (Oxford, 2012), 205–7.
39 L. Scott, 'Buckingham's Republic of Letters: Defining the Limits of Free

Expression in British Calcutta, 1818–1832' (University of Ottawa MA Thesis, 2017).

40 J. Buckingham, *A Faithful History of the Late Discussions in Bengal*, 17 (1823), 3–4, 1. In contrast, Zastoupil describes the connection between Buckingham's *Calcutta Journal* and Rammohun Roy's *Kaumudi*; the former reprinted tables of contents and excerpts from the latter. See L. Zastoupil, *Rammohun Roy and the Making of Victorian Britain* (2010).

41 [J. Hogg,] 'Mr. Buckingham's Claims', *House of Commons Debate of 7 June 1836*, 34 (1836), 177.

42 J. Kaye, *Selections from the Papers of Lord Metcalfe* (1855), 312.

43 He is promoted to second and then first assistant to the examiner, both in 1836, and becomes Examiner in 1856. See Martin Moir, 'Introduction', *CWJSM*, XXX, vii–liv at xii–xxix.

44 BL, IOR, E/4/1048, fol. 160.

45 BL, IOR, G/34/195, fols 75, 78–9.

46 J. S. Mill, 'The East India Company's Charter', *CWJSM*, XXX, 70.

47 See J. Malcolm, 'Speech of Sir John Malcolm, G.C.B., &c. &c., Delivered at a General Court of Proprietors of East India Stock, on Friday, July 9, 1824', in *The Political History of India, from 1784 to 1823* (1826), II, ccxl–ccxlii. The Charter of 1813 opened India to tradespeople unaffiliated with the Company. Malcolm estimates that about three thousand English in India were not in civil or military service (II, 313). Buckingham estimates that in 1823 over half of those composing the public in India are in the service of the company (Buckingham, *A Faithful History*, 1). For Mill on dependencies, see Mill, 'Considerations on Representative Government', 563–7; Urbinati, 'The Many Heads of the Hydra', 75. For a related interpretation pitting Whig recognition of an Indian public against the Tory recognition of an English-speaking EIC public, see N. Cassels, *Social Legislation of the East India Company: Public Justice Versus Public Instruction* (New Delhi, 2010), 365–80.

48 [Hogg,] 'Mr. Buckingham's Claims', 178. As a member of the Supreme Council in 1828, Metcalfe (discussed below) takes the opposite position: 'that the only class of persons who feel any interest in the Company's Government shall be utterly precluded from the employment of their talents in the operation of the Press, appears to be very impolitic'. Kaye, *Papers of Lord Metcalfe*, 311. For Mill's dispatch applying this policy, see BL, IOR, E/4/720, 471–90.

49 A. Ahmed, *Social Ideas and Social Change in Bengal, 1818–1835* (Leiden, 1965), 73; L. Colley, *Captives: Britain, Empire, and the World, 1600–1850* (2004).

50 Malcolm, *Political History*, 308–9. Malcolm makes it clear that he is talking about both liberties of speech and the press. *Commenting* upon local administration; *animadverting* upon functionaries; *publishing* complaints; *discussing* questions; *exposing* native religion to ridicule all create 'insubordination, contention, and disaffection' (309; Malcolm's own words are in italics).

51 Ibid., II, ccxxxii. Kaye, *Life and Correspondence*, II, 559–60.

52 Malcolm, *Political History*, II, ccxxxiii–ccxxxiv.

53 One might ask for a more nuanced distinction, for example, between a socioeconomic class and intellectual rank, see T. Ball, 'Introduction', in J. Mill, *Political Writings*, ed. Ball, xx–xxi.

54 [Hogg,] 'Mr. Buckingham's Claims', 178–9.
55 Malcolm, *Political History*, II, ccxxxv. See also P. Sonwalkar, 'Indian Journalism in the Colonial Crucible', *Journalism Studies* 16 (2015), 624–36.
56 L. Zastoupil, *John Stuart Mill and India* (Stanford, 1994), 56. For Zastoupil, 'they were ... Whigs transformed by the imperial experience' (72).
57 Quoted in J. Kaye, *The Life and Correspondence of Charles, Lord Metcalfe, A New and Revised Edition* (1858), II, 149. See also Cassels, *Social Legislation*, 364, 379; Zastoupil, *Mill and India*, 66 n. 53; S. Sanial, 'The History of Journalism in India', *Calcutta Journal* 251 (1908), 92–144.
58 L. Stanhope, *Sketch of the History and Influence of the Press in British India* (1823), 25–6, 5. The September–October republication of Stanhope's pamphlet was the final nail in the coffin for the *Calcutta Journal*, whose licence was revoked in November 1823, after both Buckingham and the journal's assistant editor had been transmitted to England. See Sanial, 'History of Journalism', 97.
59 Stanhope, *Sketch*, 193.
60 Ibid., 11.
61 C. Maclean, *The Affairs of Asia, Considered in their Effects of the Liberties of Britain* (1806), 22, 118, 156, 165, comparing all the charges against Hastings in the scales with one charge levied by Maclean against Wellesley, that of extinguishing the free press.
62 O'Rourke, *John Stuart Mill*, 153.
63 This document is reprinted in 'Extract Minute by the Right Honourable the Governor (Lord Harris), Dated the 20th June 1857, in support of Disraeli's press restrictions in India (Act no. 25, 1857), *Accounts and Paper: East India*, XXIX (1857), appendix C.
64 J. S. Mill, 'Minute on the Black Act (1836)', *CWJSM*, XXX, 14–15. This observation is reinforced by several other dispatches criticising the use of aggressive or excessive force, or the practice of using (or turning a blind eye to the use of) forced labour in public works projects. I am currently working on essays covering these and related areas of colonial malfeasance.
65 Mill, 'On Liberty', 284.
66 Ibid., 242, 269, 267.
67 Mill praises liberal government's interceding when foreign despots suppress popular uprisings that serve the good of the people (in Hungary in 1849, when Russia intervened) but never to my knowledge does he connect this argument to the EIC's suppression of native participation and learning in India. See 'A Few Words on Non-intervention', *CWJSM*, XXI, 124.
68 J. S. Mill, *CWJSM*, XIX, 606.
69 J. S. Mill, 'Remarks on Whewell's Philosophy', *CWJSM*, X, 179.
70 The multi-step process from no-rule to democracy is described in S. Holmes, 'Making Sense of Liberal Imperialism', in N. Urbinati and Z. Zakaras (eds), *J.S. Mill's Thought: A Bicentennial Reassessment* (Cambridge, 2007), 322–5.
71 Mill 'On Liberty', 269.
72 Mill, 'The Subjection of Women', *CWJSM*, XXI, 294–5.
73 J. Mill, *History of British India*, third edition (1826), V, 489.
74 J. Mill, 'Jurisprudence', in *Political Writings*, ed. Ball, 88 (emphasis added).
75 Mill, *History of British India*, 543 (emphasis added).

76 Mill, 'The East India Company's Charter', 33; P. Joyce, *The State of Freedom: A Social History of the British State since 1800* (Cambridge, 2013), 147–50. Even James Fitzjames Stephen, not a liberal, sees that J. S. Mill should say that even 'wild savages' are capable of some improvement via discussion. See J. Stephen, *Liberty, Equality, Fraternity*, ed. S. Warner (Indianapolis, 1993), 29.
77 J. S. Mill, 'England and Ireland', *CWJSM*, VI, 519.
78 B. Kinzer, *England's Disgrace: J.S. Mill and the Irish Question* (Toronto, 2001).
79 J. S. Mill, 'To John Pringle Nichol', *CWJSM*, XII, 365.
80 J. S. Mill, 'What is to be Done with Ireland?' *CWJSM*, VI, 499; Mill, 'England and Ireland', 505–32.
81 Good places to begin are his 'Spirit of the Age' essays from the 1830s, and his 1832 essay 'Comparison of the Tendencies of French and English Intellects', *CWJSM*, XXII, 442–7.
82 Mill, 'Notes on the Newspapers', 342.
83 J. S. Mill, 'The Close of the Session in France', *CWJSM*, XXIII, 457.
84 Ibid., 456.
85 K. Mantena, 'The Crisis of Liberal Imperialism', *Histoire@Politique* 2 (2010): www.cairn.info/revue-histoire-politique-2010-2-page-2.htm, accessed 26 October 2019.
86 J. Majeed, 'James Mill's History of British India: A Reevaluation', in M. Moir, D. Peers and L. Zastoupil (eds), *J.S. Mill's Encounter with India* (Toronto, 1999), 66.
87 See Ahmed, *Social Ideas*, 71–3, and C. Bayly, *Recovering Liberties: Indian Thought in the Age of Liberalism and Empire* (Cambridge, 2012), 79, for the estimate of a five thousand to ten thousand person public in Bengal in the 1820s.
88 Malcolm, *Political History*, 320–1.

Index

Abigail 50
Adam, John 245
Adams, John 197, 204
Addison, Joseph 181, 182
Admonition to Parliament (1572) 102
Aeropagitica (1644) 14, 17, 109, 110, 121, 135, 172, 175, 180, 181
Aeschylus 35
Ahab 96 n. 63
Alexander the Great 50
Alford, Francis 93
Amhurst, Nicholas 174
Anne, Queen 172
Annett, Peter 158
Arbuthnot, John 176, 188 n. 86
Arendt, Hannah 171
Aristippus 38, 39, 45 n. 100
Arnall, William 174, 176
Articles of Confederation (1781) 206 n. 11
Askew, Egeon 54
Athanasian Creed 156, 157
Atterbury, Francis 153, 157
Austin, John 230 n. 40

Babington Plot (1586) 68
Bacon, Anthony 91
Bacon, Francis, 11, 77, 194
Bailey, Samuel 19, 211–35
Bancroft, Richard (archbishop of Canterbury) 73

Barber, John 119
Barclay, John 77
Barnard, John 175
Bastwick, John 11, 87, 89, 90, 92
Bayle, Pierre 140, 141, 143, 144–5
Bellarmino, Roberto (cardinal) 71
Bentham, Jeremy 211, 212, 230 n. 40
Bernard, Jean-François 138
Biddle, John 159
Bignon, Jean-Paul (abbé) 138
Bill of Rights (1689) 18, 207 n. 11
Bill of Rights (1791) 192, 198, 201, 209 n. 49
Blackstone, Sir William (judge) 18, 19, 192, 193, 196, 199, 200, 201, 204, 205, 209 n. 42
Blasphemy 3, 16, 49, 52, 53, 123, 151–70, 173, 185 n. 21
Blasphemy Act (1698) 136–7, 138
Blasphemy Bill (1721) 16, 151–70
Blount, Charles 16
Boileau, Nicolas 138
Bolingbroke, viscount, *see* St John
Bolton, Robert 49, 52, 53
Boyer, Abel 175
Bridges, John 66
Brooke, Henry 175, 186 n. 43
Bruen, John 47, 49, 58
Buckingham, duke of, *see* Villiers
Buckingham, James Silk 242, 243, 254 n. 47, 255 n. 58

Index

Burgess, John 70
Burghley, Lord, *see* Cecil
Burke, Edmund 177
Burnet, Gilbert (bishop of Salisbury) 136, 138
Burton, Henry 11, 87–9, 90, 92, 97 n. 63, 107, 116 n. 14
Bye Plot (1603) 74

Cairo Declaration on Human Rights (1990) 4
Calves-Head Club 155
Campbell, Hugh Hume, third earl of Marchmont 179
Campeggio, Lorenzo 32
Campion, Edmund 71
Canning, Charles (governor-general of India) 246
Carleton, George (bishop of Chichester) 116 n. 14
Carr, Robert 79
Carter, John 53
Carter Jr, John 55
Cartwright, Thomas 71, 73
Catherine of Aragon 35
Cecil, William, Lord Burghley 68, 71, 75
Cecil's Commonwealth (tracts) 67, 75, 78, 91
Chandler, Edward (bishop of Lichfield and Coventry) 169 n. 79
Charles I 10, 11, 81, 82, 84–7, 90, 92, 101, 102, 104, 106.
Charles II 15, 123
Charles V 35
Charlie Hebdo 3
Chesterfield, earl of, *see* Stanhope
Cicero 68, 196
Clarendon, earl of, *see* Hyde
Clarke, Samuel 156, 162
Clitus 50
Colclough, David 12, 13, 29, 30, 40, 44 n. 74, 48, 67, 100
Collins, Anthony 126, 127, 128, 139, 140
Collinson, Patrick 73
Comte, Auguste 236, 241
Convocation 136, 153, 157, 159, 162, 163

Cooper, Anthony Ashley, third earl of Shaftesbury 140, 182
Cosin, John 103
Cotton, John Hynde 175
Courteville, Ralph 176
Covenanters, Scottish 106
Cowell, Herbert 217
Cowper, William, first earl Cowper 160
Craftsman 17, 174, 175, 176, 179, 187 n. 62, 189 n. 86
Cudworth, Ralph 51
Curll, Edmund 17

Daneau, Lambert 17
Danvers, Sir Joseph 173
David (prophet) 51
Declaration of Independence (1776) 194, 196, 197, 204, 208 n. 31
Declaration of the Rights of Man and the Citizen (1789) 121, 132
Defoe, Daniel 1, 17, 143–4, 173, 181, 189 n. 103, 190 n. 116
Dering, Edward 70
Dering, Sir Edward 107, 108
Des Maizeaux, Pierre 138
Devereux, Robert, second earl of Essex 74
Dexter, Gregory 107, 108
Diderot, Denis 141, 183
Dionysius 38–40, 45 n. 100
Dod, John 51, 55
Dow, Christopher 87
Dyer, John 189 n. 103

East India Company 237, 240, 241, 243, 244–7, 250, 255 n. 67
Eglisham, George 82
Eliot, Sir John 83–4
Elizabeth I 9, 65, 66, 67
Elton, Edward 53, 59
Elton, Sir Geoffrey 93 n. 6
Elyot, Thomas 12, 28–46
Erasmus, Desiderius 31, 32, 33, 34
Erskine, Thomas, Baron Erskine (Lord High Chancellor) 19
Essex, earl of, *see* Devereux
Euripides 120

Index

European Court of Human Rights 3, 4
Evans, John (bishop of Meath) 161
Everard, John 70, 80
Excise Crisis (1733) 174
Exclusion Crisis (1679–82) 15

F.S. (author) 52
Faulkner, George 52
Felton, John 83, 84
Field, John 71, 72, 102
Fielding, Henry 174, 191 n. 125
Filmer, Sir Robert 122, 128
Finch, Daniel, second earl of
    Nottingham 153, 156–7, 158, 161,
    162–3, 166 n. 15.
Floyd, Edward 93
Fog's Weekly Journal 173
Fontenelle, Bernard le Bovier de 140
Forced Loan (1626–7) 82, 85
Ford, John 79
Francklin, Richard 174, 175, 185 n. 32,
    190 n. 106
Frederick II of Prussia 140
Froude, James Anthony 217
Fulke, William 71

Gardiner, Samuel 52, 53
Gataker, Thomas 50, 58
Gay, John 174, 176
George I 155
Gibson, Edmund (bishop of Lincoln and
    bishop of London) 162
Godwin, William 171
Gondomar, count of, *see* Sarmiento
Gordon, Thomas 122
Grindal, Edmund (archbishop of
    Canterbury) 65
Gunpowder Plot (1605) 74
Gustav II of Sweden 178

Habermas, Jürgen 6, 172
Haines, Henry 175
Hale, Matthew (judge) 151
Hall, Arthur, 93
Hall, Joseph 158
Hamilton, William 221
Hanson, Laurence 179

Hardwicke, earl of, *see* Yorke
Harley, Robert, first earl of Oxford
    (secretary of state) 17, 128, 129, 130,
    153, 187 n. 54, 189 n. 103
Harrington, earl of, *see* Stanhope
Harrington, James 122
Hastings, Francis Rawdon, first
    marquess of Hastings 242, 255 n. 61
Heath, Sir Robert (attorney general) 103,
    105–6
Hell-Fire Club 155, 160
Helvétius, Claude-Adrien 141, 145
Henrietta Maria 86
Henry, duke of Guise 68, 69
Herod 55
Hervey, John, Baron Hervey 176
Heylyn, John 154
Heylyn, Peter 87–9, 96 n. 63, 101–2,
    104, 105, 116 n. 14
High Commission, Court of 8, 11, 73
Hildersam, Arthur 55, 56
Hill, Christopher 7
Hinde, William 47
Hobbes, Thomas 122, 124, 128, 140
Hogg, James 243, 244
Holmes, Oliver Wendell 205 n. 3, 226
Holt, Sir John (lord chief justice) 17, 173
Horace 129
Howard, Frances 79
Howard, Henry, first earl of
    Northampton 78
Howard, Thomas, fourth duke of
    Norfolk 67, 68, 91
Humboldt, Wilhelm von 121, 126
Hume, David 17, 19, 142, 144, 171–91,
    245
Hume-Campbell, Alexander 179
Hyde, Edward, first earl of Clarendon
    122

Indian Penal Code (1838) 239
*International Covenant on Civil and
    Political Rights* (1966) 121
Isocrates 28, 31, 34, 43 n. 53, 44 n. 74

Jackson, John 162
James I 8, 9, 13, 65, 73, 76, 77, 82, 88

259

Index

Jaucourt, Louis 141–2, 144, 145, 146
Jeanes, Henry 53
Jefferson, Thomas 204–5
John of Salisbury 42 n. 28
Johnson, Robert 48
Johnson, Samuel 176, 186 n. 43
Jones, Inigo 86–7
Jonson, Ben 11, 75, 77, 86–7
Joshua 51
Julian the Apostate 97 n. 63
Jyllands-Posten (2005) 3

kairos 28–46
Kant, Immanuel 183
Kennett, White (bishop of Peterborough) 161, 169 n. 79, 170 n. 94
Khomeini, Ayatollah 3
King, William (archbishop of Dublin) 156
King, William (Oxford Jacobite) 174
King's Bench, Court of 157, 168 n. 62

Lambe, John 83
La Roche, Michel de 139
Laud, William (archbishop of Canterbury) 11, 87, 89, 101, 107
Le Clerc, Jean 139
Lee, Richard Henry 200
Leicester's Commonwealth (1584) 67, 75, 79, 82
Leighton, Alexander 104–6, 109, 111, 112
Leslie, Charles 172, 173
L'Estrange, Sir Roger 15
Levellers 14, 15, 113
Lewis, Erasmus 120
Ley, Roger 52, 59
Leycester, John 47
Licensing Acts 5, 6, 16, 110, 119, 136 172, 175
Licensing Ordinance (1643) 108, 109
Lilburne, John 11, 110–13
Livy 196
Locke, John 140, 221, 222
Lopez, Rodrigo 68
Lupset, Thomas 33–4
Luther, Martin 32

Luzac, Elie 140, 149 n. 31
Lyttelton, George 179, 186 n. 40

Mabbott, Gilbert 14–15
Macaulay, Thomas Babington 5–6, 239
Machiavelli, Niccolo 196, 197
Maclean, Charles 242, 246, 253 n. 38, 255 n. 61
Madison, James 171, 209 n. 49
Main Plot (1603) 74
Malcolm, Sir John 244, 245, 250, 254 n. 47, n. 50
Mallet, David 177
Mansfield, earl of, *see* Murray
Marchmont, earl of, *see* Campbell
Marprelate Tracts (1588) 9, 73, 107
Marret, Paul 139
Mary Stuart, Queen of Scots 66, 67, 78, 90, 93
Matthews, John 173
Metcalfe, Charles Theophilus 240, 243, 245, 254 n. 48
Mettrie, Julien Offray de La 140–1, 142
Mill, James 211
Mill, John Stuart 5, 19–20, 121, 126, 130, 211, 212, 213, 216–17, 219–20, 223, 224, 225, 226, 228, 236–56
Milton, John 5, 14, 16, 17, 107, 110, 112, 121, 135, 137, 142, 146, 172, 175, 180, 181, 200, 232 n. 73
Mist, Nathaniel 161, 173
Mist's Weekly Journal 173, 185 n. 28
Montagu, Richard (bishop of Norwich) 11, 81, 101–3
Montaigne, Michel de 140
Montesquieu, baron de, *see* Secondat
More, Thomas 32, 34
Mourdant, Charles, third earl of Peterborough 160
Muhammad (prophet) 3
Munro, Thomas (governor of Madras) 246
Murray, William, first earl of Mansfield (lord chief justice) 18

Nabal 50
Neale, Sir John 65

Nedham, Marchamont 197
Nehemias 96 n. 63
New York Times v. Sullivan (1964) 210 n. 63
Nicene Creed 155, 156, 158
Nine Years War (1688–97) 177
Norfolk, duke of, *see* Howard
Northampton, earl of, *see* Howard
Notestein, Wallace 90
Nottingham, earl of, *see* Finch

O'Connell, Daniel 238
Onslow, Arthur 160
Orford, earl of, *see* Walpole
Overbury, Sir Thomas 79
Overton, Richard 107, 111, 117 n. 39
Oxford, earl of, *see* Harley

Paine, Thomas 19
Paley, William 122
parrhesia 12, 28–32, 34–5, 38, 40, 64, 67, 77, 80, 88, 89, 92, 97 n. 63, 100, 104, 106, 112, 113, 118 n. 48, 120, 130, 131
Parry Plot (1585) 68
Parsons, Robert 71
Passerano, Alberto Radicati di 138
Paul, St. 54
Peacham, Henry 30
Perez, Antonio 90
Perkins, William 51, 55–7, 62 n. 81, 62 n. 85
Peterborough, earl of, *see* Mourdant
Petition of Right (1628) 83, 87
Phillip II of Spain 69
Pickering, Lewis 77
Pitt, James 176
Plato 29, 33, 38–40, 45 n. 100
Plautus 47
Playhouse Bill (1735) 174
Plutarch 28, 31, 32, 34
Pole, Reginald (cardinal and archbishop of Canterbury) 33
Pontius Pilate 55
Pope, Alexander 119, 129, 176, 182
Price, Richard 122, 176, 202
Prideaux, Humphrey 136

Pride's Purge (1648) 113
Proast, Jonas 222
Prynne, William 8, 9, 10, 11, 14, 87, 88, 89, 90, 92, 102, 103, 104, 106, 107, 115 n. 14
Pulteney, William 174, 176, 190 n. 123
Puttenham, George 30

Quintilian 29

Ramsay, David 199
Randall, John 57
Rex v. Taylor (1676) 151, 152
Reyner, Edward 61 n. 56
Ridolfi Plot (1571) 68
Ritchie, D.G. 217
Robinson, John (bishop of London) 169 n. 79
Rous, Francis 116 n. 14
Rushdie, Salman 3
Russell, Conrad 79, 80, 83, 84

Sacheverell, Henry 17, 160, 173
St John, Henry, first viscount Bolingbroke (secretary of state) 172, 174, 175, 176, 177, 178, 179, 185 n. 31, 187 n. 62, 188 n. 79, 188 n. 86
Sallust 196
Sander, Nicholas 71
Sarmiento de Acuña, Diego, count of Gondomar 80
Schatz, Albert 235 n. 114
Sclater, William 52
Scott, Thomas 11, 12, 79, 81
Scriblerian Club 188 n. 86
Secondant, Charles-Loius de, baron de Montesquieu 181, 196, 197, 198, 239
Sedition Act (1798) 204
Shaftesbury, earl of, *see* Cooper
Shakespeare, William 75, 77, 175, 229 n. 3
Sharpe, Kevin 69, 85, 87, 92
Siebert, F.S. 7
Societies for the Reformation of Manners 154, 155
Socinianism 137, 156
Solomon 55

Index

South Sea Bubble (1720) 153, 154
Spanish Match (1614–23) 12, 70, 78, 80, 82, 85, 92
Sparke, Michael 102–4, 105, 106, 116 n. 23
Spencer, Charles, third earl of Sunderland 158, 159–60
Spinoza, Benedict 124
Squire Plot (1597) 68
Stamp Act (1712) 173
Stanhope, Leicester, fifth earl of Harrington 245, 246
Stanhope, Philip, fourth earl of Chesterfield 175, 186 n. 40
Stapleton, Thomas 71
Star Chamber, Court of 8, 11, 73, 103, 105, 116 n. 23, 202
Starkey, Thomas 33–4, 38
Stationers' Company 8–9, 14, 15–16, 99, 110
Steele, Richard 119
Stephen, James Fitzjames 130, 217, 219, 249, 256 n. 76
Stephen, Leslie 228
Stock, Richard 58
Story, Joseph (Supreme Court judge) 192
Struensee, Johann Friedrich 188 n. 72
Sunderland, earl of, *see* Spencer
Swift, Jonathan 16, 119–34, 173, 176, 182, 188 n. 79, 188 n. 86

Taylor, Harriet 238
Tenison, Thomas (archbishop of Canterbury) 137
Theseus 120
Thomson, James 175, 177, 180, 181, 182
Throckmorton Plot (1583) 68
Timoleon 202–3, 210 n. 58
Tindal, Matthew 128, 180, 181
Tocqueville, Alexis de 213, 214, 215, 216, 217, 247
Toland, John 18, 122, 136, 137, 140, 143
Toleration Act (1689) 136, 156, 158, 159, 160
Tombes, John 54–5, 59
Treatise of Treasons (1572) 67, 75, 82

Trelawney, Jonathan (bishop of Winchester) 169 n. 79
Trenchard, John 122, 176, 190 n. 120, 196, 197, 198
Trevor, Thomas, Baron Trevor 153, 154
True Briton 173
Trueman, Richard 50–1
Tucker, St George 201–2
Tutchin, John 17, 173
Tyler, Wat 195

U.S. Constitution (1789) 121, 192–210
Udall, John 89
Unitarianism 137
Universal Declaration of Human Rights (1948) 2, 121, 132 n. 15

Van Dyck, Anthony 86
Verney, George (dean of Windsor) 151
Verstegan, Richard 81
Villiers, George, first duke of Buckingham 81, 82–3, 84, 85, 92, 101
Voltaire 140, 142, 146, 211

Wake, William (archbishop of Canterbury) 153–6, 158–9, 161–2, 164–5
Waldron, Jeremy 4–5
Walpole, Horatio 176
Walpole, Robert, first earl of Orford 173, 174, 175, 176, 177, 179, 182, 183
Walwyn, William 14, 108–10, 112
War of Jenkins's Ear (1739–48) 177
War of the Austrian Succession (1740–48) 177
War of the Spanish Succession (1701–14) 177
Ward, Samuel 80, 116 n. 14
Washington, George 197
Waters, Edward 119
Webster, John 79
Wellesley, Richard, first marquis Wellesley 242
Wharton, Philip James, first duke of Wharton 155, 160, 173
Whiston, William 156–7

262

Whitaker, William 71
Whitehead, Paul 174, 177
Whitgift, John 66, 72, 73
Wilcox, Thomas 71, 102
Wilkes, John 18, 19, 184 n. 4
Willet, Andrew 70, 80
William III 159
Williams, John (bishop of Lincoln) 87, 90
Williams, Roger 107
Wilson, James 194, 207 n. 11
Wilson, Thomas 30
Wither, George 12

Wolseley, Sir Charles 123
Wolsey, Thomas 34
Woolston, Thomas 158, 164
Worrall, Thomas 103
Wotton, Anthony 116 n. 14
Wren, Matthew (bishop of Norwich and bishop of Ely) 85
Wyndham, Sir William 175–6

Yorke, Philip, first earl of Hardwicke (lord chancellor) 174, 181, 190 n. 108

Zenger, John Peter 181

EU authorised representative for GPSR:
Easy Access System Europe, Mustamäe tee 50,
10621 Tallinn, Estonia
gpsr.requests@easproject.com